PROMOTING SPONTANEOUS USE OF LEARNING AND REASONING STRATEGIES

In this book, scholars from around the world develop viable answers to the question of how it may be possible to promote students' spontaneity in the use of learning and reasoning strategies. They combine their expertise to put forward new theories and models for understanding the underlying mechanisms; provide details of new research to address pertinent questions and problems; and describe classroom practices that have proven successful in promoting spontaneous strategy use. This book is a must for educators and researchers who truly care that schooling should cultivate learning and reasoning strategies in students that would prepare and serve them for life.

A seminal resource, this book will address the basic problem that many educators are well acquainted with: that students can learn how to effectively use learning and reasoning strategies but not use them of their own volition or in settings other than the one in which they learned the strategies.

Emmanuel Manalo is a professor at the Graduate School of Education at Kyoto University, Japan.

Yuri Uesaka is an assistant professor in the Division of Educational Psychology at the Graduate School of Education at the University of Tokyo, Japan.

Clark A. Chinn is a professor in the Department of Educational Psychology at Rutgers University, USA.

Routledge Research in Achievement and Gifted Education

PROMOTING SPONTANEOUS USE OF LEARNING AND REASONING STRATEGIES

Theory, Research, and Practice for Effective Transfer

Edited by Emmanuel Manalo,
Yuri Uesaka, and Clark A. Chinn

Routledge
Taylor & Francis Group

LONDON AND NEW YORK

First published 2018
by Routledge
2 Park Square, Milton Park, Abingdon, Oxon OX14 4RN

and by Routledge
711 Third Avenue, New York, NY 10017

Routledge is an imprint of the Taylor & Francis Group, an informa business

British Library Cataloguing in Publication Data
A catalogue record for this book is available from the British Library

Library of Congress Cataloging in Publication Data
A catalog record for this book has been requested

ISBN: 978-1-138-68063-0 (hbk)
ISBN: 978-1-138-68064-7 (pbk)
ISBN: 978-1-315-56402-9 (ebk)

Typeset in Bembo
by Book Now Ltd, London

Dedicated to Celina, Shoko, and Lisa.

CONTENTS

TABLES

FIGURES

ABOUT THE CONTRIBUTORS

Joshua Adams, MS, is a graduate student in the Learning Literacies and Technologies program in the Teachers' College at Arizona State University, USA, and a member of its Learning and Cognition Lab. His research interests include collaborative learning and statistical modeling. Email: jradam12@asu.edu

Rainer Bromme, PhD, is a professor at the Psychology Department of the University of Münster, Germany. He teaches educational psychology within the BSc and MSc Psychology programs. His research is focused on communication and understanding between science and the public, the development of professional expertise, expert-layperson communication, and learning with(in) the Internet. Email: bromme@uni-muenster.de

Lynn A. Bryan, PhD, is a professor at Purdue University, USA, where she holds a joint appointment in the Department of Curriculum and Instruction and the Department of Physics and Astronomy. She also is the director for the Center for the Teaching and Learning of STEM (CATALYST). Her current research interests focus on science teacher education, teaching science at the nanoscale, and teaching science through modeling-based inquiry approaches. Email: labryan@purdue.edu

Carol K. K. Chan, PhD, is a professor in the Division of Learning, Development and Diversity at the Faculty of Education, University of Hong Kong. During her career, she has extensively investigated computer-supported knowledge building as a collaborative and inquiry-based approach to education. Her research area is the learning sciences, and her research interests include knowledge building, computer-supported collaborative learning, conceptual change, teacher learning, and the Chinese learner. Email: ckkchan@hku.hk

Michelene T. H. Chi, PhD, is the Dorothy Bray Endowed Professor of Science and Teaching in the MLF Teachers' College and Director of the Learning and Cognition Lab at the Institute for the Science of Teaching and Learning at Arizona State University, USA. She is also an elected member of the American Academy of Arts and Sciences and the National Academy of Education. Her research focuses on understanding how students learn and ways to improve their learning. Email: Michelene.Chi@asu.edu

Clark A. Chinn, PhD, is a professor in the Graduate School of Education at Rutgers University, USA. His research focuses on reasoning and argumentation, epistemic practices and epistemic cognition, conceptual change, and collaborative learning. He has worked extensively to design and investigate model-based inquiry environments in middle school science classes. Email: clark.chinn@gse.rutgers.edu

Ravit Golan Duncan, PhD, is an associate professor in the Graduate School of Education and the School of Environmental and Biological Science at Rutgers University, USA. Her research interests focus on learning progressions in science and designing instruction to promote student engagement with scientific inquiry practices. She coordinates and teaches in the Certification Program in Biological Science Education. Email: ravit.duncan@gse.rutgers.edu

Catherine Eberbach, PhD, is a program director at the United States National Science Foundation. Her research interests lie at the intersection of scientific reasoning practices in informal and formal settings. Email: ceberbac@nsf.gov

Megan L. Franke, PhD, is a professor of education at the University of California, Los Angeles, USA. Her research focuses on understanding and supporting teacher learning for both preservice and inservice teachers. She designs, prepares, and studies the preparation of early childhood to sixth-grade mathematics teachers. Email: mfranke@ucla.edu

Tatsushi Fukaya, PhD, is currently an associate professor at the Graduate School of Education of Gunma University in Japan. His research aims to understand how to promote and foster students' metacognition in and out of the classroom. He also conducts research on teacher education. Email: fukaya@gunma-u.ac.jp

Marcus Henning, PhD, is a senior lecturer and postgraduate academic advisor at the Centre for Medical and Health Sciences Education at the University of Auckland, New Zealand. He is actively engaged in research, and his specific interests include quality of life, motivation to teach and learn, organizational behavior, conflict management, and professional integrity. Email: m.henning@auckland.ac.nz

Andreas Hetmanek, DPhil, is research assistant at TUM School of Education of the Technical University Munich, Germany. He is involved in developing the German "Clearing House Effective Teaching in STEM" and teaching teacher educators. His research interests include scientific reasoning and argumentation, philosophy of science and research methods in education as well as fostering teacher skills. Email: andreas.hetmanek@tum.de

Cindy E. Hmelo-Silver, PhD, is director of the Center for Research on Learning and Technology, Barbara B. Jacobs Chair of Education and Technology, and professor of Learning Sciences at Indiana University, USA. Her research focuses on collaborative problem-based learning about complex phenomena and the role of technology in supporting collaborative learning and inquiry. Email: chmelosi@indiana.edu

Shin'ichi Ichikawa, PhD, is a professor at the Graduate School of Education of the University of Tokyo. He was a president of Japanese Association of Educational Psychology and has been a member of the National Council of Education in Japan. His main research interests are the analysis of teaching–learning processes and its applications to educational practices. Email: ichikawa@p.u-tokyo.ac.jp

Marsha Ing, PhD, is an associate professor at the Graduate School of Education at the University of California, Riverside, USA. She teaches assessment, research design, and statistics to graduate students. Her research interests include measuring mathematics teaching and learning. Email: marsha.ing@ucr.edu

Takeshi Ishizaki is a math teacher at Niitsuru Junior High School in Japan. Through teaching mathematics, he is interested in developing students' skills in memorizing and in solving problems that have survival value in future life in society. Email: shi62@sd.dcns.ne.jp

Nicholas C. Johnson is a doctoral candidate in urban schooling at the University of California, Los Angeles, USA. He studies teaching and learning through the lens of children's mathematical thinking and supports teachers to make use of children's thinking in their practice. Email: nicko@ucla.edu

Rebecca Jordan, PhD, is a professor in the Departments of Human Ecology and Ecology, Evolution, and Natural Resources at Rutgers University, USA. Her research initiatives focus on understanding how individuals reason with scientific data. In particular, she is seeking to understand how individuals generate and test explanations for complex phenomena. Email: rebecca.jordan@rutgers.edu

Seokmin Kang, PhD, is a postdoctoral researcher working at the Wisconsin Center for Education Research, University of Wisconsin-Madison, USA. Email: skang79@wisc.edu

Manu Kapur, EdD, is a professor and chair of Learning Sciences and Higher Education at ETH Zurich, Switzerland. His research and teaching interests lie at the intersection of the learning sciences, educational psychology, and mathematics education. He is widely known for his research on *productive failure*. For more information: www.manukapur.com

Matthew Lancaster, PhD, is an assistant professor of psychology at Lourdes University, USA. His research interests include cognitive engagement, category learning and usage, development of expertise, and knowledge transfer. Email: MLancaster@lourdes.edu

June Lee is a research associate from the Mathematics and Mathematics Education Department of the National Institute of Education of Singapore. She has been involved in the Institute's Productive Failure research program since its inception in Singapore, supporting ways to effect deeper learning of mathematics through this teaching method. Email: june.lee@nie.edu.sg

Ngan Hoe Lee, PhD, is an assistant professor at the National Institute of Education, Nanyang Technological University, Singapore. He teaches pre- and in-service courses as well as graduate courses in mathematics education and supervises postgraduate students pursuing masters and PhD degrees. Email: nganhoe.lee@nie.edu.sg

Chunlin Lei, PhD, is an associate professor at the School of Foreign Languages, Shanghai University of International Business and Economics. He has been teaching in higher institutions in China over 20 years, pivoting on improvement of students' academic literacy, especially collaborative inquiry and English writing skills. Email: leichunlin@suibe.edu.cn

Na Li, PhD, is a curriculum development advisor who currently works for Guangdong Country Garden School in China. Her research interests include STEM education, active learning, and technology-enhanced learning. Email: nl2284@tc.columbia.edu

Emmanuel Manalo, PhD, is a professor at the Graduate School of Education of Kyoto University in Japan. He teaches educational psychology and academic communication skills to undergraduate and graduate students. His research interests include the promotion of effective learning and instructional strategies, student diagram use, and critical thinking. Email: manalo.emmanuel.3z@kyoto-u.ac.jp

Katherine L. McEldoon, PhD, is an educational research consultant who led a state-wide research pilot with the educational technology company YouScience and the State of Georgia, USA. Her research interests include optimizing instructional design for learning, cognitive engagement, active learning, knowledge transfer, and implementing research-based educational interventions into practice. Email: K.McEldoon@alumni.vanderbilt.edu

Yoshinori Oyama, PhD, is an associate professor in the Department of Education at Chiba University in Japan. He is in charge of teacher education for students training to become teachers in elementary through to high schools. His main research areas include teachers' questioning skills training and development of students' questioning skills to enhance spontaneous use. Email: y_oyama@chiba-u.jp

Joseph Oyler, EdD, is an induction coordinator in the Center of Pedagogy and a research associate in the Department of Educational Foundations at Montclair State University, USA. Dr. Oyler worked as a classroom facilitator utilizing the Philosophy for Children program, helped design professional development programs, and served as a practitioner coach. Email: oylerj@mail.montclair.edu

Alina Reznitskaya, PhD, is a professor in the Department of Educational Foundations at Montclair State University, USA. She teaches courses in educational psychology, quantitative methodology, and educational measurement. Her research focuses on designing measures of argument literacy and examining teacher professional development programs that help improve the quality of argumentation during class discussions. Email: reznitskayaa@mail.montclair.edu

Ronald W. Rinehart, PhD, is an instructor in the Department of Educational Psychology and Foundations at the University of Northern Iowa, USA. He has worked on the PRACCIS (Promoting Reasoning and Conceptual Change In Science) project during the last several years and has also co-developed the AIR model of epistemic cognition. His research interests include epistemic cognition, reasoning, learning through inquiry, and conceptual change. Email: ron.rinehart@uni.edu

Jean-François Rouet is a research director with the French National Center for Scientific Research. He holds a position at the University of Poitiers in France. His research interests include the cognitive underpinnings of reading literacy and skilled uses of information technology. He also serves as an expert as part of the OECD PISA and PIAAC studies. Email: jean-francois.rouet@univ-poitiers.fr

Ala Samarapungavan, PhD, is a professor of educational psychology in the Department of Educational Studies at Purdue University. Her research program examines the interplay of disciplinary knowledge and epistemic reasoning in course of science learning from childhood through adulthood. Email: ala@purdue.edu

Mikiko Seo, PhD, is an associate professor in the Department of Education of Japan Women's University, Japan. She teaches educational psychology to undergraduate and graduate students. Her research interests include promotion of effective learning strategies, lesson induction, and elaboration. Email: seom@fc.jwu.ac.jp

Keita Shinogaya, PhD, is an associate professor in the College of Economics at Nihon University, Japan. His main research interest is in finding out how to effectively connect learning at home and learning at school. His other research interests include examining the relationships between students' learning strategies and teachers' teaching strategies. Email: shinogaya.keita@nihon-u.ac.jp

Suparna Sinha, PhD, is a postdoctoral associate at the Center for Math, Science and Computer Education at Rutgers University, USA. She is interested in understanding influences of technological affordances (of simulations, hypermedia, and modeling tools) on collaborative engagement and subsequently how students' collaborative engagement in technology intensive learning environments influences individual transfer of learning. Email: suparna.sinha@docs.rutgers.edu

Marc Stadtler, PhD, is a researcher (Akademischer Oberrat) at the Department of Psychology at Münster University in Germany. He teaches educational psychology in bachelor and master programs of psychology. His research interests include reading in digital media, science understanding, and the development of classroom interventions promoting advanced reading skills. Email: marc.stadtler@uni-muenster.de

Glenda S. Stump, PhD, is an educational research consultant who currently works with the Strategic Education Initiatives Group in the Office of Digital Learning at Massachusetts Institute of Technology, USA. Her research interests include teacher beliefs and pedagogic choices, strategies for teacher professional development, and student motivation. Email: gsstump@mit.edu

Yuan Sun is an associate professor at the Information and Society Research Division of the National Institute of Informatics, and the Graduate University for Advanced Studies in Japan. She teaches statistics and bibliometrics to graduate and undergraduate students. Her research interests include measurement in education and psychology, learning analytics, and institutional assessment. Email: yuan@nii.ac.jp

Masayuki Suzuki, PhD, is a lecturer at Yokohama National University in Japan. He teaches educational psychology and psychometrics to undergraduate and graduate students. His current research interests include assessment, feedback and social comparison. Email: suzuki-masayuki-mt@ynu.ac.jp

Etsuko Tanaka, PhD, is an assistant professor in the Program for Leading Graduate Schools, "PhD Professional: Gateway to Success in Frontier Asia", of Nagoya University in Japan and contributes to fostering young professionals to becoming global leaders. Her research interests include class design for the development of interest in learning. Email: tanaka.etsuko@h.mbox.nagoya-u.ac.jp

Angela C. Turrou, PhD, is a senior researcher in the UCLA Graduate School of Education and teaches in the UCLA Teacher Education Program. Her research interests focus on the interaction among teachers, students, and children's mathematical thinking, spanning early childhood through elementary school. Email: achan@gseis.ucla.edu

Yuri Uesaka, PhD, is an assistant professor at the Graduate School of Education of the University of Tokyo, Japan. Her interest is in using psychological approaches to develop effective instructional environments for enhancing the quality of student learning. She also participates in studies focused on practical applications of research in real school settings. Email: y_uesaka@p.u-tokyo.ac.jp

Mengting Wang was a masters student at the Graduate School of Education of the University of Tokyo, Japan, when she participated in the research project reported in this book. Her interest is in the development of effective instructional environments for enhancing the use of metacognitive learning strategies. Email: wangmt2014@163.com.

Noreen M. Webb, PhD, is a professor of education at the University of California, Los Angeles, USA. Her research spans domains in learning and instruction and measurement theory and applications, with a particular focus on the measurement of learning and teaching processes and performance of individuals and groups in classroom settings. Email: webb@ucla.edu

Christof Wecker, DPhil, is an interim professor at the University of Passau, Germany. His teaching focuses on learning and instruction and research methods. His research interests include instructional strategies, cross-domain skills, and pre-requisites for and obstacles to evidence-based practice in education. Email: christof.wecker@uni-passau.de

Ian A. G. Wilkinson, PhD, is a professor in the Department of Teaching and Learning at Ohio State University, USA. He teaches courses on literacy learning and teaching and conducts research on the impact of classroom talk on students' reading comprehension and the implications for professional development of teachers. Email: wilkinson.70@osu.edu

Jamison Wills is a doctoral student in educational psychology at Purdue University, USA. His research interests include how students think and reason with scientific evidence, instructional strategies that promote students' science learning, and mixed-methods approaches to studying learning. Email: willsj@purdue.edu

Dongchen Xu, MA, is a graduate student in the Cognitive Science program of the Psychology Department, Arizona State University, USA. Email: dongche1@asu.edu

David Yaghmourian, BS, is a research analyst who currently works in the Learning and Cognition Lab at the Institute for the Science of Teaching & Learning, Arizona State University, USA. Email: dyaghmou@asu.edu

Yawen Yu is working as a curriculum developer and designer at Manpower Group China. Before joining Manpower Group, Yawen's major research interests included how technological tools support students' collaborative learning of complex concepts. Yawen received her master's training from Rutgers University and Boston University.

ACKNOWLEDGMENTS

This book has only been made possible because of the generous help of many people. We would like to sincerely thank the following colleagues who freely gave of their time and knowledge to read and provide constructive comments on papers during the double-blind peer review process:

Mary Ainley, University of Melbourne, Australia

Na'ama Av-Shalom, Rutgers University, USA

Carol K. K. Chan, University of Hong Kong, China

Dexter Da Silva, Keisen Jogakuen University, Japan

Iain Doherty, Deakin University, Australia

Rachel Dryer, Charles Sturt University, Australia

Amanda Durik, Northern Illinois University, USA

Hebbah El-Moslimany, Rutgers University, USA

Susan Golbeck, Rutgers University, USA

Peter Gu, Victoria University of Wellington, New Zealand

Richard Hamilton, University of Auckland, New Zealand

Marcus Henning, University of Auckland, New Zealand

Andreas Hetmanek, Technical University Munich, Germany

Eunsook Hong, University of Nevada, USA

Leah C. C. Hung, Rutgers University, USA

May Jadallah, Illinois State University, USA

Marilar Jimenez-Aleixandre, University of Santiago de Compostela, Spain

Nate Kornell, Williams College, USA

Alistair Kwan, University of Auckland, New Zealand

Debbie Leader, Massey University, New Zealand

Chunlin Lei, Shanghai University of International Business and Economics, China

Brandon Mauclair-Augustin, Rutgers University, USA

Toshio Mochizuki, Senshu University, Japan

Kou Murayama, University of Reading, UK

Michael Paton, University of Sydney, Australia

Maria Helena T. Pedrosa-de-Jesus, University of Aveiro, Portugal

Sarah Pérez-Kriz, George Mason University, USA

Ronald W. Rinehart, University of Northern Iowa, USA

Bennett Schwartz, Florida International University, USA

David Sears, Purdue University, USA

Jonathan Shemwell, University of Maine, USA

Chris Sheppard, Waseda University, Japan

Heidrun Stöger, Regensburg University, Germany

Yoshinori Sugiura, Hiroshima University, Japan

Hiroshi Toyota, Nara University of Education, Japan

Maria Tulis, University of Augsburg, Germany

Randi Zimmerman, Rutgers University, USA

The work undertaken by Emmanuel Manalo and Yuri Uesaka in producing this book was supported by grants-in-aid (23330207, 15H01976, 26560113, 15K13126) received from the Japan Society for the Promotion of Science. The work undertaken by Clark A. Chinn was supported in part by the National Science Foundation under Grant No. 1008634. Any opinions, findings, and conclusions or recommendations expressed in this book are those of the authors and do not necessarily reflect the views of the Japan Society for the Promotion of Science or the National Science Foundation.

INTRODUCTION

Addressing the problem of inadequate spontaneity in students' use of learning and reasoning strategies

Emmanuel Manalo, Yuri Uesaka, and Clark A. Chinn

Description of the problem

The problem that this book addresses is familiar to most educators: students can be taught how to use learning and reasoning strategies but subsequently fail to use these on their own volition. For example, many students fail to use diagrams in situations when their teachers are not present to tell them to use diagrams (e.g., Uesaka, Manalo, & Ichikawa, 2007). Situations like this arise when they are learning at home, taking tests, or attempting to solve real problems in daily life. The failure to use this strategy spontaneously is of concern because the use of external resources such as diagrams is a very important strategy that students should acquire because of its utility in everyday situations. Students usually see many good examples of diagrams in class, as well as receive some encouragement for their use from their teachers, so it is not a matter of them being unaware of the strategy.

This problem of spontaneity occurs not only in learning strategy use but also with reasoning strategies. For example, adolescents—who have learned the strategy of controlling variables in school—often fail to use this strategy to evaluate studies in which variables are not controlled (Klaczynski, 2000). Similarly, students who have learned practices of argumentation often fail spontaneously to argue when they have an opportunity to do so (Chinn & Clark, 2013). And people who are aware of strategies for sourcing documents often fail to spontaneously use those strategies (Metzger, 2007).

These examples could be viewed as failures of contextual transfer (e.g., Pea, 1987) in which students do not use the strategies in settings other than those in which they learned the strategies. To provide another example: a student could learn how to use elaboration in history but not make use of the strategy in another subject like geography or English, or in dealing with a historical issue or problem outside of school. However, the problem of inadequate spontaneity in strategy use is not limited to contextual transfer failure: in many cases, even though the context or situation does not significantly change, students simply fail to use the strategy again at a later time. Students may be aware that they could use particular strategies, but they misuse those strategies, fail to work out how they could use the strategies, or simply decide that the cost of effort in using the strategies is not worth the anticipated benefit. Or it may not occur to them to use the strategies at all.

One of the earliest research reports that explicitly addressed the spontaneity of learning strategy use was by Keeney, Cannizzo, and Flavell (1967). In their study, they found that some children spontaneously used verbal rehearsal when presented with a nonverbal serial recall task, whereas other children did not—and consequently performed poorer in the task. The nonrehearsers were provided training in rehearsal and were quickly able to use the strategy and perform at essentially the same level as the rehearsers in the recall task. However, when the nonrehearsers were no longer required by the experimenters to use the rehearsal strategy, the majority of them abandoned the strategy in subsequent trials. Keeney et al. stressed that this was a case of "production deficiency" rather than a problem of inability-to-use as the children were able to use the strategy following training. They also considered this as a developmental problem in children, although it has become apparent since then that the problem also occurs widely in adults (e.g., Garner, 1990).

Since then, it has also become clear that there are degrees to which students may use or fail to use strategies spontaneously. In some cases, there is total failure of spontaneous use, such as when a student simply fails to use diagrams when it would be beneficial to do so in solving a mathematical story problem. In other cases, strategy use occurs, but there is failure in applying all that has been learned in appropriately using the strategy, such as when a student constructs a diagram but does so poorly, failing to use learned procedures for representing the necessary elements of the story problem onto the diagram. Some failures of spontaneous use occur when there are no cues at all to use the strategy, such as when a student fails to use a strategy outside of school. Other failures occur even when there are some implicit cues, such as when students fail to use diagrams in solving story problems on a test. Even though their teacher may not have explicitly prompted use of diagrams, the students might be expected to know that the teacher who has been exhorting diagram use in recent weeks might implicitly expect them to use diagrams on the test (and hence administer problems on which diagram use will improve solutions).

Background of the problem

The term "spontaneous strategy use" was employed by Borkowski, Carr, and Pressley (1987) to refer to unprompted strategy use by children. They were particularly interested in cases where such spontaneity does not occur and "production deficiency" is instead manifested. They proposed that for spontaneous strategy use to occur, the child needs to possess essential knowledge about the strategies, knowledge about higher-level (metacognitive) coordinating strategies, and motivational beliefs that provide the incentives necessary for deploying the strategies. In other words, the child needs to have sufficient knowledge about a strategy (e.g., elaboration) to be able to use it in the first place, and such knowledge is usually acquired through appropriate training experiences. But knowledge only about the strategy is not enough for spontaneous use to occur: the child also needs to develop understanding that would enable him or her to assess the demands of a task and to match those with the appropriate strategy on the basis of shared features. For instance, to better remember new concepts taught in science class, it would be helpful to elaborate on their meanings and to think about examples—because features of those concepts are similar to concepts encountered in geography which were remembered well following use of the elaboration strategy. Furthermore, the child needs to possess knowledge about the efficacy of strategies in order to be motivated to use them. More specifically, the child requires an appreciation of the value of using strategies—that the extra effort in using them pays off (e.g., elaborating on the new science concepts would take a bit more time and effort, but it would more likely lead to better understanding and retention—and to a better performance in an upcoming test).

Garner (1990) considered further why both children and adults might not use learning strategies when they should. In a review of research findings, she identified five reasons. The first is poor cognitive monitoring: the learner simply fails to notice that he or she is not learning, and consequently fails to employ an appropriate strategy to remedy the situation. Garner pointed out that, apart from a lack of understanding about how to evaluate one's own learning, this problem could occur for a number of other reasons, including absence of a requirement for the learner to respond to the instruction, working memory resources being strained (and hence leaving no cognitive resources to use for such monitoring), and the learner viewing the task as unimportant. The second reason consisted of "primitive routines that get the job done" (p. 519), which simply means that learners have a tendency to keep using strategies that are ineffective but nevertheless generate a product—albeit an inferior or useless one. She described the example of simply copying when learners are supposed to be summarizing (i.e., instead of extracting important points and integrating those with what they already know). The copying strategy is ineffective for learning, but it requires minimal effort and it generates text that can be shown to the teacher if required. The third reason is absence of non-strategy knowledge: sometimes learners do not use strategies not because they lack knowledge about those strategies but because of other knowledge deficiencies that hinder strategy use. Examples include not being able to use appropriate strategies in preparing for a test because the teacher failed to provide information about test format, not being able to use a dictionary to find the meaning of a word because of lack of knowledge about initial letters that make up the word, and not being able to meaningfully sort items because of inadequate knowledge about those items. The fourth reason is environmental lack of support for strategy use. This problem pertains particularly to classroom situations in which strategic activity (e.g., understanding the meaning and uses of new vocabulary words) is not rewarded because the teacher expects responses that require shallow processing approaches (e.g., rote verbatim memorization of the definitions provided by the teacher). Garner pointed out that classroom learning goals directly affect student strategy use, and students generally do not persist in using time- and effort-consuming strategies that do not deliver the desired results in their classroom performance. The fifth and final reason is minimal transfer: when students are taught the use of a strategy, they tend to only use it in the same situational context which they received the instruction. Hence, they may only use elaboration strategy in geography if the teacher taught use of that strategy in geography, but not in science if the teacher never taught that strategy in science. This reason is similar to the requirement of possessing sufficient higher-order coordinating strategies that Borkowski et al. (1987) proposed.

Persistence of the problem, and more recent findings in contextual transfer

Despite these challenges being proposed over a quarter of a century ago, insufficient spontaneous transfer of strategies continues to be a problem. Students' propensity to employ strategies that are deemed ineffective remains a prevalent and widely recognized problem (e.g., Dunlosky, Rawson, Marsh, Nathan, & Willingham, 2013; Karpicke, Butler, & Roediger, 2009). Furthermore, a search through educational research databases reveals that very few studies focusing explicitly on the issue of spontaneous strategy use have been undertaken since the Borkowski et al. (1987) and Garner (1990) papers. In this volume, explicit focus is placed on the question of how spontaneous strategy use can be promoted with the aim of contributing to addressing these ongoing problems.

In the related arenas of research on transfer, more research has since been conducted. One line of research has demonstrated that spontaneous transfer is most likely to occur when elements of the training situation are similar to elements of the testing situation (Singley & Anderson, 1989). In fact, surface forms of similarity promote transfer of strategies—even when such transfer is inappropriate (Ross, 1987). Surface forms of transfer were referred to by Salomon and Perkins (1989) as *low-road transfer*. A second line of research has shown that spontaneous transfer is facilitated by reflection on the similarities and differences across learning cases (Alfieri, Nokes-Malach, & Schunn, 2013). Such reflections can promote abstract understanding of strategies that can facilitate future transfer—a form of transfer called *high-road transfer* by Salomon and Perkins (1989).

Recent lines of work—all of which are reflected in chapters in this volume—have explored new approaches to promoting spontaneous transfer of learning strategies. Research on preparation for future learning (Schwartz & Martin, 2004) and productive failure (Kapur, 2016) has emphasized that there are forms of transfer other than the traditional paradigm of sequestered problem solving, in which students learn strategies or principles in one context and then apply them to analogous problems in another context. Students may also use information learned in one context to facilitate learning in a second context (such as learning from reading a text); one can often demonstrate spontaneous transfer to these tasks even when transfer to a problem solving task does not occur. Actor-oriented or situative approaches to learning place the focus on what learners actually do transfer from one situation to another, rather than focusing on failures of transfer (Lobato, 2012). Important insights have arisen from these lines of research, with studies documenting that students often transfer much more than has been recognized from studies using traditional empirical paradigms. Finally, many research efforts situated in classrooms have focused on promoting communities of learners that develop and apply community norms across settings (e.g., Cobb, Stephan, & McClain, 2001), which may increase transfer from one setting to another through the appropriation of norms to which the students are deeply committed.

These findings from research traditions on transfer are indispensable in considering the question of how it may be possible to promote greater spontaneity in students' use of effective learning and reasoning strategies, as many of the chapters contained in this volume will demonstrate. However, focusing on the more specific requirements of spontaneous strategy use promotion is necessary as not all transfer issues are relevant to spontaneity.

Importance of addressing the problem, and how this book aims to do that

Promoting the spontaneous use of learning and reasoning strategies is crucial in current educational environments worldwide, in which there is growing awareness that *learning how to learn* and *how to think* are just as important as acquiring subject content knowledge. This shift in emphasis over the past several decades is reflected in the "key competencies" that the OECD (Organisation for Economic Cooperation and Development) has proposed as being necessary to nurture in school and to continue developing throughout the course of life (OECD, 2016). A central idea that holds these key competencies together is the need to develop individuals who are able to think for themselves and take responsibility for their own learning. In fact, many of the competence areas that have been identified as being common across different countries—such as autonomous learning, mastery of learning strategies, and metalearning and reflection (cf. Rychen, Salganik, & McLaughlin, 2003)—directly pertain to the concept of spontaneous strategy use. It is useful to note here that the aims of another highly influential group in education, the twenty-first-century skills movement, are congruent with the OECD ideals, including the incorporation of "life and career skills" in school education to prepare all learners for "a world where change is constant and learning never stops" (P21 Partnership for 21st Century Learning, n.d.). A common thread in these developments is the importance they place on learners' predispositions and ability to use appropriate learning and reasoning strategies in various contexts, including novel, unfamiliar situations they will encounter in the future. They therefore point to the importance not only of learning about the strategies but also of being able to spontaneously use them in situations where it would be advantageous to do so. Hence, if there are impediments to such use of strategies, then solutions need to be found—and that is the impetus for this book.

The book comprises three sections: theory, research, and practice. The theory section contains five chapters that extend current understanding and provide new insights about the spontaneous use of particular strategies in the authors' areas of research activity and expertise. In Chapter 1, Manu Kapur, Ngan Hoe Lee, and June Lee explain how the "productive failure" instructional design elicits students' spontaneous production of prior knowledge and constructive ideas that can then be leveraged to provide them the opportunity for the development of deeper levels of understanding and transfer. In Chapter 2, Yoshinori Oyama draws from both the Japanese and international research literatures in reviewing the importance of developing learners' questioning skills, describing the different instructional approaches that have been used, and proposing possible ways of promoting spontaneity in the use of this strategy. In Chapter 3, Mark Stadtler, Rainer Bromme, and Jean-Francois Rouet argue for the embedding of multiple document reading skills training in school education, and they describe components of intervention modules they have developed so that learners can more spontaneously and autonomously apply the skills to comprehend the multiple documents they frequently need to deal with in our information society. In Chapter 4, Yuri Uesaka and Emmanuel Manalo review research in instructional methods to address the lack of spontaneity in students' use of diagrams in math word problem solving and in written communication, and they propose some educational principles that may be effective in addressing the problem of spontaneity not only in the use of diagrams but also other learning strategies. In the final chapter of this section, Chapter 5, Christof Wecker and Andreas Hetmanek consider the reasons for learners' lack of sustained strategy use and propose seven recommendations for strategy training programs that can encourage students to spontaneously use newer and better strategies instead of older and more ineffective strategies.

The research section contains six reports of new findings from primary research studies that examine various factors that affect learners' spontaneity in strategy use. In Chapter 6, Emmanuel Manalo and Marcus Henning describe evidence suggesting that use of poor strategies in second language vocabulary learning is brought about and maintained by experiences of greater effort not leading to better outcomes in assessments, which in turn result from poor knowledge and beliefs about what constitutes effective learning strategies. In Chapter 7, Etsuko Tanaka reports on findings that suggest that certain teaching styles—namely, encouraging and allowing time for students to think, building knowledge connections, and linking information learned to real-life experiences—promote learners' use of deep processing strategies. Chapter 8 describes evidence obtained by Masayuki Suzuki and Yuan Sun that students' perception of test value is a key influence in their spontaneous use of more effective strategies in test situations. In Chapter 9, Tatsushi Fukaya reports on his finding that awareness of lack of understanding significantly predicts students' spontaneity in effective learning strategy use, and that explanation generation and self-evaluation are effective in improving such awareness. Chapter 10 then describes Keita Shinogaya's investigation into the connection between teachers' teaching strategies and learners' learning strategies; his main finding is that teachers' classroom teaching behaviors directly influence the frequency and quality of students' preparation for upcoming class sessions. In Chapter 11, the final chapter in this section, Chunlin Lei and Carol Chan describe and discuss their findings about how a computer-based knowledge-building environment successfully facilitates students' use of self-regulated and co-regulated learning strategies.

In line with the book's intention of promoting spontaneous strategy use in real educational settings, the practice section is the book's largest, with eight chapters describing classroom practices that the various authors have developed and investigated. In Chapter 12, Shin'ichi Ichikawa, Yuri Uesaka, and Emmanuel Manalo explain three approaches—cognitive counseling, incorporation of learning strategy instruction in the curriculum, and facilitation of the thinking-after-instruction approach in class—that have proven to be effective in enhancing students' spontaneous use of appropriate learning strategies. In Chapter 13, Glenda S. Stump, Na Li, Seokmin Kang, David Yaghmourian, Dongchen Xu, Joshua Adams, Katherine L. McEldoon, Matthew Lancaster, and Michelene T. H. Chi describe an online module that teaches secondary school teachers how to modify their classroom activities to elicit a higher level of student engagement—identifying what worked and what did not, and suggesting strategies for improving the rate of successful teacher implementation. Chapter 14 is about a program to enhance learning strategy use: Mikiko Seo, Mengting Wang, Takeshi Ishizaki, Yuri Uesaka, and Shin'ichi Ichikawa describe its development and successful implementation in one school in Japan, including their finding that the majority of students subsequently used the strategies taught in their own learning contexts. In Chapter 15, Clark A. Chinn, Ravit Golan Duncan, and Ronald W. Rinehart discuss principles of epistemic design that have been used in the PRACCIS (Promoting Reasoning and Conceptual Change in Science) project and how application of those principles fosters transferrable epistemic growth in school students. Ala Samarapungavan, Jamison Wills, and Lynn A. Bryan in Chapter 16 report evidence from a number of projects that shows transfer of inquiry strategies emerging contextually in content-rich inquiry classrooms, and they discuss principles that enhance this transfer. In Chapter 17, Cindy Hmelo-Silver, Rebecca Jordan, Suparna Sinha, Yawen Yu, and Catherine Eberbach take both traditional and actor-oriented theoretical perspectives to describe the application of the PMC-2E (phenomena-mechanisms-components) framework in designing a technology-rich curriculum related to aquatic ecosystems, and they report evidence that embedding a conceptual representation in instruction can promote transfer of conceptual understanding to novel contents. Chapter 18 addresses the questions of how students can interact with each other in beneficial ways when the teacher is not present to provide guidance, and what moves the teacher can make to promote the emergence of such interactions. These issues are discussed in the context of findings from a fourth-grade mathematics classroom in research presented by Noreen M. Webb, Megan L. Franke, Nicholas C. Johnson,

Angela C. Turrou, and Marsha Ing. Finally, in Chapter 19, Alina Reznitskaya, Ian A. G. Williamson, and Joseph Oyler describe a research and professional development program they designed to identify and evaluate instructional activities and materials that support teachers' spontaneous use of talk moves during inquiry dialogue in their classrooms.

By examining theory, research, and practice relevant to promoting spontaneous transfer of learning and reasoning strategies, the authors of the chapters in this volume seek to promote a better understanding of how to address the problems that have been discussed in this introduction. Although the chapters have been grouped into these three sections, readers will also find that the themes of theory, research, and practice crosscut the sections. The chapters in each section touch on all three aspects. Collectively, the chapters advance a variety of recommendations for practice that are grounded in both theory and research. Both researchers and practitioners will find a trove of ideas in this volume for improving spontaneous transfer in a variety of educational settings.

References

Alfieri, L., Nokes-Malach, T. J., & Schunn, C. D. (2013). Learning through case comparisons: A meta-analytic review. *Educational Psychologist, 48*(2), 87–113.

Borkowski, J., Carr, M., & Pressley, M. (1987). "Spontaneous" strategy use: Perspectives from metacognitive theory. *Intelligence, 11*(1), 61–75.

Chinn, C. A., & Clark, D. B. (2013). Learning through collaborative argumentation. In C. E. Hmelo-Silver, C. A. Chinn, C. K. K. Chan, & A. M. O'Donnell (Eds.), *International handbook of collaborative learning* (pp. 314–332). New York, NY: Routledge.

Cobb, P., Stephan, M., & McClain, K. (2001). Participating in classroom mathematical practices. *Journal of the Learning Sciences, 10*(1–2), 113–163.

Dunlosky, J., Rawson, K. A., Marsh, E. J., Nathan, M. J., & Willingham, D. T. (2013). Improving students' learning with effective learning techniques: Promising directions from cognitive and educational psychology. *Psychological Science in the Public Interest, 14*(1), 4–58.

Garner, R. (1990). When children and adults do not use learning strategies: Toward a theory of settings. *Review of Educational Research, 60*(4), 517–529.

Kapur, M. (2016). Examining productive failure, productive success, unproductive failure, and unproductive success in learning. *Educational Psychologist, 51*(2), 289–299.

Karpicke, J. D., Butler, A. C., & Roediger, J. D. III. (2009). Metacognitive strategies in student learning: Do students practise retrieval when they study on their own? *Memory, 17*(4), 471–479.

Keeney, T. J., Cannizzo, S. R., & Flavell, J. H. (1967). Spontaneous and induced verbal rehearsal in a recall task. *Child Development, 38*(4), 953–966.

Klaczynski, P. A. (2000). Motivated scientific reasoning biases, epistemological beliefs, and theory polarization: A two-process approach to adolescent cognition. *Child Development, 71*(5), 1347–1366.

Lobato, J. (2012). The actor-oriented transfer perspective and its contributions to educational research and practice. *Educational Psychologist, 47*(3), 232–247.

Metzger, M. J. (2007). Making sense of credibility on the web: Models for evaluating online information and recommendations for future research. *Journal of the American Society for Information Science and Technology, 58*(13), 2078–2091.

OECD. (2016). *Definition and Selection of Competencies (DeSeCo).* Retrieved from www.oecd.org/edu/skills-beyond-school/definitionandselectionofcompetenciesdeseco.htm

P21 Partnership for 21st Century Learning. (n.d.). *Framework for 21st century learning.* Retrieved from www.p21.org/about-us/p21-framework

Pea, R. D. (1987). Socializing the knowledge transfer problem. *International Journal of Educational Research, 11*(6), 639–663.

Ross, B. H. (1987). This is like that: The use of earlier problems and the separation of similarity effects. *Journal of Experimental Psychology: Learning, Memory, and Cognition, 13,* 629–639.

Rychen, D. S., Salganik, L. H., & McLaughlin, M. E. (Eds.). (2003). *Contributions to the second DeSeCo symposium.* Neuchâtel, Switzerland: Swiss Federal Statistical Office.

Salomon, G., & Perkins, D. N. (1989). Rocky roads to transfer: Rethinking mechanisms of a neglected phenomenon. *Educational Psychologist, 24*(2), 113–142.

Schwartz, D. L., & Martin, T. (2004). Inventing to prepare for future learning: The hidden efficiency of encouraging original student production in statistics instruction. *Cognition and Instruction, 22*(2), 129–184.

Singley, M. K., & Anderson, J. R. (1989). *The transfer of cognitive skill.* Cambridge, MA: Harvard University Press.

Uesaka, Y., Manalo, E., & Ichikawa, S. (2007). What kinds of perceptions and daily learning behaviors promote students' use of diagrams in mathematical problem solving? *Learning and Instruction, 17,* 322–335.

PART I
Theory

1

ELICITING AND BUILDING UPON STUDENT-GENERATED SOLUTIONS

Evidence from productive failure

Manu Kapur, Ngan Hoe Lee, and June Lee

Introduction

A commitment to a constructivist epistemology requires that we build upon learners' prior knowledge. Therefore, understanding students' conceptions prior to instruction is important, because one cannot build upon prior knowledge if one does not know what this knowledge is in the first place. Given that students may have some prior knowledge about a concept they have yet to learn, it follows that the burden of the instructional designer is to first understand the *nature* of learner's prior knowledge structures. The design of design tasks and activities, therefore, must seek to elicit the kinds of knowledge—representations, solutions, strategies, ideas—that students can spontaneously generate using their formal as well as intuitive prior knowledge.

Not surprisingly, a prominent area in mathematics education research is to uncover the nature of student's prior knowledge structure, and this is evidenced by research delving into students' intuitive or informal problem strategies, alternative conceptions, and misconceptions prior to instruction in many mathematical content domains. These areas cover important K–12 mathematical topics such as addition and subtraction (e.g., Carpenter, Franke, Jacobs, Fennema, & Empson, 1998; Carpenter, Hiebert, & Moser, 1981), multiplication and division (e.g., Kouba, 1989; Mulligan & Mitchelmore, 1997; Outhred & Mitchelmore, 2000), proportional reasoning (e.g., Lamon, 1993, 1996), and algebra (e.g., Carraher, Schliemann, Brizuela, & Earnest, 2006; Johanning, 2004).

In statistics education, students' thinking about various statistical concepts, such as central tendencies, probability, and covariance, has also received attention in education research (e.g., Shaughnessy, 2007). Underlying many statistical concepts is the notion of variability, and researchers have pointed out that it should play a central role in statistics education (e.g., Loosen, Lioen, & Lacante, 1985). Note, however, that the work that is relevant here is research that examines students' pre-instructional ideas about variance, that is, before they learn the concept of variance, and not their general literacy and statistical thinking. Some areas of research regarding students' pre-instructional ideas about variability include:

(a) examining their predictions of the outcomes in sampling situations (e.g., Kelly & Watson, 2002; Reading & Shaughnessy, 2004; Shaughnessy, Canada, & Ciancetta, 2003; Shaughnessy, Ciancetta, & Canada, 2004),

(b) gaining an insight into their thinking about variability in the outcomes of a probability experiment (Shaughnessy & Ciancetta, 2002; Watson & Kelly, 2004), and

(c) their reasoning when comparing data sets or distributions of samples (Ben-Zvi, 2004; Gal, Rothschild, & Wagner, 1989; Noll & Shaughnessy, 2012; Watson & Moritz, 1999).

Much as it is important to understand students' spontaneous generation of conceptions of variability prior to instruction, it is only the first step. What is also important is *how* we can leverage these conceptions effectively in and for teaching and learning. As our review of research will show, past research does a good job of describing students' conceptions of variability, but remains relatively silent in how such elicitation of conceptions can be designed for and, in turn, used for subsequent teaching and learning of variability.

This gap in research sets up the case for the *productive failure* (PF; Kapur, 2008) instructional design as a possible method for teachers to not only elicit students' pre-instructional conceptions about variability but also build upon these to teach the targeted concept of variance.

While illustrating the PF design forms the main aim of the chapter, we begin with a brief review of past research on students' thinking and reasoning about variability to better situate our work on PF. Following that, we describe and present evidence from classroom-based studies that show students learning the concept of variance using the PF learning design. We end by discussing the findings and drawing implications for theory and research.

Students' thinking about variability

Research on students' pre-instructional thinking and reasoning about variability can be conceived to include two main areas: one that examines students' reasoning with variability, and another that investigates students' notions of how variability is measured.

In the studies examining students' reasoning with variability in data, prediction tasks were typically employed. For example, Shaughnessy et al. (2004) classified students' reasoning as predominantly additive, proportional, or distributional. "Additive" reasoners attended to the absolute numbers of a mixture rather than the population proportion, while "proportional" reasoners defended their predictions by referring to the population proportions. Students who reasoned "distributionally" attempted to account for both the centres and variability when making repeated sampling predictions.

Gal et al. (1989) examined the reasoning of grade 3 and 6 students when judging which data exhibited better performance (e.g., which class has a better test score). They found that very few students reasoned statistically (e.g., summaries of the data in each group, or synthesizing various features of the set), and most used proto-statistical strategies (e.g., focused on some features of the data such as the mode, but not considering the value). Extending Gal et al.'s (1989) research, Watson and Moritz (1999) found that students' strategies to the task ranged from numerical (e.g., retrieving scores from graphs to calculate totals or means) to visual (e.g., looking at a single feature such as the highest value), either employed individually or in conjunction with each other.

The second area of research on students' pre-instructional conceptions on variability concerns how students measure variability (Lehrer & Kim, 2009; Lehrer, Kim, & Jones, 2011; Lehrer, Kim, & Schauble, 2007). Findings revealed that grade 5 and 6 students were able to produce different measures of "precision." Some of the representative measures reported in Lehrer and Kim (2009) and Lehrer et al. (2011) include examining the percentage of cases in the central clump, looking at the range, summing of pair-wise differences among the ordered set of measures, and computing the deviations of the measures from the median.

In summary, research shows that students have rich constructive resources to spontaneously generate formal and intuitive conceptions of variability. However, research is relatively silent on: (a) the design features of tasks and activities that help elicit such conceptions, (b) exactly *how* students' conceptions could be used for instruction, that is, a systematic framework for teachers to engage with and review the various students' solutions, as well as utilizing them to teach the canonical concept of variance.

In the following sections, we describe the PF learning design (Kapur & Bielaczyc, 2012) as a method for teachers to not only elicit students' pre-instructional conceptions about variability but also build upon these to teach the targeted concept of variance. Thus, the goal of PF is not only to design tasks and activity structures that afford students to spontaneously generate multiple representations and solutions to carefully designed problems, but also how these conceptions can be used by the teacher for subsequent instruction.

PF in learning the concept of variance

PF engages students in generating solutions to novel problems first before teaching them the concept. Before learning a concept, students are afforded the opportunity to generate multiple representations and solutions, even if these solutions are not canonically correct. Although students typically fail in their problem-solving efforts to produce the correct solution, their sub-optimal representation solution methods (RSMs) can be a productive resource in preparing them to learn better from subsequent instruction (Kapur, 2010, 2012, 2014a, 2014b; Loibl & Rummel, 2014).

The PF learning design embodies four core, interdependent mechanisms: (a) activation and differentiation of prior knowledge in relation to the targeted concepts, (b) attention to critical conceptual features of the targeted concepts, (c) explanation and elaboration of these features, and (d) organization and assembly of the critical conceptual features into the targeted concepts (for a fuller explication of the design principles, see Kapur & Bielaczyc, 2012). These mechanisms are embodied in a two-phase design: a generation and exploration phase (phase 1) followed by a consolidation phase (phase 2). Phase 1 affords opportunities for students to spontaneously generate and explore the affordances and constraints of multiple RSMs, wherein activation and differentiation of prior knowledge affords noticing of the critical features of the concept, whereas phase 2 affords opportunities for organizing and assembling the relevant student-generated RSMs into canonical RSMs, wherein the activated knowledge creates the conceptual hooks for the new knowledge to be integrated and assembled. The designs of both phases were guided by the following core design principles that embody the above mentioned mechanisms:

(1) create problem-solving contexts that involve working on complex problems that challenge but do not frustrate, rely on prior mathematical resources, and admit multiple RSMs (mechanisms a and b);
(2) provide opportunities for explanation and elaboration (mechanisms b and c);
(3) provide opportunities to compare and contrast the affordances and constraints of failed or sub-optimal RSMs and the assembly of canonical RSMs (mechanisms b–d).

The PF learning design has been employed in the instruction of the targeted concept of variance in the mathematics classrooms in Singapore since 2009, and its efficacy compared to the traditional direct instruction (DI) has been demonstrated in several studies (Kapur, 2010, 2012, 2014a, 2014b, 2015a; Kapur & Bielaczyc, 2012). In such comparisons, the same teacher taught students in the PF and DI conditions. The experimental manipulation was in the sequence of problem solving and instruction. In the DI condition, students received instruction on the concept of variance followed by problem solving. In the PF condition, students engaged in problem solving first before being instructed on the concept of variance (for a fuller description of the design of the conditions, please see the cited studies). The main findings from these studies are:

(1) Despite seemingly failing in their collective and individual problem-solving efforts, PF students significantly outperformed their counterparts in the traditional DI classrooms in conceptual understanding and transfer, without compromising procedural fluency (Kapur, 2010, 2012, 2014a, 2014b, 2015a; Kapur & Bielaczyc, 2012).

(2) Students with significantly different mathematical abilities were not as different in terms of their ability to generate multiple RSMs to complex problems posed during the generation and exploration phase (Kapur, 2012, 2014b), challenging the strong and persistent belief among the teachers we have worked with that such design problem solving is more appropriate for students with high mathematics problem-solving ability, as measured by national standardized problem-solving tests in mathematics.

(3) The number of RSMs generated was positively and significantly correlated with learning gains, showing that students' RSM generation capacity predicted how much they learnt from PF (Kapur, 2012, 2014a, 2014b, 2015a). In several studies, we had found that the number of RSMs generated by the groups in the PF condition had significant effects on procedural fluency, conceptual understanding, and transfer items on the post-test.

Taken together, these findings evidence the mechanisms embodied in the PF design. Specifically, the spontaneous generation of RSMs represents an activation and differentiation of prior knowledge. Such activation and differentiation creates the necessary conditions for students to notice the critical features of the concept, which then affords opportunities for better encoding and elaboration during instruction. The significant correlation between the number of RSMs and effects on learning outcomes further support these explanations. In particular, effects on transfer suggest that such spontaneous generation of RSMs also affords students to assemble knowledge in ways that allow better cueing and retrieval in novel problem-solving contexts. In other words, spontaneous generation aids noticing and encoding of critical domain information, as well as its retrieval in novel contexts (Kapur, 2015b).

Given the empirically demonstrated efficacy of the PF learning design (Kapur, 2012, 2014a, 2014b, 2015a), we will next describe how it was employed in the teaching and learning of the concept of variance. We will describe the types of students' pre-instructional conceptions that were elicited using the design and how these conceptions were built upon during the consolidation lesson.

Eliciting and building upon student-generated conceptions

The data reported here comes from the quasi-experimental research conducted in the eighth- and ninth-grade mathematics classes in Singapore (Kapur, 2012, 2014b). In these studies, students in intact classes were assigned to the PF condition, in which they learnt the variance concept using the PF learning design. The concept of variance is typically taught in the tenth grade, and therefore all students had no instructional experience with the targeted concept—variance—prior to the study, although they had learnt the concepts of mean, median, and mode in grades 7 and 8. The medium of instruction is English throughout the Singapore school system.

Research design and intervention

As per the PF design, PF students experienced the *generation and exploration* phase followed by the *consolidation and knowledge assembly* phase. In the *generation and exploration* phase, PF students worked in small groups (dyads and triads) to generate as many representation and solution methods (RSMs) as possible to a complex problem targeted at the variance concept (see Appendix). The problem is designed to trigger prior knowledge activation and differentiation as evidenced in the RSMs students generate. The problem presented a distribution of goals scored each year by three soccer players, and students were asked to design a quantitative index to determine the most consistent player. In line with the PF design principles (Kapur & Bielaczyc, 2012), no extra support or scaffolds were provided during these two periods other than affective encouragement to persist in the generation made explicit: Students were told that they may not be able to generate the canonical solution and that they should generate as many RSMs as possible even if their RSMs were suboptimal or incorrect.

In the *consolidation and knowledge assembly* phase, the teacher led a whole-class discussion to compare and contrast the various student-generated RSMs to the targeted canonical concept. Comparing and contrasting was designed to help students notice critical features of the concept, so that students not only encode what is critical but also understand what gets encoded better in relation to what they already know. After teaching the concept of variance, the teacher then devoted some time for problem-solving practice.

Process measures

The group work artifacts and discussion transcripts were used to determine the maximal set of RSMs generated by the PF groups using an analytical scheme developed in previous work on PF (Kapur & Bielaczyc, 2012).

Process results—students' RSMs

In the generation and exploration phase, students on average generated six to seven RSMs (Kapur, 2012, 2014b). To adequately reflect the diversity of the RSMs produced, a bottom-up categorization procedure was used to examine the full set of student-generated RSMs based on the mathematical approaches and concepts they deployed. The detailed procedures, including coding reliabilities, have been described in the cited studies. For the present purposes, we describe the four major and progressively sophisticated categories that emerged: (a) central tendencies, (b) qualitative/graphing methods, (c) frequency/counting methods, and (d) deviation methods.

Category 1: Central tendencies: Typically, groups started by using mean, median, and, in some cases, mode for data analysis. However, relying on central tendencies alone was not sufficient to generate a quantitative index for variance because the problem was designed in a way to keep the central tendencies invariant. Therefore, the design of the problem "forced" students to note that their current problem-solving strategy was inadequate, as well as to adapt or revise to consider alternative methods for generating an index for consistency.

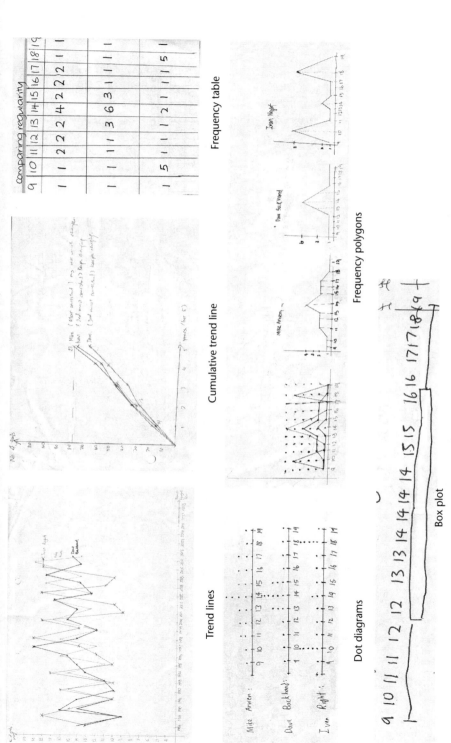

FIGURE 1.1 Examples of qualitative/graphical RSMs for measuring consistency. Students generated a diversity of representational forms such as trend lines, frequency tables, dot diagrams, frequency polygons, and box plots.

Category 2: Qualitative/graphing methods: Groups generated graphical and tabular representations that organized the data visually and were able to discern which player was more consistent. Typical examples of these qualitative/graphing methods, as shown in Figure 1.1, include dot diagrams, histograms, frequency tables, and trend lines. Evidently, the visual representations afforded a qualitative comparative analysis among the players, but they did not provide a quantitative index for consistency, even though the ideas of spread and clustering are important qualitative conceptual underpinnings for the concept of variance. Once again, the PF problem was designed to afford a problem-solving strategy of qualitative and visual

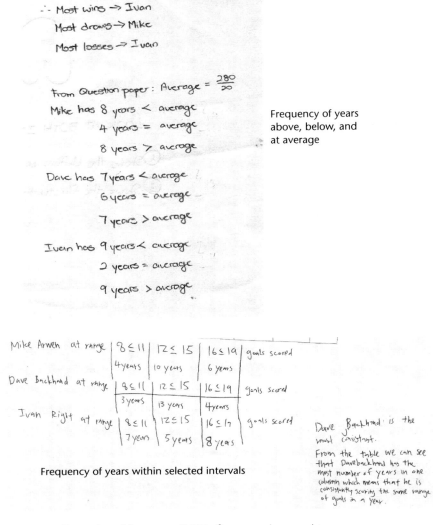

FIGURE 1.2 Examples of frequency RSMs for measuring consistency.

analysis of data. Note that although this strategy afforded noticing of critical distributional level features, it was not sufficient to fully encapsulate and measure consistency in the manner asked in the PF problem. Therefore, the design of the PF problem once again helped students notice what is critical in their spontaneous generation of RSMs but also a need to adapt and build upon their problem-solving strategies for generating RSMs.

Category 3: Frequency/counting methods: Groups built on the qualitative methods to develop frequency-based measures of consistency, and examples of these are shown in Figure 1.2. Some groups counted the frequency with which a player scored above, below, and at the mean, and concluded that the player with the highest frequency of scores at the mean had the most consistent performance. The design of the problem, therefore, afforded students to generate graphical representations and, based on the salient features they noted in those representations, adapt their problem-solving strategies to quantify those patterns. Frequency methods demonstrated that students could quantify the clustering trends that the qualitative representations revealed.

Category 4: Deviation methods: In their attempts to reason which player was consistent, groups also generated deviation methods, and examples of these are shown in Figure 1.3.

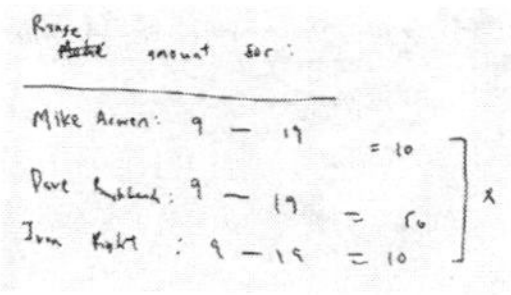

Range (DI)

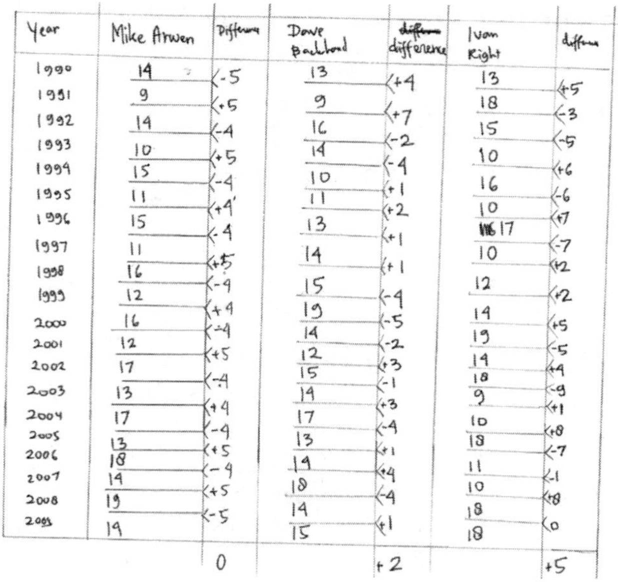

Year	Mike Arwen	Difference	Dave Backland	difference	Ivan Right	difference
1990	14	-5	13	+4	13	+5
1991	9	+5	9	+7	18	-3
1992	14	-4	16	-2	15	-5
1993	10	+5	14	-4	10	+6
1994	15	-4	10	+1	16	-6
1995	11	+4	11	+2	10	+7
1996	15	-4	13	+1	17	-7
1997	11	+5	14	+1	10	+2
1998	16	-9	15	-4	12	+2
1999	12	+4	19	-5	14	+5
2000	16	-4	14	-2	19	-5
2001	12	+5	12	+3	14	+4
2002	17	-4	15	-1	18	-9
2003	13	+4	14	+3	9	+1
2004	17	-4	17	-4	10	+8
2005	13	+5	13	+1	18	-7
2006	18	-9	14	+4	11	-1
2007	14	+5	18	-4	10	+8
2008	19	-5	14	+1	18	0
2009	14		15		18	
		0		+2		+5

Sum of deviations year-on-year deviations (D2)

FIGURE 1.3 Examples of deviation-based RSMs.

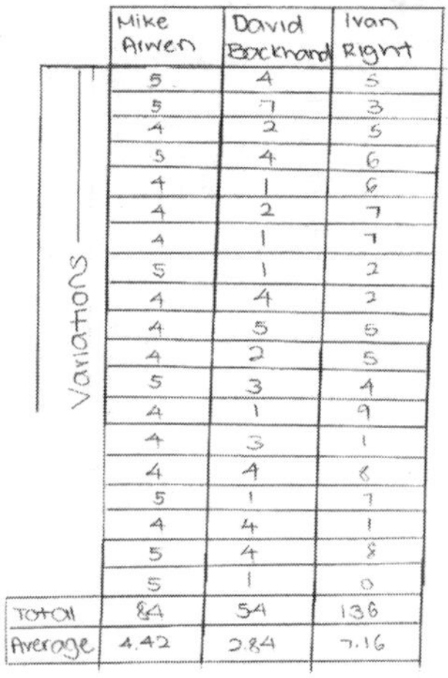

Variations	Mike Aiwen	David Bockhard	Ivan Right
	5	4	5
	5	7	3
	4	2	5
	5	4	6
	4	1	6
	4	2	7
	4	1	7
	5	1	2
	4	4	2
	4	5	6
	4	2	5
	5	3	4
	4	1	9
	4	3	1
	4	4	8
	5	1	7
	4	4	1
	5	4	8
	5	1	0
Total	84	54	136
Average	4.42	2.84	7.16

Average of year-on-year
absolute deviation (D3, D5)

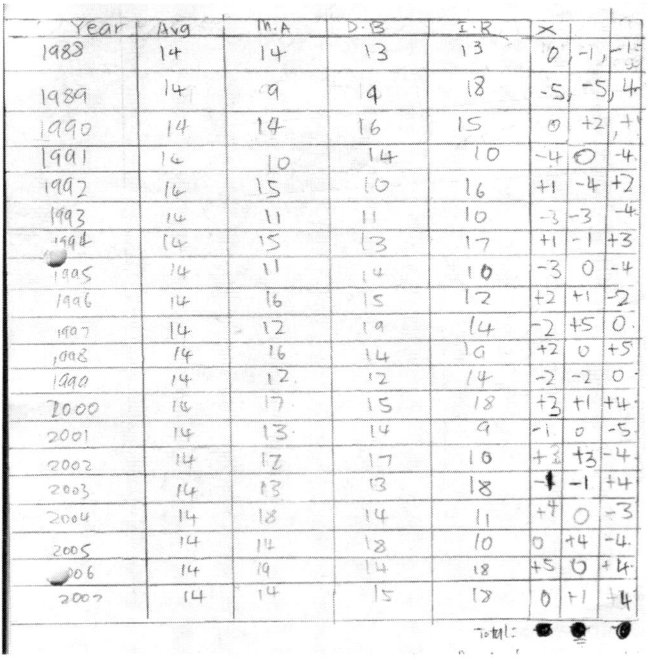

Year	Avg	M.A	D.B	I.R	X		
1988	14	14	13	13	0	-1	-1
1989	14	9	14	18	-5	-5	4
1990	14	14	16	15	0	+2	+1
1991	14	10	14	10	-4	0	-4
1992	14	15	10	16	+1	-4	+2
1993	14	11	11	10	-3	-3	-4
1994	14	15	13	17	+1	-1	+3
1995	14	11	14	10	-3	0	-4
1996	14	16	15	12	+2	+1	-2
1997	14	12	19	14	-2	+5	0
1998	14	16	14	16	+2	0	+5
1999	14	12	12	14	-2	-2	0
2000	14	17	15	18	+3	+1	+4
2001	14	13	14	9	-1	0	-5
2002	14	17	17	10	+3	+3	-4
2003	14	13	13	18	-1	-1	+4
2004	14	18	14	11	+4	0	-3
2005	14	14	18	10	0	+4	-4
2006	14	19	14	18	+5	0	+4
2007	14	14	15	18	0	+1	+4
				Totals			

Sum of deviation
about the mean
(D4)

FIGURE 1.3   *(Continued)*

The simplest deviation method generated was the range (deviation method 1, or simply D1). The problem was designed to activate this intuitive knowledge. However, by
keeping the range the same, the design of the problem also helped them see that the
range is not an optimal solution, and that they needed to adapt their problem-solving
strategy once again. Some groups calculated the sum of year-on-year deviations (D2)

of the goals scored by the players, and argued that the greater the sum, the lower the consistency of the players' performance. There were also groups that considered absolute year-on-year deviations (D3) to avoid deviations of opposite signs cancelling each other—an important conceptual leap toward understanding variance. Finally, there were some groups that calculated deviations about the mean (D4) only to find that they sum to zero. Like groups in the D3 category, a few groups further refined the calculations in D4 to consider not the sum of the deviations but the average (D5). Again, their aim was to find the player with the smallest deviation.

These four categories of student-generated RSMs suggested that the PF design afforded students the opportunity to generate multiple RSMs. It did so by (a) activating their formal and intuitive knowledge, (b) making the problem unsolvable by their formal and intuitive knowledge, (c) making them see and reason about how and why the problem-solving strategies did not work, and (d) generate new and progressively sophisticated problem-solving strategies.

Consolidation

In the consolidation and assembly phase, teachers built upon the student-generated RSMs that were activated during the generation and exploration phase. A spontaneous generation of representations and solutions is good only to the extent that teachers can engage students in comparing and contrasting among the various student-generated solutions, as well as between the student-generated solutions with the canonical solutions (e.g., average deviations from the mean, SD) (Kapur & Rummel, 2012; Loibl & Rummel, 2014). Through a whole-class discussion, teachers compared and contrasted the affordances and constraints of the RSMs and in the process engaged students to attend to and notice the critical features of the targeted concept. The explanation and elaboration of these features further aided students in the encoding process, allowing them to develop a deep understanding of the concept. Once all the critical features were being attended to, teachers then explained how these critical features were assembled in the canonical SD formula.

Attention to the critical features: Comparing and contrasting the RSMs

Teachers afforded students the opportunity to attend to the following critical features of the targeted concept of variance that were necessary to develop a deep understanding of the concept:

1 What is the difference between the mean and the distribution around the mean?
2 What is the difference between a qualitative description of the data (e.g., dot diagram and line graphs) and a quantitative description (e.g., range and SD)?
3 What is the difference between the frequency of a point and its position relative to a fixed reference point?

4 Why must we take deviations from a fixed point?
5 Why is the mean usually the fixed point; why can't it be the maximum or the minimum point, or even the median or the mode?
6 Why must we take deviations from the mean for all the points; why not just choose the maximum and the minimum point, or simply the range?
7 Why must deviations from the mean be made positive?
8 Why must we divide the sum of the squared deviations by n; why not simply work with their sum?
9 Why must we take the square root of the average of the squared deviations?
10 How do outliers affect SD?

Comparing central tendencies (e.g., mean) with qualitative/graphical methods, frequency methods with the qualitative/graphical methods, and frequency/counting methods with deviation methods afforded students opportunities to attend to the first three critical features respectively. The comparing and contrasting of the various deviation methods (see the descriptions of RSMs D1 to D5 in the previous section) provided students with opportunities to notice the critical features 4 to 8 above. Critical features 9 and 10 were attended to after the introduction of the canonical concept of SD. A comparison of the SD with average of deviations from the mean (D5) and the range (D1) afforded students the opportunity to attend to critical features 9 and 10, respectively.

Explanation and elaboration of the critical features

As teachers engaged students in noticing the critical features, teachers went on to explain and elaborate them to help students with the encoding process. In their elaboration and explanations, teachers further highlighted the affordances and constraints of the RSMs that were compared; the following elucidates how the explanation and elaboration of the SD unfolded:

1 In drawing students' attention to the critical feature of distribution about the mean when comparing the mean with qualitative/graphical methods, showing that the latter provided more information on the distribution about the mean, teachers further explained that central tendencies cannot convey information about variance, and that different distributions with the same mean can have the same variance. As students attended to the critical feature of the quantification when comparing qualitative/graphical methods with the frequency/counting methods, teachers elaborated the need of a precise value when determining the measure of consistency.
2 The notion of deviation was invoked after teachers elaborated on the need to consider the distance among points in a distribution as they got students to attend to the feature of relative position when comparing the frequency methods with the deviation methods. Teachers then went on to get students to attend to the critical features that examined where deviations could be best

taken from. For example, comparing between the sum of absolute year-on-year deviations (D3) and the sum of deviations about the mean (D4) allowed students to notice the need for a fixed reference point (e.g., the mean), and allowed teachers to explain why this was important—the consistency index would otherwise be sensitive to the ordering of data. Contrasting the range (D1) with the other deviation measures (D2 to D4) afforded students the chance to attend to the feature that maximum and minimum values may not be ideal reference points, prompting teachers to further explain that the range tells nothing about the distribution within the data, or in the center. Teachers proceeded to get students to notice the critical feature of why deviations must be made positive; this was achieved through comparing the methods that computed absolute year-on-year deviations or deviations about the mean (D3 and D5) with year-on-year deviations or deviations about the mean that kept the signs intact (D2 and D4). Following the explanation and elaboration of these two critical features, teachers went on to get students to attend to the next two critical features on making deviations positive and the need to take an average deviation. Comparing methods that computed absolute year-on-year deviations or deviations about the mean (D3 and D5) with year-on-year deviations or deviations about the mean that kept the signs intact (D2 and D4), teachers explained and elaborated on the cancelation effects that resulted when signs are kept intact, resulting in a case where the variance could be highly underestimated. When comparing the sum of and average deviation methods, teachers explained the affordance of averaging all deviations in allowing one to compare samples of different sizes.

3   The final two critical features of the need to take the square root of the average squared deviations and the effect of outliers on SD were elaborated after teachers introduced the canonical concept of SD. Teachers explained the need to reduce units into the same dimensionality with the taking of the square root and elaborated on the SD's sensitivity to the outliers.

Organization and assembly of the critical features into the targeted concept

Once all the critical features were noticed and elaborated upon, teachers then demonstrated how these features were organized and assembled in the canonical concept of the SD. Details of the design of the instructional materials and consolidation can be found in Kapur (2012, 2014b). Suffice it to say here that the consolidation lessons afforded students the opportunity to attend to the critical features of SD through the comparing and contrasting of the RSMs that they produced, to engage in the explanation and elaboration of the features, and to develop an understanding of why the canonical SD formula was assembled the way it is (also see Loibl & Rummel, 2014). Indeed, as noted earlier, the efficacy of PF in engendering better conceptual understanding and transfer has been established through several studies (Kapur, 2012, 2014a, 2014b, 2015a).

Discussion

In this chapter, we described the PF learning design (Kapur & Bielaczyc, 2012) as a possible method for teachers to not only elicit students' pre-instructional conceptions about variability but also build upon these to teach the targeted concept of variance.

In the generation and exploration phase of the PF learning design, the focus was on affording students the opportunity to leverage their formal as well as intuitive prior knowledge and resources. The PF problem was designed in a way that would activate students' problem-solving strategies based on their formal and intuitive knowledge. Yet, the problem would remain unsolvable based on such problem-solving strategies. Thus, the PF design afforded students to spontaneously generate a diversity of solutions. Because these solutions did not optimally succeed, the PF design "forces" them to notice and reason about how and why the solutions did not work. Such noticing and reasoning, in turn, potentiated further generation of solutions, where students could generate new problem-solving strategies having noticed the drawbacks of their earlier strategies. In the consolidation and assembly phase, students were afforded the opportunity for organizing and assembling the relevant student-generated RSMs into canonical RSM.

As described earlier, the role of the teacher was to: (a) direct student attention to get them to notice the critical conceptual features, (b) explain and elaborate upon the critical features by engaging students in the discussion, and (c) organize and assemble the critical features into the canonical solution. In addition, teachers set the expectations that the discussion of student-generated RSMs was not to assess them as correct or incorrect. Instead, it was to get students to appreciate why and understand what conditions some RSMs are better than others. In this way, teachers helped establish appropriate socio-mathematical expectations and norms in the classroom, which was critical in ensuring productive participation and discussion.

Researchers have previously highlighted that the measure of variance and variability (i.e., the SD) is computationally complex and difficult to motivate in instruction (delMas & Liu, 2005; Reading & Shaughnessy, 2004). Typically, instruction tended to concentrate on the procedural aspects of the formula, getting the students to practice with performing calculations and tying the SD to the empirical rule of normal distributions (delMas & Liu, 2005). As pointed out by Reading and Shaughnessy (2004), part of the difficulty in the instruction of the SD is the lack of accessible models and metaphors for students' conceptions of the SD. The challenge, therefore, is to help students coordinate the notions of center, spread, and deviation, and relate these together to conceive the SD as a measure of the relative density of values about the mean.

By engaging with and building upon students' prior conceptions about variability before formal instruction, the PF learning design might mitigate some of these issues faced by educators. With PF, as evidence from the PF studies cited earlier suggests, teachers were able to harness the various sub-optimal RSMs that students generate, compare and contrast them, and in the process get students to notice the critical features and discuss how these features are related to one another (Kapur & Rummel, 2012). Teachers then get students to see how these critical features were coordinated and assembled in the SD formula. In this process, students learn not only what works and does not work with their incorrect or sub-optimal solutions, but also why it does not work in comparison with the canonical solutions (Loibl & Rummel, 2014).

Conclusion

The PF tasks and activity structures are designed in principled ways of eliciting the spontaneous generation of multiple representations and solutions. The PF design affords the generation of problem-solving strategies because it is designed to activate the formal and informal, intuitive prior knowledge structures. Because the design also makes the problems unsolvable by these strategies, it affords the deployment of noticing and reasoning strategies, where students get to notice and understand how and why their solutions were sub-optimal. In turn, such noticing and understanding create the need to adapt and generate new problem-solving strategies, as evidenced by the various solutions students generated. Of course, merely understanding what students can generate is not sufficient for learning. Research on PF suggests that getting students to notice and coordinate the critical features by comparing and contrasting the various solutions with the canonical concept is just as critical. Herein, the PF design advances a principled way for teachers to build upon spontaneous student production and, in doing so, affords students the opportunity to develop deeper levels of understanding and transfer (Kapur, 2015b, 2016). At the same time, PF allows for more divergent ways of thinking about a concept, while engaging them in the disciplinary practices of mathematics (Bielaczyc & Kapur, 2010; Bielaczyc, Kapur, & Collins, 2013).

References

Ben-Zvi, D. (2004). Reasoning about variability in comparing distributions. *Statistics Education Research Journal, 3*(2), 42–63.

Bielaczyc, K., & Kapur, M. (2010). Playing epistemic games in science and mathematics classrooms. *Educational Technology, 50*(5), 19–25.

Bielaczyc, K., Kapur, M., & Collins, A. (2013). Building communities of learners. In C. E. Hmelo-Silver, A. M. O'Donnell, C. Chan, & C. A. Chinn (Eds.), *International handbook of collaborative learning* (pp. 233–249). New York, NY: Routledge.

Carpenter, T. P., Franke, M. L., Jacobs, V. R., Fennema, E., & Empson, S. B. (1998). A longitudinal study of invention and understanding in children's multidigit addition and subtraction. *Journal for Research in Mathematics Education, 29*(1), 3–20.

Carpenter, T. P., Hiebert, J., & Moser, J. M. (1981). Problem structure and first-grade children's initial solution processes for simple addition and subtraction problems. *Journal for Research in Mathematics Education, 12*(1), 27–39.

Carraher, D. W., Schliemann, A. D., Brizuela, B. M., & Earnest, D. (2006). Arithmetic and algebra in early mathematics education. *Journal for Research in Mathematics Education, 37*(2), 87–115.

delMas, R., & Liu, Y. (2005). Exploring students' conceptions of the standard deviation. *Statistics Education Research Journal, 4*(1), 55–82.

Gal, I., Rothschild, K., & Wagner, D. A. (1989). *Which group is better? The development of statistical reasoning in elementary school children.* Paper presented at the Meeting of the Society for Research in Child Development, Kansas City, KS.

Johanning, D. I. (2004). Supporting the development of algebraic thinking in middle school: A closer look at students' informal strategies. *The Journal of Mathematical Behavior, 23*(4), 371–388.

Kapur, M. (2008). Productive failure. *Cognition and Instruction, 26*(3), 379–424.

Kapur, M. (2010). Productive failure in mathematical problem solving. *Instructional Science, 38*(6), 523–550.

Kapur, M. (2012). Productive failure in learning the concept of variance. *Instructional Science, 40*(4), 651–672.

Kapur, M. (2014a). Productive failure in learning math. *Cognitive Science, 38*(5), 1008–1022.

Kapur, M. (2014b). Comparing learning from productive failure and vicarious failure. *The Journal of the Learning Sciences, 23*(4), 651–677.

Kapur, M. (2015a). The preparatory effects of problem solving versus problem posing on learning from instruction. *Learning and Instruction, 39*, 23–31.

Kapur, M. (2015b). Learning from productive failure. *Learning: Research and Practice, 1*(1), 51–65.

Kapur, M. (2016). Examining productive failure, productive success, unproductive failure, and unproductive success in learning. *Educational Psychologist, 51*(2), 289–299.

Kapur, M., & Bielaczyc, K. (2012). Designing for productive failure. *The Journal of the Learning Sciences, 21*(1), 45–83.

Kapur, M., & Rummel, N. (2012). Productive failure in learning and problem solving. *Instructional Science, 40*(4), 645–650.

Kelly, B. A., & Watson, J. M. (2002). Variation in a chance sampling setting: The lollies task. In B. Barton, K. C. Irwin, M. Pfannkuch, & M. O. J. Thomas (Eds.), *Mathematics education in the South Pacific: Proceedings of the 25th Annual Conference of the Mathematics Education Research Group of Australasia* (Vol. 2, pp. 366–373). Sydney, Australia: MERGA.

Kouba, V. L. (1989). Children's solution strategies for equivalent set multiplication and division word problems. *Journal for Research in Mathematics Education, 20*(2), 147–158.

Lamon, S. J. (1993). Ratio and proportion: Connecting content and children's thinking. *Journal for Research in Mathematics Education, 24*(1), 41–61.

Lamon, S. J. (1996). The development of unitizing: Its role in children's partitioning strategies. *Journal for Research in Mathematics Education, 27*(2), 170–193.

Lehrer, R., & Kim, M.-J. (2009). Structuring variability by negotiating its measure. *Mathematics Education Research Journal, 21*(2), 116–133.

Lehrer, R., Kim, M.-J., & Jones, R. (2011). Developing conceptions of statistics by designing measures of distribution. *ZDM, 43*(5), 723–736.

Lehrer, R., Kim, M.-J., & Schauble, L. (2007). Supporting the development of conceptions of statistics by engaging students in measuring and modeling variability. *International Journal of Computers for Mathematical Learning, 12*(3), 195–216.

Loibl, K., & Rummel, N. (2014). Knowing what you don't know makes failure productive. *Learning and Instruction, 34*, 74–85.

Loosen, F., Lioen, M., & Lacante, M. (1985). The standard deviation: Some drawbacks of an intuitive approach. *Teaching Statistics, 7*(1), 2–5.

Mulligan, J. T., & Mitchelmore, M. C. (1997). Young children's intuitive models of multiplication and division. *Journal for Research in Mathematics Education, 28*(3), 309–330.

Noll, J., & Shaughnessy, J. M. (2012). Aspects of students' reasoning about variation in empirical sampling distributions. *Journal for Research in Mathematics Education, 43*(5), 509–556.

Outhred, L. N., & Mitchelmore, M. C. (2000). Young children's intuitive understanding of rectangular area measurement. *Journal for Research in Mathematics Education, 31*(2), 144–167.

Reading, C., & Shaughnessy, J. M. (2004). Reasoning about variation. In D. Ben-Zvi & J. Garfield (Eds.), *The challenge of developing statistical literacy, reasoning and thinking* (pp. 201–226). Dordrecht, The Netherlands: Kluwer.

Shaughnessy, J. M. (2007). Research on statistics learning and reasoning. In F. K. Lester (Ed.), *Second handbook of research on mathematics teaching and learning: A project of the National Council of Teachers of Mathematics* (Vol. 2, pp. 957–1009). Charlotte, NC: Information Age Publishing.

Shaughnessy, J. M., & Ciancetta, M. (2002). Students' understanding of variability in a probability environment. In B. Phillips (Ed.), *Proceedings of the sixth International Conference on Teaching Statistics: Developing a statistically literate society* (pp. 295–312). Voorburg, The Netherlands: International Statistical Institute.

Shaughnessy, J. M., Canada, D., & Ciancetta, M. (2003). Middle school students' thinking about variability in repeated trials: A cross-task comparison. In N. Pateman, B. Dougherty, & J. Zilliox (Eds.), *Proceedings of the 27th Conference of the International Group for the Psychology of Mathematics Education* (Vol. 4, pp. 159–166). Honolulu, HI: University of Hawaii.

Shaughnessy, J. M., Ciancetta, M., & Canada, D. (2004). Types of student reasoning on sampling tasks. In M. J. Høines & A. B. Funglestad (Eds.), *Proceedings of the 28th Conference of the International Group for the Psychology of Mathematics Education* (Vol. 4, pp. 177–184). Bergen, Norway: Bergen University Press.

Watson, J. M., & Kelly, B. A. (2004). Expectation versus variation: Students' decision making in a chance environment. *Canadian Journal of Science, Mathematics and Technology Education, 4*(3), 371–396.

Watson, J. M., & Moritz, J. B. (1999). The beginning of statistical inference: Comparing two data sets. *Educational Studies in Mathematics, 37*(2), 145–168.

APPENDIX: Example of a complex problem targeted at the variance concept

The organizers of the Premier League Federation have to decide which one of the three players—Mike Arwen, Dave Backhand, and Ivan Right—should receive the "The Most Consistent Player for the Past 20 Years" award. The following table shows the number of goals that each striker scored between 1992 and 2011.

Year	Mike Arwen	Dave Backhand	Ivan Right
1992	14	13	13
1993	9	9	18
1994	14	16	15
1995	10	14	10
1996	15	10	16
1997	11	11	10
1998	15	13	17
1999	11	14	10
2000	16	15	12
2001	12	19	14
2002	16	14	19
2003	12	12	14
2004	17	15	18
2005	13	14	9
2006	17	17	10
2007	13	13	18
2008	18	14	11
2009	14	18	10
2010	19	14	18
2011	14	15	18

The organizers agreed to approach this decision *mathematically* by designing a *measure* of *consistency*. They decided to get your group's help. Here is what you must do:

(1) Design as many different measures of consistency as you can.
(2) Your measure of consistency should make use of all data points in the table.
(3) Show all working and calculations on the papers provided.

All the best. And remember, do not give up until you have developed several ways of calculating consistency!

2

PROMOTING LEARNERS' SPONTANEOUS USE OF EFFECTIVE QUESTIONING

Integrating research findings inside and outside of Japan

Yoshinori Oyama

Introduction

Numerous studies have been undertaken to elucidate effective pedagogical methods for cultivating questioning skills in students (e.g., King, 1995; Yeşil & Korkmaz, 2010; Yuzawa, 2009). However, considerations about effective methods for teaching questioning skills in real classroom settings have only recently gained some popularity, and the adoption of any method for teaching questioning strategies has gained little attention in regular classrooms around the world. One of the reasons for the low impact of questioning research on school practices is that the studies have generally not considered how students might use the questioning strategy of their own accord (i.e., spontaneously). Therefore, this chapter seeks to build upon the findings of previous studies in its attempts to address this issue.

The need for teaching questioning skills

The importance of learners' questioning skills has been stated in numerous studies. Seker and Kömür (2008), for example, pointed out the need to analyze the questions asked by teachers and students in the classroom and suggested that good practices relating to questioning should be incorporated into pre-service teacher training programs. Teixeira-Dias, Pedrosa-de-Jesus, Neri de Souza, and Watts (2005) listed three reasons why generating questions contributes to student learning: First, questions can lead to improvements in understanding and retention of information that a student encounters. Second, questions can drive classroom learning and are highly effective in increasing student interest, enthusiasm, and engagement. And third, learners' questions can be diagnostic of their understanding. Furthermore, quoting previous studies (King, 1994; Ikuenobe, 2001), Pedrosa-de-Jesus and Moreira (2009) reported that the act of formulating questions develops students' critical thinking, metacognition, autonomy, and decision making. Moreover, Chin and Osborne's (2008) review of questioning in science education suggested that, for students, questioning advances their comprehension of science; and for teachers, students' questions can be used as indicators of the students' understanding and thinking.

For a long time, traditional education has focused on the acquisition of knowledge and the memorization of facts, mathematical formulas, and historical events. However, the meaning of what constitutes knowledge has altered in recent decades due to—among other things—changes in the accessibility of information through technological developments such as the Internet. Greater emphasis is now being placed on the utilization of knowledge rather than the retention of knowledge. Therefore, the methods used in education provision also need to shift from mere promotion of "knowledge memorization" to development of skills in "knowledge utilization"—skills such as critical thinking, cooperative learning, and project management. Another skill essential to knowledge utilization is "question generation." As King (1994) reported, when students formulate their own questions, it makes those students actively engage in learning, and as a result, there are positive influences on achievement. In addition, the questions that students generate can be helpful to teachers in evaluating their students' understanding.

Oyama (2012) proposed a Question Learning Cycle (QLC) to indicate how learners' question generation is a crucial and integral part in the process of promoting self-regulated learning. According to this model, in order for leaners to become "self-regulated," they need to become sufficiently skilled in question generation. First, through practice, learners come up with their own questions pertinent to the task they are dealing with. Second, learners search for answers to such questions. And third, learners accomplish their exploratory learning, or another pertinent question arises and searching for answers begins again. In this cycle, teaching questioning skills is very important as learners need to be able to generate questions that are pertinent to their requirements, and that would enable the possibility of continued inquiry beyond the present time and requirements.

One indispensable objective of education should be the cultivation of students' questioning skills. However, many teachers tend to be uncertain about what to teach and how to teach their students questioning skills. Numerous studies have proposed categorization schemes of different types of questions

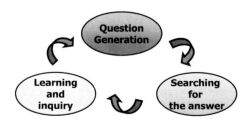

FIGURE 2.1 Question Learning Cycle (QLC).

(e.g., Eshach, Dor-Ziderman, & Yefroimsky, 2014; McTighe & Wiggins, 2013; Yeşil & Korkmaz, 2010), and some classification schemes can be useful in planning how to teach questioning skills. Therefore, in the next section, considerations about classification of questions are discussed.

Types of questions

In terms of classifying different types of questions, the most influential classification system has been Bloom's taxonomy (Bloom, Engelhart, Furst, Hill, & Krathwohl, 1956). The taxonomy suggests that questions can be categorized based on the hierarchy of thought involved in the generation of the question, and six levels are proposed: knowledge, comprehension, application, analysis, synthesis, and evaluation. This taxonomy has since been revised by Anderson and Krathwohl (2001) who proposed two dimensions: cognitive and knowledge. Concerning the cognitive aspect, six categories have been proposed: remembering, understanding, application, analysis, evaluation, and creation. On the other hand, four categories have been proposed for the knowledge aspect: factual, conceptual, procedural, and metacognitive. According to this revision, questions can then be categorized according to the cognitive processes and the knowledge aspects that they entail.

With regard to the content of the question, Scardamalia and Bereiter (1992) categorized questions based on their sources, proposing the following categories: text-based questions (i.e., questions that students ask as part of their study of a text), and knowledge-based questions (i.e., questions based only on the students' prior knowledge). In addition, Pedrosa-de-Jesus, Teixeira-Dias, and Watts (2003) categorized questions into two types: confirmation questions and transformation questions. Confirmation questions seek to clarify information and detail and attempt to differentiate between fact and speculation. In contrast, transformation questions signal some restructuring or reorganization of the student's understanding. They mentioned that both types of questions are important and they are interrelated. In another study, Yeşil and Korkmaz (2010) categorized questions generated by university students studying social studies as "lower order" questions and "higher order" questions, the basic distinction being that lower-order questions ask mere definition or meaning of new terms, while higher-order questions ask about the relationships between factors, possible applications, and comparisons to deepen thought. Eshach et al. (2014) distinguished between questions in a similar manner, but they used three categories: "low-order" questions (LOQ), "mid-order" questions (MOQ), and "high-order" questions (HOQ). LOQs are questions pitched at the knowledge and understanding level; MOQs are questions concerning the implementation level; and HOQs are questions requiring analysis, synthesis, and evaluation. Eshach et al. (2014) reported that teachers ask about twice as many MOQs and around a third more HOQs than students.

From a school teacher's perspective, a former Japanese junior and high school teacher, Onishi (1998), categorized teachers' questioning into three types: open questions, big questions, and organization questions. Open questions allow students to think freely, alert them to their perplexity, and locate problems. Asking students' opinion on the material used in the lesson is one example of an open question. Onishi (1998) pointed out that open questions are not suitable for inputting particular knowledge for students. Big questions, on the other hand, have similar characteristics to open questions, but, unlike open questions, big questions direct students' thinking. Asking students "What does 'A' symbolize?" in a literature class is an example of a big question. Finally, organization questions literally organize students' pre-existing knowledge, in order for students to realize what is known and what should be known for learning the current subject matter. Asking students "Which country has a larger population?" is one of the example of an organization question. Also, a former Japanese elementary school teacher, Noguchi (2011), described six functions of teacher questions: alerting (students notice new ways of viewing things), modification of thinking (students notice pitfalls in their thinking and modify those), deepening (triggered by a teacher's question, students think deeper and expand their thoughts), acquisition (by teachers' questioning, students acquire new knowledge), promotion of expertise (teachers' questions such as "Why is A superior to B?" make students notice the difference and seek a higher level of understanding), and application (teachers' questions make students notice what they learn in the class is applicable to the real world).

Such taxonomies are useful in describing the questioning phenomena in classrooms. However, they do not directly address the pedagogical question of what to do in teaching activities to promote the development of students' questioning skills. Concerning this aspect, Yuzawa (2009) classified learners' questions into three types: "contents comprehension questions," "contents structure questions," and "contents application question." A contents comprehension question aims to clarify the point where one's understanding of the material is not sufficient. In contrast, a contents structure question aims to clarify the crucial point of the material. Finally, a contents application question applies the learning contents using 'how' and 'why.' Yuzawa applied this classification scheme to teaching practice at the junior high school level: he asked students to generate as many questions as they liked. Next, using 'self-question' cards, he asked students to write down the questions and the reasons for generating those questions. Lastly, he asked the students to classify the questions into the categories described above. If the students' understanding of the material was insufficient, the teacher additionally asked them to generate more of the three types of questions—as appropriate. He then collected the students' 'self-question' cards. In the next class, the teacher introduces some of the questions students had generated to the whole class and asks the students' opinions about those questions and provides comments about them.

Also concerning teaching application, Niime and Arita (1987) classified teachers' questioning according to three learning phases: grasping, exploring, and summarizing. In the grasping phase, the aim is to get students to grasp the issue that the learning activity or instruction is targeting. Therefore, during this phase, the teacher should be asking questions that call upon learners' prior knowledge and stimulate awareness of any preconceptions that the learners may possess. In the exploring phase, the teacher should ask questions about relationships, similarities, differences, causes, and results of the phenomena being considered. In the summary phase, teachers should ask questions that prompt learners to *generalize* what has been learned, to generate and determine their own opinion, and to transfer acquired knowledge and skills to new settings.

More recently, McTighe and Wiggins (2013) described insightful questions as "essential questions" and distinguished them from "non-essential questions." According to McTighe and Wiggins (2013), an essential question has features such as stimulating ongoing thinking and inquiry, raising more questions, and sparking discussion and debate. They explained, for example, that a typical question in social studies on the topic of "the Constitution" is "What is the Second Amendment?" However, such questions can be considered non-essential and would not stimulate learners' curiosity. On the other hand, an essential question such as "Where is the balance between personal freedom and the common good?" could stimulate further thought and discussion on the topic. McTighe and Wiggins (2013) referred to specific essential questions as "topical" and more general essential questions as "overarching" (p. 9). They pointed out that "overarching essential questions transcend the particular subject matter to point toward broader, transferable understandings that cut across unit (and even course) topics" (p. 10). For instance, an essential question on the topic of science is "How does the structure of various insects help them to survive?" On the other hand, an overarching essential question is "How are structure and function related?" Another example of an overarching essential question is "What are common factors in the rise and fall of powerful nations?" while a topical essential question is "Why did the Soviet Union collapse?" (p. 9). These kinds of essential questions stimulate leaners' curiosity, and they enhance their likelihood of engaging in self-regulatory learning behaviors. Although retaining knowledge is a fundamental part of learning, generating questions assists learners to become effective knowledge users. Viewed this way, equipping learners with essential questioning skills can be considered an indispensable objective in the current educational environments, and students' spontaneity in generating essential questions should be promoted. Table 2.1 summarizes some of the key points in studies introduced in this section.

Teaching questioning strategy

As mentioned in the previous section, the objective of education needs to shift from "teaching knowledge" to "teaching how to utilize knowledge," and teaching learners ways to generate questions is one possible direction to foster the development of learners as "question askers" rather than merely as "question responders." However, numerous studies at different educational levels generally indicate that learners tend to avoid asking questions. For instance, Pedrosa-de-Jesus, Silva Lopes, Moreira, and Watts (2012) reported in their study that one student did not ask questions because he did not want to interrupt the rhythm of the teacher's talk. In addition, Eshach et al. (2014) reported that 84.5% of teacher questions and 82% of

TABLE 2.1 Summary of studies on classification of questions

Study	Classification of questions	Implication
Niime and Arita (1987)	Grasping, exploring, and summarizing	Teachers' questioning can be classified based on learners' three learning phases
Scardamalia and Bereiter (1992)	Text-based and knowledge-based questions	Knowledge-based questions promote construction of knowledge from various sources, and have more educational potential than text-based questions (e.g., they promote construction of knowledge from various sources)
Onishi (1998)	Open questions, big questions, and organization questions	From the teacher's perspective, questions can be categorized based on the teacher's intention in the lesson
Anderson and Krathwohl (2001)	Remembering, understanding, application, analysis, evaluation, and creation	Questions can be categorized based on the cognitive processes and thought levels they entail
Pedrosa-de-Jesus, Teixeira-Dias, and Watts (2003)	Confirmation questions and transformation questions	Both types of questions are important and interrelated; sometimes transformation questions come after confirmation questions, but the reverse process is also possible
Yuzawa (2009)	Contents comprehension questions, contents structure questions, and contents application questions	Classification of questions not only helps in facilitating deeper thinking in leaners but also helps teachers in evaluating the levels of understanding of their students
Yeşil and Korkmaz (2010)	Lower-order and higher-order questions	Asking student group to bring their questions, and teaching the classes by simply answering the students' questions increases generation of higher-order questions
Noguchi (2011)	Alerting, modification of thinking, deepening, acquisition, promoting expertise, and application	Teachers' questions can be categorized based on the functions they serve in learners
McTighe and Wiggins (2013)	Essential questions, overarching questions, and topical questions	Both teachers and students should ask essential questions in the classroom to achieve curriculum objective
Eshach, Dor-Ziderman and Yefroimsky (2014)	Low-order questions (LOQs), mid-order questions (MOQs), and high-order questions (HOQs)	Reported that teachers typically ask about twice as many MOQ and around a third more HOQ than students

student questions were low-quality questions. Moreover, Ikuta and Maruno (2004) found that pupils at grades 4 and 6 do not ask questions not because they hesitate to ask questions but because they do not have questions in the first place. This result suggests a dire need for question generation training even for elementary school children who are generally considered frequent question askers.

Many researchers have endeavored to teach questioning skills to learners (see Table 2.2). In the late 1970s, the focus of teaching questioning skills had mostly been on reading comprehension (André & Anderson, 1979; Frase & Schwartz, 1975). In the 1990s, a few studies were conducted to promote learners' questioning skills in lecture comprehension (e.g., King, 1992). Also, Rosenshine, Meister, and Chapman's (1996) meta-analysis of intervention studies compared the effects of question type (i.e., text-explicit, text-implicit, and schema-based questions), story grammar categories (i.e., setting, main character, character's goal, obstacle, main idea), signal words (i.e., "who," "what," "where," "when"), and generic questions (e.g., How are _____ and _____ alike?, What is the main idea of _____?, and How is _____ related to _____?). The result of their meta-analysis revealed that using signal words and generic questions produced the largest effect size.

Another group of researchers studied the effects of teaching questioning skills in a university lecture setting. Keeley, Ali, and Gebing (1998) encouraged psychology students to go beyond the "sponge" (memory-emphasis) model and gave students question-generating assignments. Students submitted three to six questions based on their readings. They found three categories in the questions that the students generated: "Clear-Evaluative Questions" (e.g., How reliable are their measures?), "Implication/Curiosity Questions" (e.g., What does the success rate of the drug treatment say about the cause of depression?), and "Ambiguous-Evaluative Questions" (e.g., Who were the therapists?). After question generation practice, the results showed an increase in clear-evaluative and ambiguous-evaluative questions. This finding confirm that questioning is a teachable skill.

Essential questions (McTighe & Wiggins, 2013; Wiggins & McTighe, 2005) can also be incorporated and used in designing a curriculum framework. Obenchain, Orr, and Davis (2011) reported on a teaching practice that adopted use of essential questions (EQ). They proposed a formula (EQ + historical topic = HQ) for developing historical questions (HQs). In this formula, HQs were directly related to specific content and to a specific EQ to help teachers develop HQs. History teachers from elementary to high school levels were asked to use essential questions as a core framework of the curriculum. For example, the essential question "Should liberty be limited?" could be vertically framed for different class levels. At the elementary school level, for example, "Should liberty be limited?" could be framed into a question such as "Were the British justified in limiting the liberty of colonists who protested against new taxes?" At the middle school level, the question could be: "Was the North justified in limiting the liberties of southern property owners in the civil war?" And at the high school level, the question could be: "During the Vietnam War, should the liberties of press, speech, and protest have been limited?" Based on their results, they concluded that essential questions could reframe a history curriculum to broaden and deepen the history taught in the classroom.

It is considered important for teachers to ask high-quality questions (e.g., Niime & Arita, 1987). Because of this, the effect of teaching questioning skills to pre-service teachers has also been examined. In Yeşil and Korkmaz's (2010) study, pre-service teachers were divided into three groups and were taught and asked to use three different teaching methods for six weeks. In experiment group I, the instructor asked the pre-service teachers to bring their questions, and the classes were taught only by answering those questions. In experiment group II, the instructor taught the class based on questions that the instructor prepared. Finally, in experiment group III, pre-service teachers in the class were taught by using both their own questions and the instructor's questions. Pre-service teachers' questions were collected before and after the intervention and analyzed. The results showed that the teaching method based on student questions positively contributed to the students' question-asking skills with regard to the explicitness of the objective of the questions they generated, thus confirming the importance of providing opportunities for students to generate their own questions in classroom teaching.

In Japan in the late 1980s, Akita (1988) examined the effects of self-questioning on the reading comprehension of students. She assigned 117 seventh-graders in junior high school to three treatment groups: a question group generated questions on the passage, an answer group responded to questions provided by the researcher, and a control group simply read the passage. Comparing the students' comprehension of the macrostructure of the reading material, the results showed that question generation facilitated better comprehension of the main ideas, and the effect was larger for lower and middle verbal ability students than for those with higher verbal ability.

The studies that have been reviewed here show that teaching questioning skills has an effect of assisting in the development of leaners' abilities to generate useful questions. However, most of these studies have reported the positive effects right after their training sessions ended: hence, they lack examination of learners' subsequent spontaneous use of the questioning strategy. As McTighe and Wiggins (2013, p. 59) noted, "a long-term goal of using essential questions is that students eventually become the askers and pursuers of such questions without being directed by the teacher." The ultimate objective of teaching the questioning strategy should be that of promoting learners' spontaneous use of questioning, not just fostering short-term usage of the strategy. In the next section, possible methods for promoting learners' spontaneity in using questioning will be discussed.

Promoting learners' spontaneous use of questioning

Teachers' questions are potential models for students in generating their own high-quality questions. However, focusing on the differences between experienced and novice teachers' question generation, Tienken, Goldberg, and DiRocco (2010) reported that the number of productive questions generated by beginning teachers

TABLE 2.2 Summary of studies on teaching questioning strategy

Study	Participants	Subject	Findings
Akita (1988)	117 junior high school students	Reading	Question generation facilitated the comprehension of main ideas, and the effect was larger for lower verbal ability students than for higher verbal ability students
King (1992)	57 college students	Remedial reading and study skills	Three groups' (question training, lecture summarizing, note taking) lecture comprehension and information retention performance were compared. Participants in the question training group were provided generic question stems and were found to outperform the other two groups
Rosenshine, Meister, and Chapman (1996)	Review paper	Review paper	The results of the meta-analysis show that using signal word and generic question stems has the highest effect size
Keeley, Ali, and Gebing (1998)	Total of 107 university students	Abnormal psychology	After the training, the numbers of clear-evaluative and ambiguous-evaluative questions generated by students increased. However, the number of implication/curiosity questions decreased
Yeşil and Korkmaz (2010)	71 university students	Social studies	Use of student-generated questions positively contributed to the students' question-asking skills with regard to the explicitness of the objective of questions they subsequently asked. On the other hand, use of teacher-generated questions had a more negative effect on students' question-asking skills
Obenchain, Orr, and Davis (2011)	History teachers	History	Essential questions can reframe history curriculum to broaden and deepen the contents taught in the classroom

was significantly low. Moreover, Ahtee, Juuti, Lavonen, and Suomela (2011) revealed that almost half of the student teachers in their study generated inappropriate or no questions at all. However, questioning is a skill that teachers can acquire through training. Therefore, especially for student teachers, it is necessary to provide training programs to improve their questioning skills so that they, in turn, can provide their students the necessary modeling in generating high-quality questions.

In addition to teacher training programs, the findings from a number of Japanese research studies could potentially contribute to the formulation of strategies for promoting learners' spontaneous use of questioning. The accumulated findings from these previous studies suggest that, in order to promote learners' spontaneous use of questioning, three features are essential: (1) multiple steps to scaffold learners in generating essential questions, (2) interaction between learners, and (3) formative and summative assessments of generated questions.

Multiple steps to scaffold learners in generating questions

Sato (1998) analyzed students' learning strategy use as well as the cognitive cost associated with the use of the strategies and found that when students perceive a high cost to using a strategy, they tend not to use that strategy. Therefore, one possible direction in interventions for promoting learners' questioning is to provide multiple steps to decrease the perceived cognitive cost associated with question generation. For instance, in a real educational setting, Ikuta and Maruno (2005) taught questioning skills to pupils at a Japanese elementary school by adopting a three-step approach. In the first step, the instructor asked pupils to read the material and underline the points they did not understand. In the second step, the instructor handed out a list of question stems (e.g., "What is the main idea of …?," "How does … relate to …?"; King, 1992) to assist pupils in generating their own questions. In the third step, the instructor asked the pupils to express their questions and to communicate among classmates to improve the quality of the questions they had made. The result of this study showed that the pupils' eagerness to "know more" increased after this intervention.

Considering Ikuta and Maruno's (2005) study, it would appear logical and beneficial to take a step-by-step approach to teaching questioning skills to students. First, 5W1H-type (i.e., who, what, when, why, when, and how) questions could be taught by adapting the question stems that King (1992) used. Next, students could be shown a large number of essential questions as model questions, so that they start appreciating the important qualities of such questions. Finally, they could be provided with instruction in generating questions in their real subject matter. This way the cognitive load on the learners could be lightened and they would feel less burdened when creating questions and thus possibly maintain the questioning habit even after training.

Reciprocal teaching

The next essential feature in promoting learners' spontaneous use of questioning is to provide opportunities for them to interact with other learners via questioning. In practice, Michita's (2011) study is distinctive in that it attempted to train undergraduate students' questioning skills not by providing question stems but through activities undertaken during university lectures in psychology. The 173 students in the study were required to give group presentations on lecture topics. The assigned presenter group gave their presentation, and students in the other groups listened to the presentation and discussed it to generate questions. Afterward, the presenter group answered the questions raised by the listener groups. The result showed that students' amount of questions and attitude toward questioning improved.

In another research study, Kiriyama (2009) asked undergraduate students to give group presentations in class. He distributed "question assessment sheets" for two reasons: to categorize questions raised by assigned students into who-, what-, when-, why-, and how-type questions; and to rate the appropriateness of the questions raised (5 = very appropriate; 4 = appropriate; 3 = moderate; 2 = not appropriate; 1 = not appropriate at all). Concerning appropriateness of the questions (level 1 to level 5), a chart describing appropriateness criteria was distributed to assist students in formulating their questions. The results showed that students improved in judging the quality of questions through the semester. This, therefore, is another study that showed the effectiveness of including peer-to-peer interaction in fostering the development of students' skills in using the questioning strategy.

Michita (2011) and Kiriyama (2009) did not describe the possible details of the mechanism behind the results they obtained. However, it was assumed that through the experience of giving and receiving questions in peer presentation activities, the participants realized that questioning has positive effects in critically viewing classmates' presentation and meta-cognitively viewing one's own presentation. The presenters most likely expected possible questions coming up from their audience, and this expectation of questions might have assisted in activating presenters' meta-cognition to ask self-questions such as "Are there any points still unclear?" and "Do any of the words need to be defined?" Also, it is possible that by comparing questions generated by peers, students gradually grasped the essence of high-quality questioning. Future research needs to investigate the mechanism of how and why peer interactions appear to improve learners' attitude to questioning and the quality of questions they generate. It is also plausible that learners' attitude change could lead to longer-term use of the questioning strategy, and teaching practice utilizing peer-interaction to questioning could be the key to promoting spontaneous use of the questioning strategy.

Formative and summative assessment

The third feature that could be useful to incorporate in a students' training program is assessment. It is still uncommon to evaluate questions that leaners have generated. However, assessment is a powerful tool and it can change students' behavior (cf. Murayama, 2003). In assessing learners, there are broadly two kinds of assessment that can be used: formative and summative assessment (Kitao, Nakajima, Hayashi, Hirose, Takaoka, & Ito, 2008, p. 137). The objective of formative assessment is to promote student learning through the feedback and suggestions that are provided. In contrast, a summative assessment's main objective is to assign a grade to students' performance at the end of a particular session (Kitao et al., 2008).

In a practical setting, Pedrosa-de-Jesus and Moreira (2009) used formative and summative assessments as tools for fostering students' questioning behaviors. In a seminar tutorial class, they asked students to solve one problem-based chemistry case as a formative assignment. During the class, students could talk to peers and the teacher to generate questions. After the class, written feedback was given to each student to improve the quality of the questions and to help the student create better questions. In relation to summative assessment, chemistry-based multiple-choice questions, a chemistry case study, and a problem-based case for question generation (similar to the formative assignment) were given to the students.

The students' questions were assessed in terms of (1) the number of questions at the cognitive level, (2) the relationship with the problem, and (3) the orientation to the problem. Pedrosa-de-Jesus and Moreira concluded that the use of student questions for assessment purposes improved students' learning and questioning skills.

A Japanese researcher, Tanaka (1999), developed a method that he referred to as the "question card method." It is distinct from other assessment methods in that the course grade that students receive is based only on the question cards students turn in after every lecture. The details of the question card method are as follows. First, students write questions on the lecture topics and background explanation of why he/she generated the question(s). Second, the instructor reads all of the students' questions and rates the appropriateness from 0 to 1. No matter how many questions are generated, "0" is given to questions unrelated to the lecture topic, "0.5" is given to questions without background explanation, and "1" is given to appropriate questions with background explanation. Third, the instructor responds to the students' questions in the next lecture. There are two types of responses. One is to respond to an individual question, and the other is to bind similar kinds of question into a common question and respond to them as one question. Finally, there are no mid-term or final exams, and the course grade awarded to students is based on the accumulation of the points that have been given for the questions they have generated. Tanaka (1999) reflected on his practice and concluded that, through question generation, students' thinking skills improved and they gradually became better at seeing things from multiple perspectives.

As Pedrosa-de-Jesusa and Moreira's (2009) and Tanaka's (1999) studies have shown, assessment is a powerful tool in changing learners' behavior. However, if learners stop asking questions right after the assessment ends, this practice essentially fails. The crucial point that teachers need to emphasize when using assessment for promoting questioning is the value of learners' self-assessment of questions. For instance, in addition to teacher assessment, the instructor might ask learners to assess the quality of their own questions on a scale from 1 to 5, such as what was used in Kiriyama's (2009) study, and to analyze how they might be able to improve the quality of the questions. This way, learners may develop skills for generating questions even after the training ends, and this in turn could help them maintain use of the questioning strategy.

Conclusion

As previously noted, teachers' questions are potentially a valuable resource for learners to learn "high-quality questioning" such as the generation of "essential questions" (McTighe & Wiggins, 2013; Wiggins & McTighe, 2005). Models of high-quality questioning could enable learners to experience deeper thinking and to consider questioning as an effective cognitive tool. Those learners in turn might spontaneously ask questions even after the training session ends. Moreover, in classroom settings, teachers are the ones who could show ideal models of questioning and lead question training in multiple steps, facilitate reciprocal teaching, and assess the quality of learners' questions. Therefore, what teachers do could be considered a key factor to promoting learners' spontaneous use of questioning.

In summary, this chapter introduced research findings and classroom practice conducted by Japanese researchers and teachers. By integrating research outcome outside of Japan, this chapter showed that, for developing self-regulated learners, promoting the ability to generate "essential questions" should be a target in teaching questioning in the classroom. Also, in order for students to generate such high-quality questions, by combining the findings of studies inside and outside of Japan, this chapter proposed using multiple steps to scaffold leaners to generate questions, reciprocal teaching, and assessment to give leaners feedback to improve the quality of the questioning. This chapter has argued the possibility that these pedagogical methods promote learners' spontaneous use of questioning and self-regulatory learners.

References

Ahtee, M., Juuti, K., Lavonen, J., & Suomela, L. (2011). Questions asked by primary student teachers about observations of a science demonstration. *European Journal of Teacher Education, 34*(3), 347–361.

Akita, K. (1988). The effects of self-questioning on comprehension of an expository passage. [Shitsumon zukuri ga setsumeibun no rikai ni oyobosu eikyo]. *Japanese Journal of Educational Psychology, 36*(4), 307–315.

Anderson, L. W., & Krathwohl, D. R. (Eds.). (2001). *A taxonomy for learning, teaching, and assessing: A revision of Bloom's taxonomy of educational objectives.* New York, NY: Longman.

André, M. E. D. A., & Anderson, T. H. (1979). The development and evaluation of a self questioning study technique. *Reading Research Quarterly, 14*(4), 605–623.

Bloom, B. S., Engelhart, M. D., Furst, E. J., Hill, W. H., & Krathwohl, D. R. (1956). Taxonomy of educational objectives: The classification of educational goals. In B. S. Bloom (Ed.), *Handbook I: Cognitive domain.* New York, NY: David McKay Company.

Chin, C., & Osborne, J. (2008). Students' questions: A potential resource for teaching and learning science. *Studies in Science Education, 44*(1), 1–39.

Eshach, H., Dor-Ziderman, Y., & Yefroimsky, Y. (2014). Question asking in the science classroom: Teacher attitudes and practices. *Journal of Science Education and Technology, 23*(1), 67–81.

Frase, L. T., & Schwartz, B. J. (1975). Effect of question production and answering on prose recall. *Journal of Educational Psychology, 67*(5), 628–635.

Ikuenobe, P. (2001). Questioning as an epistemic process of critical thinking. *Educational Philosophy and Theory, 33*(3&4), 325–341.

Ikuta, J., & Maruno, S. (2004). Does the child generate a question in elementary school class? Relation between interrogative feeling and the question generation, and expression [Shougakusei wa jyugyo chu ni sitsumon wo omoitsuite iru noka]. *Kyushu University Psychological Research, 5*, 9–18.

Ikuta, J.,& Maruno, S. (2005). Change of children questioning in elementary school class through question generation centered instruction [Sitsumon dukuri wo chushin ni shita shidou ni yoru jido no jyugyo shu no sitsumon seisei katudo no henka]. *Japanese Society for Educational Technology, 29*, 577–586.

Keeley, S. M., Ali, R., & Gebing, T. (1998). Beyond the sponge model: Encouraging students' questioning skills in abnormal psychology. *Teaching of Psychology, 25*(4), 270–274.

Kiriyama, S. (2009). Development of evaluation methods aiming at better questions from students [Gakusei no sitsumon ryoku kojyo wo neratta hyouka houhou no kaihatsu]. *Journal of Japanese Society for Engineering Education, 57,* 99–102.

Kitao,T., Nakajima, M., Hayashi, R., Hirose, T., Takaoka, M., & Ito, M. (2008). *Educational psychology [Seisen compact kyoiku shinrigaku].* Kyoto, Japan: Kitaouji Shobou.

King, A. (1992). Comparison of self-questioning, summarizing, and notetaking-review as strategfies for learning from lectures. *American Educational Research Journal, 29*(2), 303–323.

King, A. (1994). Guiding knowledge construction in the classroom: Effects of teaching children how to question and how to explain. *American Educational Research Journal, 31*(2), 338–368.

King, A. (1995). Inquiring minds really do want to know: Using questioning to teach critical thinking. *Teaching of Psychology, 22*(1), 13–17.

McTighe, J., & Wiggins, G. (2013). *Essential questions: Opening doors to student understanding.* Alexandria, VA: Association for Supervision and Curriculum Development (ASCD).

Michita, Y. (2011). Effect of question-asking training in a college lecture class on learners' attitudes and ability to ask questions [Jyugyo ni oite samazama na sitsumon keiken wo surukotoga sitsumon taido to sitsumon ryoku ni oyobosu kouka]. *Japanese Journal of Educational Psychology, 59,* 193–205.

Murayama, K. (2003). Test format and learning strategy use [Test keisiki ga gakushu houryaku ni ataeru eikyo]. *Japanese Journal of Educational Psychology, 51*(1), 1–12.

Niime, K., & Arita, K. (1987). *Questioning skill for children's deep thinking in social studies [Shakaika kangae saseru hatsumon no gijyutsu].* Tokyo: Meiji Tosho.

Noguchi, Y. (2011). *Questioning technics for teachers. [Kyoshi no tame no hatsumon no sahou].* Tokyo: Gakuyo Shobou.

Obenchain, K. M., Orr, A., & Davis, S. H. (2011). The past as a puzzle: How essential questions can piece together a meaningful investigation of history. *The Social Studies, 102*(5), 190–199.

Onishi, C. (1998). *Ways to improve questionings [Hatsumon Jyotatsu hou].* Tokyo: Minshusha.

Oyama, Y. (2012). Review of effects of self-questioning [Jiko sitsumon no kouka to kongo no kadai]. In Y. Uesaka & E. Manalo (Eds.), *Symposium: Promoting students' use of effective learning strategies: Findings from the first year of a JSPS supported research project* (pp. 15–22). Tokyo: The University of Tokyo.

Pedrosa de Jesus, H., & Moreira, A. C. (2009). The role of students' questions in aligning teaching, learning and assessment: A case study from undergraduate sciences. *Assessment & Evaluation in Higher Education, 34*(2), 193–208.

Pedrosa de Jesus, H., Silva Lopes, B., Moreira, A., & Watts, M. (2012). Contexts for questioning: two zones of teaching and learning in undergraduate science. *Higher Education, 64,* 557–571.

Pedrosa de Jesus, H., Teixeira-Dias., & Watts, M. (2003). Questions of chemistry. *International Journal of Science Education, 25*(8), 1015–1034.

Rosenshine, B., Meister, C., & Chapman, S. (1996). Teaching students to generate questions: A review of the intervention studies. *Review of Educational Research, 66*(2), 181–221.

Sato, J. (1998). Effects of learners' perceptions of utility and costs, and learning strategy preferences. [Gakushu houryaku no yuko sei no ninchi, cost no ninchi, konomi ga gakushu houryaku no siyou ni oyobosu eikyo]. *Japanese Journal of Educational Psychology, 46*(4), 367–337.

Scardamalia, M., & Bereiter, C. (1992). Text-based and knowledge-based questioning by children. *Cognition & Instruction, 9*(3), 177–199.

Seker, H., & Kömür, S. (2008). The relationship between critical thinking skills and in-class questioning behaviours of English language teaching students. *European Journal of Teacher Education, 31*(4), 389–402.

Tanaka, H. (1999). *Farewell to lecture style education: Introduction to the question card method [Sayonara Furui Kogi]*. Hokkaido: Hokkaido University Press.

Teixeira-Dias, J., Pedrosa de Jesus, H., Neri de Souza, F., & Watts, M. (2005). Teaching for quality learning in chemistry. *International Journal of Science Education, 27*(9), 1123–1137.

Tienken, C. H., Goldberg, S., & DiRocco, D. (2010). Questioning the questions. *Education Digest, 75*(9), 28–32.

Wiggins, G., & McTighe, J. (2005). *Understanding by design (Expanded 2nd ed. USA)*. Alexandria, VA: Association for Supervision and Curriculum Development (ASCD).

Yeşil, R., & Korkmaz, Ö. (2010). A comparison of different teaching applications based on questioning in terms of their effects upon pre-service teachers' good questioning skills. *Procedia – Social and Behavioral Sciences, 2*, 1075–1082.

Yuzawa, M. (2009). Improvement of application skill thorough self-question generation. In H. Yoshida & E. De Corte (Eds.), *Application of children' logic into classroom practice: Educational practical psychology in designing class [Kodomo no ronri wo ikasu jyugyo zukuri]*. Kyoto, Japan: Kitaouji Shobou.

3

LEARNING FROM MULTIPLE DOCUMENTS

How can we foster multiple document literacy skills in a sustainable way?

Marc Stadtler, Rainer Bromme, and Jean-François Rouet

Introduction

While you are reading these lines, take a look around your desk: many readers of this chapter will find a plethora of documents lying around, some of which may be connected with each other. These documents may shed light on a topic from different angles and thus nurture your comprehension of the topic, given that you establish connections, uncover similarities, and identify contradictions. The present volume on the promotion of spontaneous transfer of students' proficient use of learning strategies offers yet another chance for learning by reading multiple documents.

In our information society, learning from multiple documents has become a widespread way of accessing knowledge provided by others. A survey sponsored by the European Commission has, for instance, found that 85% of 9 to 16-year-old children in Europe reported using the Internet for schoolwork on a regular basis (Livingstone, Haddon, Görzig, & Ólafsson, 2011). The Internet may qualify as a resource for autonomous and self-determined learning because students can select their own paths through a multitude of perspectives following their interests and needs.

At the same time, learning from multiple documents places high demands on students' reading skills (Britt & Gabrys, 2000; Rouet, 2006). As a result, an increasing number of intervention procedures aiming at improving the skills of multiple document comprehension have recently been devised. The goal of the present chapter is, first, to introduce the skills necessary to learn from multiple documents. In so doing, we also delineate the difficulties that learners at different age levels experience. We then give an overview of the existing instructional interventions designed to promote these skills. In so doing, we shall highlight the extent to which the interventions are successful in terms of having learners execute learning strategies on their own volition. We thus seek to study the focal question of how instructors may promote spontaneous use of learning strategies in an applied context: learning from multiple documents.

What are the skills necessary when learning from multiple documents?

Learning from multiple documents presents considerable challenges to an individual's text-processing skills. The sheer amount of information that is accessible with just a few mouse-clicks requires learners to locate information relevant to their learning goals. Furthermore, Internet-based publications still lack comprehensive editorial quality control, which is often seen in traditional print media (Bromme & Goldman, 2014). For example, an online reader seeking information about the pros and cons of vaccination will find answers from experts but also claims which would not hold up under scientific inquiry (Tozzi, et al., 2010). Hence, another important skill for the learning from multiple documents lies in the evaluation of the information and its sources. After all, learning from multiple documents requires individuals to form coherence within and across documents, which requires a high degree of integration processes (Perfetti, Rouet, & Britt, 1999). In the following sections, we shall introduce the skills of searching for information, evaluation, and integration as well as comment on common problems that some readers face.

The skill of information search

The search for information in text documents is a multifaceted skill, which readers increasingly acquire from elementary grades to secondary education (Cerdán, Gilabert, & Vidal-Abarca, 2011; Dreher & Sammons, 1994; Rouet & Coutelet, 2008). Factors responsible for the development of this skill include an increase of topic knowledge, a more differentiated knowledge of metatextual elements (e.g., titles, paragraphs, or tables of contents) as well as the development of basic reading skills (i.e., decoding, accessing the mental lexicon).

A comprehensive depiction of the sequence of steps used when dealing with research tasks in multiple documents is provided by the cognitive process model MD-TRACE developed by Rouet and Britt (2011). According to the authors, readers must first form a mental representation of the search task. This includes information about what has to be searched for, what is already known, and what resources in terms of time and the information repositories are available. During the next step, readers must evaluate whether the search task can be completed using their own prior knowledge or if they must consult external sources. If readers decide to consult external sources, they will need to evaluate the relevance of the available information—a task that younger readers especially have great difficulties with. For example, Rouet, Ros, Goumi, Macedo-Rouet, and Dinet (2011) reported that fifth and seventh graders are strongly influenced by surface features, such as the position of a document on a results page or visual characteristics (i.e., emphasis through bold print). This effect, however, fades with ninth graders and high school seniors, who increasingly use the semantic content of the textual claims when making relevance judgments. In the final step, the reader must determine to what degree the search result (aggregated from various sources) fulfills the task requirements. Depending on this information, readers can then decide whether to continue searching for more information or put an end to their search. This is a self-regulatory process, which relies mainly on metacognitive skills.

Thus, the search for information is a complex task that places high demands on content-related prior knowledge, metatextual knowledge, self-regulatory skills, working memory capacity, and basal reading skills. Hence, especially when dealing with complex tasks as well as with an increasing amount of irrelevant information, readers show deficits that suggest that specific interventions are necessary to optimize these searching skills.

The skill of evaluating information and its sources

The goal of evaluating information is to critically examine knowledge claims in regard to their validity. Bromme, Kienhues, and Porsch (2010) differentiated between two main approaches of validity assessments: Readers can first evaluate knowledge claims on the basis of their own topic comprehension (evaluation in terms of "what is true?"). For example, readers can compare claims in terms of their consistency with their own prior knowledge or assess the quality of the presented arguments. The skills to evaluate arguments have been extensively described in the research program on critical thinking and will not be further elaborated in this chapter (for an overview, see King & Kitchener, 1994).

A different approach to evaluating the validity of knowledge claims uses a detour via the evaluation of source characteristics, i.e., information that surrounds the production of a document (source evaluation in terms of "whom to believe?"). This includes, for example, information about the location and time of publishing, expertise and the perceived intentions of the author, the employed genre (i.e., report, commentary, gloss), or the intended readership of a document (Britt, Rouet, & Braasch, 2012).

Because readers often use the Internet to inform themselves about unfamiliar science-related issues, one could assume that they rely heavily on the evaluation of the source in their validity judgments. However, according to Maier and Richter (2014), readers use their prior knowledge routinely to decide upon the validity of a text, and not only with topics they are familiar with. Especially when scientific information is presented in a popularized way and seems easy to comprehend, readers rely on their own comprehension of the subject (Scharrer, Bromme, Britt, & Stadtler, 2012).

In contrast, however, readers pay relatively little attention to source information such as author characteristics or the publishing date (Britt & Aglinskas, 2002; Gerjets, Kammerer, & Werner, 2011; Stadtler & Bromme, 2008; Strømsø, Bråten, Britt, & Ferguson, 2013; Wineburg, 1991). Moreover, readers encode source information incompletely (Britt et al., 2012) and use this only rarely, when they have to reach an informed decision (Barzilai, Tzadok, & Eshet-Alkala, 2015; Stadtler, Scharrer, Brummernhenrich, & Bromme, 2013) or when they have to justify their validity judgments (Stadtler, Scharrer, Macedo-Rouet, Rouet, & Bromme, 2016). However, the extent to which readers pay attention to sources varies depending on the personal characteristics of the reader, such as his or her epistemic beliefs (e.g., Bråten, Britt, Strømsø, & Rouet, 2011). In particular, readers who realize that they depend on others when acquiring knowledge and believe knowledge to be uncertain and tentative tend to evaluate sources in regard to their expertise and their cooperative motives (Bråten et al., 2011).

The deficit of spontaneous attention to sources is puzzling because in developmental psychology research, children as young as five years already have the insights that knowledge is unequally distributed and that their own qualification as a source of knowledge varies depending on the situation (Danovitch & Keil, 2004). Furthermore, studies show that both school students and adults may possess skepticism about the media, which is often explained through the open publishing principal of the Internet (Kuiper, Volman, & Terwel, 2009). While knowledge about the necessity of source evaluation seems abundant, readers usually fail to translate this into concrete actions during reading. Instructional interventions can begin here in order to achieve a more intensive use of source characteristics in the service of making validity judgments.

The skill of integrating information

The integration of text information with one's prior knowledge and with the evolving discourse model is another central element of learning from text (Kintsch, 1998). A special characteristic of learning from multiple documents is that integration is not limited to the connection of information within one single text. For example, if someone is searching for information on the Internet about the influence of cholesterol on cardiovascular disease, he or she might start searching in an online encyclopedia for threshold levels of elevated cholesterol. In addition, the website of a pharmaceutical company might offer information about proper treatment with medications, while another source offers information about the side effects of common medications, as well as information about alternative medical treatments. Finally, students may search Internet forums in which affected lay people exchange personal experiences in regard to heightened cholesterol levels. To achieve a comprehensive understanding of an issue, students must combine the information they have gathered into an increasingly complete picture by going beyond the margins of a single document. It is important that the information is then interconnected and that rhetorical relations such as contradiction or corroboration are discovered (Wineburg, 1991).

What makes cross-textual integration even more demanding is that learners cannot rely on linguistic coherence markers (e.g., "compared to," "similarly") to the same extent as when learning from a single document, in which the author usually highlights coherence relations (Stadtler, Scharrer, & Bromme, 2011). Thus, one can assume that in addition to automatic, memory-based integration processes as described by Kintsch (1998), strategic integration attempts are also necessary for coherence formation in complex information environments. Wineburg (1991), for instance, provided a detailed description of how historians and novices approach multiple documents on a historical controversy. When historians encountered insecure information, they actively searched for comparable information in other documents and identified both affirming and contradictory accounts of a situation—a strategy which Wineburg calls "corroboration." Unlike expert historians, high school students rarely used this strategy and frequently missed conflicts between different accounts of the same situation (see also Stahl, Hynd, Britton, McNish, & Bosquet, 1996).

Stadtler and colleagues (e.g., Stadtler, Scharrer, Skodzik, & Bromme, 2014; Stadtler et al., 2013) provided further evidence that these integration strategies are seldom used even among experienced learners. A main finding of their studies investigating conflict detection was that university students with little prior topic knowledge often overlook conflicts unless these are signaled by linguistic coherence markers or students are encouraged to integrate information across texts by appropriate reading tasks. Similarly, Wiley and Voss (1999) showed that when learners do not follow a task encouraging them to integrate information, they often form poorly integrated mental representations of a text.

In summary, it can be noted that learners of different ages rarely deliberately integrate information across sources. This breeds the danger that one-sided and unconnected text representations are created, which inadequately reflect the discursive character of scientific knowledge.

How can we foster the skills to learn from multiple documents?

Fostering the search for information in multiple documents

Teachers may counter their students' difficulties in searching for information through a variety of measures. In webquests (Segers & Verhoeven, 2009), for instance, learners search for the answer to a problem in a limited set of web documents that have been preselected by the teacher. This design avoids the cognitive strain due to excessive irrelevant information and lack of fit of the information with the readers' levels of prior knowledge. Moreover, it is no longer necessary to formulate adequate search terms, which often overtaxes the capacities of younger readers (i.e., MaKinster, Beghetto, & Plucker, 2002). Thus, webquests simplify the information environment rather than teaching learning strategies. This, however, may be a first step for younger learners to spontaneously apply strategies they already have at their disposal without being overwhelmed by an information overload.

To improve students' relevance judgments, it has proven to be helpful to encourage readers to deeply reflect on their search goals while searching for information (de Vries, van der Meij, & Lazonder, 2008; Rouet et al., 2011). This can be achieved, for example, by instructing readers to write down everything they already know about their search subject, thus highlighting both prior knowledge resources and knowledge deficits.

Gerjets and Hellenthal-Schorr (2008) introduced a comprehensive training program called "Competent information search in the World Wide Web" (CIS-WEB). In CIS-WEB, seventh and eighth graders acquire declarative and procedural knowledge necessary to solve information problems on the web. In this training, both teacher- and leaner-centered phases alternate in six modules over a course of three consecutive school days. Central search strategies are introduced by the teacher; students then individually work on practice questions, worked-out examples, and knowledge tests with immediate feedback. The empirical evaluation of the program showed a positive effect on search performance: The training led to improvement on search tasks which, for example, required readers to locate relevant information within a single website. Because there was no further prompting or scaffolding during the testing phase, one may conclude that students had internalized the search strategies to a sufficient degree so that they were able to execute them spontaneously when necessary. However, it should be noted that performance was observed on an immediate post-test. This leaves open the question to what extent CIS-WEB participants would still spontaneously apply their newly learned searching skills after a longer period of time.

Fostering the evaluation of information and its sources

While numerous interventions focusing on the evaluation of information have been developed in the research program on critical thinking (e.g., Halpern, 1998; King & Kitchener, 1994), the number of interventions focusing on the optimization of source evaluations has notably risen only in the past years. In the following brief literature review, we focus on the presentation of interventions that promote source evaluation. (For overviews of programs that focus more broadly on the evaluation of information, see Halpern, 1998; King & Kitchener, 1994).

Recently, a number of source evaluation programs have been developed and evaluated with students at grades 4–6 (i.e., de Vries et al., 2008; Kuiper, Volman, & Terwel, 2008; Macedo-Rouet, Braasch, Britt, & Rouet, 2013), grades 7–10 (Gerjets & Hellenthal-Schorr, 2008; Kammerer, Meier, & Stahl, 2016; Mason, Junyent, & Tornatora, 2014; Stadtler, Paul, Globoschütz, & Bromme, 2015; Walraven, Brand-Gruwel, & Boshuizen, 2013), grades 11–13 (Braasch, Bråten, Strømsø, Anmarkrud, & Ferguson, 2013; Britt & Aglinskas, 2002; Nokes, Dole, & Hacker, 2007; Stadtler et al., 2013), and university students (e.g., Brand-Gruwel & Wopereis, 2006; Graesser et al., 2007; Stadtler & Bromme, 2008; Wiley et al., 2009). While some of these programs focus exclusively on the evaluation of sources, others can be seen as comprehensive interventions that foster other skills in addition to evaluating sources, such as formulating search terms, locating information on websites, or monitoring one's own progress (de Vries et al., 2008; Gerjets & Hellenthal-Schorr, 2008; Kuiper et al., 2008; Nokes et al., 2007).

Many training programs focus on the identification and evaluation of source characteristics: During class, teachers and students develop comprehensive checklists of evaluation criteria (i.e., last update, presence of publishing information, profession of author name) by which documents should then be evaluated and subsequently ranked (i.e., Kuiper et al., 2008; Walraven et al., 2013). A problem with this approach may be that the training of source evaluation takes place in a rather decontextualized way, i.e., detached from the focal question of the validity of knowledge claims. Thus, Kuiper et al. reported that many fifth-grade students do not notice how the evaluation of sources may help their own understanding of a topic, and they do not see the benefit of this action. Similarly, Walraven et al. (2013) reported from her training with ninth-graders that students learn to apply evaluation strategies in a familiar topic but fail to transfer the same strategies to a new content domain.

To overcome the gap between tacit knowledge about evaluation strategies and their practical application, training programs might use the reader's information need as a starting point and encourage students to search for supporting evidence for central knowledge claims. Evidence for the validity of a claim may be derived not only from supporting empirical data but also from the presence of favorable source characteristics (Wiley et al., 2009).

Such an approach was selected by Macedo-Rouet et al. (2013) as well as Stadtler et al. (2016). Macedo-Rouet et al. confronted fourth- and fifth-graders with controversial knowledge claims, for instance, about the necessity of a snack during lunch breaks at school. Controversial claims were presented by different sources that both had an interest in the subject. However, only one of the authors possessed the level of expertise necessary to make valid assertions on the topic. For example, the controversial claims in regard to healthy snacks were presented by a nutritionist and the mother of a student. In the 30-minute training phase, students reflected in group discussions on the way people gain expertise. They then practiced with some example controversies, in which they had to identify which of the two conflicting sources had the greater topic-related expertise. Through the practice of "faded instruction," controversies were first solved under the guidance of the teacher and then were increasingly solved individually. In the ensuing test phase, the students whose performance on a standardized reading comprehension test was below the median demonstrated significantly better identification of the more qualified source compared to a control group. Moreover, these students performed better on a source memory test, which required the correct assignment of knowledge claims to their respective source. Students whose performance in the reading comprehension test was above the median already performed well on the pre-test (better identification of the source with greater expertise as well as better source memory); their performance remained at the same high level without increasing after participating in the training program. Macedo-Rouet and colleagues concluded that their training helped weaker readers notice "expertise-markers" in texts and then use these to identify the more competent of two conflicting sources. Most importantly, their students applied these strategies without further prompting on a post-test with new materials. Because the post-test was administered directly after the intervention, it remains an open question how stable these effects are over time and to what extent learners would spontaneously apply their newly acquired evaluation strategies in a variety of contexts.

Stadtler et al. (2016) developed a slightly modified version of this training for vocational students with poor general reading ability. One variation on the Macedo-Rouet et al. study was that the conflicting sources all had an academic background. Differences in competence resulted from the sources representing academic disciplines that were more or less pertinent with regard to the issue (Bromme et al., 2010). For example, conflicting claims dealing with the controversy of cleaning oil spills with oil-eating bacteria were introduced by a microbiologist (highly pertinent) and a ship-building engineer (lowly pertinent). To identify the source with greater competence, the readers must draw on their intuitive assumptions about the division of cognitive labor—i.e., their assumptions about the graded pertinence of scientific disciplines in relation to the topic of interest (Bromme et al., 2010; Danovitch & Keil, 2004). Thus, it was not possible to identify the most competent source by simply choosing the person with the highest academic rank.

During a kick-off presentation, the participants of the experimental group were made aware of the unequal distribution of knowledge in our society ("division of cognitive labor," Bromme et al., 2010). As seen in Macedo-Rouet et al., participants then practiced identifying the more pertinent source by first solving sample controversies in group discussions. In these, the experimenter initially modeled how to identify the most pertinent source. Learners then gradually took over the task of reflecting on the underlying expertise. Finally, students solved further sample controversies individually, following the principle of faded instruction. In the final test phase, students were presented with another set of controversies. They were to indicate with which claims they agreed and provide reasons for their choices in a short essay. The students of the training group more frequently selected the source with the pertinent source and more frequently referred to source expertise in their written justifications compared to the untrained students of the control group. The findings allow for some optimism as they show a positive effect of a brief intervention on the spontaneous application of sourcing strategies among learners with poor reading skills (average score at the 33rd percentile on a standardized reading comprehension test). However, tests of the long-term effects of the trainings have yet to be conducted.

Our brief literature survey reveals an increasing number of interventions aiming to foster source evaluation. While secondary (and even younger) students can successfully evaluate source information when prompted to do so, younger students especially do not always put their strategy knowledge into action spontaneously. Differences between the interventions may be interpreted in terms of conditions that promote the spontaneous application of source evaluation strategies. In this regard, the principle of faded instruction used by Macedo-Rouet et al. and Stadtler et al. may be especially helpful. It provides ample opportunity for learners to practice their newly acquired skills and requires them to increasingly take over the responsibility for strategy execution. Furthermore, it may be especially helpful to associate source evaluation strategies with a concrete goal, such as judging the validity of knowledge claims. Otherwise, interventions may run the risk of teaching students checklists of criteria for source evaluation without the conditional and procedural knowledge of when and how to apply them during learning. It needs to be stressed, however, that no study has yet examined the long-term effects of teaching students source evaluation strategies. This leaves open the question how sustainable the observed results are over time and in a variety of contexts.

Fostering the integration of information

Existing approaches to counter the described lack of cross-textual integration often focus on the tasks with which learners approach a set of documents. Thus, the idea is not to explicitly teach integration strategies but to create task conditions that afford an especially high degree of integration on the part of the learner. From this research it has emerged that an increased amount of intertextual integration often results from argument tasks. These require leaners to reconstruct an explanation for a specific (historic, social, or scientific) phenomenon from multiple documents (i.e., Bråten & Strømsø, 2009; Cerdán & Vidal-Abarca, 2008; Stadtler et al., 2011; Wiley & Voss, 1999). On the other hand, tasks that require the identification of specific information or that focus on general comprehension contribute less to the formation of highly integrated mental representations (Bråten & Strømsø, 2009; Cerdán & Vidal-Abarca, 2008; Stadtler et al., 2011; Wiley & Voss, 1999). Whether a learning task is beneficial for the integration of information also seems to depend on reader characteristics, such as their amount of prior knowledge and their epistemic beliefs. Gil, Bråten, Vidal-Abarca, and Strømsø (2010), for example, reported that only learners with high prior knowledge benefitted from an argument task. Learners with little prior knowledge seemed overwhelmed by the argument task and formed a more coherent mental representation when their goal was to write a summary. Similarly, Bråten and Strømsø (2009) reported that learners who conceived of knowledge as uncertain and complex benefited from argument tasks. In contrast, learners who viewed knowledge as unchanging and as comprising simple facts developed a poorly integrated representation from argument tasks. In a series of studies, the research group of Bråten and Strømsø presented further evidence for the central role of epistemic beliefs while integrating information from multiple documents (for a summary, see Bråten et al., 2011). Even though the findings are not always consistent, the studies reported in Bråten et al. could be summarized as follows: Beliefs relating to the dimensions "simplicity vs. complexity" of knowledge (i.e., knowledge as a collection of facts vs. knowledge as a web of related concepts) and "certainty vs. preliminarity" (i.e., unchangeable knowledge vs. tentative knowledge) can predict the degree of integration activity. Learners who believe knowledge to be complex and tentative make more intensive efforts to integrate information from different sources, compared to readers who view knowledge as simple and certain.

The reported studies show that task instructions are powerful tools with which teachers can support the integration efforts of their students. Moreover, modifying task instructions (in comparison to extended strategy training) are rather economic interventions which may be easily integrated into daily teaching practice. One can question, however, the extent to which learners internalize task instructions that they learn in school, and whether learners are able to transfer these onto other learning contexts (for instance, in informal learning contexts outside of schools). Thus, task instructions constitute an effective short-term intervention for fostering integrative activity which might be complemented by comprehensive strategy training. The findings on the interaction between task instructions and learners' epistemic beliefs suggest the value of taking learner characteristics into account when designing more comprehensive strategy training. Appropriate epistemic beliefs are needed in order to ensure favorable motivational preconditions for spontaneously applying integration strategies (Kienhues, Stadtler, & Bromme, 2011).

Summary

Recent cohorts of students are often described as "digital natives" because they have socialized with digital media from their early childhood on (OECD, 2011). However, empirical findings show that the skills necessary to learn from multiple documents dealing with complex scientific issues cannot be taken for granted among students who are well-versed with different types of media (i.e., Macedo-Rouet et al., 2013; OECD, 2011; Walraven et al., 2013). Against this background, we have reviewed research on how to foster information search, source evaluation, and the integration of information.

Our review revealed that there is an increasing number of training approaches targeting the skills necessary to learn from multiple documents. Many of these approaches, however, are short-term interventions with immediate tests of skill acquisition. Interventions that investigate spontaneous and autonomous application of the taught skills in the longer run are rare. Nevertheless, some hypotheses about what might promote the acquisition of multiple document comprehension skills in a sustainable way can be derived from the empirical database.

In line with socio-constructionist approaches to learning, a first principle is to teach multiple document learning skills in an applied context (Palincsar, 1998). Evaluation skills, for instance, could be taught in the context of reading multiple documents about a scientific controversy. In so doing, instructors could demonstrate that evaluating an author's competence or intentions is not a goal in itself but a means to acquire valid knowledge about the world. This may help learners realize the benefit of investing time and effort into an unfamiliar and sometimes demanding strategy. The studies of Macedo-Rouet et al. (2013) and Stadtler et al. (2016) additionally suggest that learners at different age levels may benefit from external support that fades from modeling target skills to unobtrusive supervision of individual strategy execution. Learners can thus acquire procedural knowledge about how to execute a strategy and have ample practice time. However, the aforementioned didactic principles might only be beneficial to the extent that they are paired with favorable learner characteristics. The research reviewed suggests that epistemic beliefs might play an important role. Learners who acknowledge the uncertain, complex, and socially constructed nature of knowledge may be especially motivated to search, integrate, and evaluate information from multiple documents (Bråten et al., 2011). This also includes an awareness of how knowledge is distributed in the form of written documents. Learners who access multiple documents need to be aware that texts are artifacts produced by authors with different intentions and levels of competence and that they are used to convey meaning, rather than being direct depictions of reality. Learners also need to be aware of publication principles, online and offline, including the fact that Internet-based publications still lack the principle of comprehensive editorial quality control that is often seen in traditional print media (Bromme & Goldmann, 2014). The question is then whether classroom interventions aiming at multiple document learning skills should always address learners' epistemic beliefs to assure that instruction falls on fruitful grounds.

As one limitation of our literature review, we have portrayed the skills necessary to learn from multiple documents in separation from one another. The skills of searching, integrating, and evaluating multiple documents, however, are closely intertwined and may enrich each other. For example, during successful integration of information, the detection of a conflict between two sources often stimulates processes of source evaluation (Braasch, Rouet, Vibert, & Britt, 2012). Moreover, information integration enables readers to determine to what extent a knowledge claim is backed up by a source and can thus be used for validity evaluations (Wineburg, 1991). After all, search skills are necessary to even localize (source) information on a website, which can then be integrated and evaluated. Thus, the skills involved when reading multiple documents are connected with one another in complex ways. Depending on the task, the first step of this process is usually the search for information. Evaluation and integration processes become relevant in the course of dealing with the contents of the opened document and may trigger new search processes (Rouet & Britt, 2011).

An aspect which we left mostly untouched is the discipline specificity of search, evaluation, and integration skills. Admittedly, there is almost no research subject in which one or more of these three skills could be regarded as unimportant. Therefore, the skills of search, evaluation, and integration may be regarded as generic reading skills, at least to some extent. However, Goldman et al. (2016) rightfully argued that each academic discipline develops its own forms of knowledge representation and text genres. The knowledge of such conventions is pivotal for the process of making meaning from multiple documents in a given discipline. In history, for example, experts but not novices have been shown to alter their reading strategies according to whether they process primary or secondary information sources (Wineburg, 1991). In science, readers often face the challenge of interpreting multiple forms of knowledge representations, including texts, graphs, and data charts (Tabak, 2015). Knowing how to interpret a specific graphical representation of an imaging method such as functional magnetic resonance imaging, for example, will be essential to integrate this information with the accompanying written explanation in a textbook.

Furthermore, the reported dependency of strategy selection on discipline-specific epistemic beliefs can be interpreted as a further indication for the context dependency of reading multiple documents. To develop sound intervention programs, it could thus be especially fruitful to integrate the acquisition of multiple document reading skills into the respective school subject (in the sense of "science meets reading"). This is how it could be ensured that the acquisition of skills takes place in the course of interacting with discipline-specific representation formats and is based upon adequate epistemic beliefs. For example, during a history class, students could answer questions regarding historical controversies using authentic documents, in which they must search, evaluate, and connect information. Students could be supported by observing experts using reading strategies in their respective domains and subsequently reflect upon their proper use (cf. "Project Reading, Evidence, and Argumentation in Disciplinary Instruction; www.projectreadi. org). Spontaneous transfer of these strategies requires ample discipline-specific knowledge and experience.

At the beginning of our chapter, we argued that the skill of being able to read multiple documents is a key competence in our information society. We wish to end this chapter emphasizing that strong readers possess both: well-routinized basic reading skills as well as advanced skills in searching, evaluating, and integrating multiple documents. Readers who already have difficulties when dealing with easy texts in terms of decoding, accessing the mental lexicon or with propositional integration on the sentence level, will most likely have even greater difficulties in complex reading environments such as the Internet. These readers will most likely feel frustrated and feel less motivated when dealing with complex reading tasks (Kuiper et al., 2009). In this sense, our plea for embedding the training of multiple document reading skills in school education is also meant as a plea for the development of programs seeking to strengthen basic reading abilities, which form the basis of the more complex reading skills described in this contribution.

Note

This chapter is an extended and modified adaptation of the following German journal publication: Stadtler, M., Bromme, R., & Rouet, J.-F. (2014). "Science meets reading": Worin bestehen die Kompetenzen zum Lesen multipler Dokumente zu Wissenschaftsthemen und wie fördert man sie? *Unterrichtswissenschaft, 52.*

References

Barzilai, S., Tzadok, E., & Eshet-Alkalai, Y. (2015). Sourcing while reading divergent expert accounts. *Instructional Science, 43*(6), 737–766.

Braasch, J., Bråten, I., Strømsø, H. I., Anmarkrud, Ø., & Ferguson, L. E. (2013). Promoting secondary school students' evaluation of source features of multiple documents. *Contemporary Educational Psychology, 38*, 180–195.

Braasch, J., Rouet, J.-F., Vibert, N., & Britt, M. (2012). Readers' use of source information in text comprehension. *Memory & Cognition, 40*(3), 450–465.

Brand-Gruwel, S., & Wopereis, I. (2006). Integration of the information problem-solving skill in an educational programme: The effects of learning with authentic tasks. *Technology, Instruction, Cognition, and Learning, 4*(3&4), 243–263.

Bråten, I., & Strømsø, H. I. (2009). Effects of task instruction and personal epistemology on the understanding of multiple texts about climate change. *Discourse Processes, 47*(1), 1–31.

Bråten, I., Britt, M. A., Strømsø, H. I., & Rouet, J.-F. (2011). The role of epistemic beliefs in the comprehension of multiple expository texts: Toward an integrated model. *Educational Psychologist, 46*(1), 48–70.

Britt, M. A., & Aglinskas, C. (2002). Improving student's ability to identify and use source information. *Cognition & Instruction, 20*(4), 485–522.

Britt, M. A., & Gabrys, G. (2000). Teaching advanced literacy skills for the World Wide Web. In C. Wolfe (Ed.), *Webs we weave: Learning and teaching on the World Wide Web* (pp. 73–90). New York: Academic Press.

Britt, M. A., Rouet, J. F., & Braasch, J. L. (2012). Documents as entities. In M. A. Britt, S. R. Goldman, & J.-F. Rouet (Eds.), *Reading: from words to multiple texts* (pp. 160–179). New York, NY: Routledge.

Bromme, R., & Goldman, S. (2014). The public's bounded understanding of science. *Educational Psychologist, 49*(2), 59–69.

Bromme, R., Kienhues, D., & Porsch, T. (2010). Who knows what and who can we believe? Epistemological beliefs are beliefs about knowledge (mostly) attained from others. In L. Bendixen & F. Feucht (Eds.), *Personal epistemology in the classroom: Theory, research, and implications for practice* (pp. 163–193). Cambridge, MA: Cambridge University Press.

Cerdán, R., & Vidal-Abarca, E. (2008). The effects of tasks on integrating information from multiple documents. *Journal of Educational Psychology, 100*(1), 209–222.

Cerdán, R., Gilabert, R., & Vidal-Abarca, E. (2011). Selecting information to answer questions: Strategic individual differences when searching texts. *Learning and Individual Differences, 21*(2), 201–205.

Danovitch, J. H., & Keil, F. C. (2004). Should you ask a fisherman or a biologist? Developmental shifts in ways of clustering knowledge. *Child Development, 75*(3), 918–931.

de Vries, B., van der Meij, H., & Lazonder, A. W. (2008). Supporting reflective web searching in elementary schools. *Computers in Human Behaviour, 24*(3), 649–665.

Dreher, M. J., & Sammons, R. B. (1994). Fifth graders' search for information in a textbook. *Journal of Reading Behavior, 26*(3), 301–314.

Gerjets, P., & Hellenthal-Schorr, T. (2008). Competent information search in the World Wide Web: Development and evaluation of a web training for pupils. *Computers in Human Behavior, 24*(3), 693–715.

Gerjets, P., Kammerer, Y., & Werner, B. (2011). Measuring spontaneous and instructed evaluation processes during Web search: Integrating concurrent thinking-aloud protocols and eye-tracking data. *Learning & Instruction, 21*, 220–231.

Gil, L., Bråten, I., Vidal-Abarca, E., & Strømsø, H. I. (2010). Summary versus argument tasks when working with multiple documents: Which is better for whom? *Contemporary Educational Psychology, 35*(3), 157–173.

Goldman, S. R., Britt, M. A., Brown, W., Cribb, G., George, M., Greenleaf, C., . . . Project READI. (2016). Disciplinary literacies and learning to read for understanding: A conceptual framework for disciplinary literacy. *Educational Psychologist, 51*(2), 219–246.

Graesser, A., Wiley, J., Goldman, S., O'Reilly, T., Jeon, M., & McDaniel, B. (2007). SEEK Web tutor: Fostering a critical stance while exploring the causes of volcanic eruption. *Metacognition and Learning, 2*(2), 89–105.

Halpern, D. F. (1998). Teaching critical thinking for transfer across domains. *American Psychologist, 53*(4), 449–455.

Kammerer, Y., Meier, N., & Stahl, E. (2016). Fostering secondary-school students' intertext model formation when reading a set of websites: The effectiveness of source prompts. *Computers & Education, 102*, 52–64.

Kienhues, D., Stadtler, M., & Bromme, R. (2011). Dealing with conflicting or consistent medical information on the Web: When expert information breeds laypersons' doubts about experts. *Learning & Instruction, 21*, 193–204.

King, P. M., & Kitchener, K. S. (1994). *Developing reflective judgement: Understanding and promoting intellectual growth and critical thinking in adolescents and adults.* San Francisco, CA: Jossey-Bass.

Kintsch, W. (1998). *Comprehension: A paradigm for cognition.* Cambridge, MA: Cambridge University Press.

Kuiper, E., Volman, M., & Terwel, J. (2008). Integrating critical Web skills and content knowledge: Development and evaluation of a 5th grade educational program. *Computers in Human Behavior, 24*, 666–692.

Kuiper, E., Volman, M., & Terwel, J. (2009). Developing Web literacy in collaborative inquiry activities. *Computers & Education, 52*, 668–680.

Livingstone, S., Haddon, L., Görzig, A., & Ólafsson, K. (2011). *Risks and safety on the internet: The perspective of European children: Full findings.* Retrieved from http://eprints.lse. ac.uk/33731/

Macedo-Rouet, M., Braasch, J., Britt, M. A., & Rouet, J.-F. (2013). Teaching fourth and fifth graders to evaluate information sources during text comprehension. *Cognition & Instruction, 31*, 204–226.

Maier, J., & Richter, T. (2014). Lernen mit multiplen Texten zu kontroversen wissenschaftlichen Themen: Die Rolle der epistemischen Validierung. *Unterrichtswissenschaft, 43*, 24–38.

MaKinster, J. G., Beghetto, R. A., & Plucker, J. A. (2002). Why can't I find Newton's third law? Case studies of students' use of the Web as a science resource. *Journal of Science Education and Technology, 11*, 155–172.

Mason, L., Junyent, A. A., & Tornatora, M. C. (2014). Epistemic evaluation and comprehension of Web-source information on controversial science-related topics: Effects of a short-term instructional intervention. *Computers and Education, 76*, 143–157.

Nokes, J. D., Dole, J. A., & Hacker, D. J. (2007). Teaching high school students to use heuristics while reading historical texts. *Journal of Educational Psychology, 99*, 492–504.

OECD. (2011). *PISA 2009 Results: Students on line: Digital technologies and performance (Volume VI).* Paris, France: OECD.

Palincsar, A. S. (1998). Social constructivist perspectives on teaching and learning. *Annual Review of Psychology, 49*, 345–375.

Perfetti, C. A., Rouet, J.-F., & Britt, M. A. (1999). Toward a theory of documents representation. In H. van Oostendorp & S. R. Goldman (Eds.), *The construction of mental representations during reading* (pp. 99–122). Mahwah, NJ: Lawrence Erlbaum Associates.

Rouet, J.-F. (2006). *The skills of document use: From text comprehension to Web-based learning.* Mahwah, NJ: Lawrence Erlbaum Associates.

Rouet, J.-F., & Britt, M. A. (2011). Relevance processes in multiple document comprehension. In M. T. McCrudden, J. P. Magliano, & G. Schraw (Eds.), *Text relevance and learning from text* (pp. 19–52). Charlotte, NC: Information Age Publishing.

Rouet, J.-F., & Coutelet, B. (2008). The acquisition of document search strategies in grade school students. *Applied Cognitive Psychology, 22,* 389–406.

Rouet, J.-F., Ros, C., Goumi, A., Macedo-Rouet, M., & Dinet, J. (2011). The influence of surface and deep cues on primary and secondary school students' assessment of relevance in Web menus. *Learning and Instruction, 21,* 205–219.

Scharrer, L., Bromme, R., Britt, M. A., & Stadtler, M. (2012). The seduction of easiness: How science depictions influence laypeople's reliance on their own evaluation of scientific information. *Learning & Instruction, 22,* 231–243.

Segers, E., & Verhoeven, L. (2009). Learning in a sheltered Internet environment: The use of WebQuests. *Learning & Instruction, 19,* 423–432.

Stadtler, M., & Bromme, R. (2008). Effects of the metacognitive computer-tool met.a.ware on the Web search of laypersons. *Computers in Human Behavior, 24,* 716–737.

Stadtler, M., Paul, J., Globoschütz, S., & Bromme, R. (2015). Watch out! – An instruction raising students' epistemic vigilance augments their sourcing activities. In D. C. Noelle, R. Dale, A. S. Warlaumont, J. Yoshimi, T. Matlock, C. D. Jennings, & P. P. Maglio (Eds.), *Proceedings of the 37th Annual Conference of the Cognitive Science Society* (pp. 2278–2283). Austin, TX: Cognitive Science Society.

Stadtler, M., Scharrer, L., & Bromme, R. (2011). How reading goals and rhetorical signals influence recipients' recognition of intertextual conflicts. In L. Carlson, C. Hoelscher, & T. F. Shipley (Eds.), *Proceedings of the 33rd Annual Conference of the Cognitive Science Society* (pp. 1346–1351). Austin, TX: Cognitive Science Society.

Stadtler, M., Scharrer, L., Brummernhenrich, B., & Bromme, R. (2013). Dealing with uncertainty: Readers' memory for and use of conflicting information from science texts as function of presentation format and source expertise. *Cognition & Instruction, 31,* 130–150.

Stadtler, M., Scharrer, L., Macedo-Rouet, M., Rouet, J.-F., & Bromme, R. (2016). Improving vocational students' consideration of source information when deciding about science controversies. *Reading and Writing, 29,* 705–729.

Stadtler, M., Scharrer, L., Skodzik, T., & Bromme, R. (2014). Comprehending multiple documents on scientific controversies: Effects of reading goals and signaling rhetorical relationships. *Discourse Processes, 51,* 93–116. doi:10.1080/0163853X.2013.855535

Stahl, S. A., Hynd, C. R., Britton, B. K., McNish, M. M., & Bosquet, D. (1996). What happens when students read multiple source documents in history? *Reading Research Quarterly, 31*(4), 430–456.

Strømsø, H. I., Bråten, I., Britt, M. A., & Ferguson, L. (2013). Spontaneous sourcing among students reading multiple documents. *Cognition & Instruction, 31*(2), 176–203.

Tabak, J. (2015). Functional scientific literacy: Seeing the science within the words and across the Web. In L. Corno & E. M. Anderman (Eds.), *Handbook of educational psychology* (3rd ed., pp. 269–280). London: Routledge.

Tozzi, A. E., Buonuomo, P. S., degli Atti, M. L. C., Carloni, E., Meloni, M., & Gamba, F. (2010). Comparison of quality of internet pages on human papillomavirus immunization in Italian and in English. *Journal of Adolescent Health, 46*(1), 83–89.

Walraven, A., Brand-Gruwel, S., & Boshuizen, H. A. (2013). Fostering students' evaluation behaviour while searching the internet. *Instructional Science, 41*(1), 125–146.

Wiley, J., & Voss, J. F. (1999). Constructing arguments from multiple sources: Tasks that promote understanding and not just memory for text. *Journal of Educational Psychology, 91*(2), 301–311.

Wiley, J., Goldman, S. R., Graesser, A. C., Sanchez, C. A., Ash, I. K., & Hemmerich, J. A. (2009). Source evaluation, comprehension, and learning in Internet science inquiry tasks. *American Educational Research Journal, 46*, 1060–1106.

Wineburg, S. S. (1991). Historical problem solving: A study of the cognitive processes used in the evaluation of documentary and pictorial evidence. *Journal of Educational Psychology, 83*(1), 73–87.

4

HOW TO ADDRESS STUDENTS' LACK OF SPONTANEITY IN DIAGRAM USE

Eliciting educational principles for the promotion of spontaneous learning strategy use in general

Yuri Uesaka and Emmanuel Manalo

Introduction

The problem of lack of spontaneity in learning strategy use

Many learners—unless explicitly prompted by their teachers or other people—tend not to use appropriate learning strategies in situations where it would be advantageous for them to do so. This is despite their apparent knowledge or awareness about the strategies through instruction they have received, or even through prior use of those strategies. This problem was identified five decades ago by Flavell, Beach, and Chinsky (1966). An important observation they made was that children who did not spontaneously use learning strategies were *not* transformed into spontaneous strategy users by the mere provision of instruction. Although a number of authors since then have attempted to explain why the failure to use learning strategies occurs (e.g., Borkowski, Carr, & Pressley, 1987; Garner, 1990), little has been reported in the research literature about how to effectively promote spontaneity in such use. One reason is that the learning strategy research area has tended to focus more on revealing motivational, perceptual, and other factors that are related to strategy use (e.g., Murayama, 2003; Pintrich, 2003; Sato, 1998). However, many of these kinds of investigation have not sufficiently considered the conversion of the findings to instructional methods or interventions that can be applied and tested in real classroom settings. In cases where enhancement of learning strategies had been the focus of the investigation (e.g., Guthrie, Van Meter, Hancock, Alao, Anderson, & McCann, 1998; Sawyer, Graham, & Harris, 1992), measurement of success had focused on academic achievement resulting from the enhancement of the learning strategies, rather than on whether the students were subsequently able to use the strategies spontaneously in their own real learning situations.

Although, by and large, learning strategy research has not explicitly focused on the promotion of spontaneous use, there are a small number of studies that have made the promotion of such spontaneity their main concern. Those studies include investigations into the promotion of spontaneous diagram use in math word problem solving and in written communication—areas in which, apart from the current authors, very few researchers are working on. Math word problems, also known as "story problems," provide background or contextual information about the math problem in text rather than math notations. They are considered important in math education, with one reason being that they link acquired math knowledge and skills to real-world situations depicted in the stories attached to the problems (e.g., Reed, 1999; Schoenfeld, 1985). Written communication, on the other hand, pertains to the translation of thought to verbal language and the symbolic systems used in writing (e.g., Britton, Burgess, Martin, McLeod, & Rosen, 1975; Keys, 1999). It is considered an essential component of literacy in modern societies. For both math problem solving and written communication, diagram use is considered efficacious (e.g., Ainsworth, Prain, & Tytler, 2011; Hembree, 1992; Mayer, 2003; Schoenfeld, 1985), but students' lack of spontaneity in such use has been identified as a problem (e.g., Dufour-Janvier, Bednarz, & Belanger, 1987; Manalo, Uesaka, Pérez-Kriz, Kato, & Fukaya, 2013). This chapter provides a brief review of the pertinent findings from those studies, which deal with students ranging from the junior high school through to the university levels, including the instructional methods that have been found to be effective in promoting spontaneous use. At the end of this chapter, educational principles that can be elicited from those studies to promote spontaneous strategy use *in general* are considered.

Promotion of spontaneous diagram use in math word problem solving

Following a brief explanation of the lack of spontaneity problem in students' use of diagrams in math word problem solving, this section outlines the learner- and task-related factors that have been found to affect students' diagram use and then describes instructional strategies that have been found to be effective in promoting the desired spontaneity in diagram use.

Lack of spontaneity in diagram use when solving math word problems

Diagram use is one of the most effective strategies that students can employ in solving math word problems (e.g., Hembree, 1992; Polya, 1945; Schoenfeld, 1985). Furthermore, the ability to effectively use diagrams can be considered an essential skill in twenty-first-century environments. For example, a report concerning twenty-first-century skills from the National Academy of Sciences in the United States recommended that students should "learn to use a wide range of problem solving strategies" including "heuristic processes such as drawing a diagram" (Pellegrino & Hilton, 2012, p. 125). However, there is evidence that students generally lack spontaneity in using diagrams when problem solving. For example, Dufour-Janvier et al. (1987) pointed out that few students use diagrams spontaneously when they encounter difficult problems even though their teachers often use diagrams when explaining how to solve such types of problems. Problems in lack of spontaneous use have also been reported in case studies and student assessments. For example, Uesaka (2014) reported three cases in which students' failure to spontaneously use diagrams was identified as one of the primary reasons for their failure to solve math problems; and Uesaka, Suzuki, Kiyokawa, Seo, and Ichikawa (2014) reported that, while many students in school can correctly use diagrams when the instructions provided in assessments explicitly encourage their use, the majority do not spontaneously use diagrams when there is no explicit instruction or encouragement to do so—and as a consequence many fail to correctly solve the problems given.

Learner- and task-related factors that influence spontaneous diagram use in problem solving

To consider how it may be possible to promote students' spontaneity in using diagrams, the following subsections examine both learner- and task-related factors that have an influence on such spontaneity.

Learner-related factors

To better understand the learner-related factors, Uesaka, Manalo, and Ichikawa (2007) administered math word problem-solving tasks and questionnaires to more than 600 junior high school students from Japan and New Zealand. The problems were ones for which diagram use would be beneficial. The questionnaire items assessed student perceptions about various issues relating to diagram use.

The analysis revealed that the New Zealand students used more diagrams compared to the Japanese students in problem solving. Furthermore, a higher proportion of Japanese students did not use diagrams and failed to solve the problems given. The students' responses to the questionnaire items were examined in relation to their math problem-solving performance. This analysis revealed that the students' perception of diagrams as tools for their own use (i.e., tools they use for tasks like problem solving) was correlated with diagram use, whereas perception of diagrams as teachers' tools (i.e., tools that teachers use in tasks like teaching) was uncorrelated with diagram use. Furthermore, a higher proportion of the Japanese students tended to view diagrams as teacher's instructional tools rather than their own problem-solving tools. In addition, the perception of cost in using diagrams negatively correlated with diagram use, and the Japanese students perceived a higher cost involved in using diagrams. These findings suggest that, to promote spontaneity in diagram use, it might be important to enhance students' perception of the efficacy of diagram use for one's own problem solving and to decrease their perception of the cost involved in such use.

Uesaka et al. (2007) also discussed the influence of instruction, which differed between the two countries. The national curriculum in New Zealand at the time not only stressed the importance of teaching how to understand diagrams but also considered the use of diagrams as a communication tool as being one of the crucial goals of algebra. In contrast, the Japanese national curriculum at the time only emphasized understanding of diagrams and target mathematical concepts, but not the use of diagrams as tools for problem solving and communication.

Task-related factors

Uesaka and Manalo (2012) critically examined a previous suggestion that students' spontaneity in using diagrams is affected by the length-relatedness of the story context of math word problems (i.e., whether the problem is about distance or other measurement of length; Reed, 1999). They proposed an alternative explanation: that the cognitive cost required in translating the concrete situations described in math word problems to effective diagrams is the more important determinant of whether a diagram will be used. In constructing appropriate diagrams, it is necessary to identify information that is directly relevant to solving the problem. In this process, if the diagram that is appropriate for solving the problem is similar to the concrete situation described in the problem, then the cognitive cost of translation is low and diagrams will likely be used. However, the 'appropriate diagram' is often not similar to the concrete situation described in the problem, as it is often a more abstract representation such as a table or a graph. In such cases, the cognitive cost of translation becomes high, and diagrams are less likely to be used. For example, students are more likely to draw a more concrete illustrative diagram (or sketch) showing the relative positions and distances of characters described in a problem (see Figure 4.1). However, they are less likely to construct a more abstract table to work out change in quantities relative to time that may be required to solve another problem. In the former, the diagram resembles the appearance of the situation described in the problem. In the latter, however, the diagram does not look anything like the situation described in the problem and, therefore, requires more cognitive translational steps (abstraction and re-representation of relevant components) to construct.

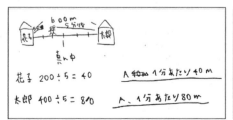 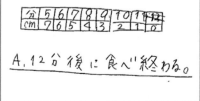

FIGURE 4.1 Examples of illustration (left) which is more concrete, and table (right) which is more abstract, that students have constructed to help them solve math word problems.

The results of two studies that Uesaka and Manalo (2012) conducted with junior high school students supported the cognitive cost explanation they proposed. That explanation is congruent with cognitive load theory, which suggests that learners resort to using less effective—but also less demanding—strategies when faced with more complex tasks that impose a greater load on working memory (e.g., Sweller, van Merrienboer, & Paas, 1998). In terms of application, the findings of the Uesaka and Manalo study suggest that it would be important to enhance students' skills in diagram construction to reduce perceptions of a high and prohibitive cognitive cost associated with such construction (cf. Sweller et al., 1998).

Instructional strategies for improving spontaneous use of diagrams

Promoting both perception of the efficacy of using and skills in constructing diagrams

The findings from the previous studies referred to in the preceding sections suggest that students spontaneously use diagrams in problem solving if (a) they perceive diagrams as useful and a part of their own repertoire of tools to use in problem solving, and (b) they possess sufficient skills to construct the diagrams they want to use, including diagrams that depict information more abstractly, such as tables and graphs. These requirements are clearly aligned with the basic mechanisms of the expectancy-value theory of motivation (e.g., Wigfield & Eccles, 2000), which posits that an individual will not likely engage in a task (in this case, using diagrams in problem solving) unless the individual perceives some clear value in undertaking that task, as well as expects that he or she will likely succeed in it. The influence of students' beliefs about the usefulness of particular learning strategies on their actual use of those strategies had also been observed by a number of researchers such as Nolen and Haladyna (1990); various studies have also demonstrated that appropriate and sufficient instruction on learning skills is necessary for students to more willingly apply them to their work (e.g., meta-analysis by Graham & Perin, 2007, on writing skills).

Based on the above-mentioned indications from their previous research, Uesaka, Manalo, and Ichikawa (2010) designed and tested an intervention in which a teacher incorporated two manipulations into the usual instruction provided in a math class to improve *both the perception of the efficacy of using diagrams and skills in constructing more abstract diagrams*. This framework of providing students with encouragement to enhance awareness of the effectiveness of the target strategy, combined with skills training, is similar to the concept of "informed training" proposed by Brown, Bransford, Ferrara, and Campione (1983), where students are provided not only with training on the strategy but also information about why it is effective and the expected beneficial outcomes from its use. Uesaka et al. (2010) conducted five days of classes for 86 eighth-grade students and demonstrated that the interventions used improved both awareness of the efficacy of diagram use and skills in constructing diagrams, which in turn improved participants' spontaneous use of diagrams in the groups that received both forms of interventions. An interesting additional finding from this study was that students' process orientation moderated the effects of the interventions provided. Process orientation pertains to students' beliefs about learning: whether they value the process of understanding to arrive at the correct answer, or simply getting the correct answer. In the Uesaka et al. study, for students who believed that getting the correct answer was all that mattered, the intervention had little beneficial effect. This finding is congruent with previous research findings in the area of learning strategy use suggesting that intervention effects are influenced by students' beliefs about learning (e.g., Shinogaya, 2008).

Effects of peer instruction on promoting spontaneous use of diagrams in solving math word problems

The Uesaka et al. (2010) study provided concrete suggestions for how it may be possible to promote spontaneous diagram use in problem solving. It is important, however, to consider teaching methods that can more naturally be employed in real classroom situations. Diagrams are tools not only for problem solving but also for effective communication. As Uesaka and Manalo (2007) suggested, it is possible that viewing diagrams as tools for communication can lead to promoting the spontaneous use of diagrams in problem solving.

Uesaka and Manalo (2007, 2008a) examined this hypothesis by conducting five days of experimental classes for eighth-grade students. All students received instruction about the efficacy of using diagrams in math word problem solving. Their findings were that only students who received opportunities to explain how to solve the problems to other students (in peer instruction sessions) evidenced significant improvements in spontaneous diagram use in subsequent problem-solving assessments. (Note that in this study, the control group received exactly the same instruction as the experimental students—except that they did not get opportunities to explain how to solve the problems to other students in peer instruction sessions.) In a later study, Uesaka and Manalo also demonstrated that the *problem-solving performance* of junior high school students in a condition with peer instruction (similar to that of the previous study) was higher than that of students in other conditions without peer instruction (Uesaka & Manalo, 2011).

Uesaka and Manalo (2007, 2008a) discussed the process by which peer instruction likely promotes improvement in the spontaneity with which students use diagrams. Firstly, by setting the situation in which a student needs to explain to a peer how to solve problems, the student's likelihood of using diagrams increases, as it is difficult to sufficiently explain what to do through the use of only verbal language. The resulting increase in diagram use contributes to improving the student's diagram construction skills. Secondly, as Ainsworth and Th Loizou (2003) also pointed out, explaining with the use of diagrams improves understanding of the nature of the problem. Furthermore, the student may receive questions and non-verbal feedback from his or her peer. By answering those questions—during which diagram use is likely to be involved—the student further deepens his or her understanding of the problem, in addition to recognizing more clearly the benefits of using diagrams in problem solving. Because of these experiences and resulting insights (which likely contribute to enhancing the student's perception about the usefulness of diagrams, and his or her skills in constructing appropriate diagrams), the student becomes more likely to spontaneously use diagrams in future problem-solving situations. Other researchers have also pointed out that peer interaction facilitates the acquisition of strategies because the interaction helps students realize the value and significance of strategies in problem solving (e.g., Azmitia, 1988). The efficacy of this peer instruction approach has since then been demonstrated in educational practices that were implemented in real classroom settings (e.g., Uesaka, 2014; Uesaka & Manalo, 2008b).

Promotion of spontaneous diagram use in written communication

Students' general lack of spontaneity in diagram use is also an issue with written communication. In this section, the possible reasons for the problem are considered, and then instructional strategies aimed at promoting the desired spontaneity are described, including research findings about their effectiveness.

Lack of spontaneity in diagram use in writing explanations

As in problem solving, diagrams are considered efficacious in communication (e.g., Ainsworth, 2006; Ainsworth et al., 2011; Mayer, 2003). In simple terms, when visual representations are used together with verbal representations, both visual and verbal channels of the message recipient's working memory receive the message to be conveyed. Thus, the message is not only read or heard but also seen. When the words that are read or heard are integrated with the images that are seen, understanding the intended message likely becomes easier. It should be noted, however, that not all diagrams included with verbal communication would necessarily be helpful. Some diagrams—and some verbal information for that matter—can be extraneous or redundant, and they tend to overload the verbal and/or visual channels of working memory instead (Mayer & Moreno, 2003). Thus, in combining verbal and visual representations in communication, it is important to consider how those representations can optimally be used to promote understanding of the intended message.

A more pressing problem, however, for the development of students' communicative competence is lack of spontaneity in diagram use. While some students do spontaneously use diagrams when taking notes for their own selves, a significantly lower proportion spontaneously use diagrams when producing explanations for other people (Manalo et al., 2013). Manalo et al. suggested that a possible reason for this lack of spontaneity in using diagrams is educational socialization: in schools, there is a general expectation that, when students are required to explain what they have learned (e.g., in tests and in reports), they have to use words—and diagrams are at most optional to include. Thus, students may develop a perception that, while words are essential, diagrams are hardly necessary when they have to communicate knowledge. However, apart from educational socialization, there are also learner- and task-related factors that influence diagram use in written communication.

Learner- and task-related factors that influence spontaneous diagram use in written communication

Learner- and task-related factors influence spontaneous diagram use in written communication because those factors affect the cognitive processing cost of generating both verbal and visual representations of the information to be communicated (Manalo & Uesaka, 2012). A learner-related factor that has been found to influence diagram use is language proficiency. Manalo and Uesaka (2012, 2014) reported evidence that when students have to use a second language to explain information they have learned, diagram use is significantly related to their proficiency in that language: if they are not so proficient in the second language, they are more likely to use *only words*. This may sound counter-intuitive in that one would expect that a student who is not so proficient in a language would resort more to using other means—such as representing information diagrammatically—to compensate for their shortcomings in using the language. However, perhaps because of the previously mentioned educational socialization, such students tend to focus on producing verbal representations (i.e., words, phrases, sentences) in the language they are not proficient. Because of that inadequate proficiency, the production of verbal representations uses up more of the limited processing resources available in working memory, and as a consequence, little or no resources remain for the construction of any diagrams (Manalo & Uesaka, 2012).

The same explanation applies to task-related factors. One task-related factor that Manalo and Uesaka (2012, 2014) reported was imageability of the information to be explained (i.e., how easy it is to visually imagine that information). If it is easy to imagine (e.g., tangible information like the layout of a room, or the commonly known organs of the human body), then diagrams are more likely to be used as constructing a diagram for such information would not be so resource-intensive and there would likely be sufficient cognitive processing resources available for it. However, if the information is hard to imagine (i.e., more abstract information such as procedures, or conceptual organization), diagrams are less likely to be used as the production of diagrams for such information would be more resource-intensive, and there may not be adequate resources available for such production.

These findings indicate that learner- and task-related factors can affect (a) the amount of cognitive resources available in working memory for diagram production (e.g., little available when also using a language in which proficiency is low) and/or (b) the cognitive cost entailed in constructing the necessary diagram (e.g., high cost for hard-to-imagine information). However, apart from these factors, it is likely that other reasons—such as those that Garner (1990) proposed—would also explain why spontaneous diagram use is low in written communication. For example, students may lack knowledge about the appropriate diagrams to use or how to construct such diagrams (i.e., including lack of confidence in drawing), they may not perceive the value or benefit of using diagrams, and so on. Manalo and Uesaka (2014) also found that the intended audience of the communication mattered: students were more likely to use diagrams when making notes for their own selves, and less likely when writing explanations of the same information for other people. To explain this finding, Manalo and Uesaka suggested that it may be more difficult to discern the kinds of diagrams that other people would understand in such communication, and students may perceive greater diagram utility in taking notes (e.g., summarizing, connecting ideas) than in writing an explanation.

Instructional strategies for improving spontaneous diagram use

As in math word problem solving, Uesaka and Manalo (2014) found that interactive peer communication can increase spontaneous diagram use. However, the spontaneous use was limited to the interactive context: students only spontaneously used diagrams when they were interactively explaining to each other; later, in an explanation writing context, they no longer made use of diagrams (Manalo, Uesaka, & Sheppard, 2015)—hence, no transfer occurred. This finding suggests that some essential requirements of spontaneous diagram use may not be adequately addressed by the mere provision of interactive peer communication. For such spontaneous use to occur, students may need more comprehensive knowledge and skills in diagram use, as well as to more clearly perceive the value of such use in different contexts.

Based on the above considerations, Manalo and Uesaka (2016) examined the effectiveness of providing a hint, instruction, and practice in diagram use to find out if the combination of those interventions would be adequate in promoting spontaneous diagram use in students' explanation writing. The participants in their study were 21 undergraduate university students in a real education studies course in which, for homework, they had to regularly write a one-page explanation of what they had learned. In the first few weeks of the course (baseline), almost none of the students used diagrams in the explanations they produced. When the hint was provided (in the form of written feedback—"including diagrams could make your explanation easier to understand"—on their explanation homework), diagram use significantly increased. Still, fewer than half of the students evidenced diagram use in their explanation writing. When instruction was provided (in the form of a lecture on the various ways in which diagrams could be used to enhance written communication), diagram use increased slightly—but not significantly—compared to the level reached following the hint provision. It was not until practice in constructing appropriate diagrams was provided (in the form of a workshop, plus an additional homework in constructing different types of diagrams) that the majority of students started using diagrams in their explanation writing. This increase in diagram use in the students' explanation writing was maintained for the remainder of the semester, even though no further hints, instruction, or practice was provided. Furthermore, 62% of the students spontaneously used diagrams in explaining various points in their final test at the end of the semester.

The findings of this study indicate that providing a hint to make students realize that diagrams could be useful, instruction to improve their knowledge about how to use diagrams, and practice to develop their procedural knowledge for using diagrams can be effective in promoting spontaneous diagram use in written communication. These findings are congruent not only with the findings reported in the preceding sections of this chapter about diagram use in problem solving, but also with previous reports about the influence of perception of usefulness and possession of adequate skills on students' use of learning strategies (e.g., Graham & Perin, 2007; Nolen & Haladyna, 1990). It is worth noting also that the Manalo and Uesaka (2016) study referred to here was conducted as part of a real course, using authentic materials that the students had to learn and explain, and thus ecological validity and potential for use in other similar teaching situations are high.

Discussion

General framework for the promotion of spontaneous learning strategy use

Promoting perceptions about efficacy and skills in learning strategy use

Two instructional components, shown in Figure 4.2, have been identified from the present authors' program of research as crucial in promoting greater spontaneity in diagram use. The first component is the encouragement of student perceptions about the efficacy of diagram use. This means that it is necessary to cultivate explicit knowledge or awareness in the students that use of the learning strategy is efficacious, and also to provide them with information or some other means for understanding why the learning strategy is efficacious. The second component is the enhancement of diagram construction skills. Such skills require the possession of both declarative and procedural knowledge—in other words, knowing what diagrams to use and how to create such diagrams.

The important point that needs to be emphasized here is that only providing verbal encouragement or skills training is not enough: combining the two components is necessary. Uesaka et al. (2010) found that participants' spontaneous use of diagrams under conditions with only verbal encouragement or with only skills training was the same as in the control group. On the other hand, when both components were provided in addition to the usual subject instruction, students' use of the strategy—of their own volition—was promoted, even in contexts that were different from those of the regular classes, such as in tests. This fact was also confirmed by the findings of Manalo and Uesaka (2016). In this study, the spontaneous use of diagrams in written communication was not sufficiently promoted by providing only verbal encouragement in the form of a hint, or even after instruction about the effective use of diagrams had been provided. The reason was that, even if the students knew that diagrams were useful and could be used in particular ways to facilitate better communication, they remained deficient in their

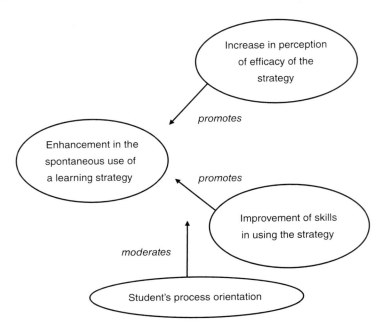

FIGURE 4.2 Instructional components in the promotion of the spontaneous use of learning strategies.

diagram construction skills. Thus, it was not until they also received practice—in effect, enhancing their procedural knowledge about how to use diagrams—that the majority of the students spontaneously used diagrams.

The components of the framework proposed here have been put forward in previous research, but usually separately or without placing equivalent emphasis on the two components. For example, Kennedy and Miller (1976) reported that providing verbal feedback to enhance students' perception of the value of using a strategy resulted in those students persisting in the use of that strategy in subsequent trials. Their findings, therefore, emphasized the importance of the perception-of-efficacy component, but not the improvement-of-skills component. In contrast, researchers such as Borkowski and Cavanaugh (1979) and Stokes and Baer (1977) have instead emphasized the importance of providing comprehensive instruction in strategy use to improve learners' ability to reliably apply the strategy—but without explicit consideration of their perceptions about the strategy's efficacy.

As depicted in Figure 4.2, students' process orientation—which pertains to their beliefs about what is important in learning—is another crucial factor to consider. The Uesaka et al. (2010) study revealed that it moderated the effects of the two instructional components, suggesting that such orientation affects decisions about strategy use. In broader terms, this indicates that student attitudes toward learning need to be addressed also in educational interventions if improvements in their learning behaviors—such as using learning strategies more spontaneously—are desired.

As previously alluded to, the framework proposed here is like an application of the expectancy-value theory (Wigfield & Eccles, 2000) to addressing the question of how it may be possible to promote greater spontaneity in students' use of learning strategies. This is a new idea in the topic area of spontaneous diagram use, and a reformulation of prior findings and suggestions where the broader topic area of spontaneous use of learning strategies *in general* is concerned. The present authors believe that this two-component combination is particularly important in real education settings. In fact, evidence already exists that the application of this framework has been effective in a program for improving the spontaneous use of learning strategies (other than diagram use) in a school (see Chapter 14 in this book). However, further research would be helpful in confirming the broader usefulness of this framework.

Effects of peer instruction in promoting spontaneous use of a learning strategy

A series of studies by Uesaka and Manalo (Uesaka & Manalo, 2007, 2008a, 2011; Uesaka, 2014) demonstrated the effects of peer instruction on the spontaneous use of diagrams in students' own learning. The findings of these studies suggest that the experience of diagram use in peer instruction leads to the internalization of diagram use as part of the student's repertoire of learning strategies. It is possible that, like the framework described in the previous subsection, peer instruction can help facilitate spontaneous use not just of diagrams but also other learning strategies. In fact, findings from a recent study by Fukaya, Uesaka, Tanaka, Shinogaya, Nishio, and Ichikawa (2016) suggest that peer instruction can promote the spontaneous use of other learning strategies—such as self-explanation—in students' daily learning situations.

It is important to stress, however, that peer instruction on its own, without the associated instruction and skills development in the use of the target learning strategy, would likely not be effective. The studies by Uesaka and Manalo, referred to above, all combined peer instruction activities with learning strategies instruction and relevant skills development in use of the strategy.

Some possible directions for future research

A topic worth examining in future research is the interaction between learner-related and task-related factors. With regard to task-related factors, Uesaka and Manalo (2012) demonstrated the influence of transformational costs in the construction of useful diagrams from the descriptions provided in math word problems. However, both perceived and actual cognitive cost might differ depending on students' diagram construction skills. Thus, the effect of skills instruction and training on such costs of using learning strategies would be valuable to examine in future research.

Finally, enhancing the quality of strategy use is as important as improving the frequency of strategy use. For example, in the case of diagram use in math word problem solving, it is necessary to select the appropriate types of diagrams.

However, as Grawemeyer and Cox (2004) demonstrated, novices make poor decisions and are biased in the kinds of diagrams they choose. To address such problems, Uesaka and Manalo (2006) proposed an instructional method that included active comparison of diagrams used in problem solving, and demonstrated the effectiveness of this method in promoting students' subsequent construction of appropriate diagrams. The method proved effective because the comparisons undertaken made salient the important features that make different diagrams appropriate for solving different types of problems. The attention to such features likely helped the students to form abstract conditional rules they could apply when considering what diagrams to use in subsequent problem solving. Garner (1990) discussed the necessity of developing conditional knowledge about learning strategies if learners are to be able to make appropriate decisions about when and what kinds of strategies to use. Topics such as how to improve conditional knowledge about other learning strategies, and how to promote the quality of learning strategy use, should be examined more in future research in this area—alongside the issue of spontaneous use.

References

Ainsworth, S. (2006). DeFT: A conceptual framework for considering learning with multiple representations. *Learning and Instruction, 16*(3), 183–198.

Ainsworth, S., Prain, V., & Tytler, R. (2011). Drawing to learn in science. *Science, 333*(6046), 1096–1097.

Ainsworth, S., & Th Loizou, A. (2003). The effects of self-explaining when learning with text or diagrams. *Cognitive Science, 27*(4), 669–681.

Azmitia, M. (1988). Peer interaction and problem solving: When are two heads better than one? *Child Development, 59*(1), 87–96.

Borkowski, J., Carr, M., & Presseley, M. (1987). "Spontaneous" strategy use: Perspectives from metacognitive theory. *Intelligence, 11*(1), 61–75.

Borkowski, J. G., & Cavanaugh, J. C. (1979). Maintenance and generalization of skills and strategies by the retarded. In N. R. Ellis (Ed.), *Handbook of mental deficiency: Psychological theory and research* (pp. 569–611). Hillsdale, NJ: Erlbaum.

Britton, J., Burgess, A., Martin, N., McLeod A., & Rosen, R. (1975). *The development of writing abilities* (pp. 11–18). London: Macmillan.

Brown, A. L., Bransford, J. D., Ferrara, R., & Campione, J. (1983). Learning, remembering, and understanding. In P. H. Mussen (series Ed.) & J. H. Flavell & E. M. Markman (vol. Eds.), *Handbook of child psychology: Vol. 3. Cognitive development* (4th ed., pp. 77–166). New York, NY: Wiley.

Dufour-Janvier, B., Bednarz, N., & Belanger, M. (1987). Pedagogical considerations concerning the problem of representation. In C. Janvier (Ed.), *Problems of representation in the teaching and learning of mathematics* (pp. 110–120). Hillsdale, NJ: Erlbaum.

Flavell, J. H., Beach, D. R., & Chinsky, J. M. (1966). Spontaneous verbal rehearsal in a memory task as a function of age. *Child Development, 37*(2), 283–299.

Fukaya, T., Uesaka, Y., Tanaka, E., Shinogaya, K., Nishio, S., & Ichikawa, S. (2016). Effects of a high school peer-tutoring program on the quality of students' interaction and learning strategy use. *Japanese Journal of Educational Psychology, 64*(1), 88–104.

Garner, R. (1990). When children and adults do not use learning strategies: Toward a theory of settings. *Review of Educational Research, 60*(4), 517–529.

Graham, S., & Perin, D. (2007). A meta-analysis of writing instruction for adolescent students. *Journal of Educational Psychology, 99*(3), 445–476.

Grawemeyer, B., & Cox, R. (2004). The effect of knowledge-of-external-representations upon performance and representational choice in a database query task. *Lecture Notes in Artificial Intelligence, 2980*, 351–354.

Guthrie, J. T., Van Meter, P., Hancock, G. R., Alao, S., Anderson, E., & McCann, A. (1998). Does concept-oriented reading instruction increase strategy use and conceptual learning from text? *Journal of Educational Psychology, 90*, 261–278.

Hembree, R. (1992). Experiments and relational studies in problem-solving: A meta-analysis. *Journal for Research in Mathematics Education, 23*(3), 242–273.

Kennedy, B. A., & Miller, D. J. (1976). Persistent use of verbal rehearsal as a function of information about its value. *Child Development, 47*(2), 566–569.

Keys, C. W. (1999). Revitalizing instruction in scientific genres: Connecting knowledge production with writing to learn in science. *Science Education, 83*(2), 115–130.

Manalo, E., & Uesaka, Y. (2012). Elucidating the mechanism of spontaneous diagram use in explanations: How cognitive processing of text and diagrammatic representations is influenced by individual and task-related factors. *Lecture Notes in Artificial Intelligence, 7352*, 35–50.

Manalo, E., & Uesaka, Y. (2014). Students' spontaneous use of diagrams in written communication: Understanding variations according to purpose and cognitive cost entailed. *Lecture Notes in Artificial Intelligence, 8578*, 78–92.

Manalo, E., & Uesaka, Y. (2016). Hint, instruction, and practice: The necessary components for promoting spontaneous diagram use in students' written work? *Lecture Notes in Artificial Intelligence, 9781*, 157–171.

Manalo, E., Uesaka, Y., Pérez-Kriz, S., Kato, M., & Fukaya, T. (2013). Science and engineering students' use of diagrams during note taking versus explanation. *Educational Studies, 39*(1), 118–123.

Manalo, E., Uesaka, Y., & Sheppard, C. (2015). *Can interactive communication promote students' use of diagrams in explaining what they have learned?* Paper presented at the EARLI Conference, August 25–29, Cyprus University of Technology, Limassol, Cyprus.

Mayer, R. E. (2003). The promise of multimedia learning: Using the same instructional design methods across different media. *Learning and Instruction, 13*(2), 125–139.

Mayer, R. E., & Moreno, R. (2003). Nine ways to reduce cognitive load in multimedia learning. *Educational Psychologist, 38*, 43–52.

Murayama, K. (2003). Learning strategy use and short- and long-term perceived utility. *Japanese Journal of Educational Psychology, 51*(2), 130–140.

Nolen, S. B., & Haladyna, T. M. (1990). Personal and environmental influences on students' beliefs about effective study strategies. *Contemporary Educational Psychology, 15*(2), 116–130.

Pellegrino, J. W., & Hilton, M. L. (2012). *Education for life and work: Developing transferable knowledge and skills in the 21st Century*. Washington, DC: National Academies Press.

Pintrich, P. R. (2003). A motivational science perspective on the role of student motivation in learning and teaching contexts. *Journal of Educational Psychology, 95*(4), 667–686.

Polya, G. (1945). *How to solve it: A new aspect of mathematical method*. Princeton, NJ: Princeton University Press.

Reed, S. K. (1999). *Word problems: Research and curriculum reform*. Mahwah, NJ: Erlbaum.

Sato, J. (1998). Effects of learners' perception of utility and costs, and learning strategy preferences. *Japanese Journal of Educational Psychology, 46*(4), 367–376.

Sawyer, R. J., Graham, S., & Harris, K. R. (1992). Direct teaching, strategy instruction, and strategy instruction with explicit self-regulation: Effects on the composition skills and self-efficacy of students with learning disabilities. *Journal of Educational Psychology, 84*, 340–352.

Schoenfeld, A. H. (1985). *Mathematical problem solving*. San Diego, CA: Academic Press.

Shinogaya, K. (2008). Effects of preparation on learning: Interaction with beliefs about learning. *Japanese Journal of Educational Psychology, 56*(2), 256–267.

Stokes, T. F., & Baer, D. M. (1977). An implicit technology of generalization. *Journal of Applied Behavior Analysis, 10*(2), 349–367.

Sweller, J., van Merrienboer, J. J. G., & Paas, F. G. W. C. (1998). Cognitive architecture and instructional design. *Educational Psychology Review, 10*, 251–296.

Uesaka, Y. (2014). *Supporting mathematics problem solving by encouraging the strategy of diagram utilization: Development of the "REAL approach", linking theory and practices.* [Japanese title: Suugakuteki mondaikaiketsu ni okeru zuhyou katsuyou no shien]. Tokyo: Kazama-shobo.

Uesaka, Y., & Manalo, E. (2006). Active comparison as a means of promoting the development of abstract conditional knowledge and appropriate choice of diagrams in math word problem solving. *Lecture Notes in Artificial Intelligence, 4045*, 181–195.

Uesaka, Y., & Manalo, E. (2007). Peer instruction as a way of promoting spontaneous use of diagrams when solving math word problems. In D. S. McNamara & J. G. Trafton (Eds.), *Proceedings of the 29th Annual Cognitive Science Society* (pp. 677–682). Austin, TX: Cognitive Science Society.

Uesaka, Y., & Manalo, E. (2008a). Does the use of diagrams as communication tools result in their internalization as personal tools for problem solving? In B. C. Love, K. McRae, & V. M. Sloutsky (Eds.), *Proceedings of the 30th Annual Conference of the Cognitive Science Society* (pp. 1711–1716). Austin, TX: Cognitive Science Society.

Uesaka, Y., & Manalo, E. (2008b). School curriculum development to promote student spontaneous diagram use in problem solving. *Lecture Notes in Computer Science, 5223*, 437–439.

Uesaka, Y., & Manalo, E. (2011). The effects of peer communication with diagrams on students' math word problem solving processes and outcomes. In L. Carlson, C. Hoelscher, & T. Shipley (Eds.), *Proceedings of the 33rd Annual Conference of the Cognitive Science Society* (pp. 312–317). Austin, TX: Cognitive Science Society.

Uesaka, Y., & Manalo, E. (2012). Task-related factors that influence the spontaneous use of diagrams in math word problems. *Applied Cognitive Psychology, 26*(2), 251–260.

Uesaka, Y., & Manalo, E. (2014). How communicative learning situations influence students' use of diagrams: Focusing on the spontaneous construction of diagrams and student protocols during explanation. *Lecture Notes in Artificial Intelligence, 8578*, 93–107.

Uesaka, Y., Manalo, E., & Ichikawa, S. (2007). What kinds of perceptions and daily learning behaviors promote students' use of diagrams in mathematics problem solving? *Learning and Instruction, 17*(3), 322–335.

Uesaka, Y., Manalo, E., & Ichikawa, S. (2010). The effect of perception of efficiency and diagram construction skills on students' spontaneous use of diagrams when solving math word problems. *Lecture Notes in Artificial Intelligence, 6170*, 197–211.

Uesaka, Y., Suzuki, M., Kiyokawa, S., Seo, M., & Ichikawa, S. (2014). Using COMPASS (componential assessment) to reveal Japanese students' actual competence in the fundamentals of mathematics: Is it true that "students are generally fine with the fundamentals and the problems exist only in applications"? *Japanese Journal of Educational Technology, 37*, 397–417.

Wigfield, A., & Eccles, J. S. (2000). Expectancy-value theory of achievement motivation. *Contemporary Educational Psychology, 25*(1), 68–81.

5

OBSTACLES TO THE USE OF LEARNING STRATEGIES AFTER TRAINING (AND SOME APPROACHES TO OVERCOME THEM)

Christof Wecker and Andreas Hetmanek

The Problem

Consider the following situation: Ninth-grade students have participated in a four-week curriculum unit about the genetic engineering of crops (for research on such a curriculum unit, see Kollar, Wecker, Langer, & Fischer, 2013; Wecker, Kollar, Fischer, & Prechtl, 2010). Their task was to develop a reasoned position on the question of whether genetic engineering of crops should be allowed or forbidden. To this purpose, they have read background information about some fundamentals of genetics underlying genetic engineering. In dyads, they have collaboratively conducted several web searches in order to back up potential arguments concerning economic, health-related, and environmental issues of the genetic engineering of crops. During these searches, they received computer-based scaffolding on how to conduct a good web search: to develop an initial sketch of a potential argument concerning the decision; to derive a kind of schema of the information needed to back up this argument; to generate search terms that would maximize the retrieval of relevant information while minimizing the retrieval of irrelevant information; to skim through search engine results and screen the entries for their topical relevance, trustworthiness, and impartiality based on title, text excerpt, and URL; to navigate to some of the web pages retrieved and locate relevant information by using site navigation bars and search functions; to extract and document the provenience of relevant pieces of information; and to further develop this information into a full-fledged argument.

After each cycle of web search, the students engaged in class-level discussions in which they could exchange and challenge the arguments they developed and enriched during their web searches. During these discussions, they were scaffolded by their teacher to back up their positions with detailed information found on the web and to challenge each other's views on grounds of relevance, trustworthiness, and impartiality.

The teacher finds that the students were quite successful in applying the heuristics for a good web search suggested by the computer-based scaffolds, and that, on average, from one plenary discussion to the next, the quality and amount of detail in their argument as well as their critical questions concerning each other's positions and the reasons put forward to support them have improved steadily.

However, two weeks after this unit in a class discussion on a different topic, the teacher observes that the quality of students' spontaneous arguments and the level of critical challenges of each other's positions has dropped considerably. Furthermore, informal discussions with students reveal that since the end of the curricular unit on genetic engineering they have hardly ever employed the heuristics for good web search that were taught during this unit. What has gone wrong?

Paradigmatic cases of teaching imply that learners are led from a state of relative incompetence to competence. There are, however, many skills—often not tied to a particular content domain, such as *argumentation, information problem solving, learning strategies*—for which the situation is quite different. Learners do not necessarily start from a state which they perceive as one of incompetence (in contrast, say, to reading or mathematics): Only under quite unusual circumstances, a search engine will yield zero results, and most students manage to obtain a satisfactory set of results for almost any topic that is of interest to them. Likewise, at least on a superficial level, participation in a discussion requires little more than to say *something* at certain points in exchange with a partner. Hence, the problem is not one of teaching learners new strategies for dealing with tasks they could not deal with otherwise. The problem is rather one of teaching the learners new strategies for dealing with tasks they can already handle in some way on the basis of strategies they already have. Hence, new strategies and one or several older strategies compete with each other (Siegler & Jenkins, 1989, pp. 99, 101). The question then is: Under which conditions is a newly taught strategy likely to "win" over older strategies that may be sufficient to obtain subjectively satisfactory outcomes? In the following section, we will first discuss two distinct modes of processing by which strategies are selected during and after training. Subsequently, we will deal with factors influencing the selection of a new strategy after training, before we finally turn to some practical implications.

Modes of strategy selection

Obstacles to maintaining a new strategy can be elucidated drawing on the distinction between controlled and automatic processing, so we begin with a discussion of these two modes of processing.

Controlled vs. automatic processing

Automatic processing is "a fast, parallel, fairly effortless process that is not limited by short-term memory capacity, is not under direct subject control, and performs well-developed skilled behaviors. It typically develops when subjects process stimuli in consistent fashion over many trials; it is difficult to suppress, modify, or ignore, once learned" (Shiffrin & Schneider, 1984, p. 269). In our example, applying older strategies is a case of automatic processing: Typically, learners rely on routines they have developed over a myriad of trials when conducting a web search or engaging in a discussion rather than exerting conscious control, and they apparently have difficulty suppressing, modifying, or ignoring these strategies, at least as soon as they return to such tasks in their everyday lives.

In contrast, controlled processing is "often slow, generally serial, effortful, capacity limited, subject regulated, and is used to deal with novel or inconsistent information. It is needed in situations where the responses required to stimuli vary from one trial or situation to the next, and is easily modified, suppressed, or ignored at the desire of the subject" (Shiffrin & Schneider, 1984, p. 269). This kind of processing occurs in our example when learners try to employ the computer-based prompts they receive during their web searches or try to make use of the scaffolding during the plenary discussions. They slowly generate behavior in reaction to these kinds of support, which often overwhelms their processing capacities, and actively influence the degree to which they follow (or ignore) these hints.

To some extent, learners may switch between automatic and controlled processing. In a situation in which older and newer strategies compete with each other, the selection of one of these strategies often depends on the mode of processing (see Figure 5.1): When learners are relying on automatic processing, the strategy that has attained the highest degree of automaticity will be employed automatically without being deliberately selected. This will typically be an older, well-practiced strategy. Controlled processing, in contrast, involves the conscious selection, application, and monitoring of strategies by means of metacognition (Borkowski, Carr, & Pressley, 1987, p. 63). Hence, a different strategy may be selected based on a conscious assessment of its functionality for attaining a learner's current goal. These

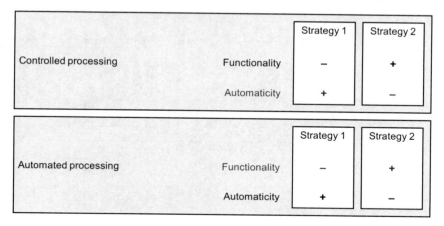

FIGURE 5.1 Competition between an old strategy (strategy 1) and a new strategy (strategy 2) with controlled vs. automatic processing before the automatization of the new strategy.

may also include satisfying the teachers' requirements for dealing with a task. The ease with which the strategies can be used plays only a secondary role in this case. In our example, most learners switch to controlled processing during the curricular unit and select the new strategies suggested by the computer-based prompts during the web searches and by the teachers' scaffolding during the plenary discussions, even if they are harder for them to implement due to lack of practice.

This distinction between automatic and controlled processing parallels several other distinctions from the literature (see Stanovich, 2011, p. 18), such as the one between system I and system II (Kahneman, 2011). (Although they differ in emphasis, these differences do not affect our current argument.) The distinction between automatic and controlled processing also plays a role in skill acquisition. Theories of skill acquisition assume that during the early phase of skill acquisition, tasks are solved by means of conscious, interpretive application of declarative information. In later phases, this information is compiled into a procedural format that can be executed unconsciously and becomes more and more automated with practice (Anderson, 1982; 1987; Anderson & Lebiere, 1998). Hence, skill acquisition can be regarded as a transition between controlled and automatic processing (see Figure 5.2). A central question is whether strategies such as searching for arguments and evaluating information found on the Internet can become automatic or will always require controlled processing. We assume that these strategies do not differ from other cognitive skills in terms of the amenability to automatization through practice, in particular, with respect to their regulatory components: Although searching for an argument or evaluating a piece of information may require switches to controlled processing at certain points in highly complicated cases even at later stages of skill acquisition, detecting a need for evidence and invoking strategies of argument search and information evaluation can become a fully automatic routine.

However, the strategies that have long since reached a state in which they are employed fully automatically will typically be the older ones that are supposed to

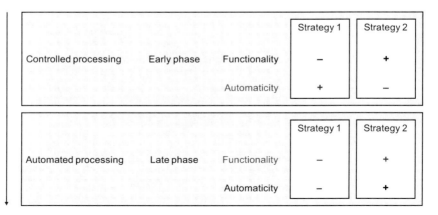

FIGURE 5.2 Automatization of a new strategy (strategy 2) that competes with an old strategy (strategy 1).

be supplanted by more functional strategies through instruction. As a consequence, the most likely reason for the "lack of transfer" of newly taught strategies to everyday situations is that these older strategies continue to "win" over new strategies.

Strategy selection during and after training

Humans tend to take the line of least resistance. This certainly applies to dealing with cognitive tasks, too. Nevertheless, learners seem to be quite capable of switching to controlled processing in educational settings: When asked by a teacher, they can "decompile" their automated strategies, i.e., split them up into their component parts to execute them in a controlled way, and work in a kind of "debug mode" to satisfy teachers' demands. This capacity enables them to interpret the instructions they receive and employ new strategies in the context of educational settings. A prerequisite for this alternative mode of functioning is that learners suppress habits that guide their everyday behavior and are triggered immediately by environmental signals (Munakata, Snyder, & Chatham, 2012, p. 72). In our example, such habits comprise the learners' spontaneous ways of interacting with a search engine or contributing to a discussion. Studies show that the selection of strategies is in fact associated with inter-individual differences in inhibition (Hodzik & Lemaire, 2011, p. 341). Thus, the controlled processing employed in an educational setting enables learners to try out new strategies and engage in some initial practice of their application.

After leaving the educational setting, such newly practiced strategies compete with the older strategies that have a long history of practice before the training (Siegler & Jenkins, 1989, pp. 99, 101). Depending on the motivation to continue using the newly acquired strategy, a learner may either quickly relapse into automatic processing or try to sustain controlled processing. In the former case, a relapse into older strategies is quite likely because in most cases these have attained a far higher degree of automaticity than any newly acquired strategy that has been practiced only to a limited extent during an educational intervention. In this case, a change toward consistent use of the new strategy is effectively prevented. In the case of sustained controlled processing, there is some chance that the newly acquired strategy is selected on appropriate occasions and receives further practice. Eventually, it may become as automated as old strategies have been prior to the training, whereas old strategies may slowly become less automated due to lack of practice (see Figure 5.2). Under these circumstances, the new strategy may supplant the older one. The duration of this development depends on many different factors, such as the complexity of the newly learned strategy, the frequency of rehearsal opportunities, or the persistence in rehearsal and practice.

To prevent old strategies from winning over a new strategy immediately after training, it is, therefore, important to inhibit the use of old strategies and make sure the new strategy is continuously selected until it has attained a sufficient degree of automaticity even outside of educational settings. As elaborated above, this applies particularly to the regulatory components that invoke a new strategy: Even if parts of a new strategy still require controlled processing in complicated cases, the strategy itself needs to be invoked automatically in order to receive further practice after explicit training in educational settings. In the subsequent section, we will discuss some beneficial conditions for overcoming this obstacle.

Factors determining the use of a new learning strategy after training

There is a long-standing tradition of research on the transfer and maintenance of learning strategies, such as strategies for memorization, which can be applied to the problem discussed in this chapter. Based on the preceding considerations, this section is divided into two parts: In the first part, we discuss conditions for maintaining controlled processing after the end of training in a new strategy as long as necessary to provide sufficient practice for the new strategy. In the second part, we cover conditions that contribute to the continued selection of a new strategy instead of old ones. In these two parts, both cognitive and motivational issues play a role.

Conditions for maintaining controlled processing (for a while)

Learners will only maintain controlled processing after training if they experience a certain need to change the current habit. During training, their awareness needs to be raised that the proposed change in the way they approach certain tasks is necessary for fully transparent reasons. There are at least two necessary conditions for such raised awareness:

(1) *Learners need to perceive the learning tasks as something valuable outside of the classroom rather than just "doing schoolwork."*

This condition concerns the basic motivational framing of training in new strategies. Primarily it is most likely to be fulfilled if tasks are selected that are intrinsically motivating for students, such as tasks that trigger learners' curiosity because they experience discrepancies and cognitive conflict, or tasks that allow learners to satisfy their basic needs for competence, autonomy, and relatedness (Ryan & Deci, 2000, p. 57), or tasks that reveal the utility of knowledge about the topic of the curricular unit as well as of the new strategy for learners' everyday lives (Pressley, Borkowski, & Schneider, 1989, p. 865).

A task such as the one of forming a reasoned position concerning genetic engineering has considerable potential to be motivating for adolescents whose political interests have started developing because it is very likely that they will be affected by this technology in their everyday lives. Nevertheless, an educational setting such as the one described here may still be experienced as "doing schoolwork" if web searches and plenary discussions are experienced mainly as the retracing of existing positions and arguments.

An approach that may be used when tasks and the use of corresponding new strategies are not motivating for learners in the first place is having learners themselves reflect on the potential utility of the new strategy for their everyday lives in short essays. This method has been shown to increase not only learners' interest in the new strategy, but also later performance (Hulleman & Harackiewicz, 2009; Hulleman, Godes, Hendricks, & Harackiewicz, 2010). In doing so, they have to link a strategy to personally meaningful outcomes that may act as an incentive to engage in controlled processing even after training. This kind of reflection also touches upon expectations about the outcomes of old and new strategies, which brings us to our second point.

(2) *Learners need to become aware of the fact that their previous strategies do not produce satisfactory results, and understand why* (Pressley et al., 1989, p. 859).

This condition concerns the specific aspect that motivation for a certain action can only be high if there is little expectation that the situation as it is will end up satisfactorily anyway. Research on strategies has shown that new strategies replace older ones if learners notice that the old strategy produces erroneous or otherwise unsatisfactory results (Siegler & Jenkins, 1989, pp. 104–105). A particular obstacle in the case of the skills discussed in this chapter often lies in the fact that learners have to deal with ill-structured problems with unclear demands or quality standards. This is the flip side of and the main reason for the fact mentioned above that, in these contexts, learners typically possess old strategies that appear to function sufficiently well and enable them to get along just fine. For example, it is often not particularly clear to most students what a good web search or a really strong argument in a plenary discussion looks like. However, in solving an ill-structured problem, part of the solution often involves developing constraints, demands, and quality standards step-by-step as the solution of the problem unfolds (see Simon, 1973, p. 189). Furthermore, in such areas typically there is no upper bound to the quality of performance. Hence, part of teaching a new strategy in an area of ill-structured problems is to help learners grasp and accept certain quality standards they have previously not been aware of. A complementary part of the task is to help them become aware of the fact that their current performance may not meet high standards yet.

Hence, learners might benefit from tasks that make shortcomings of their performances fully obvious (see Schank, Berman, & Macpherson, 1999; Siegler & Jenkins, 1989, pp. 113–114). This approach makes use of the idea of "productive failure" (Kapur, 2008). That is, learners first try to solve problems on their own and may experience certain impasses. Only after they have made these initial attempts at problem solving do they receive instruction in strategies for solving the type of problems in question (Kapur, 2008). In the context of our example, something similar could be achieved by choosing a certain discussion format—for instance, a debate—in which learners are at a clear disadvantage if they fail to name the sources of their arguments upon request. In addition to raising learners' awareness about applicable standards as well as unsatisfactory performance, it may be helpful not only to recognize *that* one's old strategies produce unsatisfactory results but also *why* they do. This insight parallels an aspect of learners' understanding of the utility of the new strategy that is an important prerequisite not primarily for maintaining controlled processing but, in particular, for securing the continued selection of the new learning strategy under appropriate conditions after training.

Conditions for maintaining the selection of the new learning strategy under appropriate conditions (forever)

When learners maintain controlled processing even after the training of a new strategy, there is a chance that they will select the new strategy rather than reverting to their older, automated strategies. There is, however, no guarantee that they will choose this option spontaneously. The following conditions must be fulfilled for this choice to be the most likely one:

(3) *Learners must have become aware of the fact that the use of the new strategy produces satisfactory results, and must have understood why* (see Pressley et al., 1989, p. 865).

This condition concerns another motivational aspect, namely that the motivation for a certain action can only be high if the person has the expectation that the action in question will lead to a satisfactory outcome. This is the idea underlying so-called "informed training," i.e., training in which learners are not only told how to execute a strategy but also given some information about the significance of the strategy (Brown, Campione, & Day, 1981, p. 15). First of all, general knowledge about the value of strategies plays a role in this respect: General strategy knowledge increases learners' understanding that their learning outcomes will improve if appropriate strategies are employed in the right circumstances (Borkowski et al., 1987, pp. 63, 66–67). In addition, more specific knowledge about the value of a particular strategy increases the likelihood that the new strategy is selected. This is the case if learners can actually detect improved results of the application of the strategy (Borkowski et al., 1987, pp. 65–66). Consequently, feedback that testifies such improvement in learning outcomes has been shown to foster the application of the new strategy (see Ringel & Springer, 1980, pp. 329–330). Such feedback may benefit not only learners' specific beliefs about the functionality of a strategy as such for obtaining desired outcomes, but also their personal confidence that they are able to implement the strategy with sufficient "fidelity" as to actually obtain these outcomes. On top of general and specific knowledge about the functionality of strategies in general or the specific new strategy in particular, learners' continued selection of the new strategy benefits from insight into the particular conditions and causes of these effects of the new strategy on the desired outcomes. Research on strategies has shown that strategy use is increased when learners are provided with information about the conditions under which a strategy produces these effects and about how it produces them, in comparison to information about the fact *that* it produces these effects (Borkowski et al., 1987, pp. 64–65; O'Sullivan & Pressley, 1984, pp. 280–281; Paris, Newman, & McVey, 1982, pp. 496–499; 504–506). In one of these studies (Paris et al., 1982), a micro-genetic analysis approach (five days with two observations each day) was used in the context of memory skills to investigate whether elaborated instruction on the usefulness and significance of strategy use affects the subsequent study behavior and test performance in memory tasks. Thirty first- and second-grade children (mean age = 7.25 years) participated in the study and were randomly assigned to one of two training conditions (elaborated strategy training vs. strategy training only). All children worked with five different sets of memory cards on five days. On day 3, all children received a strategy training. In the elaborated training condition, the modelling of the strategies was enriched by verbal explanations of the usefulness of each strategy and personalized feedback attributing study success to strategy application. Throughout the study, strategy application was observed first during the learning phase (coding for active vs. passive studying behavior), and second during recall tasks focusing on *clustering* as one of the strategies. In addition, metacognitive judgments were coded from interviews after completing the recall tasks (Paris et al., 1982, pp. 493–495). Results showed a distinct advantage of the elaborated condition: Understanding the usefulness and significance of strategies contributed significantly to improvement of learning behavior as well as to task performance. Path-analytic analyses additionally established a link between the design of the training, the metacognitive judgments of the students, their subsequent study behavior, and the resulting recall performance (Paris et al., 1982, pp. 496–499, 504–506). Such enriched information can even raise the level of later strategy use to the level that is obtained by immediately reminding the learners to apply the strategy (O'Sullivan & Pressley, 1984, pp. 283–284). Furthermore, it can effectively suppress the application of old strategies (Paris et al., 1982, pp. 499–500; Waters, 1982, pp. 188–189; for less strong evidence, see Rao & Moelly, 1989, p. 344).

In line with these considerations, specific features that are present during a strategy training can promote the continued selection of the newly taught strategy after the training, such as emphasizing the significance of the strategy for producing outcomes of high quality, or feedback to learners that attributes reaching high levels of quality to the application of the new strategy (or not reaching high levels of quality to the lack of application of the new strategy) (Borkowski et al., 1987, pp. 68–69; Ringel & Springer, 1980, pp. 329–330; Schunk & Rice, 1993). The effect of these components of instruction on continued strategy use is mediated motivationally to a large extent: They foster appropriate and functional attributions of success and failure, self-confidence, and control beliefs. Via the expectation that using the new strategy will lead to desired outcomes, these cognitions increase the motivation to employ the new strategy. Putting effort into the application of the new strategy is likely to yield the desired outcomes. Hence, the conviction that the application of the new strategy promotes one's desired outcomes will foster its application as well as its actual outcomes, which in turn will stabilize this conviction, thereby creating a virtuous circle of strategy use (Borkowski et al., 1987, pp. 67–68).

The previous condition operates in phases in which learners still engage in controlled processing. The long-term dominance of the new strategy over the old strategy, however, requires that the new strategy becomes automatized itself. This is the final condition for the continued use of the new strategy:

(4) *Learners need to automatize the new strategy at least to the same extent as the old strategies it has to supplant* (Pressley et al., 1989, pp. 860, 862).

This condition has a processing-related and a motivational aspect: Concerning processing, automatization implies greater fluency in applying a strategy. Hence, the better the new strategy is practiced and thereby automatized, the greater the ease and accuracy with which this strategy can be applied. The motivational side of greater fluency is that the strategy can be performed nearly without effort, which makes it more likely that a learner will spontaneously select the strategy and stick to it rather than trying to avoid it due to high demands on effort. Not only the duration of practice (Borkowski et al., 1987, p. 65) but also the variety of tasks used plays an important role in the likelihood of later strategy transfer (Borkowski et al., 1987, p. 64). Only if the new strategy is practiced well enough to arrive at a high level of automatization, the new strategy has a good chance of winning out over older strategies. In fact, the more the new strategy is practiced exclusively, the more the older strategies will become less automatized to time, and finally become inferior to the new strategy as far as automatization is concerned (see Figure 5.2).

Practical implications

Before turning to practical implications, we need to begin this concluding section with a disclaimer: Not all kinds of learning strategies at different levels of complexity have been covered with equal comprehensiveness in research. In particular, learning strategies that are rather tightly interwoven with technology-based practices of information search, such as online search skills, or that play a role in social learning settings, such as argumentation skills, have not been investigated from the perspective of strategy maintenance after training very much. Instead, most of the reasoning we presented in this chapter is based on research about metacognition and memory strategies in cognitive developmental psychology. We had to extrapolate from this earlier research to arrive at assumptions about learners' processing and their likely continued use of strategies that still have some anchoring in empirical research. However, the findings we relied on may not all be generalizable to more complex strategies such as those used when conducting web searches or contributing arguments in discussions. Nevertheless, there is good reason to expect that the described basic mechanisms of cognition and motivation are applicable to a broad range of strategies, although certainly more research is needed on more complex strategies.

In the introduction to this chapter, we presented a scenario many teachers are familiar with. In the main part of this chapter, we identified possible reasons for the lack of sustained, spontaneous strategy use and delineated some ideas how these problems might be overcome. These approaches can be summarized and condensed as follows:

1 Use tasks that are personally meaningful to the learners and that they will not regard as "doing school work."
2 Help learners to realize that the quality of their current performance is less than optimal or even unsatisfactory.
3 Help learners to realize that the quality of their current performance is less than optimal or even unsatisfactory *because they employ suboptimal strategies*.
4 Help learners to inhibit their previously used strategies.
5 Help learners to *realize that* the new strategy produces performance of high quality that satisfies applicable quality standards.
6 Help learners to *understand why* the new strategy produces performance of high quality that satisfies applicable quality standards.
7 Provide learners with ample occasions and a broad array of diverse tasks to practice the application of the new strategy in order to automatize it.

References

Anderson, J. R. (1982). Acquisition of cognitive skill. *Psychological Review, 89*(4), 369–406.

Anderson, J. R. (1987). Skill acquisition: Compilation of weak-method problem solutions. *Psychological Review, 94*(2), 192–210.

Anderson, J. R., & Lebiere, C. (1998). *The atomic components of thought*. Mahwah, NJ: Erlbaum.

Borkowski, J. G., Carr, M., & Pressley, M. (1987). "Spontaneous" strategy use: Perspectives from metacognitive theory. *Intelligence, 11*(1), 61–75.

Brown, A. L., Campione, J. C., & Day, J. D. (1981). Learning to learn: On training to learn from texts. *Educational Researcher, 10*(2), 14–21.

Hodzik, S., & Lemaire, P. (2011). Inhibition and shifting capacities mediate adults' age-related differences in strategy selection and repertoire. *Acta Psychologica, 137*(3), 335–344.

Hulleman, C. S., Godes, O., Hendricks, B. L., & Harckiewicz, J. M. (2010). Enhancing interest and performance with a utility value information. *Journal of Educational Psychology, 102*(4), 880–895.

Hulleman, C. S., & Harackiewicz, J. M. (2009). Promoting interest and performance in high school science classes. *Science, 326*, 1410–1412.

Kahneman, D. (2011). *Thinking, fast and slow*. New York, NY: Macmillan.

Kapur, M. (2008). Productive failure. *Cognition and Instruction, 26*(3), 379–424.

Kollar, I., Wecker, C., Langer, S., & Fischer, F. (2013). When instruction supports collaboration, but does not lead to learning – the case of classroom and small group scripts in the CSCL classroom. In N. Rummel, M. Kapur, M. Nathan, & S. Puntambekar (Eds.), *To see the world and a grain of sand: Learning across levels of space, time, and scale: CSCL 2013 conference proceedings. Vol. 1: Full papers & symposia* (pp. 256–263). Madison, WI: International Society of the Learning Sciences.

Munakata, Y., Snyder, H. R., & Chatham, C. H. (2012). Developing cognitive control: Three key transitions. *Current Directions in Psychological Science, 21*(2), 71–77.

O'Sullivan, J. T., & Pressley, M. (1984). Completeness of instruction and strategy transfer. *Journal of Experimental Child Psychology, 38*(2), 275–288.

Paris, S. G., Newman, R. S., & McVey, K. A. (1982). Learning the functional significance of mnemonic actions: A microgenetic study of strategy acquisition. *Journal of Experimental Child Psychology, 34*(3), 490–509.

Pressley, M., Borkowski, J. G., & Schneider, W. (1989). Good information processing: What it is and how education can promote it. *International Journal of Educational Research, 13*(8), 857–867.

Rao, N., & Moely, B. E. (1989). Producing memory strategy maintenance and generalization by explicit or implicit training of memory knowledge. *Journal of Experimental Child Psychology, 48*(3), 335–352.

Ringel, B. A., & Springer, C. J. (1980). On knowing how well one is remembering: The persistence of strategy use during transfer. *Journal of Experimental Child Psychology, 29*(2), 322–333.

Ryan, R. M., & Deci, E. L. (2000). Intrinsic and extrinsic motivations: Classic definitions and new directions. *Contemporary Educational Psychology, 25*(1), 54–67.

Schank, R. C., Berman, T. R., & Macpherson, K. A. (1999). Learning by doing. In C. M. Reigeluth (ed.), *Instructional design theories and models. Vol. 2: A new paradigm of instructional theory* (pp. 161–181). Mahwah, NJ: Erlbaum.

Schunk, D. H., & Rice, J. M. (1993). Strategy fading and progress feedback: Effects on self-efficacy and comprehension among students receiving remedial reading services. *The Journal of Special Education, 27*(3), 257–276.

Shiffrin, R. M., & Schneider, W. (1984). Automatic and controlled processing revisted. *Psychological Review, 91*(2), 269–276.

Siegler, R. S., & Jenkins, E. (1989). *How children discover new strategies.* Hillsdale, NJ: Erlabum.

Simon, H. A. (1973). The structure of ill structured problems. *Artificial Intelligence, 4,* 181–201.

Stanovich, K. E. (2011). *Rationality and the reflective mind.* Oxford, UK: Oxford University Press.

Waters, H. S. (1982). Memory development in adolescence: Relationships between meta-memory, strategy use, and performance. *Journal of Experimental Child Psychology, 33*(2), 183–195.

Wecker, C., Kollar, I., Fischer, F., & Prechtl, H. (2010). Fostering online search competence and domain-specific knowledge in inquiry classrooms: Effects of continuous and fading collaboration scripts. In K. Gomez, L. Lyons, & J. Radinsky (Eds.), *Learning in the disciplines: Proceedings of the 9th International Conference of the Learning Sciences (ICLS 2010). Vol. 1: Full papers* (pp. 810–817). Chicago, IL: International Society of the Learning Sciences.

PART II

Research

6

SECOND LANGUAGE VOCABULARY LEARNING

Are students cognitive misers and, if so, why?

Emmanuel Manalo and Marcus Henning

Introduction

The centrality of vocabulary acquisition in second language (L2) learning has been demonstrated in numerous research studies. Nation (2006) reported, for example, that a learner of English as an L2 would need an 8,000 to 9,000 word-family vocabulary (where a word-family pertains to a base word and its derivatives) to understand written text without assistance, and a 6,000 to 7,000 word-family vocabulary to understand spoken text. L2 vocabulary knowledge has also been reported to significantly correlate with L2 speaking competence (Oya, Manalo, & Greenwood, 2009), and with academic achievement among non-native primary age children and university students (Loewen & Ellis, 2005; Saville-Troike, 1984).

Research in L2 vocabulary learning has also revealed that some approaches to learning are more effective than others. Experimental studies have shown that effective L2 vocabulary learning strategies are those that entail deeper processing through form and meaning associations[1] (e.g., Avila & Sadoski, 1996; Brown & Perry, 1991; Sagarra & Alba, 2006). In real educational settings, the strategies that have been reported as being effective include contextual guessing and skilled use of dictionaries (e.g., Fan, 2003; Gu & Johnson, 1996), word analysis (use of knowledge about grammar and morphology; Fan, 2003), note taking, paying attention to word formation, contextual encoding, activation of newly learned words (Gu & Johnson, 1996), mnemonic strategies (association, elaboration), and self-testing (Manalo, 1999). In contrast, simple repetition strategies have been found to be ineffective: Gu and Johnson (1996), for example, reported that visual repetition (e.g., trying to remember a word by writing it repeatedly) was the strongest *negative* predictor of vocabulary size and general proficiency in English, while Fan (2003) found repetition strategies to be related to poor learning.

It should briefly be noted here that, although general distinctions can be made between "effective" and "ineffective" strategies, what might prove "effective" in real-life situations would depend to some extent on learner characteristics and situational contexts. Gu (2003), for example, explained how motivations and preferences for styles of learning could result in the use of very different approaches—but with similarly successful outcomes. Murayama (2003a) also pointed out that the format of tests could influence how students learn target information, and whether they use deep or shallow processing strategies. Hence, such distinctions between effective and ineffective are not absolute, and strategies that are usually considered ineffective or involving shallow processing can be considered appropriate in some situations (e.g., the use of rote memorization to prepare for tests that require simple regurgitation of information). In fact, Ellis (1994) emphasized that, while acquiring the semantic and conceptual aspects of vocabulary requires explicit learning processes in which deep processing approaches are effective, reproduction and production aspects depend to a large extent on implicit learning—which includes repetitive exposure to the target vocabulary. There are neurobiological explanations for the role of repetition in learning (see, e.g., Kandel, 2001), but a discussion of those is outside the scope of this chapter.

Studies that have investigated the spontaneous strategies that L2 learners use in real vocabulary learning situations have revealed mixed results as far as the use of effective strategies is concerned. For example, while Gu and Johnson (1996) found that Chinese university students used a wide variety of vocabulary learning strategies, both those that can be considered effective and those that can be considered ineffective, Kudo (1999) and Lawson and Hogben (1996) reported that the majority of students were using ineffective strategies. Among Japanese senior high school students, Kudo found that cognitively shallower strategies such as repetition were popular; and with Australian university students learning Italian, Lawson and Hogben found that the majority were simply repeating words and their meanings during their attempts at learning. The present authors are also aware of many instructors in university learning contexts who complain about the majority of their students being poor at L2 vocabulary building and persisting in the use of simple rote memorization and other shallow processing strategies.

The research and anecdotal evidence on the strategies that students use in learning L2 vocabulary brings up one important question: Why do many students spontaneously use poor strategies for learning? An intuitive answer might suggest that such strategies are easier and require far less effort to execute compared to strategies involving deeper processing. In fact, there is support for such an answer in cognitive educational research. Perceived cost efficiency of strategies affects students' decisions on their use (McCombs, 1988), and both Murayama (2003b) and Sato (1998) have reported evidence indicating that perceived high cost is a deterrent to the use of learning strategies. More recently, Uesaka and Manalo (2012) have pointed out that cognitive cost is an important determinant in students' spontaneous use of diagrams when attempting to solve math word problems. Even though diagram use has been proven to be the most efficacious toward obtaining a correct solution in such situations (see, e.g., Hembree, 1992), Uesaka and Manalo found significantly lower rates of diagram use when students were attempting to solve problems that required the construction of more abstract diagrams (e.g., graphs and tables, compared to more concrete diagrams like topographic scene illustrations). They explained that the construction of more abstract diagrams require more transformational steps, from understanding the terms of the problem to abstractly representing pertinent aspects of that problem in the diagram constructed (e.g., time represented on the x-axis and volume on the y-axis of a line graph). Those additional transformational steps not only demand greater competence, but also entail greater cost in terms of the cognitive resources required—thus making them prohibitive to use for many students in problem solving situations. Manalo and Uesaka (2012) and Manalo, Uesaka, Pérez-Kriz, Kato, and Fukaya (2013) also observed the effect of cognitive cost on students' spontaneous use of diagrams when writing explanations of what they had learned. When having to explain information of lower imageability, the rate of spontaneous diagram use was significantly lower compared to when explaining information that was easier to imagine—presumably because more cognitive resources would have been required to construct an appropriate diagram for the hard-to-imagine information.

This explanation, however, appears counter-intuitive when the likely poor outcomes of shallow processing strategies are considered (i.e., poor learning, leading to poor test results and poor grades). Especially at the university level, when the grades that students obtain usually lead to more salient consequences in qualification achievement and career-related options, students would more likely be willing to invest greater effort in the use of strategies that would bring about better outcomes. Even though explanations of human performance based on economic concepts (such as supply and demand) assume that people are predisposed to avoid or minimize cognitive workload (e.g., Allport, 1954), they also suggest that the use of available resources is influenced by intended performance (e.g., Navon & Gopher, 1979; Norman & Bobrow, 1975). In other words, if people are aiming to perform well (e.g., students aiming to get good grades), they would be willing to deploy more resources to achieve such aims (e.g., use more effective learning strategies even if such strategies might entail higher cognitive workload).

In the present study, the objectives were two-fold. First, the study sought to confirm that, in learning L2 vocabulary, many university students tend to spontaneously use learning strategies that are of the shallow processing type, involving mainly repetition and indicative of low cognitive effort. In other words, the aim was to find out if students really have a tendency toward being "cognitive misers" or cognitive processing cost minimizers (cf. Gronich, 2006; Uesaka & Manalo, 2012) when undertaking vocabulary learning to prepare for tests. It sought to confirm this with Japanese university students in science and engineering who could be considered as generally being more serious and aiming for higher levels of achievement (explained further in "Participants" description below). Even though Lawson and Hogben (1996) had earlier reported the use of poor L2 vocabulary learning strategies among university students, their participant group comprised of only 15 students. Also, as previously noted, the participants in Kudo's (1999) study were Japanese high school rather than university students. If it were confirmed that students in the present study were cognitive misers in L2 vocabulary learning, the study's second objective was to elucidate likely reasons for this. As previously explained, the use of such poor strategies would seem untenable if students were aiming to perform well in their studies.

Method

Participants

The participants were 84 Japanese undergraduate university students (female = 24, male = 60) who were taking a second year compulsory course in academic reading in English (the students' L2). The students were all enrolled in one university's science and engineering faculty, and they were recruited from two classes of the academic reading course. They were fairly homogenous in age, all being about 20 years old.

In Japan, it is generally well known that significant proportions of university students are poorly motivated and do not work hard in their studies (e.g., Manalo, Koyasu, Hashimoto, & Miyauchi, 2006; Shimoyama, 1996). However, as noted in the preceding section, the students who comprised the participants of this study could be considered as generally more serious and better motivated to achieve good grades. The reason is that, in the faculty where they were enrolled, there is a selection process into specialist subject courses and professor laboratories at the senior level, which depends on grades and is highly competitive. Passing with mediocre grades usually results in not being accepted into their subject/laboratory of choice, and being relegated instead to studying under unpopular professors in unpopular subjects/topic areas. Grades in English are particularly important as senior members of the faculty have repeatedly expressed a commonly held view that such grades are indicative of students' ability to think logically and critically. Thus, although no direct measurement of the participants' learning motivation was taken, and it is acknowledged that there would have been variations in such motivation among the student cohort, it would nevertheless be reasonable to claim that the majority of the participants were serious in their studies and aiming to achieve good grades—at least more so than other Japanese university students not facing a grade-based selection process.

Procedure

In the English academic reading course they were taking, the students were required to learn Coxhead's (2000) academic words lists. They were administered bi-weekly tests on selected words from those lists. The tests were in two parts: the first part comprised of 10 multi-choice questions in which the students had to choose from five options the most appropriate word to fill in a blank in a given sentence, and the second part comprised of 10 cued recall questions that required them to write the appropriate word given two sentences with blanks for those words and cues of the form "this word begins with [letter] and means [very brief definition of the word]".

The students' performance in two consecutive tests was examined in this research. The tests were of the form described above, and were each scored out of 20.

Following each test, the students were administered a brief, one-page questionnaire (in Japanese) that asked about the test study strategy they used, as well as their view about the difficulty level of the strategy, how confident they were of their ability to use the strategy, and their expectations about its effectiveness. The strategy question was an open-ended question: the students were provided space to briefly write a description of the strategy they used. The difficulty, confidence, and effectiveness questions sought responses on 5-point Likert-type scales, with only the end points anchored (i.e., 1 = "very easy to use" to 5 = "very difficult to use" for the difficulty question; 1 = not confident at all" to 5 = "completely confident" for the confidence question; and 1 = "not effective" to 5 = "very effective" for the effectiveness question).

In addition, in the questionnaire administered following the first test, the students were asked if they could think of a more effective strategy for learning L2 vocabulary words for the class tests: to briefly describe the strategy if they could, or to explain their answer if they could not. They were also asked to provide ratings for difficulty, confidence, and effectiveness for the strategy (if they described one). In the questionnaire administered following the second test, the students were additionally asked if they had used the "more effective" strategy they might have described when completing the questionnaire following the previous test, and to explain their answer either way.

Note that there was an implicit expectation that the students might spontaneously use a "more effective" strategy in the second test, particularly if they had not used an effective strategy in the first test and became aware of that as a consequence of answering the questionnaire. Garner (1990) pointed out that one important reason why children and adults do not use effective strategies in learning is that they simply do not notice that the strategies they are using are not delivering optimal outcomes. In other words, they are poor at cognitive monitoring, and they fail to detect any problem in what they are doing and the results they are getting—especially if the problem is not serious enough (e.g., they may not be failing yet, but the test scores they are getting may be quite poor). Thus, by alerting the students to any shortcomings in the learning strategies they were using, it was expected that they might make some adjustments to the strategies they would subsequently use.

Results

Were the students cognitive misers in learning L2 vocabulary?

The basic answer to this question appears to be "yes". The difficulty question they were asked was: "How easy or difficult is this strategy for you to use?" On the scale of 1 to 5 they were presented, 3 was the middle point. However, the students' mean reported difficulty level was below this, tending more toward "very easy to use" ($M = 2.49$, $SD = 1.06$). Furthermore, their responses to the confidence ($M = 3.02$, $SD = .86$) and effectiveness ($M = 3.23$, $SD = .94$) questions suggest that they were using a study strategy that they were neither fully confident with nor certain about its effectiveness.

When the descriptions of strategies that the students' used were examined, this revealed that 50% of the strategies comprised solely of repetition and other shallow processing approaches (e.g., "I read the words and sample sentences", "I read over and over again", "I look at the words"). Forty-two point nine per cent (42.9%) of the strategies described entailed or included looking up word meanings (e.g., "I look up the words using an English dictionary", "I look up the words and write the meaning", "I examine the meaning of each word and read the sample sentences"). Only 7.1% of the strategies described entailed or included elaboration, association, and/or active self-testing (e.g., "I look up the meaning and use them in sentences", "I look at the sample sentences, predict meaning, and look up if necessary"). Note that if the description that a student wrote contained mention of any elaboration, association, or active self-testing methods—even if it also included mention of repetition or finding the meaning of words—it was included in the third category for the purposes of classifying the responses. Likewise, if the description included looking up the meanings of words—even combined with repetition or other shallow processing strategies—it was included in the second category.

In response to the question about whether they could think of a more effective strategy to use, 62% of the students indicated that they could. On average, they rated the new strategy they described as being more difficult to use compared to the ones they had been using: $M = 3.67$, $SD = 1.01$ for the new strategy; $t_{(56)} = 5.56$, $p < .001$. The new strategies were also perceived as potentially being more effective: $M = 4.08$, $SD = .90$ for the new strategies; $t_{(58)} = 7.23$, $p < .001$. Their confidence level in being able to use the new strategies was somewhat lower, but not significantly so: $M = 2.69$, $SD = .92$ for the new strategies; $t_{(57)} = 1.27$, $p = .209$.

Why the cognitive miserliness?

Analysis of the students' test performance and responses to the questions asked revealed that a possible reason for the students' cognitive miserliness was a mismatch between the difficulty levels of the strategies they were using and the resulting test outcomes. This basically means that, when they used more difficult strategies, it did not lead to better test results. The students' perceptions about their confidence in and effectiveness of the strategies they had used in the first test both significantly (positively) correlated with their scores in that test: $r = .22$, $p = .044$; and $r = .29$, $p = .007$; respectively (see Figure 6.1). This suggests that when they felt more confident in the strategy they were using and considered it more effective, they also tended to obtain better scores in the test. However, the correlation between their scores in that test and their perceptions of the difficulty levels of the strategies they used was *not* significant: $r = -.07$, $p = .504$. This suggests that even when they were using what they perceived to be a more difficult strategy, it was not paying off in terms of producing better results.

As reported above, the "better" strategies that the students could think of (when they were asked following the first test) were perceived as significantly more difficult than the strategies they used in the first test. However, these better strategies were in fact mostly shallow processing and repetition strategies: an examination of the students' descriptions of those strategies revealed that 55.1% of them were so (e.g., "Write down all the sample sentences", "Write the words over and over again", and "Look at the words over and over again"). Only 20.4% involved looking up word meanings, and 24.5% involved some form of elaboration, association, and/or active self-testing (e.g., "Make my own quiz", "Make my own sentences and read out loud; use words in daily life"). The distribution between these kinds of strategies was not proportionately different from the distribution of the kinds of strategies they reported using in the first test: $\chi^2(4, N = 49) = 5.16$, $p = .271$.

Furthermore, most of the students did not subsequently use the "better" strategies they had described. In the second test, 71% of the students reported using exactly the same strategy they had used in the first test. Of the ones who reported using a different strategy, only 22% indicated that they used the "better" strategy they described following the first test.

There was a positive average normalized gain score ($M = .05$, $SD = .95$) when comparing the students' scores in the first and second tests (see Crouch & Mazur, 2001, for the method used to compute the average normalized gain score). Comparing the actual means they obtained in test 1 ($M = 15.48$, $SD = 2.79$) and test 2 ($M = 16.42$, $SD = 2.88$) showed a significant difference: $t_{(83)} = -3.27$, $p = .002$. However, across the two tests, there were no significant changes in the students' perceptions about the difficulty of, their confidence in, and the effectiveness of the vocabulary learning strategies they employed.

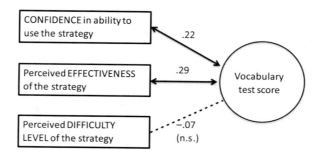

FIGURE 6.1   Significant correlations between student vocabulary test scores and their ratings of confidence in ability to use the strategy and perceived effectiveness of the strategy; perceived difficulty level of the strategy was not significantly correlated.

Discussion

What the findings suggest

Based on the findings of this study, cognitive cost appears to influence students' strategy use in learning L2 vocabulary words for tests. In particular, three aspects of the students' test behavior and questionnaire responses indicate this cognitive cost influence. First, the use of repetition and shallow processing strategies was prevalent in both the first and the second tests: at least half of the students reported relying solely on such strategies for their preparation. Second, the level of effort the students reported using was, on average, low. And third, the majority of students could think of "better" strategies to use—but they subsequently did not use those strategies. The fact that those "better" strategies were also perceived as being more difficult provides a viable partial explanation for why they were not used.

If students are serious in their studies and concerned about the grades they get, however, one would expect that they would be willing to invest greater effort—cognitive or otherwise—into test preparation to achieve better results. So why was this apparently not the case with the science and engineering university students in the current study? A possible reason is that many of the students might have had experiences that have led them to the conclusion that deploying more effort in L2 vocabulary learning does not usually lead to better outcomes. The finding that the perceived difficulty level of strategies the students were using was not significantly correlated with test outcome strongly suggests this. Furthermore, the mismatch between effort and outcome may occur because the students were generally poor in their views—and perhaps knowledge—about what effective learning strategies for L2 vocabulary learning might involve. The findings revealed that, for many of them, "better" strategies simply pertained to deploying more effort in implementing basically the same or similar repetitive, shallow processing strategies they had been using. Thus, the cycle shown in Figure 6.2 is perpetuated.

Previous research has demonstrated the importance of motivation in all stages of the vocabulary learning process (i.e., the instigation, sustenance, and evaluation stages; Tseng & Schmitt, 2008). The results of the present study suggest that if there is a mismatch between effort put in and subsequent outcomes, motivation could be detrimentally affected and students could end up investing little effort into such learning. In cases where demotivation has already occurred, it would be necessary to break any negative cycles, such as the one shown in Figure 6.2, if students are to be dissuaded from being cognitive misers in their vocabulary learning. The cycle depicted in Figure 6.2 illustrates how the investment of little effort and use of poor strategies are likely to combine in producing poor test outcomes for a student. As a consequence, the student might feel that she needs to "try harder" and actually invest more effort in preparing for a subsequent test. However, despite the greater effort, if the student continues to use poor strategies, she is likely to obtain poor outcomes in the test. Such a disappointing result (i.e., result obtained is not commensurate with the effort put in) is likely to lead to her concluding that "there is no point in trying so hard". So the student reverts

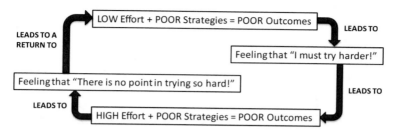

FIGURE 6.2 Possible process explanation for why students continue making low cognitive effort in L2 vocabulary learning.

back to investing little effort in preparing for tests. At some point in the future (e.g., when a teacher might say to the student, "You need to work harder!"), the student might again put more effort in; but without the use of more effective strategies, this negative cycle is likely to simply repeat.

Implications for practice

Attempts at breaking the negative cycle shown in Figure 6.2, would essentially require combining the deployment of greater effort with the use of effective strategies so that successful outcomes would ensue and the development of feelings about the futility of effort could be avoided. To do so, students would need to be provided instruction, training, and practice in the use of effective, appropriate strategies for L2 vocabulary learning.

It should be stressed here that simply telling students about effective learning strategies is unlikely to be sufficient: students may find it difficult to effectively use strategies even if they learn about them. Nassaji (2003), for example, found that students generally experienced difficulties in inferring the meanings of unknown words from context—even after finding out that such use of inference is considered effective for vocabulary learning. Hence, explicit training and provision of adequate practice would likely be required, to ensure that students are able to develop the necessary confidence and proficiency in use.

Another potential hurdle to be wary of is that students may simply not appreciate the value of employing deeper processing strategies. Lawson and Hogben (1996) pointed out, for example, that students might not use some vocabulary learning strategies because they lack awareness of the associated advantages. In fact, Uesaka, Manalo, and Ichikawa (2007, 2010) stressed the importance of developing students' appreciation of the value of using an effective strategy. Therefore, where L2 vocabulary learning is concerned, it would be important for teachers to not only teach and provide practice for the use of the strategies, but also to try to facilitate experiences that would allow students to more tangibly appreciate the value of using those strategies.

So, in practical terms, what might a teacher do in class to promote more spontaneous use of effective strategies in vocabulary learning? First, the teacher needs to ensure that students have adequate knowledge about what is effective for such learning: directly assessing such knowledge may be necessary. If a sufficient proportion of the students is deficient in such knowledge, then instruction should be provided. But, as stressed above, the students should be provided not only instruction but also training and practice in actually using the strategies. Unfamiliarity with strategies is likely to lead to uncertainty, errors and/or failure in correctly applying them to real learning contexts, as well as perceptions of higher cognitive cost in using them (i.e., unfamiliar strategies would likely appear more difficult and troublesome to use). During the provision of training and practice, it is important for the teacher to identify any difficulties students may be experiencing, and to provide advice and/or additional instruction as may be required.

As noted above, students also need to appreciate the personal value of using the more effective learning strategies. One practical way to facilitate this would be to ensure that test formats used are such that they evaluate students' deeper understanding of meaning and use of the target words. Thus, use of the effective strategies should lead students to experiences of being able to achieve better in the tests that they sit. The teacher could also encourage appropriate use of the newly acquired vocabulary words in other coursework. For example, the teacher could award additional grade points for correct use of the target words in reports that students write and/or presentations they make. That way, students would not view vocabulary learning as simply for the short-term purpose of passing vocabulary tests (for which the use of shallow processing strategies may be adequate).

Note

1 Form here pertains to the word's pronunciation (spoken form), spelling (written form), and component parts, like its prefix, root, and suffix. Meaning, on the other hand, pertains to what the word refers to, and what comes to mind when people think of that word (Lessard-Clouston, 2013),

References

Allport, G. W. (1954). *The nature of prejudice*. New York: Addison Wesley.
Avila, E., & Sadoski, M. (1996). Exploring new applications of the keyword method to acquire English vocabulary. *Language Learning, 46*(3), 379–395.
Brown, T. S., & Perry, F. L., Jr. (1991). A comparison of three learning strategies for ESL vocabulary acquisition. *TESOL Quarterly, 25*(4), 655–670.
Coxhead, A. (2000). A new academic word list. *TESOL Quarterly, 34*(2), 213–238.
Crouch, C. H., & Mazur, E. (2001). Peer instruction: Ten years of experience and results. *American Journal of Physics, 69*, 970–977.
Ellis, N. (1994). Consciousness in second language learning: Psychological perspectives on the role of conscious processes in vocabulary acquisition. *AILA Review, 11*, 37–56. Retrieved April 4, 2016 from www.aila.info/en/publications/aila-review/reviev-volumes/73-aila-review-issue-11.html
Fan, M. Y. (2003). Frequency of use, perceived usefulness, and actual usefulness of second language vocabulary strategies: A study of Hong Kong learners. *The Modern Language Journal, 87*(2), 222–241.

Garner, R. (1990). When children and adults do not use learning strategies: Toward a theory of settings. *Review of Educational Research, 60*(4), 517–529.

Gronich, L. H. (2006). *The cognitive miser theory and decisions for war and peace.* Paper presented at the 2006 Annual Meeting of the International Studies Association, March 22–25, San Diego, CA. Retrieved November 1, 2013 from www.allacademic.com//meta/p_mla_apa_research_citation/1/0/0/8/5/pages100859/p100859-1.php

Gu, P. Y. (2003). Fine brush and freehand: The vocabulary-learning art of two successful Chinese EFL learners. *TESOL Quarterly, 37*(1), 73–104.

Gu, Y., & Johnson, R. K. (1996). Vocabulary learning strategies and language learning outcomes. *Language Learning, 46*(4), 643–679.

Hembree, R. (1992). Experiments and relational studies in problem-solving: A meta-analysis. *Journal for Research in Mathematics Education, 23*(3), 242–273.

Kandel, E. R. (2001). The molecular biology of memory storage: A dialogue between genes and synapses. *Science, 294*(5544), 1030–1038.

Kudo, Y. (1999). *L2 vocabulary learning strategies (NFLRC NetWork #14)* [PDF document]. Honolulu, HI: University of Hawai'i, Second Language Teaching & Curriculum Center.

Lawson, M. J., & Hogben, D. (1996). The vocabulary-learning strategies of foreign-language students. *Language Learning, 46*(1), 101–135.

Lessard-Clouston, M. (2013). *Teaching vocabulary.* Alexandria, VA: TESOL International Association.

Loewen, S., & Ellis, R. (2005). Second language vocabulary and academic achievement in undergraduate university students. In E. Manalo & G. Wong-Toi (Eds.), *Communication skills in university education: The international dimension* (pp. 260–276). Auckland, New Zealand: Pearson Education.

Manalo, E. (1999). Spontaneous mnemonic use in simulated foreign word learning. *Psychologia, 42,* 160–169.

Manalo, E., Koyasu, M., Hashimoto, K., & Miyauchi, T. (2006). Factors that impact on the academic motivation of Japanese university students in Japan and in New Zealand. *Psychologia, 49*(2), 114–131.

Manalo, E., & Uesaka, Y. (2012). Elucidating the mechanism of spontaneous diagram use in explanations: How cognitive processing of text and diagrammatic representations is influenced by individual and task-related factors. In P. Cox, P. Rodgers, & B. Plimmer (Eds.), *Diagrammatic representation and inference (Lecture Notes in Artificial Intelligence 7352)* (pp. 35–50). Berlin, Germany: Springer-Verlag.

Manalo, E., Uesaka, Y., Pérez-Kriz, S., Kato, M., & Fukaya, T. (2013). Science and engineering students' use of diagrams during note taking versus explanation. *Educational Studies, 39*(1), 118–123.

McCombs, B. L. (1988). Motivational skill training: Combining metacognitive, cognitive, and affective learning strategies. In C. E. Weinstein, E. T. Goetz, & P. A. Alexander (Eds.), *Learning and study strategies: Issues in assessment, instruction, and evaluation* (pp. 141–169). San Diego, CA: Academic Press.

Murayama, K. (2003a). Test format and learning strategy use. *Japanese Journal of Educational Psychology, 51*(1), 1–12.

Murayama, K. (2003b). Learning strategy use and short- and long-term perceived utility. *Japanese Journal of Educational Psychology, 51,* 130–140.

Nassaji, H. (2003). L2 vocabulary learning from context: Strategies, knowledge sources, and their relationship with success in L2 lexical inferencing. *TESOL Quarterly, 37*(4), 645–670.

Nation, I. S. P. (2006). How large a vocabulary is needs for reading and listening? *The Canadian Modern Language Review, 63*(1), 59–81.

Navon, D., & Gopher, D. (1979). On the economy of the human-processing system. *Psychological Review, 86*(3), 214–255.

Norman, D. A., & Bobrow, D. J. (1975). On data-limited and resource-limited processes. *Cognitive Psychology, 7*(1), 44–64.

Oya, T., Manalo, E., & Greenwood, J. (2009). The influence of language contact and vocabulary knowledge on the speaking performance of Japanese students of English. *The Open Applied Linguistics Journal, 2*(1), 11–21.

Sagarra, N., & Alba, M. (2006). The key is in the keyword: L2 vocabulary learning methods with beginning learners of Spanish. *The Modern Language Journal, 90*(2), 228–243.

Sato, J. (1998). Effects of learners' perceptions of utility and costs, and learning strategy preferences. *Japanese Journal of Educational Psychology, 46*(4), 367–376.

Saville-Troike, M. (1984). What really matters in second language learning for academic achievement? *TESOL Quarterly, 18*(2), 199–219.

Shimoyama, H. (1996). A review of studies on student apathy. *Japanese Journal of Educational Psychology, 44*(3), 350–363.

Tseng, W. T., & Schmitt, N. (2008). Toward a model of motivated vocabulary learning: A structural equation modeling approach. *Language Learning, 58*(2), 357–400.

Uesaka, Y., & Manalo, E. (2012). Task-related factors that influence the spontaneous use of diagrams in math word problems. *Applied Cognitive Psychology, 26*(2), 251–260.

Uesaka, Y., Manalo, E., & Ichikawa, S. (2007). What kinds of perceptions and daily learning behaviors promote students' use of diagrams in mathematics problem solving? *Learning and Instruction, 17*(3), 322–335.

Uesaka, Y., Manalo, E., & Ichikawa, S. (2010). The effects of perception of efficacy and diagram construction skills on students' spontaneous use of diagrams when solving math word problems. In A. K. Goel, M. Jamnik, & N. H. Narayanan (Eds.), *Diagrammatic representation and inference (Lecture notes in artificial intelligence 6170)* (pp. 197–211). Berlin, Germany: Springer-Verlag.

7

THE EFFECT OF TEACHING STYLES ON STUDENTS' LEARNING STRATEGY USE AND INTEREST IN STUDYING SCIENCE

Etsuko Tanaka

Introduction

Importance of focusing on learning strategies that students use

In most learning situations, the learning strategy that is used has a crucial role. For example, the use of cognitive learning strategies (e.g., rehearsal, elaboration) is considered an essential component of self-regulated learning behavior (Pintrich, 1999). Many previous studies have pointed out that the learning strategy used influences the resulting quality of learning, and that some strategies lead to good achievement while others do not (e.g., Dinsmore & Alexander, 2012; Vermunt & Vermetten, 2004). Various classification schemes of learning strategies have been proposed, with many of these schemes making a distinction between three large categories: cognitive, metacognitive, and resource management strategies (e.g., Berger & Karabenick, 2011; Pintrich, Smith, Garcia, & McKeachie, 1993; Uesaka, 2010). Regarding cognitive strategies, we can distinguish between deep and surface processing learning strategies. Deep processing strategies focus on meaning understanding, while surface processing strategies place little emphasis on meaning understanding and focus instead on repetition and retention (e.g., Ichihara & Arai, 2006; Marton & Säljö, 1976). For example, Marton and Säljö (1976) identified different levels of processing of information: surface-level and deep-level processing. On the basis of this distinction, Drew and Watkins (1998) showed that a surface approach to learning has a negative effect on academic achievement; in contrast, a deep approach has a positive effect. In their review of literature on patterns of student learning, Vermunt and Vermetten (2004) pointed out that the majority of studies have shown that meaning-directed learning is positively associated with study achievement, while reproduction–directed learning has a negative correlation with achievement. On the basis of such findings, it would appear important to encourage students to use deep processing strategies.

Interventions for encouraging students to use learning strategies, and their limitations

Previous studies have identified various factors that affect learning strategy use (e.g., Garner, 1990; Murayama, 2003; Sato, 1998; Uesaka, Manalo, & Ichikawa, 2010). For example, Berger and Karabenick (2011) showed that self-efficacy in mathematics affects use of elaboration, metacognition, and time and study management strategies. Sato (1998) confirmed that learners who perceive high utility in a learning strategy tend to use that learning strategy more frequently; on the other hand, learners who perceive high costs in a strategy tend not to use the strategy. Furthermore, Murayama (2003) divided the perceived utility of learning strategies into long- and short-term perceived utility and found that not long-term but short-term perceived utility directly affects strategy use. The Expectancy-Value theory (e.g., Wigfield, 1994; Wigfield & Eccel, 2000) similarly emphasizes the importance of competence belief and subjective task value (utility and cost) on achievement-related choices.

Based on such findings, various interventions aimed at encouraging students to use effective learning strategies have been designed and implemented. For example, Suzuki, Tanaka, Murayama, and Ichikawa (2011) and Suzuki and Ichikawa (2011) taught students how to efficiently solve math problems. They provided students the necessary information about some problem-solving strategies, asked them to use and practice those strategies, and administered a test containing similar problems in order to assess the students' use of those strategies. One month later, they gave the students another similar test in order to confirm the effect of the intervention and whether the students were still making use of the strategies. The results showed that some students used the strategies to solve similar math problems after the intervention and they showed achievement improvements. However, two months afterward, the students were found not to use the strategies any more in their attempts at solving similar math problems. Note that this intervention was only provided once within a limited amount of class time, and hence limitations of its impact would be expected. However, the results lend support to previous indications that unless major changes are made to daily classroom practices and encouragement for using the strategies are continuously provided, it appears difficult to effect transfer of strategy use to other learning contexts and for that use to maintain over time.

Ames and Archer (1988) pointed out that interventions aimed at training of learning strategies might not have lasting effects if the classroom does not support the targeted outcomes of the intervention. Also, more recent research has shown that uptake of cognitive and metacognitive strategies tends to be low in many classrooms (Askell-Williams, Lawson, & Skrzypiec, 2012). Uesaka (2010) noted that in order to improve students' strategy use, the strategies that are taught should work well together with the daily lessons that are provided. Finding practical classroom activities that can encourage students to spontaneously use deep processing strategies is therefore important.

Distinctions between types of interest

Apart from the effect of instruction or the teacher, individual motivational factors also have an effect on learning strategy use (e.g., Alexander, Graham, & Harris, 1998; Berger & Karabenick, 2011; Meece, Blumenfeld, & Hoyle, 1988; Pintrich & de Groot, 1990; Simons, Dewitte, & Lens, 2004). The research described in this chapter focused on the individual factor of interest in the subject being learnt. Previous studies have found that when the learning material is interesting, learners tend to learn it more deeply (e.g., McDaniel, Waddill, Finstad, & Bourg, 2000; Schiefele, 1996). Interest is very similar to the concept of intrinsic motivation. People who have interest in the contents of a learning task tend to engage in the task without any need for external pressure or incentive. However, the concept of interest contains some points of difference. For example, interest is evoked as a result of interaction with the subject content (e.g., Hidi & Renninger, 2006), which is not necessary where intrinsic motivation is concerned. Essentially, intrinsic motivation is a broader concept, which also includes general personality traits such as curiosity. Interest researchers, however, deal with more specific aspects of intrinsic motivation, and currently much of the research undertaken regarding interest aims to differentiate types of interest.

One key research in this area was conducted by Hidi (1990), and in this research, she classified interest into individual interest and situational interest. She explained the types of interest thus: "Individual interest develops slowly over time and tends to have long-lasting effects on a person's knowledge and values. Situational interest, on the other hand, tends to be evoked more suddenly by something in the environment and may have only a short term effect" (p. 551). Silvia (2006) also suggested the same classification using different terms, "interests" and "interest," where the former pertains to individual interest, while the latter pertains to situational interest as a temporal state. In this study, we focused on individual interest: not the momentary psychological state but the personal trait.

Another perspective in classifying types of interest is whether it is caused by emotional change or by perception of value (e.g., Ainley & Ainley, 2011; Mitchell, 1993; Schiefele, 2009). We can trigger interest by emotional change caused by novelty, complexity, uncertainty, or conflict relating to the object (Silvia, 2006) or by positive feeling. But the interest may last just for a while. A lot of previous research suggests that perceiving the value of learning contents is important for interest development (e.g., Hidi & Renninger, 2006; Krapp, 2002; Mitchel, 1993). Linnenbrink-Garcia et al. (2010) demonstrated that interest based on the emotional aspect and interest based on the value aspect depend on different factors. Therefore, it appears important to deal with interest in a way that considers distinctions along those lines. Harackiewicz, Durik, Barron, Linnenbrink-Garcia, and Tauer (2008) showed that interest based on emotion does not directly predict later engagement with the object, but interest based on the value aspect does. In the present study, therefore, one prediction made was that interest based on the value aspect would be more related to learning strategy use than interest based on the emotion aspect.

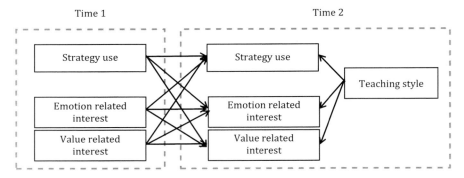

FIGURE 7.1 Model that was tested in this study.

Overview of this study

In this study, we considered it important to focus on the particular subject that students are learning because previous research has shown that students' interest depends on the specific object under consideration (Hidi & Renninger, 2006; Renninger & Su, 2012). We focused here on science as the subject. Kjærnsli and Lie (2011) pointed out that science is generally regarded as being very important in meeting societal needs, and low recruitment in scientific professions is a concern in many countries. Also, a decline in interest and attitude toward science with increase in age has numerous times been documented (Krapp & Prenzel, 2011; Potvin & Hasni, 2014).

The purpose of this study was to reveal the teaching styles used by teachers that affect students' use of deep processing strategies in science study. We were also interested in the relationship between learning strategy use and two kinds of interest: emotion-related interest and value-related interest. We predicted that value-related interest would be more related to learning strategy use than emotion-related interest. We also expected that perceived teaching style would affect interest in science as well as learning strategy use. In addition, we expected that students who were interested in the learning content based on its value would be more willing to focus on the meaning of it. In turn, learning strategy use could affect value-related interest because students would be able to deepen their interest in the content through deepening their knowledge about it. The model we tested in this research is represented in Figure 7.1.

Preliminary data collection and construction of the perceived teaching style scale

Before the main study described in this chapter was conducted, work was undertaken on the development of a new "perceived teaching style" scale and on establishing its structure and reliability. Some previous research studies have presented various scales to measure teachers' teaching style (e.g., Bru, Stornes, Munthe, & Thuen, 2010; Smimou & Dahl, 2012; Wagner, Göllner, Helmke, Trautwein, & Lüdtke, 2013). These previous scales were designed to measure various aspects of teaching style, but they were not subject specific and they did not focus on issues that may be pertinent when considering teaching style in science. Although the Programme for International Student Assessment (2007) measured students' perception of science teaching and learning, a robust structure for categorizing the survey items was lacking. For example, these two items "students spend time in the laboratory doing practical experiments" and "students are required to design how a school science question could be investigated in the laboratory" are both in the same cluster of "Hands-on activities in science teaching and learning". However, these items would have different influences on spontaneous use of learning strategies as the first one could demand the use of many different strategies depending on the exact requirements of the experiments the students need to do, while the second one specifically demands the use of strategies associated with thinking for oneself and designing one's own experiments. Hence these previous scales were not deemed as adequate for identifying what teaching styles used by teachers might affect students' use of learning strategies in science, and for subsequently making proposals for enhancing teachers' science classroom conduct. Thus, a new scale for assessing students' perceptions of teaching style in science was constructed. This construction process is described briefly in the following paragraphs.

Possible scale items were collected to construct the scale for assessing students' perceptions of the teaching styles that their science teachers use. Using questionnaires, 22 elementary school, junior high school, and high school teachers were asked what they do in their classes to improve their students' interest in science. Additionally, some items were created based on observations made of teachers' classroom behaviors while teaching science classes. Two researchers including the author compiled the responses together with the observation-items, modified the expressions of the items as appropriate, and clustered and deleted items to eliminate duplication. In total, 35 possible items for the scale were generated.

Three hundred and thirteen (313) elementary school students (from grades 5 and 6), 1,003 junior high school students (from grades 7, 8, and 9), and 402 high school students (from grade 10) were asked to respond to a questionnaire with the 35 items. They were asked to read each item (a description of teaching behavior) and to select one number from 1 (corresponding to "not true") to 5 (corresponding to "true") according to the way the students perceived their science teacher that year was teaching in class.

Exploratory factor analysis (using promax rotation and principal axis factoring) was carried out on the data that was collected. Thirteen items were excluded because their factor loadings were too low or they depended on several factors. As a result, a teaching style scale with 22 items and consisting of seven factors was created. The seven factors were: encouraging students to express their opinions, linking of information learnt to daily-life, building knowledge connections, clarifying goals and achievements, showing concrete cases of what is being learnt, encouraging students to think for themselves, and caring about students (Table 7.1). They all had reasonably high reliability coefficients ($\alpha = .75 - .90$).

A confirmatory factor analysis was carried out and goodness-of-fit measures were calculated. These were found to be indicative of a good model fit: CFI = .953, and RMSEA = .049. In addition, using multiple group structural equation modeling (divided into elementary school, junior high school, and high school), measurements of goodness of fit were calculated. Again, these returned values indicative of a good model fit: CFI = .932, and RMSEA = .033.

Method

Participants and procedure

Six hundreds and forty-three (643) junior high school students (from grades 7 to 9, which correspond to the ages of 12–15 years in Japan) from three junior high schools answered the questionnaires used in this study at an early part and then a later part of the school year. In Japan, the school year begins in April and ends in March of the following year; the questionnaires were administered first from May to June and then in March.

The author sought the necessary permissions and requested teachers in the schools to collect data from their students. Participation by both teachers and students was voluntary. Questionnaires were sent to the schools, and teachers who were willing to participate administered them to their students. The top page of the questionnaires explained that the data collected would only be used for research purposes, and that teachers would not see students' answers or use them for any grading purposes. It also explained that, if students did not want to participate, they could leave the pages of the questionnaire blank and submit them at the end without any answers. The students were provided envelopes to put their questionnaire in and submit at the end of the data collection session.

Items and scales used in the questionnaires administered

Deep processing strategies

Four items were included in the questionnaire to measure students' use of deep processing strategies. These items were based on items in questionnaires that had been constructed and used by Ichikawa, Horino, and Kubo (1998) and Ichihara and Arai (2006) in their studies. These previous studies used many more items to assess students' learning views and behaviors, but only four that the present author deemed most pertinent for the purposes of this study were selected and used. The wording of the items was also slightly modified to emphasize application to the students' science study. English translations of the items used are as follows: "When I study science, I don't only memorize but also try to understand", "When I study science, I try to think about relationships among what I have been learning", "When I study science, I try to think about reasons deeply", and "When I study science, I try to consider various ways to solve the question by myself". Students responded to these items on a 5-point scale, where 1 = "not true" and 5 = "true." These items were included in questionnaires administered to the students in both the early and the later parts of the school year. Cronbach's alpha which was calculated using the current data were $\alpha = .87$ (time 1) and $\alpha = .87$ (time 2).

TABLE 7.1 The items of the teaching style scale and factor correlations

Items	Factor loading						
	I	II	III	IV	V	VI	VII
Encouraging students to express their opinions							
In my class, I have opportunities to exchange opinions with my classmates.	**.89**	−.06	.03	−.02	.01	.03	−.05
My teacher requires me to write or say what I learn in my own words.	**.88**	.11	−.04	.02	−.07	−.07	−.03
In my class, I get time to discuss things and think together with my classmates.	**.86**	.00	−.03	−.02	.03	.06	−.08
In my class, I have opportunities to say what I understand using my own words.	**.76**	.03	.02	−.03	−.01	.02	.05
Linking of information learnt to daily-life							
My teacher provides familiar, everyday examples related to what I am learning.	.06	**.92**	−.05	−.02	−.05	−.02	.03
When learning a rule of law in science, my teacher explains it using examples from daily-life.	−.09	**.75**	.01	−.02	.07	.15	−.02
My teacher tells some news related to science.	.12	**.66**	.02	−.03	−.04	−.06	.13
My teacher explains how what I am learning is related to our life.	.01	**.64**	.11	.11	.01	.03	−.06
Building knowledge connections							
My teacher explains the connections between what I am learning and what I will be learning next.	−.10	.05	**.92**	−.04	.02	−.03	−.02
My teacher shows the connections between what I am learning and what I have learned before.	.08	.10	**.73**	−.02	−.01	−.05	−.02
My teacher does not tell us all the steps required in an experiment and requires us to think for ourselves.	.13	−.13	**.60**	−.05	−.04	.18	−.01
In my class, I get opportunities to approach a problem by remembering what I had learned before.	.14	.14	**.44**	.05	.04	−.06	.07
Clarify goals and achievements							
My teacher asks whether there is anything that I cannot understand.	−.09	.00	−.10	**.90**	−.09	.00	.02
My teacher asks me how much I can understand.	.20	−.07	.06	**.57**	.11	.00	−.06
My teacher explains clearly the purposes of experiments and observations we conduct.	−.01	.14	.07	**.51**	.17	−.01	−.02

(Continued)

TABLE 7.1 (Continued)

Items	Factor loading						
	I	II	III	IV	V	VI	VII
Showing concrete cases of what is being learnt							
My teacher shows us the real things we are learning in class.	-.08	-.04	.00	.01	**.95**	.01	-.02
My teacher shows us different kinds of experiments.	.19	.13	-.03	-.08	**.58**	-.01	.11
Encouraging students to think for themselves							
My teacher gives me enough time to think by myself.	.06	-.06	.00	.02	.05	**.72**	.07
My teacher gives me time to think through difficult problems by myself.	.02	.17	.02	-.02	-.04	**.72**	-.03
Caring about students							
My teacher conducts lessons in an amusing way.	-.17	.10	-.01	.02	-.01	.05	**.81**
My teacher gives us enjoyable activities.	.13	.06	-.03	-.07	.08	-.04	**.75**
My teacher adjusts lessons according to how much we are understanding.	.21	-.07	.15	.21	-.12	.08	**.40**
Cronbach's alpha	.90	.88	.83	.75	.79	.77	.82

Interests in science

In order to measure interest in science, an interest scale constructed by Tanaka (2015) was used. In previous studies assessing student interest in learning, items like "I enjoy learning ..." and "I think learning ... is important" had been used (e.g., Favero, Boscolo, Vidotto, & Vicetini, 2007; Tsai, Kunter, Ludthke, Trautwein, & Ryan, 2008;). However, such items may be too abstract and not sufficiently focused on experiences and other issues that may impact on students' interest in a subject. This was the motivation behind the scale constructed by Tanaka (2015), which comprised items drawn from interviews with and free descriptions obtained from large samples of students. In the interviews and questionnaire for free descriptions, students were asked what aspect of science learning was interesting to them. After collecting such items, two researchers divided the items into seven categories and made adjustments so that each category has six items. Using the resulting items, a questionnaire was constructed and administered to 1,998 students in elementary, junior high, and high schools. Factor analysis revealed that the scale consists of two main factors and six sub-factors. The two main factors are emotion-related interest and value-related interest, congruent with the structure proposed by Linnenbrink-Garcia et al. (2010). To simplify the analysis of data obtained in the present study, only these two main factors were considered (i.e., not the sub-factors).

Emotion-related interest pertains to interest associated with personal emotions and emotional responses that the student experiences from studying or learning about science (e.g., "Science is interesting because sometimes I'm surprised by the results of experiments", "Science is interesting because I feel happy when I find out what something means"). In contrast, value-related interest pertains to perceptions about the value of studying or learning about science (e.g., "Science is interesting because I can understand the explanation of rules and laws", "Science is interesting because it is linked to my own life"). All items are shown in the Appendix 1. The scale was administered to students twice: at the early part and the later part of the school year.

The Interest in Science Scale has a robust structure as reported by Tanaka (2015). In brief, each sub-factor has high reliability ($\alpha = .84 - .92$) and the goodness of fit of the model that consists of six factors is good (RMSEA = .05, CFI = .89). In this research, the mean scores, which were calculated by averaging scores of the corresponding sub-factors, were used as indices of emotion-related interest and value-related interest.

Student perceptions of teacher teaching style

This is the scale that was constructed during the preliminary research described in the earlier section of this chapter, and it consists of 22 items. The scale was administered to students only once, during the later part of the school year.

Results

Basic statistics of scales

Table 7.2 shows the means, SDs and correlations of strategy use, interest, and perceived teaching style. In order to confirm whether there was an effect of teacher on students' reports of teaching styles, an ANOVA using teacher as the predictor variable was conducted for each subscale. The results showed that all subscales have significant between-group difference depending on teacher ($F(9, 642) = 5.59 – 19.04$, $p < .001$; see Appendix 2). These results suggest that the students' responses differed according to their teacher.

Relationship between strategy use and interests, and influence of teaching style

In order to find out the relationship between use of deep processing strategies and the two types of interests, and the influence of students' perceptions of their teacher's teaching style on change in strategy use and interest, structural equation modeling was conducted. First, a full model, which included all paths between strategy use and interests, and from teaching style to strategy use and interests, was tested. Then the factors, which have no effect on any dependent variable, and the paths which were not significant, were eliminated. Standardized partial regression coefficients of the final model (Figure 7.2) are shown in Table 7.3, and goodness-of-fit indicators of both the full model and the final model are shown in Table 7.4. The results of the final model will be used because its goodness of fit is better.

Regarding the influence by teaching style, the two teaching styles of "linking of information learnt to daily-life" and "building knowledge connections" evidenced significant positive effects on learning strategy use at time 2 and both kinds of interest at time 2. "Encouraging students to think for themselves" also had a positive effect on leaning strategy use at time 2. "Showing concrete cases of what is being learnt" and "clarifying goals and achievements" had positive effects only on feeling-related interest at time 2, and it had a negative effect on learning strategy use at time 2.

Regarding the relationship between learning strategy use and the two kinds of interest, value-related interest at time 1 had a positive effect on learning strategy use at time 2 even when the effect of teaching styles was excluded. In turn, leaning strategy use at time 1 had a positive effect on value-related interest at time 2. Feeling-related interest at time 1 had no significant effect on leaning strategy use or value-related interest at time 2.

These results indicate that value-related interest is more related to learning strategy use than emotion-related interest, and students who are interested in the learning content based on its value tend to focus on the meaning of it. In turn, the learning strategy that students use has a subsequent effect on their value-related interest. Also, the results suggest that some perceived teaching styles affect interest in science as well as learning strategy use.

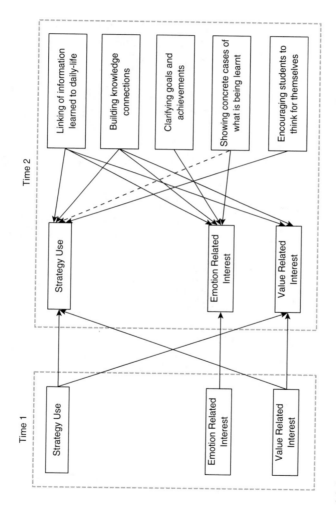

FIGURE 7.2 Final model that was tested in this study.

TABLE 7.2 The means, SDs, and correlations of strategy use, interest, and perceived teaching style

	Mean	SD	1	2	3	4	5	6	7	8	9	10	11	12	13
1 Learning strategy (Time 1)	2.98	1.00													
2 Learning strategy (Time 2)	3.11	.96	.55												
3 Emotion-related interest (Time 1)	3.45	.96	.68	.42											
4 Emotion-related interest (Time 2)	3.63	.90	.40	.62	.56										
5 Value-related interest (Time 1)	3.08	.92	.74	.50	.85	.49									
6 Value-related interest (Time 2)	3.28	.88	.46	.77	.48	.82	.54								
7 Encouraging students to express their opinions	2.96	.99	.25	.44	.26	.42	.27	.46							
8 Linking of information learnt to daily-life	3.57	.96	.37	.53	.36	.58	.41	.61	.57						
9 Building knowledge connections	3.11	.88	.27	.51	.26	.48	.32	.57	.73	.69					
10 Clarifying goals and achievements	3.29	.97	.24	.42	.28	.51	.29	.48	.54	.64	.64				
11 Showing concrete cases of what is being learnt	3.95	1.05	.28	.31	.38	.56	.31	.43	.42	.64	.48	.51			
12 Encouraging students to think for themselves	3.30	1.02	.31	.50	.30	.48	.33	.53	.62	.65	.65	.54	.46		
13 Caring about students	3.43	1.06	.32	.48	.35	.53	.34	.52	.65	.74	.69	.63	.58	.66	

TABLE 7.3 Standardized partial regression coefficients of the final model ($p < .05$)

Independent variable	Dependent variable	Standardized β
Learning strategy (Time 2)	Learning strategy (Time 1)	.37
	Value-related interest (Time 1)	.08
	Linking of information learnt to daily-life	.21
	Building knowledge connections	.23
	Showing concrete cases of what is being learnt	−.12
	Encouraging students to think for themselves	.10
Feeling-related interest (Time 2)	Feeling-related interest (Time 1)	.38
	Linking of information learnt to daily-life	.17
	Building knowledge connections	.12
	Clarifying goals and achievements	.10
	Showing concrete cases of what is being learnt	.18
Value-related interest (Time 2)	Value-related interest (Time 1)	.30
	Learning strategy (Time 1)	.08
	Linking of information learnt to daily-life	.28
	Building knowledge connections	.25

TABLE 7.4 Goodness of fit of the full model and the final model

	CFI	RMSEA	AIC
Full model	1.00	.33	208.00
Final model	.99	.02	147.93

Discussion

In this study, the effects of perceived teaching styles on students' use of learning strategies and their interest in science were examined. Also, the reciprocal relationship between strategy use and interest was investigated.

The main findings were as follows. First, some perceptions of teaching style have effects on learning strategy use and interest. In particular, student perceptions of the teacher facilitating interconnection of learning contents, and emphasizing relationships between science and daily-life, were found to have a positive effect on both interest based on value and use of deep processing strategies. Second, interest based on value was found to have a reciprocal relationship with learning strategy use, but no such relationship was found where interest based on emotion was concerned. As previous research pointed out (e.g., Ainley & Ainley, 2011; Mitchel, 1993; Schiefele, 2009), it is useful to classify types of interest from the view of whether it is caused by emotional change or perception of value.

The finding that interest based on value and learning strategy use have a reciprocal relationship suggests that we can encourage students' use of deep processing strategy by improving interest based on value, and vice versa. One possible explanation for this reciprocal relationship is that, if students perceive intrinsic value in learning science (e.g., that science is interesting because of the links to daily-life events), they may more naturally pay attention to understanding the meaning of rules, laws, and phenomenon (i.e., not just memorizing them) and, if students focus on such meaning and understanding in their approach to learning, they are likely to understand more deeply and hence appreciate the many intrinsic values of science that understanding reveals to them. This explanation is congruent with the first main finding that the same teaching styles appear to promote both value-based interest and learning strategy use.

Next, we will consider those two teaching styles found to positively influence interest based on value and learning strategy use. Both facilitating interconnection of learning contents and emphasizing relationships between science and daily-life would probably lead to elaboration and organization of students' knowledge. For example, Hulleman and Harackiewics (2009) found that relevance intervention, during which students were encouraged to make connections between their lives and what they were learning in their science courses, increased interest in science and the course grades of students who initially had low success expectations. The teaching style of encouraging students to think for themselves, which has positive effect on learning strategy use, probably also provides opportunities for students to elaborate on and organize the knowledge that they are acquiring. If students are provided lots of opportunities for knowledge elaboration and organization in their classes, they are likely to understand more deeply. This would also likely encourage them to focus more on the meaning of what they are learning.

There are a number of other findings we need to consider. First, with regard to interest based on emotion, no reciprocal relationship was found with both interest based on value and learning strategy use. This finding suggests that just by triggering positive emotion during science learning, we cannot deepen students' interest and encourage them to pay greater attention to the meaning of science contents in their approach to learning. This finding is congruent with findings from previous research on interest. Previous studies for example have pointed out that, compared to interest based on emotion, interest based on value has a greater effect on learning (e.g., Harackiewicz et al., 2008; Tanaka, 2015). The findings of the present study, however, further clarify the nature of the relationship between interest and learning strategy use. In other words, while previous research had shown only that amount of interest leads to deeper understanding, the present study distinguishes between interest based on emotion and interest based on value and shows that, not interest based on emotion, but interest based on value leads to the use of learning strategies that promote deeper understanding.

It is also important to consider the results concerning the other four teaching styles, apart from the three teaching styles that were found to positively affect learning strategy use. First, one noteworthy finding was that showing concrete cases of what is being learnt had a positive effect on interest based on emotion, but that it had a negative effect on learning strategy use. It is likely that showing concrete cases such as the conduct of an experiment, plants being studied, and movies about the topic being discussed would trigger students' positive emotion about the matter being studied. However, in order to improve interest based on value, more interventions or activities are probably needed. The finding that showing concrete cases had a negative effect on learning strategy use was unexpected. This finding might have arisen because of the way teaching styles were measured – that is, teaching styles were measured based only on student perceptions and reports. It is therefore possible that many students who pay a lot of attention to the concrete cases shown by their teacher and make judgments about that teacher according to how often he or she shows concrete cases in class, may have tendencies also to pay attention to the more superficial aspects of science lessons. This would need to be examined more carefully in future research.

Clarifying goals and achievements had a positive effect on emotion-related interest. If the teacher clarifies the goals of an experiment before students conduct the experiment, as well as checks with the students how well they can understand, the students may be able to subsequently derive greater amounts of positive emotion of achievement.

Perceptions of the teacher encouraging students to express their opinions and caring about their students did not have any discernable effects on interest and learning strategy use. Both these teaching styles may be important in classes, but the results of the present study suggest that these teaching styles may not be effective on their own. Rather than encouraging students to express their opinions as such, the more important point may be that teachers need to develop students' expression and communication skills. For example, it may be better *not* to ask students questions requiring "yes" or "no" answers, or questions that simply enquire about the 'correct' answer, but to ask students questions requiring the expression of reasons and meaning related to the matter being learnt. The effect of combining some of these teaching styles may also be worth examining in future research.

Next, we will consider the limitations of this study. First, in this study, learning strategy use was measured by the use of a self-report questionnaire. It is possible that questionnaires are limited in their capacity to measure students' real strategy use because the students may not be able to accurately judge their own learning behaviors and because social desirability issues may affect the responses they provide. In future research, it would be useful to measure learning strategy use by using behavioral indices and testing the effects examined here on such measurements.

Second, we measured only students' perception of teaching style. The effect of the teacher on students undoubtedly entails a complex and dynamic mechanism. It would include issues like beliefs of the teacher affecting his or her teaching behavior and that behavior in turn affecting students' perceptions in the classroom environment. In future research, we should examine this whole mechanism – or as much of it as possible – including factors such as teachers' beliefs and actual behaviors in their class.

Third, this study was a correlational research. We did not test the effect in the case where the teacher might change his or her teaching style into a more desirable one based on the results of this study. In future research, conducting an experimental study in the classroom to confirm the indicated cause and effect relationships would be ideal.

Finally, we will briefly describe a practical suggestion based on the findings of this study for improving students' use of leaning strategies focusing on understanding of meaning in science study. The findings suggest that teachers should make more salient the connections between science contents that students are learning and what the students have previously learned, as well as what they may have experienced in their daily-life. Also, it is important to encourage and to give students enough time to think for themselves, and not for teachers to just spend copious amounts of time explaining in a one-sided manner during classroom lessons. These teaching behaviors will likely be beneficial in improving students' interest based on the value of science. In addition, we can think not only of the direct effect of such an intervention on learning strategy use but also the indirect effect. By enhancing students' interest based on value, we can encourage students to use learning strategies focusing on understanding of meaning. Previous studies have suggested similar interventions for improving students' value-based interest (Durik & Harackiewicz, 2007; Tanaka, 2013).

References

Ainley, M., & Ainley, J. (2011). A cultural perspective on the structure of student interest in science. *International Journal of Science Education, 33*(1), 51–71.

Alexander, P. A., Graham, S., & Harris, K. R. (1998). A perspective on strategy research: Progress and prospects. *Educational Psychology Review, 10*(2), 129–154.

Ames, C., & Archer, J. (1988). Achievement goals in the classroom: Students' learning strategies and motivation processes. *Journal of Educational Psychology, 80*(3), 260–267.

Askell-Williams, H., Lawson, M. J., & Skrzypiec, G. (2012), Scaffolding cognitive and meta-cognitive strategy instruction in regular class lessons. *Instructional Science, 40*(2), 413–443.

Berger, J. L., & Karabenick, S. A. (2011). Motivation and students' use of learning strategies: Evidence of unidirectional effects in mathematics classrooms. *Learning and Instruction, 21*(3), 416–428.

Bru, E., Stornes, T., Munthe, E., & Thuen, E. (2010). Students' perceptions of teacher support across the transition from primary to secondary school. *Scandinavian Journal of Educational Research, 54*(6), 519–533.

Dinsmore, D. L., & Alexander, P. A. (2012). A critical discussion of deep and surface processing: What it means, how it is measured, the role of context, and model specification. *Educational Psychology Review, 24*(4), 499–567.

Drew, P. Y., & Watkins, D. (1998). Affective variables, learning approaches and academic achievement: A causal modeling investigation with Hong Kong tertiary students. *British Journal of Educational Psychology, 68*(2), 173–188.

Durik, A. M., & Harackiewicz, J. M. (2007). Different strokes for different folks: How individual interest moderates the effects of situational factors on task interest. *Journal of Educational Psychology, 99*(3), 597–610.

Favero, L. D., Boscolo, P., Vidotto, G., & Vicentini, M. (2007). Classroom discussion and individual problem-solving in the teaching of history: Do different instructional approaches affect interest in different ways? *Learning and Instruction, 17*(6), 635–657.

Garner, R. (1990). When children and adults do not use learning strategies: Toward a theory of settings. *Review of Educational Research, 60*(4), 517–529.

Harackiewicz, J. M., Durik, A. M., Barron, K. E., Linnenbrink-Garcia, L., & Tauer, J. M. (2008). The role of achievement goals in the development of interest: Reciprocal relations between achievement goals, interest, and performance. *Journal of Educational Psychology, 100*(1), 105–122.

Hidi, S. (1990). Interest and its contribution as a mental resource for learning. *Review of Educational Research, 60*(4), 549–571.

Hidi, S., & Renninger, K. A. (2006). The four-phase model of interest development. *Educational Psychologist, 41*(2), 111–127.

Hulleman, C. S., & Harackiewicz, J. M. (2009). Promoting interest and performance in high school science classes. *Science, 326*(5958), 1410–1412.

Ichihara, M., & Arai, K. (2006). Moderator effects of meta-cognition: A test in math of a motivational model. *Japanese Association of Educational Psychology, 54*(2), 199–210.

Ichikawa, S., Horino, M., & Kubo, N., (1998). Gakusyuuhouhouwo sasaeru gakusyuukanto gakusyuudouki [Students' beliefs and motivations about learning that support their strategy use]. In S. Ichikawa (Ed.), *Ninchikaunseringukaramita gakusyuuhouhouno soudanto shidou [Counselling and teaching study skills: A cognitive counselling approach]* (pp. 186–203). Tokyo, Japan: Brain Press.

Kjærnsli, M., & Lie, S. (2011). Students' preference for science careers: International comparisons based on PISA 2006. *International Journal of Science Education, 33*(1), 121–144.

Krapp, A. (2002). Structural and dynamic aspects of interest development: Theoretical considerations from an ontogenetic perspective. *Learning and Instruction, 12*(4), 383–409.

Krapp, A., & Prenzel, M. (2011). Research on interest in science: Theories, methods, and findings. *International Journal of Science Education, 33*(1), 27–50.

Linnenbrink-Garcia, L., Durik, A. M., Conley, A. M., Barron, K. E., Tauer, J. M., Karabenick, S. A., & Harackiewicz, J. M. (2010). Measuring situational interest in academic domains. *Educational and Psychological Measurement, 70*(4), 647–671.

Marton, F., & Säljö, R. (1976). On qualitative differences in learning: I – Outcome and process. *British Journal of Educational Psychology, 46*(1), 4–11.

McDaniel, M. A., Waddill, P. J., Finstad, K., & Bourg, T. (2000). The effects of text-based interest on attention and recall. *Journal of Educational Psychology, 92*(3), 492.

Meece, J. L., Blumenfeld, P. C., & Hoyle, R. H. (1988). Students' goal orientations and cognitive engagement in classroom activities. *Journal of Educational Psychology, 80*(4), 514–523.

Mitchell, M. (1993). Situational interest: Its multifaceted structure in the secondary school mathematics classroom. *Journal of Educational Psychology, 85*(3), 424–436.

Murayama, K. (2003). Learning strategy use and short- and long-term perceived utility. *Japanese Journal of Educational Psychology, 51*(2), 130–140.

Pintrich, P. R. (1999). The role of motivation in promoting and sustaining self-regulated learning. *Internal Journal of Educational Research, 31*(6), 459–470.

Pintrich, P. R., & de Groot, E. V. (1990). Motivational and self-regulated learning components of classroom academic performance. *Journal of Educational Psychology, 82*(1), 33–40.

Pintrich, P. R., Smith, D. A. F., Garcia, T., & McKeachie, W. J. (1993). Reliability and predictive validity of the motivated strategies for learning questionnaire (MSLQ). *Educational and Psychological Measurement, 53*(3), 801–813.

Potvin, P., & Hasni, A. (2014). Analysis of the decline in interest towards school science and technology from grades 5 through 11. *Journal of Science Education and Technology, 23*(6), 784–802.

Programme for International Student Assessment. (2007). *PISA 2006: Science competencies for tomorrow's world: Volume 1 – Analysis.* Paris: OECD Publishing.

Renninger, K. A., & Su, S. (2012). Interest and its development. In R. M. Ryan (Ed.), *The Oxford handbook of human motivation* (pp. 167–187). Oxford, UK: Oxford University Press.

Sato, J. (1998) Effects of learners' perceptions of utility and costs, and learning strategy preferences. *Japanese Journal of Educational Psychology, 46*(4), 367–376.

Schiefele, U. (2009). Situational and individual interest. In K. Wentzel, A. Wigfield, & D. Miele (Eds.), *Handbook of motivation at school* (pp. 197–222). New York: Routledge.

Silvia, P. J. (2006). *Exploring the psychology of interest.* New York: Oxford University Press.

Simons, J., Dewitte, S., & Lens, W. (2004). The role of different types of instrumentality in motivation, study strategies, and performance: Know why you learn, so you'll know what you learn! *British Journal of Educational Psychology, 74*(3), 343–360.

Smimou, K., & Dahl, D. W. (2012). On the relationship between students' perceptions of teaching quality, methods of assessment, and satisfaction. *Journal of Education for Business, 87*(1), 22–35.

Suzuki, M., & Ichikawa, S. (2011). Effects of the instruction about efficient calculation problems using an abstract strategy. *Proceedings of the 27th Annual Conference of Japan Society for Educational Technology* (pp. 643–644). Tokyo, Japan: Japan Society for Educational Technology.

Suzuki, M., Tanaka, E., Murayama, K., & Ichikawa, S. (2011). Classification of efficient calculation problems and the effect of instruction using an abstract strategy. *Educational Technology Research, 34*(1), 75–83.

Tanaka, E. (2013). Teaching strategy to improve the development of interest: Learners' positive emotion and perception of value. *The Japanese Journal of Psychology in Teaching and Learning, 9*, 12–28.

Tanaka, E. (2015). The classification of students' interests in science and relation of interests to use of deep-processing learning strategies and spontaneous learning behavior. *Japanese Journal of Educational Psychology, 63*(1), 23–36.

Tsai, Y. M., Kunter, M., Ludtke, O., Trautwein, U., & Ryan, R. M. (2008). What makes lessons interesting? The role of situational and individual factors in three school subject. *Journal of Educational Psychology, 100*(2), 460–472.

Uesaka, Y. (2010). Metaninch, gakushukan, gakusyuhouryaku [Metacognition, belief about learning and learning strategy]. In S. Ichikawa (Ed.), *Theories and applications of cognitive psychology 5: Development and learning* (pp. 182–200). Kyoto, Japan: Kitaohgi.

Uesaka, Y., Manalo, E., & Ichikawa, S. (2010). The effects of perception of efficacy and diagram construction skills on students' spontaneous use of diagrams when solving math word problems. In A. K. Goel, M. Jamnik, & N. H. Narayanan (Eds.), *Diagrams 2010, lecture notes in artificial intelligence 6170* (pp. 197–211). Berlin, Heidelberg: Springer-Verlag.

Vermunt, J. D., & Vermetten, Y. J. (2004). Patterns in student learning: Relationships between learning strategies, conceptions of learning, and learning orientations. *Educational Psychology Review, 16*(4), 359–384.

Wagner, W., Göllner, R., Helmke, A., Trautwein, U., & Lüdtke, O. (2013). Construct validity of student perceptions of instructional quality is high, but not perfect: Dimensionality and generalizability of domain-independent assessments. *Learning and Instruction, 28*, 1–11.

Wigfield, A. (1994). Expectancy-value theory of achievement motivation: A developmental perspective. *Educational Psychology Review, 6*(1), 49–78.

Wigfield, A., & Eccel, J. S. (2000). Expectancy-value theory of achievement motivation. *Contemporary Educational Psychology, 25*(1), 68–81.

APPENDIX 7.1 Items of interest in science

Emotion–related interest

Experience-based interest

Science is interesting because we can use various instruments.
Science is interesting because we can conduct experiments.
Science is interesting because we get opportunities to look at and touch real things.
Science is interesting because we get opportunities to use various chemicals.
Science is interesting because I can watch various kinds of experiments.
Science is interesting because it is possible to handle various things.

Amazement-based interest

Science is interesting because there are times when I get surprised by the results we get in experiments.
Science is interesting because I find the results of experiments amazing.
Science is interesting because we learn about things that can be surprising.
Science is interesting because it amazes me and gives me surprising discoveries.
Science is interesting because there are times when we are just surprised by what we find out.

Accomplishment-based interest

Science is interesting because I feel happy when I solve the questions and problems we get in class.
Science is interesting because I feel happy when I can fully understand something.
Science is interesting because I feel happy when I find answers on my own.
Science is interesting because I feel happy when my expectations are met.
Science is interesting because I feel happy when I reach a point of understanding something.

Value–related interest

Knowledge acquisition–based interest

Science is interesting because I can learn about various kinds of things.
Science is interesting because I can learn new things.
Science is interesting because I can find out what I previously did not know.
Science is interesting because I can increase my knowledge.

Thought deepening–based interest

Science is interesting because I can make my own predictions.
Science is interesting because I can understand the meaning of its laws and rules.
Science is interesting because I do not just have to listen to my teacher, but I can also think for myself.
Science is interesting because what we learn links to each other.
Science is interesting because it makes me think about things carefully by myself.
Science is interesting because it helps me understand that various kinds of knowledge are connected.

(Continued)

APPENDIX 7.1 (Continued)

Daily-life–related interest

Science is interesting because it is connected to our own lives.

Science is interesting because it is related to myself.

Science is interesting because it is applicable to real life.

Science is interesting because it is related to what we usually experience.

Science is interesting because it helps us to explain things around us.

Science is interesting because it is related to familiar things that happen around us.

APPENDIX 7.2 Results of ANOVA

	$F(9, 633)$
Encouraging students to express their opinions	6.70
Linking of information learnt to daily-life	9.50
Building knowledge connections	5.73
Clarifying goals and achievements	5.59
Showing concrete cases of what is being learnt	19.04
Encouraging students to think for themselves	8.86
Caring about students	10.11

8

EFFECTS OF STUDENTS' PERCEPTIONS OF TEST VALUE AND MOTIVATION FOR LEARNING ON LEARNING STRATEGY USE IN MATHEMATICS

Masayuki Suzuki and Yuan Sun

Introduction

In Japanese junior and senior high schools, regular exams are conducted four or five times per year. Because test performance in regular exams, which is important for entrance examinations at senior high schools or colleges, is highly important for students, many of them increase their study time before such exams (Matsunuma, 2009; Nagao, 2000). Despite their increased motivation, many students utilize superficial learning strategies, such as rote memorization, for the test rather than using elaboration-based learning strategies (Fujisawa, 2002). In addition, students are encouraged to review their tests in order to enhance their comprehension and monitor the effectiveness of their learning strategies after they receive feedback about their performance (e.g., Dansereau et al., 1979; Nakano, 1986). However, many students disregard the usefulness of test feedback as an opportunity to review and improve their learning (e.g., Maclellan, 2001; Suzuki, Toyota, & Sun, 2015). Therefore, it is important to identify the factors that affect students' use of learning strategies before and after a test.

In the present study, we focused on students' perceptions of test value as predictors of students' use of learning strategies. Recently, researchers have investigated students' perspectives of tests and assessments (e.g., Brown, Irving, Peterson, & Hirschfeld, 2009; Hong & Peng, 2008; Maclellan, 2001; Peterson & Irving, 2008; Rakoczy, Harks, Klieme, Blum, & Hochweber, 2013; Struyven, Dochy, & Janssens, 2005; Suzuki, 2012). For example, Hong and Peng (2008) showed that students who perceived a test as useful in learning were more likely to employ metacognitive learning strategies. However, these studies have not obtained robust evidence regarding these relationships. In fact, the majority of these studies investigated the relationship between the use of learning strategies and perceptions of test value only at a single point in time. When we predict a dependent variable at time *t* by an independent variable at time *t*–1, spuriously inflated estimates will be obtained if exogenous variables that correlate with the independent variable and affect the dependent variable are not controlled (Cole & Maxwell, 2003). In addition, previous studies have shown that motivation variables predict students' use of learning strategies. Therefore, the present study conducted two time-point surveys and examined the effects of perceptions of test value on students' use of learning strategies in testing situations after controlling for the use of learning strategies at Time 1. This study also took measurements of motivation variables as well as perceptions of test value in order to investigate their unique contributions.

Self-regulated learning

Self-regulated learners are persistent, resourceful, confident, and they are superior academic achievers (Zimmerman, 1990). According to the social cognitive perspective (Bandura, 1986), students' self-regulatory processes are divided into three cyclical phases: a forethought phase in which they analyze tasks, set goals, and select or create strategies before attempting to learn; a performance phase in which they monitor and control their behaviors during learning efforts; and a self-reflection phase involving self-evaluation based on feedback after learning efforts (Zimmerman, 2007). Self-reflection affects forethought, which completes the self-regulatory cycle.

Previous studies have shown that students' use of self-regulated learning strategies affects their academic achievement (Pintrich & DeGroot, 1990; Vermunt, 1998). However, many of these studies (e.g., Hong & Peng, 2008; Pintrich, Smith, Garcia, & McKeachie, 1993; Zimmerman & Martinez-Pons, 1986) have neither distinguished between pre- and post-test strategies nor measured post-test strategies. This is an important issue because students are encouraged to review their tests, correct mistakes, and identify the reasons for their mistakes to enhance their comprehension (Dansereau et al., 1979). Nakano (1986) showed that students who corrected and elaborated upon their responses after a test achieved higher scores. In addition, students can monitor the effectiveness of their learning strategies and react to feedback by altering strategies used during the self-reflection phase (Zimmerman, 1990). Thus, the present study categorized learning strategies into two types: pre-test strategies (corresponding to learning strategies in both the forethought and performance phases), which include metacognitive strategies and cognitive processing strategies, and post-test strategies (corresponding to learning strategies in the self-reflection phase).

Metacognitive strategies are activities that involve planning, monitoring, and controlling one's own learning process. Students' metacognitive skills are related to academic achievement, with self-regulated learners setting strategic plans and monitoring their progress in test situations (e.g., Kitsantas, 2002; Sungur, 2007; Vermunt, 1998). Cognitive processing strategies are activities for processing and storing learned information. This study focused on two cognitive processing strategies: deep processing strategies that involve semantic understanding of study materials or solutions, and surface processing strategies that involve rote memorization. The adoption of deep processing strategies is a null or positive predictor of academic achievement, while the adoption of surface processing strategies is a null or negative predictor of academic achievement (e.g., Elliot, McGregor, & Gable, 1999; Hong & Peng, 2008; Pintrich & DeGroot, 1990; Suzuki, 2013). Furthermore, the use of deep processing strategies positively affects the growth of academic achievement (Murayama, Pekrun, Lichtenfeld, & vom Hofe, 2013).

Finally, we focused on three types of post-test review strategies: checking answers, preparing for future tests, and improving future learning. More specifically, the first strategy is simply to review whether answers given in a previous test were correct and to identify reasons for mistakes. The second involves understanding how teachers organize a test. The third involves modifying learning strategies to make them more effective and to prevent future errors.

Perceptions of test value

Suzuki (2012) defined test value as tests' purposes and roles and developed a scale of test value. This scale is comprised of four subscales: (1) improvement, which is the aspect of a test that helps students to understand level of their achievement and improve learning; (2) pacemaker, which is the aspect that helps students to set goals and create a learning plan; (3) enforcement, which is the aspect that is used to enforce learning; and (4) comparison, which is the aspect that is used by teachers to identify high-performing students.

The aspects of a test that improve learning and encourage planning have positive relations with intrinsic motivation, perceived competence, and the use of effective learning strategies, whereas the aspects that enforce learning and enable the identification of excellent students have negative relations with these variables (Suzuki, 2011, 2012, 2013). For example, Suzuki (2012) found that students who considered tests as an effective way to improve their learning preferred to adopt review strategies, and those who regarded tests as an effective way to create a learning program employed metacognitive strategies. Furthermore, experimental studies (Suzuki, 2011, 2013) have shown that cultivating appropriate perceptions of test value among students promotes the use of deep processing strategies.

Motivational factors: Intrinsic and extrinsic motivation and perceived competence

Previous research studies have documented various motivations that affect use of learning strategies (e.g., Corpus, McClintic-Gilbert, & Hayenga, 2009; Elliot et al., 1999; Midgley, Kaplan, & Middleton, 2001; Nolen, 1988). We focused on three motivations in particular: intrinsic motivation, extrinsic motivation, and perceived competence. Intrinsic motivation is defined as motivation to engage in a task for the personal satisfaction derived from it. It is associated with the use of deep processing strategies and higher academic achievement (Pintrich & DeGroot, 1990; Vansteenkiste, Simons, Lens, Sheldon, & Deci, 2004). Extrinsic motivation is defined as motivation to engage in a task for external reasons. While there are numerous external reasons, such as the desire to avoid punishment or shame, or to gain rewards (e.g., Deci & Ryan, 1985; Vallerand & Bissonnette, 1992), this study only dealt with extrinsic motivation driven by academic requirements. In other words, students study subjects because teachers or parents make them do so. This kind of motivation has been linked to the use of superficial processing strategies, self-handicapping, and poor academic achievement (Corpus et al., 2009; Midgley et al., 2001; Vansteenkiste et al., 2004).

Several theories about motivation have focused on individuals' beliefs about their competence (Eccles & Wigfield, 2002). Law, Elliot, and Murayama (2012) also indicated that perceived competence is a central construct in achievement motivation. Although previous research has focused on the relationship between perceived competence and academic achievement, the findings suggest that perceived competence can be a predictor of the use of learning strategies because high perceived competence is associated with high academic achievement (e.g., Elliot et al., 2000; Marsh, 1991; Marsh & Martin, 2011), and learning strategies are also associated with academic achievement.

Aims and hypotheses of the present study

In the present study, we conducted two time-point surveys and investigated the effects of the perceptions of test value and motivation (i.e., intrinsic motivation, extrinsic motivation and perceived competence) on the use of learning strategies for mathematics study before and after a test. It was predicted that perceptions of the aspects of improvement and pacemaking would have positive relationships with the use of effective learning strategies (i.e., metacognitive, deep processing, and three-review strategies). Intrinsic motivation and perceived competence were also expected to be positive predictors of effective learning strategies use, whereas extrinsic motivation was expected to be a positive predictor of surface processing strategies use.

Methods

Participants and procedure

Participants in this study were students in 67 classes from four Japanese junior high schools. Schools were located in Tokyo and the Kanto region. Overall, 2,352 students (1,161 males, 1,187 females, 4 unspecified) participated in at least one assessment (for details, see Table 8.1). The participants completed the same questionnaire one week after taking mid-term exams in both June (T1) and September (T2).

TABLE 8.1 The number of participants at different time points

	Time 1			Time 2			Time 1 or Time 2		
	Grade 1	Grade 2	Grade 3	Grade 1	Grade 2	Grade 3	Grade 1	Grade 2	Grade 3
Males	344	342	387	347	352	366	371	376	414
Females	360	377	407	361	381	406	376	391	420
Unspecified	5	5	3	6	6	5	0	3	1
Total	709	724	797	714	739	777	747	770	835

Measures

Learning strategies use, perceptions of test value and motivations were assessed by self-reported scales at T1 and T2. All scales were in reference to mathematics (for more details regarding the items, see the Appendix).

In this paper, the data pertaining to learning strategies use at both T1 and T2 were included in the analyses. However, for perceptions of test value and motivation only the data at T1 were used in the analyses. Table 8.2 presents descriptive statistics, internal consistency estimates (coefficient omega), and correlations between variables. The subscale scores were the mean of item scores.

Metacognitive strategies

Suzuki's (2012) metacognitive strategies scale was used to assess students' use of metacognitive strategies. It consists of four items including statements such as "I create a learning plan before studying for a test". The participants responded to each item on a scale of 1 (*disagree*) to 5 (*agree*), in which higher scores indicate greater use of metacognitive strategies.

Cognitive processing strategies

Three items developed by Suzuki (2012) were used to measure the use of deep processing strategies (e.g., "I try to integrate new information with prior knowledge"). The other three items were used to assess surface processing strategies (e.g., "I simply memorize the solutions to problems"). Participants responded to these items on a scale of 1 (*disagree*) to 5 (*agree*).

Review strategies

This study also used items developed by Suzuki (2012) to assess post-test review strategies. The participants were presented with three subscales with three items each: strategies for checking correct answers (e.g., "I check the answers that I was not sure about during the test even if they turned out to be correct"), strategies to prepare for future tests (e.g., "I review tests so I can understand teachers' tendencies in organizing tests"), and strategies to improve learning (e.g., "I review tests and use it for improving my usual study methods"). The participants responded to each item on a scale of 1 (*disagree*) to 5 (*agree*).

TABLE 8.2 Descriptive statistics, internal consistencies, and correlation matrix among the variables

		n	M	SD	ω	1	2	3	4	5	6	7	8	9	10	11	12	13	14	15	16	17	18
1	Improvement	2180	4.12	0.78	.83																		
2	Pacemaker	2175	3.36	0.87	.73	.58																	
3	Enforcement	2187	2.74	1.02	.77	-.18	-.03																
4	Comparison	2209	2.42	1.12	.80	-.25	-.14	.55															
5	Intrinsic motivation	2201	2.18	0.78	.86	.37	.39	-.29	-.18														
6	Extrinsic motivation	2213	2.41	0.71	.63	-.02	.01	.39	.29	-.14													
7	Perceived competence	2190	2.59	1.14	.92	.22	.19	-.22	-.14	.54	-.10												
8	Metacognitive strategies_T1	2204	3.28	0.95	.76	.42	.43	-.25	-.16	.40	-.03	.25											
9	Deep strategies_T1	2172	3.19	0.95	.75	.34	.34	-.21	-.13	.52	-.09	.40	.50										
10	Surface strategies_T1	2155	2.73	0.94	.68	-.02	.00	.21	.10	-.18	.18	-.14	-.07	-.28									
11	Reviews for checking correct answers_T1	2196	3.21	1.04	.70	.40	.36	-.26	-.17	.46	-.08	.33	.54	.59	-.15								
12	Reviews for future tests_T1	2191	2.91	1.07	.86	.33	.36	-.12	-.06	.38	.01	.25	.50	.50	.01	.57							
13	Reviews for improving learning_T1	2186	3.18	1.07	.86	.45	.47	-.22	-.17	.45	-.01	.28	.62	.57	-.06	.63	.64						
14	Metacognitive strategies_T2	2172	3.22	0.90	.77	.34	.31	-.16	-.10	.27	.00	.17	.58	.38	-.05	.44	.40	.49					
15	Deep strategies_T2	2139	3.04	0.94	.77	.31	.26	-.20	-.12	.43	-.07	.40	.37	.58	-.28	.46	.36	.40	.48				
16	Surface strategies_T2	2172	2.77	0.86	.66	-.01	-.02	.14	.07	-.15	.19	-.12	-.04	-.22	.46	-.13	-.02	-.05	.03	.22			
17	Reviews for checking correct answers_T2	2208	3.17	0.95	.70	.32	.30	-.18	-.07	.36	-.06	.24	.42	.43	-.16	.54	.39	.46	.57	-.33	-.06		
18	Reviews for future tests_T2	2208	2.99	0.98	.82	.29	.26	-.11	-.02	.28	.02	.19	.40	.37	-.02	.40	.53	.45	.55	-.23	.03	.61	
19	Reviews for improving learning_T2	2182	3.14	0.96	.82	.35	.30	-.16	-.08	.32	-.01	.21	.47	.42	-.09	.48	.43	.54	.63	-.30	-.03	.71	.70

Perceptions of test value

Suzuki's (2012) Values of a Test Scale was used to assess students' perceptions of test value. It consists of four subscales: improvement (comprised of five items including statements such as "The purpose of math tests is to check how much we understand"); pacemaker (comprised of four items including statements such as "The purpose of math tests is to get used to planning our studies"); enforcement (comprised of four items including statements such as "The purpose of math tests is to force us to study"); and (4) comparison (comprised of three items such as "The purpose of math tests is to identify excellent students"). The participants responded to each item on a scale of 1 (*disagree*) to 5 (*agree*).

Intrinsic–extrinsic motivation

Nishimura, Kawamura, and Sakurai's (2011) Academic Motivation Scale, which is comprised of six items (three items per subscale), was used to assess students' intrinsic motivation (e.g., "I study math because studying math is fun") and extrinsic motivation (e.g., "I study math because people around me ask me to study"). The participants responded to each item on a scale of 1 (*strongly disagree*) to 4 (*strongly agree*).

Perceived competence

Four items developed by Suzuki (2012) were used to assess students' perceived competence (e.g., "I think I am good at math"). The participants responded to each item on a scale of 1 (*disagree*) to 5(*agree*).

Data analysis

We used a multilevel model (Hox, 2010) to examine how students' perceptions of test value and motivations affected their use of learning strategies after controlling for learning strategies use at T1. In this multilevel model, we also examined whether use of learning strategies, and the effects of perceptions of test value and motivations differed among the various classrooms. In the analyses, the classrooms' mean was subtracted from the corresponding individual scores.

In addition, we applied multiple imputation to deal with the missing data prior to the analyses. Due to the longitudinal design of the study, some data were missing. For handling missing data, multiple imputation and full-information maximum likelihood are currently the most favored approaches (Enders, 2010; Graham, 2009). Multiple imputation has an advantage over full-information maximum likelihood in the treatment of incomplete independent variables (Enders, 2010). We generated 20 imputed datasets and conducted multilevel analyses using *Mplus* (Muthén & Muthén, 1998–2012).

Results

Exploratory multilevel analyses showed that the intercepts of all dependent variables, except surface processing strategies, had a significant variance component between classrooms, thus indicating that the use of learning strategies differed among classrooms. The results also showed no variation between classrooms in terms of the relationship among perceptions of test value, motivation for learning, and learning strategies. In other words, the results indicated that the effects of perceptions of test value and motivation on learning strategies use were consistent. Therefore, we adopted a variance component model in which the regression intercept that represents the expected value of dependent variables for a student was allowed to vary across classrooms, while the regression slopes that represent the effects of independent variables were not (Hox, 2010). Table 8.3 presents the parameter estimates of this model.

The findings also showed that learning strategies use at T1 predicted the use at T2 (metacognitive strategies, $\hat{\gamma}_{10} = 0.50$; deep processing strategies, $\hat{\gamma}_{10} = 0.43$; surface processing strategies, $\hat{\gamma}_{10} = 0.39$; reviews strategies for checking correct answers, $\hat{\gamma}_{10} = 0.39$; reviews strategies for future tests, $\hat{\gamma}_{10} = 0.43$; reviews strategies for improving learning, $\hat{\gamma}_{10} = 0.41$). It is important to note that perceptions of test value and motivation for learning predicted learning strategies use, after controlling for learning strategies use at T1. Specifically, perceived value of tests for improvement significantly predicted metacognitive strategies ($\hat{\gamma}_{20} = .12$), deep processing strategies ($\hat{\gamma}_{20} = .11$), reviews for checking correct answers ($\hat{\gamma}_{20} = .10$), reviews for future tests ($\hat{\gamma}_{20} = .14$), and reviews for improving learning ($\hat{\gamma}_{20} = .15$). Also, pacemaker, enforcement, and comparison predicted reviews for checking correct answers ($\hat{\gamma}_{30} = .07$, $\hat{\gamma}_{40} -0.07$ and $\hat{\gamma}_{50} 0.06$). Enforcement and comparison predicted reviews for future tests ($\hat{\gamma}_{40} = 0.07$ and $\hat{\gamma}_{50} 0.07$). Intrinsic motivation and perceived competence were significant positive predictors of deep processing strategies ($\hat{\gamma}_{60} = .11$ and $\hat{\gamma}_{80} = 0.12$), whereas extrinsic motivation for learning was a significant positive predictor of surface processing strategies ($\hat{\gamma}_{70} = .13$). Intrinsic motivation for learning also predicted reviews for checking correct answers ($\hat{\gamma}_{60} = .12$). These results emphasize that students' perceptions about test value and their motivation for learning are important factors that influence their use of learning strategies.

Discussion

This study examined how students' perceptions of test value and their motivation for learning affect their use of learning strategies in testing situations. Results showed that perceived test value predicted learning strategies use after controlling for the use of learning strategies in the previous mid-term examination. More specifically, improvement items (from Suzuki's Values of a Test Scale) predicted the three review strategies and deep processing strategies. These findings are consistent with previous studies (Suzuki, 2011, 2012, 2013). It is not surprising that the students who perceived tests as being helpful for understanding the extent of their own comprehension and improving their overall learning reported using more

TABLE 8.3 Parameter estimates of perceptions of test value and motivations on the use of the different learning strategies

	Metacognitive strategies		Deep processing strategies		Surface processing strategies		Reviews strategies for checking correct answers		Reviews strategies for future tests		Reviews strategies for improving learning	
	Estimates	SE	Estimates	SE	Estimates	SE	Estimates	SE	Estimates	SE	Estimates	SE
Fixed effects												
γ_{00} Intercept	3.21**	0.02	3.03**	0.03	2.76**	0.02	3.17**	0.03	2.99**	0.03	3.13**	0.03
γ_{10} Learning strategies_T1	0.50**	0.02	0.43**	0.03	0.39**	0.02	0.39**	0.02	0.43**	0.02	0.41**	0.02
γ_{20} Improvement	0.12**	0.03	0.11**	0.03	0.04	0.03	0.10**	0.03	0.14**	0.03	0.15**	0.04
γ_{30} Pacemaker	0.01	0.03	-0.02	0.03	-0.01	0.02	0.07**	0.03	0.02	0.03	-0.01	0.04
γ_{40} Enforcement	-0.04	0.02	-0.04	0.02	-0.03	0.02	-0.07**	0.02	-0.07**	0.02	-0.06	0.03
γ_{50} Comparison	0.01	0.02	0.00	0.02	0.01	0.02	0.06**	0.02	0.07**	0.02	0.05	0.02
γ_{60} Intrinsic motivation	0.01	0.03	0.11**	0.03	-0.06	0.03	0.12**	0.03	0.04	0.03	0.07	0.04
γ_{70} Extrinsic motivation	0.03	0.02	0.02	0.03	0.13**	0.03	-0.02	0.03	0.04	0.03	0.02	0.03
γ_{80} Perceived competence	0.02	0.02	0.12**	0.02	-0.02	0.02	0.02	0.02	0.03	0.02	0.02	0.02
Random effects												
Var (u_{0j})	0.02**	0.01	0.03**	0.01	0.01	0.01	0.03**	0.01	0.02**	0.01	0.03**	0.01
Var (e_{ij})	0.52**	0.02	0.53**	0.02	0.57**	0.02	0.59**	0.02	0.65**	0.02	0.63**	0.02

Learning strategies_T1 means the use of learning strategies corresponding to dependent variables measured at time1. ** $p < .01$

review strategies and deep processing strategies. In addition, as expected, improvement items had a positive effect on metacognitive strategies. However, the finding that pacemaker items, which measure perceptions of tests being helpful for creating a learning program, had no significant correlation with metacognitive strategies use contradicts Suzuki's (2012) findings. One possible explanation for this difference could be the age and cognitive development of the participants. For example, Suzuki's (2012) survey was conducted with high school students, whereas this study was conducted with junior high school students. Both improvement and pacemaker items required the participants to reflect on the instrumental aspects of tests that encourage effective learning. Therefore, junior high school students might find it difficult to distinguish each role. As a result, when both improvement and pacemaker items are included in the analyses model, the latter's specific contribution to metacognitive strategies use may disappear.

Furthermore, enforcement items, which measure perceptions that tests force students to learn, negatively affected review strategies for checking correct answers and future tests. These findings support Suzuki's (2012) results. Students who feel that they are being controlled by a test tend to adopt impromptu learning strategies when exams draw near and not review their test results. On the other hand, the finding that comparison items, which measure perceptions that tests are used for teachers to compare students, was positively related to review strategies for checking correct answers and future tests was unexpected. Psychological literature offers no consistent evidence regarding whether competition promotes or impedes performance (Murayama & Elliot, 2012). Previous research about motivation for learning has identified the controlling context as the component that undermines motivation for learning. In Reeve and Deci's (1996) study, those who were pressured to win and received positive feedback about their performance demonstrated decreased levels of self-determination, which in turn undermined their intrinsic motivation. This finding suggests that the effects of perceived comparison depend on whether students perceive themselves as being made to learn by a test. Actually, comparison items had null or weakly negative simple correlation with review strategies use (see Table 8.2), whereas comparison items were a positive predictor of these strategies when other perceptions about test value were controlled for in the analysis. However, clarifying this point requires further research.

With regard to motivational factors, intrinsic and extrinsic motivation and perceived competence predicted some learning strategies use. More specifically, intrinsic motivation predicted the adoption of deep processing strategies and review strategies for checking correct answers. In addition, perceived competence positively affected deep processing strategies use. These results support past findings that motivational tendencies shape future learning and resulting achievement (Deci & Ryan, 1985; Marsh & Martin, 2011). On the other hand, extrinsic motivation was a positive predictor of the adoption of surface processing strategies. This result is also consistent with past findings (e.g., Vansteenkiste et al., 2004). Extrinsic motivation is typically driven by short-term benefits of learning, so it is linked to superficial strategies such as rote learning.

Finally, a comparison of the perceptual and motivational influences suggests a difference in the extent of their influence that is worth noting. Improvement items (which belong to perceptions of test value) predicted the use of *all* the learning strategies except surface processing strategies. This finding suggests that perception of test value is a more critical factor that influences students' use of learning strategies than their learning motivation.

Implications for practice

Because regular examinations are an integral part of learning in Japanese schools, how to encourage students to use exams to improve their learning is an important topic. The findings in this research suggest that students' perceptions of test value had relatively more influence on learning strategies use than their learning motivation. Therefore, educators need to attend to students' perceptions of test value and guide them to perceive test value in terms of improvement of learning rather than enforcement. Some studies have shown positive effects on interest and achievement when experimenters intervene in students' perceptions of test value (Rakoczy et al., 2013; Suzuki, 2011, 2013). These findings imply that modifying students' perceptions of test value may contribute greatly to their adoption of effective learning strategies.

Limitations and suggestions for future research

Our study has several limitations. First, the factors we focused on in this study were confined to perceptions of test value and motivation. Because numerous factors affect learning strategies use, future studies need to include other variables such as affective factors (e.g., achievement emotions; Pekrun, Elliot, & Maier, 2009) or epistemic beliefs (Schommer, 1990). Second, although this study produced evidence that students' perceptions about test value and motivation for learning influence their use of learning strategies, these relationships are only correlational. Students' perceptions about test value, motivation for learning, and the use of learning strategies are reciprocally linked to their academic achievements. Therefore, alternative approaches such as a cross-lagged model or latent change score model (McArdle, 2009) may be better suited to examine causal ordering and possible reciprocal effects. Finally, our findings pertain to junior high school students. Because this study suggests that factors affecting students' use of learning strategies differ at developmental stages, a survey of other populations, such as high school or college students, will be conducted in a future study.

Acknowledgment

We are grateful to the students for their participation in the survey. This research was supported by 8th Hakuho Research Grant for Child Education.

References

Bandura, A. (1986). *Social foundations of thought and action: A social cognitive theory.* Englewood Cliffs, NJ: Prentice Hall.

Brown, G. T. L., Irving, S. E., Peterson, E. R., & Hirschfeld, G. H. F. (2009). Use of interactive-informal assessment practices: New Zealand secondary students' conceptions of assessment. *Learning and Instruction, 19*(2), 97–111.

Cole, D. A., & Maxwell, S. E. (2003). Testing mediational models with longitudinal data: Questions and tips in the use of structural equation modeling. *Journal of Abnormal Psychology, 112*(4), 558–577.

Corpus, J. H., McClintic-Gilbert, M. S., & Hayenga, A. O. (2009). Within-year changes in children's intrinsic and extrinsic motivational orientations: Contextual predictors and academic outcomes. *Contemporary Educational Psychology, 34*(2), 154–166.

Dansereau, D. F., McDonald, B. A., Collins, K. W., Garland, J. C., Holley, C. D., Diekhoff, G. M., & Evans, S. H. (1979). Evaluation of a learning strategy system. In H. F. O'Nell, Jr., & C. D. Spielberger (Eds.), *Cognitive and affective learning strategies* (pp. 3–43). New York: Academic Press.

Deci, E. L., & Ryan, R. M. (1985). *Intrinsic motivation and self-determination in human behavior.* New York: Plenum.

Eccles, J. S., & Wigfield, A. (2002). Motivational beliefs, values, and goals. *Annual Review of Psychology, 53*(1), 109–132.

Elliot, A. J., Faler, J., McGregor, H. A., Campbell, W. K., Sedikides, C., & Harackiewicz, J. M. (2000). Competence valuation as a strategic intrinsic motivation process. *Personality and Social Psychology Bulletin, 26*(7), 780–794.

Elliot, A. J., McGregor, H. A., & Gable, S. (1999). Achievement goals, study strategies, and exam performance: A meditational analysis. *Journal of Educational Psychology, 91*(3), 549–563.

Enders, C. K. (2010). *Applied missing data analysis.* New York: Guilford.

Fujisawa, S. (2002). *Gomakashi bennkyo (jou): Gakuryoku teika wo jochou suru shisutemu.* Tokyo, Japan: Shinnyousha.

Graham, J. W. (2009). Missing data analysis: Making it work in the real world. *Annual Review of Psychology, 60*, 549–576.

Hong, E., & Peng, Y. (2008). Do Chinese students' perceptions of test value affect test performance? Mediating role of motivational and metacognitive regulation in test preparation. *Learning and Instruction, 18*(6), 499–512.

Hox, J. (2010). *Multilevel analysis: Techniques and applications* (2nd ed.). Mahwah, NJ: Erlbaum.

Kitsantas, A. (2002). Test preparation and performance: A self-regulatory analysis. *The Journal of Experimental Education, 70*(2), 101–113.

Law, W., Elliot, A. J., & Murayama, K. (2012). Perceived competence moderates the relation between performance-approach and performance-avoidance goals. *Journal of Educational Psychology, 104*(3), 806–819.

Maclellan, E. (2001). Assessment for learning: The differing perceptions of tutors and students. *Assessment and Evaluation in Higher Education, 26*(4), 307–318.

Marsh, H. W. (1991). Failure of high-ability high-schools to deliver academic benefits commensurate with their students' ability levels. *American Educational Research Journal, 28*(2), 445–480.

Marsh, H. W., & Martin, A. J. (2011). Academic self-concept and academic achievement: Relations and causal ordering. *British Journal of Educational Psychology, 81*(Pt 1), 59–77.

Matsunuma, M. (2009). Why are some high achievers on the course final exam unsuccessful on the proficiency exam in English? *The Japanese Journal of Psychology, 80*(1), 9–16.

McArdle, J. J. (2009). Latent variable modeling of differences and changes with longitudinal data. *Annual Review of Psychology, 60*(1), 577–605.

Midgley, C., Kaplan, A., & Middleton, M. (2001). Performance-approach goals: Good for what, for whom, under what circumstances, and at what cost? *Journal of Educational Psychology, 93*(1), 77–86.

Murayama, K., & Elliot, A. J. (2012). The competition-performance relation: A meta-analytic review and test of the opposing processes model of competition and performance. *Psychological Bulletin, 138*(6), 1035–1070.

Murayama, K., Pekrun, R., Lichtenfeld, S., & vom Hofe, R. (2013). Predicting long-term growth in students' mathematics achievement: The unique contributions of motivation and cognitive strategies. *Child Development, 84*(4), 1475–1490.

Muthén, L. K., & Muthén, B. O. (1998–2012). *Mplus user's guide* (7th ed.). Los Angeles, CA: Author.

Nagao, A. (2000). Kyouiku hyouka no porithikkusu bunnseki. In A. Nagao & S. Hamada (Eds.), *Kyouiku hyouka wo kanngaeru* (pp. 40–70). Kyoto, Japan: Mineruva shobou.

Nakano, Y. (1986). The effects of postfeedback interval (PFI) and its method of management at test situation. *Japanese Journal of Educational Psychology, 34*(3), 204–210.

Nishimura, T., Kawamura, S., & Sakurai, S. (2011). Autonomous motivation and meta-cognitive strategies as predictors of academic performance: Does intrinsic motivation predict academic performance? *Japanese Journal of Educational Psychology, 59*(1), 77–87.

Nolen, S. B. (1988). Reasons for studying: Motivational orientations and study strategies. *Cognition and Instruction, 5*(4), 269–287.

Pekrun, R., Elliot, A. J., & Maier, M. A. (2009). Achievement goals and achievement emotions: Testing a model of their joint relations with academic performance. *Journal of Educational Psychology, 101*(1), 115–135.

Peterson, E. R., & Irving, S. E. (2008). Secondary school students' conceptions of assessment and feedback. *Learning and Instruction, 18*(3), 238–250.

Pintrich, P. R., & DeGroot, E. V. (1990). Motivational and self-regulated learning components of classroom academic performance. *Journal of Educational Psychology, 82*(1), 33–40.

Pintrich, P. R., Smith, D. A. F., Garcia, T., & McKeachie, W. J. (1993). Reliability and predictive validity of the motivated strategies for learning questionnaire (MSLQ). *Educational and Psychological Measurement, 53*(3), 801–813.

Rakoczy, K., Harks, B., Klieme, E., Blum, W., & Hochweber, J. (2013). Written feedback in mathematics: Mediated by students' perception, moderated by goal orientation. *Learning and Instruction, 27*, 63–73.

Reeve, J., & Deci, E. L. (1996). Elements of the competitive situation that affect intrinsic motivation. *Personality and Social Psychology Bulletin, 22*(1), 24–33.

Schommer, M. (1990). Effects of beliefs about the nature of knowledge on comprehension. *Journal of Educational Psychology, 82*(3), 498–504.

Struyven, K., Dochy, F., & Janssens, S. (2005). Students' perceptions about evaluation and assessment in higher education: A review. *Assessment and Evaluation in Higher Education, 30*, 325–341.

Sungur, S. (2007). Modeling the relationships among students' motivational beliefs, meta-cognitive strategy use, and effort regulation. *Scandinavian Journal of Educational Research, 51*(3), 315–326.

Suzuki, M. (2011). Effects of a rubric: Values of a test, motivation for learning and learning strategies. *Japanese Journal of Educational Psychology, 59*(2), 131–143.

Suzuki, M. (2012). Relationship between values of a test and strategies in learning for and reviewing a test: Test approach-avoidance tendency as a mediator. *Japanese Journal for Research on Testing, 8*(1), 19–30.

Suzuki, M. (2013). Exploring the mechanism of the effects of presenting a rubric and fact patterns. *Educational Technology Research, 36*, 1–9.

Suzuki, M., Toyota, T., & Sun, Y. (2015). How learners use feedback information: Effects of social comparative information and achievement goals. In D. C. Noelle, R. Dale, A. S. Warlaumont, J. Yoshimi, T. Matlock, C. D. Jennings, & P. P. Maglio (Eds.), *Proceedings of the 37th Annual Conference of the Cognitive Science Society* (pp. 2308–2313). Austin, TX: Cognitive Science Society.

Vallerand, R. J., & Bissonnette, R. (1992). Intrinsic, extrinsic, and amotivational styles as predictors of behavior: A prospective study. *Journal of Personality, 60*(3), 599–620.

Vansteenkiste, M., Simons, J., Lens, W., Sheldon, K. M., & Deci, E. L. (2004). Motivating learning, performance, and persistence: The synergistic effects of intrinsic goal contents and autonomy-supportive contexts. *Journal of Personality and Social Psychology, 87*(2), 246–260.

Vermunt, J. D. (1998). The regulation of constructive learning processes. *British Journal of Educational Psychology, 68*(2), 149–171.

Zimmerman, B. J. (1990). Self-regulated learning and academic achievement: An overview. *Educational Psychologist, 25*(1), 3–17.

Zimmerman, B. J. (2007). Goal setting: A key proactive source of academic self-regulation. In D. H. Schunk & B. J. Zimmerman (Eds.), *Motivation and self-regulated learning: Theory, research, and applications* (pp. 267–295). New Jersey, NJ: Lawrence Erlbaum Associates.

Zimmerman, B. J., & Martinez-Pons, M. (1986). Development of a structured interview for assessing student use of self-regulated learning strategies. *American Educational Research Journal, 23*(4), 614–628.

Appendix

Items for values of a test questionnaire

<u>Instruction:</u> In your opinion, what is the purpose of math tests? For each item, circle only one number to indicate the extent to which it applies to you.

<u>Improvement</u>

The purpose of math tests is to check how much we understand.

The purpose of math tests is to help us understand our weak points.

The purpose of math tests is to review our study methods up to this point.

The purpose of math tests is to determine our ability.

The purpose of math tests is to give results to be used in our studies from now on.

<u>Pacemaker</u>

The purpose of math tests is to get used to planning our studies.

The purpose of math tests is to allow us to check our study habits.

The purpose of math tests is to encourage our motivation to learn.

The purpose of math tests is to provide regular opportunities to study.

<u>Enforcement</u>

The purpose of math tests is to force us to study.

The purpose of math tests is to make us study, even if by force.

The purpose of math tests is to make us study because without tests, we would not study.

We would not study without tests.

<u>Comparison</u>

The purpose of math tests is to identify excellent students.

The purpose of math tests is to distinguish between those who can study and those who cannot.

The purpose of math tests is to help teachers rank the students.

Items for intrinsic–extrinsic motivation questionnaire

<u>Instruction:</u> This questionnaire asks your reasons for applying yourself to your studies. For each item, circle only one number that most closely reflects how you feel to indicate the extent to which it applies to you.

Intrinsic motivation

> I study math because I enjoy solving problems.
>
> I study math because studying math is fun.
>
> I study math because it is enjoyable to discover new ways of solving math problem.

Extrinsic motivation

> I study math because people around me ask me to study.
>
> I study math because I am scolded if my grade drops.
>
> I study math because studying is something like a rule.

Items for perceived competence questionnaire

Instruction: In your opinion, to what extent are the following statements true?

> I think I am good at math.
>
> I think my math ability is excellent.
>
> I think I understand the content of my math lessons.
>
> I am confident that I will get good marks on the math test.

Items for metacognitive strategies use questionnaire

Instruction: Concerning your study methods for the regular math test:

> I create a learning plan before studying for a test.
>
> After checking the amount of time I have until the test and the range of the exam contents, I draw up a study schedule.
>
> As I check my study progress, I adjust my study pace by increasing or decreasing the amount of time for studying.
>
> As I continue with my study, I take into consideration how well I understand the study contents.

Items for cognitive strategies use questionnaire

Instruction: Concerning your usual math study methods:

Deep processing strategies

> I try to integrate new information with prior knowledge

When I come across a formula, I think about why it is structured the way it is.

I do not just memorize how to solve a problem; I always think "Why do I solve it in that way?"

Surface processing strategies

I simply memorize the solutions to problems.

I do not concern myself with how formulas work, I just memorize them.

I do not concern myself with why problems are solved the way they are.

Items for review strategies use questionnaire

Instruction: Concerning your studies after you have received your math test sheet:

Reviews for checking correct answers

In terms of incorrect answers, I try to find out why and how I made those errors.

I check the answers that I was not sure about during the test even if they turned out to be correct.

I write down the points of the problems for which I gave incorrect answers.

Reviews for future tests

I review tests so I can understand teachers' tendencies in organizing tests.

I review tests so that I can better understand the format of future regular tests.

I review tests so that I can find strategies for solving future tests.

Reviews for improving learning

I review tests and use it for improving my usual study methods.

After the test is over, I reflect whether my study methods were good.

I review tests and use it as a reference point for future study plans.

9

APPLYING METACOGNITION THEORY TO THE CLASSROOM

Decreasing illusion of knowing to promote learning strategy use

Tatsushi Fukaya

Importance of learning strategies

To achieve deep understanding, not just memorizing, we must know effective learning strategies to arrange and integrate new information with our prior knowledge. Derry and Murphy (1986, p. 2) defined a *learning strategy* as "the collection of mental tactics employed by an individual in a particular learning situation to facilitate acquisition of knowledge or skill." One category of learning strategies on which previous research has focused is cognitive strategies which referred to the way of processing new information (Corno & Mandinach, 1983; Zimmerman & Pons, 1986). Previous research has classified cognitive strategies into two sub-categories: shallow processing strategies and deep processing strategies (Marton & Säljö, 1976; Weinstein & Mayer, 1986). A shallow processing strategy involves repeating information over and over without thinking about its meaning. On the other hand, a deep processing strategy involves the mental operations such as relating information to other/prior knowledge (i.e., *elaboration, association*) and organizing information to be conceptually coherent (i.e., *organization*).

So far, evidence has been accumulated about the link between the use of learning strategies and task performance. In general, the use of a shallow processing strategy has negative or no influence on learning, whereas the use of a deep processing strategy has positive influence on learning (e.g., Pintrich & De Groot, 1990; Zimmerman & Martinez-Pons, 1990; but see Dinsmore & Alexander, 2012 for details about these relationships). In addition, Murayama, Pekrun, Lichtenfeld, and vom Hofe (2013) reported that learning strategies are important in long-term growth in school achievement. They demonstrated that rehearsal negatively predicted mathematics achievement growth from grades 5 to 10, and elaboration positively predicted growth from grades 7 to 10, even after controlling for the influence of intelligence. Thus, enhancing students' ability to use effective learning strategies has been an important theme for both educational researchers and practitioners.

Two aspects for promoting learning strategy use

Given the importance of learning strategy, the next question is "On which aspects should we focus to boost students' use of learning strategies?" The first possible aspect is knowledge about learning strategies, which has been regarded as a requisite for using learning strategies (Pressley, 1986). Obviously, we cannot use the strategy without knowing it.

However, various studies have also argued that providing knowledge about learning strategies is insufficient to change students' way of learning (e.g., Brown, Campione, & Day, 1981; Paris, Lipson, & Wixson, 1983). One possible reason is that students do not truly recognize the necessity to change from shallow processing to deep processing strategies. Imagine a student leaving class for the day: She does not fully understand the content that has been covered in class, but unfortunately, she is unaware of her own poor understanding. Thus, she continues to use an ineffective strategy, such as rote learning, because of her *illusion of knowing*. Garner (1990) suggested that inaccurate self-evaluation impedes the use of effective learning strategies.

The second possible aspect for boosting the effective use of learning strategies is conceptualized as lack of metacognition. Metacognition means cognitive functions at a high-order level that checks and controls various cognitive activities such as information processing (see also Dunlosky & Metcalfe, 2009 for a comprehensive outline of the processes involved in metacognition). Indeed, a function for evaluating our own understanding has been labeled *metacognitive monitoring* (e.g., Nelson & Narens, 1990; Thiede, Griffin, Wiley, & Redford, 2009). While metacognitive monitoring which is undertaken during the performance of a task is called *online monitoring*, monitoring which is undertaken before and after the performance of a task is called *offline monitoring* (cf. Desoete, Roeyers, & De Clercq, 2003; Veenman, Van Hout-Wolters, & Afflerbach, 2006). Because it is important to judge accurately our own understanding after finishing the task, researchers have focused on offline monitoring which occurs after the task, and which also relates to the illusion of knowing.

In this research area, the illusion of knowing, sometimes termed *bias* (Schraw, 2009), has been measured as the difference between students' subjective judgment about their own comprehension after learning and their objective test performance (e.g., Commander & Stanwyck, 1997; Glenberg, Wilkinson, & Epstein, 1982). Considerable research has demonstrated that students with lower test performance tend to overestimate their future test performance (e.g., Bol & Hacker, 2001; Hacker, Bol, Horgan, & Rakow, 2000; Nietfeld, Cao, & Osborne, 2005). Thus, their low test performance may be caused not only by the lack of learning skill but also by their lack of awareness that they are unable to accurately judge their level of understanding (cf. Dunning, Johnson, Ehrlinger, & Kruger, 2003).

Focus of this study

Considering the information presented above, a lack of metacognitive monitoring may lead to not employing more effective learning strategies when they are required.

Given its theoretical and practical importance, it is surprising that very little research has assessed how the illusion of knowing is associated with the use of learning strategies. Thus, the aim of present study was to evaluate an intervention for promoting university students' use of learning strategies in a psychology statistics course. For this purpose, we divided whole classes into pre-intervention (hereafter referred to as "pre-phase") and intervention phases, and implemented the interventions to improve students' monitoring accuracy and promote their use of learning strategies.

Our intervention was designed with reference to the study by Nietfeld, Cao, and Osborne (2006). In their intervention, they asked college students to complete exercises for realizing their bias at the end of each class. Students assessed their own understanding for their current class and answered questions in a review test. Then they received feedback about their test performance and judgments and were asked to reflect on the discrepancy in their responses. As Nietfeld et al. (2006) and other studies (e.g., Fukaya, 2013) have demonstrated, we can assume that externalizing thoughts is important for realizing one's state of understanding. Thus, in the present study, we required students to explain the statistical concepts learned in class.

However, previous studies have also suggested that many learners cannot distinguish "quality of recall" (e.g., accuracy of recalled information) when judging their own understanding. Dunlosky, Rawson, and Middleton (2005) required participants to read texts, recall the content (definition of learned concepts), and predict their test performance. The authors analyzed the accuracy of their recall and investigated whether participants could make predictions distinguishing the quality of recall. The results showed that despite participants recalling the content inaccurately, their prediction of the recalled contents was higher than the contents not recalled. Therefore, in the present study, we also asked students to evaluate their own answers based on evaluation criteria. Through this self-evaluating activity, students were expected to detect the errors in their explanations and recognize their own lack of understanding (cf. Lipko, Dunlosky, Hartwig, Rawson, Swan, & Cook, 2009).

The evaluation criteria were also expected to promote greater use of the elaboration strategy among students. For example, the criterion for the term *correlation* requires students to define it in a manner similar to "a phenomenon in which two variables co-vary," and to provide an example resembling "the more aggressive people are, the more antisocial their behavior." This method emphasizes the importance of studying both a concept's definition and example. The cognitive process of generating examples could be treated as *elaboration*, in which a concrete example is related to the abstract definition by using students' prior knowledge (cf. Wittrock, 1989).

In addition, the evaluation criteria also serve to elicit active use of organization strategy in which one identifies how concepts are related. By self-evaluating their answers based on the criteria, students would become aware of the need to organize the relationships between the statistical concepts. For instance, the criteria of *correlation coefficient* include other technical terms such as *standard deviation* and *covariance* in the formula. If they review the content after class, students also have to summarize the relationships between these terms. Thus, although the criteria do not directly inform them of the way to utilize organization strategy, the evaluation criteria might be effective in promoting their use of the strategy.

To assess this intervention's effects, we set up two dependent variables. First, the students' illusion of knowing was measured. At the end of each class, we asked students to rate how well they understood that day's content on a seven-point scale. In the next step, we instructed them to explain the statistical concepts learned that day in writing. After the explanation task, students rated their understanding again. In order to generate a measure of students' illusion of knowing, the difference between each of their comprehension ratings and their explanation task performances was calculated by changing both scores on a 0–100% scale. For example, if a certain student rated his understanding at 4 points (50%) on the scale and got no correct answers on the explanation task (0%), he showed a 50% illusion of knowing. Whether the illusion of knowing decreased was examined by asking students to rate their understanding both before and after the explanation task.

Second, students' use of learning strategies in the course was measured with a self-reported questionnaire. The elaboration and organization scale from the *Motivated Strategies for Learning Questionnaire* (MSLQ), developed by Pintrich, Smith, García, and McKeachie (1993), was used. MSLQ has been proven to have adequate reliability and validity (e.g., Pintrich et al., 1993) and has been used in numerous studies in various countries (see Duncan & McKeachie, 2005 for a review). Students responded to these scales twice—in the pre-phase and in the intervention phase.

Three hypotheses were tested regarding the effects of the explanation and self-evaluation tasks: (1) Students would lower their overestimation of comprehension after the explanation and self-evaluation tasks; (2) students' use of learning strategies would increase from the pre-phase to the intervention phase; and (3) the amount of decrease of comprehension rating through explanation and self-evaluation tasks in the intervention phase (or awareness of illusion of knowing, hereafter) would be positively associated with the increase in use of learning strategies. In other words, students who recognize their illusion of knowing would begin to use more learning strategies in the intervention phase.

Method

Participants

The participants were 67 undergraduate students enrolled in a "Statistics for Psychology I" course held at a university in Tokyo, Japan. The undergraduates included in the study attended at least 9 of the 14 class sessions offered in the course. The course level was introductory, and most students were freshmen. Missing data because of nonattendance or omissions ($M = 3.81$ for each variable) were statistically inferred according to the multiple imputation method (cf. Graham, 2009). A missing data analysis was performed with the "Missing Values" program of SPSS, ver. 21, using 20 time imputations.

Outline of the course and the intervention

In a typical lesson, a teacher (the author, in this case) first explained the statistical concepts or indexes with the corresponding definitions, the numerical expressions, and the meanings as well. We also used hypothetical data as examples in explanations and showed illustrative diagrams in power point animation. For similar indexes such as *mean deviation, variance,* and *standard deviation,* the author organized their characteristics in a table for contrast. Then, the teacher confirmed the students' understanding by requiring them to explain the concepts in their own words and solve calculation exercises. In addition, the teacher divided the students into groups of three and gave them more advanced problems to solve. The problems were designed to require them to apply acquired knowledge for solving (e.g., to explain why a U-shape curve produces low correlation). After the students had discussed the solutions, the teacher explained the answers. The teacher also encouraged their preparation and review of the lessons, and especially to promote review, providing them voluntary homework and awarding additional grade points for its correct completion.

The 14-week term was divided into three phases: pre-phase (2nd–5th week), intervention phase I (7–9th week), and intervention phase II (11–13th week). The phases were separated by two midterm examinations at the 6th and 10th weeks. Table 9.1 displays how the activities were manipulated for reflection at the end of each class. In the pre-phase, students rated their comprehension of the class on a 7-point scale, prompted by the query, *How well do you think you understand today's class?—1 (very poorly) to 7 (very well).* The teacher explained that point 1 indicated they could not explain the class content at all; point 4, they could explain half the important concepts; and point 7, they could explain all important concepts.

In the intervention phase, the explanation and self-evaluation tasks were added as activities for reflection, asking the students (1) to explain two important statistical concepts or indexes for each class (see Table 9.2) and (2) to evaluate their own answers based on the evaluation criteria. We instructed students to explain without referring to the text, and to do so in a way that people who do not know the concepts could understand. After every student had completed the explanation task, the teacher displayed the evaluation criteria, by which students scored their answers in terms of definition and example (or definition and numerical formula for statistical indexes). The students scored each of their answers, with 0 meaning that the student did not write anything or wrote incorrect definitions and explanations; 0.5 meaning the student could write only correct definitions or correct examples; and 1 point meaning the student could write both correct definitions and examples. Therefore, the total for the students' explanation task performance or self-evaluation ranged from 0 to 2 points per class during the intervention phases.

TABLE 9.1 Overview of the experimental design

Pre-phase	*Intervention phase I and II*
Activities for reflection	
1 Comprehension judgment	1 Comprehension judgment (pre)
	2 Explanation of statistical concepts
	3 Evaluation of their own answer
	4 Comprehension judgment (post)

Figure 9.1 shows an example of an explanation in which a student could write the definition for each item, but he could not write examples, so he marked his own answer 0.5. The reflection activities lasted 10–15 minutes for each class.

TABLE 9.2 Topics of class and explanation task items

		Topics of class	*Explanation task items*
Pre-phase	2	Level of measurement	
	3	Representative value	
	4	Statistical dispersion	
	5	Standardization	
	6	Short exam	
Intervention phase I	7	Scatter plot	(1) scatter plot, (2) correlation
	8	Correlation	(1) covariance, (2) correlation coefficient
	9	Nature of correlation	(1) spurious relationship, (2) causal relationship
	10	Short exam	
Intervention phase II	11	Association	(1) cross tabulation, (2) phi coefficient
	12	Regression	(1) regression coefficient, (2) residual
	13	Reliability, validity	(1) reliability, (2) convergent evidence
	14	Final exam	

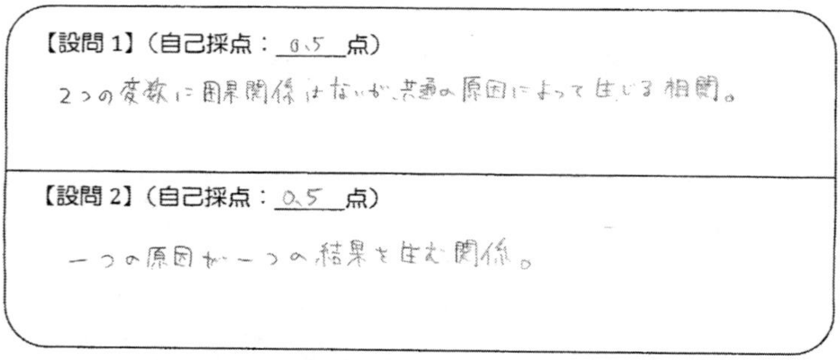

【設問1】（自己採点： 0.5 点）
2つの変数に因果関係はないが、共通の原因によって生じる相関。

【設問2】（自己採点： 0.5 点）
一つの原因から一つの結果を生む関係。

【Item 1】 (Self-rating: 0.5 points)

Spurious relationship is a correlation caused by a common cause, in which two variables are not in cause-and-effect relationship.

【Item 2】 (Self-rating: 0.5 points)

Causal relationship refers to the relationship that a cause produces an effect.

FIGURE 9.1 Example of a student's explanations in the ninth week.

The upper one in original version. The lower one in translated version.

Measures

Illusion of knowing (Pre- and Post-intervention): The index of illusion of knowing was tabulated as the difference between the participants' comprehension judgment and their explanation task performance. Participants rated their comprehension twice, both before and after explanation, so that the pre-intervention illusion of knowing was calculated based on their first comprehension judgment, whereas the post-intervention illusion of knowing was based on their second judgment. Both judgment and performance scores were converted to a percentage. Therefore, a positive score on illusion of knowing represented students' overestimation of their comprehension.

Learning strategies (elaboration and organization): Learning strategies (elaboration and organization) were measured using scales from the MSLQ (Pintrich et al., 1993). The use of learning strategies was assessed at two points in time: first, at pre-phase during the fourth week and, second, at intervention phase during the 13th week. Students were asked, "*When you prepare and review the contents of this class, to what extent do you practice the following behaviors?*" They responded on a 7-point scale to the questionnaire items, which consisted of six items of elaboration (e.g., "I try to understand the materials in this class by making connections between the readings and the concepts from the lectures") and four items of organization (e.g., "I make simple charts, diagrams, and tables to help me organize course material"). The reliability of both scales was estimated by using the data measured during the pre-intervention phase. Both scales showed acceptable levels of reliability as measured by Cronbach's alpha ($\alpha = .73$ for elaboration and $\alpha = .67$ for organization).

Results

This study tested the following hypotheses:

(1) The scores of illusion of knowing would decrease through the explanation and self-evaluation tasks in intervention phases I and II.
(2) The use of learning strategies (elaboration and organization) would increase from the pre-intervention phase to the intervention phase.
(3) Awareness of the illusion of knowing (the amount of decrease in comprehension rating through explanation and self-evaluation tasks) would be positively related to increase in use of learning strategies.

We also conducted an additional analysis because of a reason explained later.

Effect of explanation and self-evaluation on the illusion of knowing

Descriptive statistics for the variables are shown in Table 9.3. To examine the effect of explanation and self-evaluation on the illusion of knowing, within-subjects *t* tests were conducted for each intervention phase. In both intervention phases, the

TABLE 9.3 Summary of means and standard errors for the variables

	Pre-phase	Intervention phase I	Intervention phase II
Comprehension judgment (pre)	63% (1%)	61% (1%)	58% (1%)
Explanation task performance		45% (2%)	66% (2%)
Self-grading		50% (3%)	59% (2%)
Illusion of knowing (pre)		16% (2%)	-8% (2%)
Illusion of knowing (post)		6% (2%)	-13% (2%)

The values in parentheses pertain to the respective *standard errors*.

illusion of knowing significantly decreased from pre to post (t (66) = −6.70, p < .001 in intervention phase I; t (66) = −3.15, p < .001 in intervention phase II). These results support the hypothesis about the intervention effect on metacognitive monitoring. We also confirmed that correlations between students' self-grading and actual test performance were significant both in intervention phase I (r = .52, p < .01) and phase II (r = .57, p < .01), which provides an explanation for why the students could gauge their actual state of understanding. However, as given in Table 9.3, the score in intervention phase II showed that underestimation of comprehension emerged at the first comprehension rating (−8%) and became stronger through the explanation and self-evaluation tasks (−13%). The presumed mechanisms of the effects are addressed in the discussion section.

Change in use of learning strategies from pre-phase to intervention phase

For the second hypothesis, the gain in learning strategies score from pre- to intervention phase was assessed via within-subjects t tests. Contrary to our hypothesis, no significant effect on elaboration was found (t (66) = 1.05, *n.s.*). On the other hand, organization significantly increased from pre- to post-phase (t (66) = 3.35, p < .01; see Figure 9.2). In partial support of the hypothesis, this result suggests that requiring students to explain and self-evaluate statistical concepts boosts the use of organization strategy. Because students did not use elaboration more frequently after intervention, additional analysis was conducted (see below, under "Additional analysis …").

Relationship between awareness of one's own illusion of knowing and increase of learning strategy use

As explained in the previous section, our results showed that (1) explaining and self-evaluating statistical concepts made participants better aware of their own

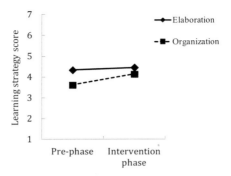

FIGURE 9.2 Use of learning strategies in pre–phase and intervention phase.

Note: Error bar refers to 95% *CI*.

illusion of knowing and (2) the use of organization strategy increased from pre- to intervention phase. To further explore the relationship between decreased illusion of knowing and increased use of learning strategy, we analyzed whether awareness of the illusion of knowing (calculated as the difference between comprehension judgments before and after the intervention) predicted the amount of change in use of organization strategy from pre- phase to intervention phase.

Multiple regression analysis was performed with awareness of illusion of know-ing in intervention phases I and II as independent variables and the amount of change in organization strategy use as the dependent variable. The results showed that awareness of illusion of knowing in intervention phase I significantly pre-dicted the increase in organization strategy use ($b* = .29$, $t = 2.09$, $p = .04$). On the other hand, awareness of illusion of knowing in intervention phase II did not significantly predict the change in organization strategy use ($b* = -.08$, $t = -0.57$, $p = n.s.$). Thus, a direct link between realizing one's own illusion of knowing and the use of learning strategies was proven.

Additional analysis on the use of elaboration strategy in explanation and homework tasks

We assumed that evaluation criteria were helpful for instructing participants that both definition and example are important for effectively studying statistical con-cepts (i.e., elaboration is a useful strategy for learning concepts). Previous analysis, however, indicated that students' use of elaboration strategy did not increase after intervention. One reason this hypothesis may not have been supported was because the questionnaire items may have been too vague to detect the target changes in study behavior. In other words, the MSLQ elaboration items (e.g., I try to understand the materials in this class by making connections between the readings and the concepts from the lectures) do not appear to specifically deal with elaboration of concepts with the use of definition and examples. Thus, the intervention effect should be examined using a different index. Hence whether students' descriptions in explanation and homework changed after the intervention began was additionally analyzed.

First, we investigated the number of times students wrote definitions and examples of statistical concepts in the explanation task of the intervention phases. In each intervention phase, students could write definitions and examples for three statistical concepts: *correlation*, *spurious relationship*, and *causal relationship* in intervention phase I; and *cross tabulation*, *reliability*, and *convergent evidence* in intervention phase II. Students' explanations were coded as 0 (nonexistent) or 1 (existent) for each definition and example, separately, and the ratios of generating definitions and examples between the two intervention phases were compared.

If the intervention gradually enabled students to write definitions and examples, there would be a difference in ratios of students who generated definitions and examples between the intervention phases. The results of McNemar's test showed that a significant difference existed in ratios in example descriptions between the two phases ($p < .001$); however, no significant effect was found for definition descriptions (see Table 9.4). Although we expected the changes in both definition and example descriptions, the results showed that students had already paid attention to definitions in intervention phase I. On the other hand, students did not at first generate examples when explaining the statistical concepts, but they became able to construct examples in intervention phase II, perhaps because they recognized their own insufficient explanations.

In addition, because the task of explaining statistical concepts was also offered in voluntary homework, the change in descriptions of these items was analyzed. Specifically, we used data from four weeks (7th and 9th in intervention phase I; 11th and 13th in intervention phase II), in which students could write definitions and examples for the following concepts: *correlation*, *spurious relationship*, and *causal relationship* in intervention phase I; and *cross tabulation*, *validity*, *reliability*, and *convergent evidence* in intervention phase II. Although the homework in the second week also included an explanation task for statistical concepts (i.e., four levels of measurement), we excluded these data because during the class, all students generated examples for each level such as nominal scale and ordinal scale. Submitting homework was optional, and to obtain reliable data on their explanations, only students who submitted the homework at least twice in four weeks were included in the analysis. Fifty-seven students met this condition.

The written explanations in the homework were analyzed similarly to the explanations for the in-class explanation task. A McNemar's test showed that the ratios of students who generated definitions and examples did not increase in either

TABLE 9.4 Students' ratios of generating definitions and examples in explanation tasks ($n = 67$)

	Definition	Example
Intervention phase I	75%	13%
Intervention phase II	83%	52%

TABLE 9.5 Students' ratios for generating definitions and examples in homework ($n = 57$)

	Definition	Example
Intervention phase I	98%	27%
Intervention phase II	98%	36%

phase (*n.s.*), because almost all students wrote definitions (98% in both phases; see Table 9.5). On the other hand, the ratios of students who wrote examples did increase from 27% to 36%, although the increase did not reach statistical significance.

Discussion

The theory of metacognition has stimulated many educational attempts at improving student learning behaviors. Note, however, that lots of application studies aimed at promoting metacognition have focused on online metacognition, which refers to the metacognitive functions when leaners engage in specific tasks at hand (e.g., Palincsar & Brown, 1984). However, Fukaya (2013) demonstrated that even if students engaged actively in online metacognition, they could not judge their own understanding after reading texts; that is, improving online-monitoring does not guarantee the improvement of offline-monitoring. That is why this study focused on offline metacognition, which involves the metacognitive activities after the completion of a learning task. In this study, the illusion of knowing and its potential negative influence on the use of learning strategies was examined.

The first finding was that explanation generation and self-evaluation effectively reduced students' illusion of knowing. Presumably, when participants could not generate explanations of statistical concepts, they realized that they had overestimated their own comprehension, or they could recognize, aided by the evaluation criteria, their lack of content details in the definitions and examples they generate. The results also showed that the use of organization strategy increased from pre-phase to intervention phase. This type of processing is effective for studying statistical concepts because to understand concepts such as *correlation coefficient*, learners also need to understand related concepts like *mean* and *deviation*. Thus, participants began to use more organization strategies.

Finally, the results revealed a direct link between the realization of one's illusion of knowing and the use of organization strategy. In other words, decreased comprehension judgment through explanation generation and self-evaluation positively predicted increased organization strategy use. From these results, we could explain the claim made in prior research that instructing strategic knowledge is not enough for enhancing students' strategic behavior (Brown et al., 1981; Paris et al., 1983). The results suggest that if students overestimate their comprehension and do not recognize a need to change their learning strategies, they do not use effective learning strategies even when teachers have provided instructions on those strategies. Thus, to design an effective intervention for promoting learning strategy use, we must consider how we can promote students' realization of their lack of understanding.

One might point out that our intervention was confounded with time in the course, so that students may become aware of their illusion of knowing over the course of a semester without the explanation and self-evaluation tasks. Although this possibility cannot be dismissed without the use of a control group, prior research has shown that students, especially with low grades, consistently overestimate their own test performance even when they have received objective feedback on their grades (Hacker et al., 2000). Therefore, we believe that the intervention utilizing explanation and self-evaluation tasks must be a critical factor in decreasing students' illusion of knowing.

Previous studies have demonstrated that interventions for metacognitive monitoring enhance not only judgment accuracy, but also test performance (e.g., Nietfeld et al., 2006). Although such findings are important in an educational context, they do not clarify what mechanisms are involved in the effect of their intervention on increased test performance. The findings of the present study provide a possible explanation: that promoting accurate metacognitive monitoring changes students' learning strategy use, which then improves their test performance.

The relationship between metacognitive monitoring and learning strategy use also provides insight for future studies on metacognition. Prior research has explored whether interventions for accurate monitoring enable participants to effectively regulate their study. These prior studies, however, focused only on the quantitative aspect of regulation, namely how long participants studied the materials (Rawson, O'Neil, & Dunlosky, 2011; Thiede, Anderson, & Therriault, 2003), and the qualitative aspect (i.e., the types of strategies used by students) had been neglected. Thus, this study provides a new perspective on the relationship between metacognitive monitoring and metacognitive control. However, we have to note that the findings of this study were based on students' self-report, and thus it would be important in future research to examine in detail how decreasing students' illusion of knowing could influence their regulation of actual strategic behavior – using a more rigid experimental approach.

The present study found that explanation generation and self-evaluation decreased the illusion of knowing. However, in intervention phase II, participants showed underestimation of their comprehension. The finding that the degree of illusion was different between the two phases could possibly be explained by differences in the difficulty levels of learned or explained concepts. According to Schommer and Surber (1986), a hard text produces more illusion of knowing compared to an easy one. Because there were several possible confounding factors between the two phases, we cannot conclude with certainty that the differential difficulty of concepts was the only causal factor, but the fact that there were also differences in the explanation task performance between the two phases support this claim (see Table 9.3). In addition to the differences between the two phases, students underestimated their understanding in intervention phase II. This result suggests that students do not rate their comprehension objectively (e.g., "I rated 4 on comprehension judgment because I was able to explain one of the statistical concepts"), but utilize subjective clues that reflect their understanding, for instance, perceived cognitive difficulties while explaining.

For elaboration strategy, this research did not find a statistically significant increase in the self-report scale, but it did find the effect in a part of the learning behavior index. The failure of the self-report scale in detecting an effect might be attributable to the items measuring elaboration being too abstract to capture learners' use of a specific learning strategy, namely relating abstract definitions of statistical concepts to concrete examples. With the measures based on the actual learning behavior, the ratio of students who wrote both definitions and examples in the explanation task increased. In contrast, in the homework task, the ratio did not increase from intervention phase I to phase II. According to Barnett and Ceci (2002), who conducted systematic reviews of research on transfer, differences in physical contexts (e.g., places in which participants study) and social contexts (e.g., studying with or without others) might have an influence on successful transfer of learning skills. This is one possible reason why transfer of elaboration skills from classroom to home did not occur in this study.

To promote the transfer from classroom to home environment, a more intensive intervention would be needed. For example, on the basis of previous findings (Uesaka, Manalo, & Ichikawa, 2010), it would likely be efficacious to instruct students more explicitly in the utility of learning strategies. As an illustration, when a teacher provides instruction on a statistical concept, she could first explain it only via definition, and then she could add an example to indicate how the example helps students understand the target definition by linking it with students' prior knowledge. As such students would realize the utility of generating examples to understand a difficult concept. Another example of how we could also apply this method would be to show students how organizing the concepts according to their similarities and differences help their comprehension. Hence, further research should be conducted to investigate whether more intensive interventions could promote the transfer of learned skills.

Finally, the question of how we might be able to use metacognitive theory in real classrooms needs to be considered. When applying metacognitive theory to real classroom settings, we must note that promoting accurate monitoring is not sufficient on its own but constitutes only one step for students to become strategic learners; that is, even if students realize their own overestimation of understanding, they are unlikely to change their learning strategies without teachers' or others' guided instruction about effective learning strategies. What is important in applied research is not to bring specific empirical finding to the classrooms, but to use a variety of findings to design effective interventions for improving student learning. As such, it is hoped that, in future studies, effective interventions both for metacognitive monitoring (awareness of the illusion of knowing) and metacognitive control (regulation of ones' own strategic behavior) could successfully be designed.

Note

A modified Japanese version of this chapter was published as Fukaya, T. (2016). Promoting offline-metacognition II (Study 4). In T. Fukaya, *Promoting and nurturing metacognition: The mechanism of and support for conceptual understanding.* Kyoto: Kitaoji Press.

References

Barnett, S. M., & Ceci, S. J. (2002). When and where do we apply what we learn? A taxonomy for far transfer. *Psychological Bulletin, 128*(4), 612–637.

Bol, L., & Hacker, D. J. (2001). A comparison of the effects of practice tests and traditional review on performance and calibration. *The Journal of Experimental Education, 69*(2), 133–151.

Brown, A. L., Campione, J. C., & Day, J. D. (1981). Learning to learn: On training students to learn from texts. *Educational Researcher, 10*(2), 14–21.

Commander, N. E., & Stanwyck, D. J. (1997). Illusion of knowing in adult readers: Effects of reading skill and passage length. *Contemporary Educational Psychology, 22*(1), 39–52.

Corno, L., & Mandinach, E. B. (1983). The role of cognitive engagement in classroom learning and motivation. *Educational Psychologist, 18*(2), 88–108.

Derry, S. J., & Murphy, D. A. (1986). Designing systems that train learning ability: From theory to practice. *Review of Educational Research, 56*(1), 1–39.

Desoete, A., Roeyers, H., & De Clercq, A. (2003). Can offline metacognition enhance mathematical problem solving? *Journal of Educational Psychology, 95*(1), 188–200.

Dinsmore, D. L., & Alexander, P. A. (2012). A critical discussion of deep and surface processing: What it means, how it is measured, the role of context, and model specification. *Educational Psychology Review, 24*(4), 499–567.

Duncan, T. G., & McKeachie, W. J. (2005). The making of the motivated strategies for learning questionnaire. *Educational Psychologist, 40*(2), 117–128.

Dunlosky, J., & Metcalfe, J. (2009). Introduction. In J. Dunlosky & J. Metcalfe (Eds.), *Metacognition* (pp. 1–8). Los Angeles, CA: Sage.

Dunlosky, J., Rawson, K. A., & Middleton, E. L. (2005). What constrains the accuracy of metacomprehension judgments? Testing the transfer-appropriate-monitoring and accessibility hypotheses. *Journal of Memory and Language, 52*(4), 551–565.

Dunning, D., Johnson, K., Ehrlinger, J., & Kruger, J. (2003). Why people fail to recognize their own incompetence. *Current Directions in Psychological Science, 12*(3), 83–87.

Fukaya, T. (2013). Explanation generation, not explanation expectancy, improves metacomprehension accuracy. *Metacognition and Learning, 8*(1), 1–18.

Garner, R. (1990). When children and adults do not use learning strategies: Toward a theory of settings. *Review of Educational Research, 60*(4), 517–529.

Glenberg, A. M., Wilkinson, A. C., & Epstein, W. (1982). The illusion of knowing: Failure in the self-assessment of comprehension. *Memory & Cognition, 10*(6), 597–602.

Graham, J. W. (2009). Missing data analysis: Making it work in the real world. *Annual Review of Psychology, 60*(1), 549–576.

Hacker, D. J., Bol, L., Horgan, D. D., & Rakow, E. A. (2000). Test prediction and performance in a classroom context. *Journal of Educational Psychology, 92*(1), 160–170.

Lipko, A. R., Dunlosky, J., Hartwig, M. K., Rawson, K. A., Swan, K., & Cook, D. (2009). Using standards to improve middle-school students' accuracy at evaluating the quality of their recall. *Journal of Experimental Psychology: Applied, 15*(4), 307–318.

Marton, F., & Säljö, R. (1976). On qualitative differences in learning: I—Outcome and process. *British Journal of Educational Psychology, 46*(1), 4–11.

Murayama, K., Pekrun, R., Lichtenfeld, S., & vom Hofe, R. (2013). Predicting long-term growth in students' mathematics achievement: The unique contributions of motivation and cognitive strategies. *Child Development, 84*(4), 1475–1490.

Nelson, T. O., & Narens, L. (1990). Metamemory: A theoretical framework and new findings. In G. Bower (Ed.), *The psychology of learning and motivation* (Vol. 26, pp. 125–173). New York, NY: Academic Press.

Nietfeld, J. L., Cao, L., & Osborne, J. W. (2005). Metacognitive monitoring accuracy and student performance in the postsecondary classroom. *The Journal of Experimental Education, 74*(1), 7–28.

Nietfeld, J. L., Cao, L., & Osborne, J. W. (2006). The effect of distributed monitoring exercises and feedback on performance, monitoring accuracy, and self-efficacy. *Metacognition and Learning, 1*(2), 159–179.

Palincsar, A. S., & Brown, A. L. (1984). Reciprocal teaching of comprehension-fostering and comprehension-monitoring activities. *Cognition and Instruction, 1*(2), 117–175.

Paris, S. G., Lipson, M. Y., & Wixson, K. K. (1983). Becoming a strategic reader. *Contemporary Educational Psychology, 8*(3), 293–316.

Pintrich, P. R., & De Groot, E. V. (1990). Motivational and self-regulated learning components of classroom academic performance. *Journal of Educational Psychology, 82*(1), 33–40.

Pintrich, P. R., Smith, D. A., García, T., & McKeachie, W. J. (1993). Reliability and predictive validity of the Motivated Strategies for Learning Questionnaire (MSLQ). *Educational and Psychological Measurement, 53*(3), 801–813.

Pressley, M. (1986). The relevance of the good strategy user model to the teaching of mathematics. *Educational Psychologist, 21*(1), 139–161.

Rawson, K. A., O'Neil, R. L., & Dunlosky, J. (2011). Accurate monitoring leads to effective control and greater learning of patient education materials. *Journal of Experimental Psychology: Applied, 17*(3), 288–302.

Schommer, M., & Surber, J. R. (1986). Comprehension-monitoring failure in skilled adult readers. *Journal of Educational Psychology, 78*(5), 353–357.

Schraw, G. (2009). A conceptual analysis of five measures of metacognitive monitoring. *Metacognition and Learning, 4*(1), 33–45.

Thiede, K. W., Anderson, M. C. M., & Therriault, D. (2003). Accuracy of metacognitive monitoring affects learning of texts. *Journal of Educational Psychology, 95*(1), 66–73.

Thiede, K. W., Griffin, T. D., Wiley, J., & Redford, J. S. (2009). Metacognitive monitoring during and after reading. In D. J. Hacker, J. Dunlosky, & A. C. Graesser (Eds.), *Handbook of metacognition in education* (pp. 85–106). New York: Routledge.

Uesaka, Y., Manalo, E., & Ichikawa, S. (2010). The effects of perception of efficacy and diagram construction skills on students' spontaneous use of diagrams when solving math word problems. *Lecture Notes in Artificial Intelligence, 6170*, 197–211.

Veenman, M. V., Van Hout-Wolters, B. H., & Afflerbach, P. (2006). Metacognition and learning: Conceptual and methodological considerations. *Metacognition and Learning, 1*, 3–14.

Weinstein, C. E., & Mayer, R. E. (1986). The teaching of learning strategies. In M. C. Wittrock (Ed.), *Handbook of research on teaching* (pp. 315–327). New York: Macmillan.

Wittrock, M. C. (1989). Generative processes of comprehension. *Educational Psychologist, 24*(4), 345–376.

Zimmerman, B. J., & Martinez-Pons, M. (1990). Student differences in self-regulated learning: Relating grade, sex, and giftedness to self-efficacy and strategy use. *Journal of Educational Psychology, 82*(1), 51–59.

Zimmerman, B. J., & Pons, M. M. (1986). Development of a structured interview for assessing student use of self-regulated learning strategies. *American Educational Research Journal, 23*(4), 614–628.

10

PREPARATORY LEARNING BEHAVIORS FOR ENGLISH AS A SECOND LANGUAGE LEARNING

The effects of teachers' teaching behaviors during classroom lessons

Keita Shinogaya

Introduction

Importance of a preparation for the next classroom lesson

For school students, preparation for the class (i.e., learning the contents of the next class beforehand) is necessary for deeply understanding the contents of the class at school. Research studies about advanced organizers have shown that reading a brief passage about the learning materials beforehand could enhance not only retention of facts contained in the materials but also understanding of the relations between those facts (Ausubel, 1960). Other previous studies have revealed that if students gained knowledge about the contents of the class beforehand, the quality of their note-taking improved and their use of metacognitive strategies (such as *monitoring*) during class increased (Shinogaya, 2008; Titsworth & Kiewra, 2004).

In addition, various learning strategies are likely involved in preparation. Although previous research studies have categorized learning strategies and examined how they influence learners' achievement (Alexander, Graham, & Harris, 1998; Elliot, McGregor, & Gable, 1999), no previous study had examined strategies during preparatory learning. Shinogaya (2010) pointed out this problem and developed a questionnaire about preparation strategies in learning English as a foreign language. Four strategies are included in the questionnaire: looking up (e.g., I look up unknown words in the English text), conjecturing (e.g., I guess the meanings of unknown words without using a dictionary), reviewing previous texts (e.g., I review my notebook when I prepare for the next class), and help-seeking (e.g., I ask a family member the meaning of unknown words). Shinogaya also examined the relationships between preparation strategies and strategy use during classroom lessons and found that students who looked up unknown words beforehand could pay better attention to important information and took notes more smoothly during the class.

Effects of school teachers on students' learning

Although preparation is an important activity promoting deep processing during class, school students often do not spontaneously prepare for upcoming classes (Shimizu, 2005). To improve students' learning, it is necessary to reveal the effects of what and how school teachers teach in daily classroom lessons on the frequency and quality of preparation that their students undertake. Previous research studies have revealed that the classroom goal structure that the teacher sets affects students' learning behaviors. Classroom goal structure pertains to the type of goal that is focused on in the classroom. According to previous research studies, there are two types of goal structures: mastery goal structure and performance goal structure. If teachers place importance on the learning process or students' learning progress in their classroom, the classroom is said to have a "mastery goal structure." On the other hand, if teachers focus not on process but learning outcomes or relative ability, the classroom is said to have a "performance goal structure" (Lyke & Young, 2006).

Nolen and Haladyna (1990) indicated that perception of mastery goal structure positively affects students' beliefs about effective learning strategies (such as elaboration and organization). Wolters (2004) also showed that mastery goal structure positively relates to cognitive and metacognitive strategy use. In contrast, students' perceptions of performance structure has no significant relation to their learning strategies use (Lyke & Young, 2006; Nolen & Haladyna, 1990; Wolters, 2004). These findings suggest that students can perceive teachers' goals and regulate their use of learning strategies accordingly.

Purpose of this chapter

As mentioned above, previous research studies about classroom goal structures have revealed that school teachers' goals affect their students' learning behaviors. But teachers' goals or classroom goal structures are not behavioral but cognitive variables. Thus, it is likely to be difficult for school teachers to clearly understand how to change their teaching behaviors based on the findings reported from such studies. Of course, there are some studies that have focused on teachers' teaching behaviors, but these studies examined the effects of how teachers teach school subjects on students' motivation and behaviors in the classroom (e.g., Tsai, 2000; Vansteenkiste, Simons, Lens, Sheldon, & Deci, 2004). The present author is aware of no previous research study that has attempted to connect teachers' teaching behaviors in classrooms and their students' learning behaviors at home. The purpose of this chapter is to reveal the effect, and the related processes, of teachers' teaching behaviors on the frequency and quality of students' preparation.

Study 1

Introduction and purpose of this study

Study 1 examined the effect of teachers' teaching behaviors on students' frequency of preparation. In this study, direct instruction of preparation and teaching style in classroom lessons were focused on as teaching behaviors. In addition, this study also measured students' perceptions about preparation. Previous research studies have shown that perceived utility about a strategy positively relates to spontaneous use of that strategy, and perceived cost negatively relates to such use. In other words, the more students think a strategy is useful for their own learning, the more they use it spontaneously, and the more students think a strategy is difficult to use, the less they use the strategy (e.g., Murayama, 2003; Sato, 1998).

Previous research studies about teachers' goals or classroom goal structures (e.g., Nolen & Haladyna, 1990) suggest that students can perceive needed learning behaviors from teachers' teaching behaviors. But there is no previous study that examined the relation between teachers' teaching behaviors and students' perceptions about learning behaviors. This study measured teachers' teaching behaviors, students' perceptions about preparation, and students' preparatory learning behaviors and then built a relation model with structural equation modeling. According to Nolen and Haladyna (1990), students' perceptions can mediate effects of teachers' teaching behaviors on students' preparatory learning. For example, if teachers deal more with difficult contents that cannot be understood without any prior knowledge, students might perceive the utility of preparation and prepare for the next class spontaneously.

Method

Participants

The participants in this study were 632 eighth-grade students in one public high school in Japan (age range, 16–17 years). Prior to the conduct of the study, the necessary participation permissions and agreements were sought and obtained. Questionnaires were sent to the school and administered in the English class. Students needed about 10 minutes to complete the questionnaire. The questionnaire was administered in April (the first month of the academic year), and students responded in the questionnaire about their learning and their teachers' teaching behaviors in the previous year.

Measures

Students' cognition and learning behaviors

Undertaking of preparation was measured with one item ("I always prepared for the next classroom lesson"). Murayama (2003) and Sato (1998) asked participants about the utility and cost of various learning strategies. In the present study, items about perceived utility and cost of "preparation" instead of "learning strategies" were created by making minor wording modifications to questionnaire items from these previous studies. Perceived utility was gauged with the use of five items (e.g., "If I undertake preparation, I can understand the class well"). To measure perceived costs of preparation, three items were used (e.g., "To prepare for the next class every time is hard for me"). Students were instructed to respond to these items on a five-point Likert-type scale (1 = *not at all true of me*; 2 = *not very true of me*; 3 = *difficult to decide either way*; 4 = *a little true of me*; 5 = *very true of me*) in consideration of their English learning.

Teachers' teaching behaviors

Items about teachers' teaching behaviors were collected in a pilot study in which teachers ($N = 26$) answered questions about the methods they used to motivate students to prepare for the class. Two graduate students who were majoring in educational psychology checked the content validity of and then categorized the teachers' responses. Based on this analysis, two factors were identified and seven items were made to measure teachers' teaching behaviors in the questionnaire for students. One factor was direct instruction about preparation and it was measured by three items (e.g., "My teacher teaches how to prepare for the next class"). The other factor was a teaching style requiring deep understanding and was measured by four items (e.g., "My teacher teaches higher level knowledge," "My teacher asks students to explain their way of thinking"). Students responded to these items on a five-point Likert-type scale which was the same as the one described previously.

Results

Table 10.1 contains the means and standard deviations for the items used in Study 1. As mentioned before, it was assumed that teachers' teaching behaviors affect students' perception about preparation and then influence students' preparation. As a first step, we generated and tested a model assuming that perceived utility and cost about preparation mediate the relationships between two teaching behaviors and students' conduct of preparation. Secondly, paths that increased model fit were added to the model. Figure 10.1 is the model that was finally adopted. It contains teachers' teaching behaviors, students' perceived utility and cost of strategy, and students' conduct of preparation. To simplify the figure, all errors have been excluded. This study assumed perceived utility and cost of preparation as mediating variables. The model showed a good fit to the data (GFI = .948, AGFI = .925, CFI = .903, RMSEA = .060). Teachers' direct instruction of preparation positively affected students' undertaking of preparation ($\beta = .236$) and negatively predicted their perceived cost of preparation ($\beta = -.200$). In addition, teachers' teaching style requesting deep understanding positively influenced both perceived utility of preparation ($\beta = .467$) and perceived cost of preparation ($\beta = .350$). Furthermore, perceived utility positively affected students' preparation ($\beta = .114$), while perceived cost showed a negative influence on it ($\beta = -.172$).

Discussion

In the final model, teachers' direct instruction of preparation positively affected students' administration of preparation. In other words, the more teachers show their students the importance of preparation, the more students prepare for the

TABLE 10.1 Study 1: Means and standard deviations

	Mean	SD
Frequency of preparation	3.30	1.28
Perceived utility about preparation (four items)		
PU1: Preparation is useful for learning	3.96	1.05
PU2: Preparation is necessary to get good marks	4.07	1.05
PU3: If I undertake preparation, I can understand the class well	4.30	0.91
PU4: If I undertake preparation, I can keep up with the lesson	4.25	0.97
Perceived cost about preparation (three items)		
PC1: I think preparation is difficult	4.29	0.99
PC2: To prepare for the next class every time is hard for me	3.92	1.04
PC3: It is hard for me to get time for preparation	3.78	1.15
Teachers' teaching behaviors		
Direct instruction of preparation (three items)		
DI1: My teacher teaches about the importance of preparation	3.18	1.32
DI2: My teacher evaluates students' preparation	2.33	1.38
DI3: My teacher teaches how to prepare for the next class	3.60	1.24
Teaching style requiring deep understanding (four items)		
TS1: My teacher teaches higher-level knowledge	3.22	1.12
TS2: My teacher asks students to explain their way of thinking	3.63	1.30
TS3: My teacher asks students if they have any questions	3.41	1.18
TS4: My teacher asks students to reflect on their understanding at the end of the class	2.74	1.33

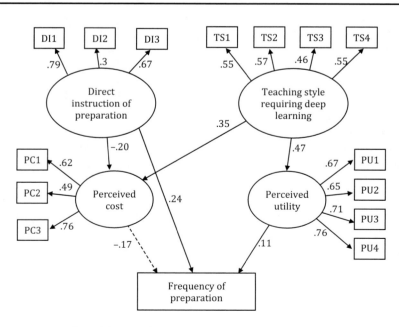

FIGURE 10.1 Final model in Study 1.

Note: T value for all paths are significant at $p < .05$.

next class. This result is not of major importance in this study because 'spontaneous' strategy use is not involved in the process: instead, it indicates that students do what their teachers ask them to do. However, this finding shows that teachers' teaching behaviors affect students' perception of preparation behaviors. Direct instruction of preparation showed a negative influence on students' perceived cost. This finding suggests that if teachers teach students how to prepare for the next class or how important preparation is, students' perceived cost decreases. Second, teachers' teaching style requiring deep understanding showed a positive influence on perceived utility and a negative influence on perceived cost of preparation.

As the model shows, perceived utility has a positive influence on the conduct of preparation. In contrast, perceived cost has a negative effect on it. These results are consistent with previous research studies that have examined the effects of students' cognition on their spontaneous strategy use (e.g., Murayama, 2003; Nolen, 1988; Sato, 1998). Thus, the results of this study suggest that teachers' teaching behaviors indirectly affects students' spontaneous preparation behaviors.

Questions that arose from Study 1

Although this study revealed teachers' teaching behaviors affect students' preparation, three problems were identified. First, Study 1 focused not on quality but frequency of students' preparation. In other words, Study 1 was not able to examine individual differences in the kinds of strategies students used during preparation. However, understanding those qualitative differences in strategy use during preparation is important toward appraising the value of the effects of the teaching behaviors examined.

Second, teachers' teaching style in this study was not sufficiently concrete and detailed. In other words, the factor "teaching style requiring deep understanding" was unclear about what and how teachers should teach in an English class. Thus, more detailed aspects of teachers' strategies of teaching English in classroom lessons needed to be measured.

Finally, students responded to items about teachers' teaching behaviors in this study. If students respond to both items about teachers' behaviors and items about their own (students') behaviors, high correlations between them could be easily found because of response bias (Murayama & Elliot, 2009). To overcome this technical problem, in the next study English teachers also responded to the questionnaire about their teaching behaviors.

Study 2

Introduction and purpose of this study

The purpose of Study 2 was to examine the effects of teachers' teaching strategies on students' learning strategies during preparation. Unlike Study 1, both students and their English teachers responded to the questionnaires in this study. Thus, the data of Study 2 had a hierarchical structure and hierarchical linear modeling (HLM) was used (Raudenbush & Bryk, 2002) for analysis.

In addition, this study also measured students' learning motives. Learning motives are reason why students learn. Horino and Ichikawa (1997) found two factors in the reasons Japanese high school students study English. One was "content-attached motive", and the other was "content-detached motive". The former motive is that students learn English with intrinsic reason (e.g., "Because to learn English is interesting"). On the other hand, content-detached motive is that students do not perceive intrinsic value in learning English, but they learn English with more extrinsic reasons (e.g., "Because I would like to be praised by my teacher and parents"). According to Horino and Ichikawa, content-attached motive positively influence the use of various cognitive strategies such as elaboration, organization, and rehearsal. Furthermore, other previous studies have revealed that students who learn with intrinsic reasons make greater use of self-regulated learning strategies such as elaboration, organization, and metacognition (e.g, Bonney, Cortina, Smith-Darden, & Fiori, 2008; Elliot, et al., 1999; Tabachnick, Miller, & Relyea, 2008).

These findings from previous research suggest that students' content-attached motive can positively influence their spontaneous strategy use during preparation. If teachers teach how to prepare for the next class or teach contents that require various preparation strategies, these teaching behaviors can increase preparatory behaviors of students with low content-attached motive. This assumption is based on the finding that students with high content-attached motive spontaneously use various strategies during preparation.

Method

Participants

The participants were 985 students from six high schools (23 classrooms) in Japan. However, as explained later, data from only 646 students were analyzed and reported here. Questionnaires were sent to each school and administered in the English class. Prior to the conduct of the study, the necessary participation permissions and agreements were sought and obtained. Not only students but also their English teachers ($N = 15$) responded to questionnaires. Students needed about 10 minutes, and teachers needed about 5 minutes, to complete the questionnaires.

Measures

Students' variables

The questionnaire for students consisted of items about learning motives and strategies in preparation. In more detail, the items are described below.

Learning motives for English   English learning motives were measured with items which were the same as in Horino and Ichikawa (1997). Five items were used for each factor, content-attached motive (e.g., "Because to learn English is interesting", "Because learning English is useful for my job in the future") and content-detached motive (e.g., "Because I would like to be praised by my teacher and parents", "Because I don't want to be scolded by my teacher and parents"). Students responded to these items on the same 5-point Likert-type scale previously described.

Learning strategies during preparation   Fifteen items from Shinogaya (2010) were used to measure students' strategies during preparation. As mentioned earlier, Shinogaya found four strategy factors in preparation for learning English as a foreign language: "looking up", "conjecturing" "reviewing previous texts", and "help seeking". Four items (e.g., "I look up unknown words in the English text") were used to measure students' use of look-up strategy, and four items (e.g., "I guess the meanings of unknown words without using a dictionary") were used to measure students' use of conjecturing strategy. Four items (e.g., "I review my notebook when I prepare for the next class") for reviewing previous texts and three items for help seeking (e.g., "I ask my family member the meaning of unknown words") were used. Students responded to these items on the same five-point Likert-type scale.

Teachers' variables

The questionnaire for English teachers consisted of 26 items about their teaching behaviors.

Direct instruction of preparation strategies   Teachers' direct instruction of preparation strategies was measured with the same 15 items as those used in the students' preparation strategies. Teachers were asked to rate the extent to which they urge their students to use each strategy during preparation on a five-point Likert-type scale which was the same as that previously described.

Teaching strategies in classroom lesson   Teachers' teaching strategies were measured using 11 items from Shinogaya (2014). In that study, four factors were found: "macro-structure approach", "micro-structure approach", "own question answering approach", and "listening approach." The macro-structure approach is explaining the structure of English texts. Three items (e.g., "I teach macro-structure of English text in the class") were used. The micro-structure approach is a teaching style focusing in detail on specific words and/or sentences. Three items (e.g., "I explain the origin of meanings of each English word") were used. The own question answering approach is to ask students to answer how to translate words or sentences in the English text during class. Three items (e.g., "I ask students to explain how they translate some sentences in the text") were used. The listening approach is to put importance on listening activities when they teach English texts. Two items ("I read the text to my students" and "I play CDs that read out the text") were used. They rated the items using the same five-point Likert-type scale.

Results

If students who learn not only at high school but also at cram school are included in the data, learning at cram school can function like preparation for the class at high school even if they report that they do not use any strategies during preparation. As it was not possible to control for this possibility in Study 1, in Study 2 data from students who reported that they also studied English at cram school were excluded from analyses. Therefore, the data of only 646 students were used in the analysis. However, the data of all teachers ($N = 15$) were used.

In Table 10.2, ω coefficients, and means and standard deviations for students' learning motives and preparation strategies are displayed. ω coefficients that are greater than 0.7 indicate adequate internal validity of items. All students' variables showed adequate reliability coefficients. The means and standard deviations for teachers' variables are displayed in Table 10.3.

TABLE 10.2 Means and standard deviations of students' variables

	ω	Mean	SD
Learning motives			
Content-attached motive	.86	3.80	0.83
Content-detached motive	.82	2.48	0.89
Preparation strategies			
Look up	.80	3.65	0.89
Conjecturing	.76	3.23	0.85
Reviewing previous notes	.70	2.85	0.90
Help-seeking	.84	3.06	1.00
$N = 646$			

TABLE 10.3 Means and standard deviations of teachers' variables

	Mean	SD
Instruction of preparation strategies		
Look up	3.32	1.05
Conjecturing	3.33	0.86
Reviewing previous notes	2.33	0.76
Help seeking	3.08	0.51
Teaching strategies in classroom lesson		
Macro-structure approach	3.95	0.55
Micro-structure approach	3.33	0.47
Own question answering approach	3.67	0.79
Listening activity	4.00	0.97
$N = 15$		

Interclass correlation coefficients (ICC)

The data of this study consisted of students' variables and their teachers' variables. Thus, the data structure represents students who are nested within a higher organizational unit (their teacher). According to previous studies, ignoring a hierarchical data structure in analysis leads to large estimation errors even if the ICC score seems as small as 0.01 (e.g., Kreft & De Leeuw, 1998). ICC was computed using τ_{00} (variance between classes) and σ^2 (variance within the classes) with equation (1).

$$ICC = \frac{\tau_{00}}{\tau_{00} + \sigma^2} \tag{1}$$

ICC scores for all dependent variables in this study were over 0.01. According to Barcikowski (1981), the risk ratio of statistical tests increases if the ICC score is over 0.01. HLM (Raudenbush & Bryk, 2002) is a sophisticated technique that can deal with such data. So this study conducted HLM in further analyses.

Level 1 model without teachers' variables

First, a model that did not contain teachers' variables at level 2 was conducted. The model is as shown below. In this model, all significance levels were set at .05. Variables used as predictors were selected by multiple regression analyses (step-wise method). For example, when each student's score of look-up strategy is a dependent variable, the regression model is as shown below.

$$Y_{ij} = \beta_{0j} + \beta_{1j} X_{1ij} + r_{ij} \quad r_{ij} \sim N(0, \sigma^2) \tag{2}$$

$$\beta_{0j} = \gamma_{00} + u_{0j} \tag{3}$$

$$\beta_{1j} = \gamma_{10} + u_{1j} \tag{4}$$

$$\begin{bmatrix} u_{0j} \\ u_{1j} \end{bmatrix} \sim N \left[\begin{pmatrix} 0 \\ 0 \end{pmatrix}, \begin{pmatrix} \tau_{00} & \tau_{01} \\ \tau_{10} & \tau_{11} \end{pmatrix} \right] \tag{5}$$

Y_{ij} is the score in look up strategy of student i whose teacher is j and X_{1ij} is the student's score of content-attached motive. β_{0j} is an intercept and β_{1j} is the slope parameter that shows the influence of content-attached motive. γ_{ij} is a randomly distributed personal effect. On the model of level 2, β_{0j} and β_{1j} are predicted as a sum of grand means (γ_{00} and γ_{10}) and random effects with each teacher (u_{0j} and u_{1j}). Equation (5) means that u_{0j} and u_{1j} are normally distributed and their variance components are shown as τ_{00} and τ_{11}.

When each student's score of look up strategy was set as a, dependent variable, the variance component associated with the intercept and slope parameter of content-attached motive (the value of τ_{00} and τ_{11}) were significant. Furthermore, variance of intercept and coefficient of content-attached motive were significant when conjecturing and reviewing notes were dependent variables. Furthermore, when help-seeking was used as a dependent variable, the intercept and coefficient of both motives were significant. These results suggest that teachers differed in how their students prepared for the next class and in the kinds of relationship between their students' content-attached motive and their strategy use. In further analyses below, the aspects of teachers' teaching behaviors that give rise to such differences were examined.

Level 2 model with teachers' variables

Multilevel models were developed to assess between-teacher differences in students' score of preparation strategies and relations among students' variables. Teachers' direct instruction of each preparation strategy and the four types of teaching strategies in classroom lesson were used as predictors in level 2 models. The equations in the level 2 model were as shown below.

$$\beta_{0j} = \gamma_{00} + \gamma_{01}W_{1j} + \gamma_{02}W_{2j} + \gamma_{03}W_{3j} + \gamma_{04}W_{4j} + \gamma_{05}W_{5j} + u_{0j} \tag{6}$$

$$\beta_{1j} = \gamma_{10} + \gamma_{11}W_{1j} + \gamma_{12}W_{2j} + \gamma_{13}W_{3j} + \gamma_{14}W_{4j} + \gamma_{15}W_{5j} + u_{1j} \tag{7}$$

$$\begin{bmatrix} u_{0j} \\ u_{1j} \end{bmatrix} \sim N \left[\begin{pmatrix} 0 \\ 0 \end{pmatrix}, \begin{pmatrix} \tau_{00} & \tau_{01} \\ \tau_{10} & \tau_{11} \end{pmatrix} \right] \tag{8}$$

Equations (6) and (7) are different from the model without teachers' variables. In this model, the intercept and slope parameter of level 1 regression were predicted by teachers' variable. For example, when look up strategy is the dependent variable, W_{1j} is direct instruction of the look up strategy and $W_{2j}, W_{3j}, W_{4j}, W_{5j}$ means teachers' score in use of the macro-structure approach, the micro-structure approach, the own question answering approach, and the listening approach, respectively. Equation 8 means that the residual component of equation (6) and (7) are normally distributed and their variance components are shown as τ_{00} and τ_{11}.

Equation 8 means that the residual components of equations (6) and (7) are normally distributed and their variance components are shown as τ_{00} and τ_{11}.

Effect of teachers' teaching behaviors on students' preparation strategies
The results indicate that teachers' macro-structure approach γ_{02} (−.219, $p < .01$), micro-structure approach γ_{03} (.257, $p < .05$), and own question answering approach γ_{04} (.229, $p < .05$) had significant influences on the intercept of the look-up strategy. This results suggest that students whose teachers explained the macro-structure of English text did not use the look-up strategy (after controlling for the influences of other variables). As teachers explained the origins of English words and made students answer their own translation, students increased their use of the look-up strategy. The analysis also showed that the score of teachers' own question answering approach positively related to the students' help-seeking score γ_{04} (.353, $p < .05$).

Interaction between teachers' teaching behaviors and students' variables The results revealed that there were some cross-level interactions between teachers' variables and students' variables. As shown in Table 10.4, teachers' teaching strategies significantly influenced the slope of students' learning motive. When students' look-up strategy was used as a dependent variable, teachers' direct instruction of the strategy $\gamma_{11}(-.102, p < .05)$ and own question answering approach γ_{13} (.177, $p < .05$) affected the slope of the students' content-attached motive. For example, as shown Figure 10.2, the relationships between content-attached motive and look-up strategy were different because of teachers' direct instruction of the strategy. This figure suggests that teachers' direct instruction of the strategy was effective for students whose content-attached motive scores were low. In the same way, Table 10.4 shows that as the teachers' score in own question answering approach increased, the slope of the content-attached motive on look-up strategy also increased.

TABLE 10.4 Results of the model showing teachers' variables

	Look up		Conjecturing		Reviewing notes		Help-seeking	
	Estimation	SE	Estimation	SE	Estimation	SE	Estimation	SE
Intercept								
Mean γ_{00}	3.666**	0.029	3.248**	0.028	2.854**	0.043	2.992**	0.125
DIS γ_{01}	0.038	0.033	−0.011	0.034	−0.161	0.113	0.026	0.334
Macro γ_{02}	−0.218**	0.055	0.031	0.077	0.124	0.114	−0.008	0.282
Micro γ_{03}	0.257*	0.084	0.208	0.105	0.200	0.133	0.195	0.353
OQA γ_{04}	0.229**	0.058	0.098	0.063	0.067	0.076	0.353**	0.247
LA γ_{05}	−0.015	0.026	0.034	0.017	0.045	0.050	−0.204	0.239
Slope of CAM								
Mean γ_{10}	0.402**	0.037	0.359**	0.043	0.386**	0.051	0.210**	0.071
DIS γ_{11}	−0.102*	0.041	0.040	0.054	−0.110	0.143	−0.103	0.182
Macro γ_{12}	0.035	0.067	0.085	0.112	0.150	0.104	0.049	0.157
Micro γ_{13}	0.210	0.096	−0.133	0.099	−0.018	0.137	0.045	0.199
OQA γ_{14}	0.177*	0.071	0.063	0.053	0.019	0.055	0.057	0.143
LA γ_{15}	−0.044	0.044	−0.074	0.047	−0.049	0.063	−0.048	0.136
Slope of CDM								
Mean γ_{20}							0.115	0.050
DIS γ_{21}							0.061	0.125
Macro γ_{22}							−0.172	0.117
Micro γ_{23}							0.111	0.140
OQA γ_{24}							−0.034	0.099
LA γ_{25}							0.075	0.095

*$p < .05$; **$p < .01$

DIS = direct instruction strategy, Macro = macro-structure approach, Micro = micro-structure approach, OQA = own question answering approach, LA = listening activity

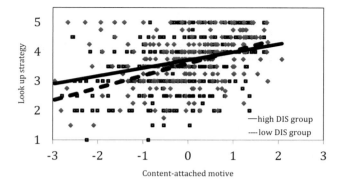

FIGURE 10.2 Relations between content-attached motive and look-up strategy.

Discussion

In Study 2, students' preparation strategies and teachers' teaching strategies were measured. The results of HLM analysis suggest that the more teachers explain the macro-structure of English texts in their class, the less students use the look-up strategy. The look-up strategy is used to find out the meanings of unknown words and sentences with the use of a dictionary; so it is not a strategy focusing on the macro-structure of English texts. So, as teachers' macro-structure approach increases, students' perception of the need to look up unknown words decreases and their score in use of the look-up strategy during their preparation decreases.

On the other hand, the results indicate that teachers' micro-structure approach positively relates to students' look-up strategy. This finding means that the more teachers explain the origin of each word's meaning, the more students examine the meanings of unknown words and sentences with a dictionary beforehand. It can be said that the micro-structure approach "tells" students that understanding the meanings of each word is important. This finding also suggests that if teachers often make students explain the meanings of English sentences, students have to prepare the "right answer" or "good translations" beforehand, which in turn increases their help-seeking behavior.

These results suggest that students perceive what is needed for preparatory behaviors from what and how their teachers teach in the classroom, and that students adopt their preparation strategies to fit to the class.

HLM analysis also showed an interesting cross-level interaction. As shown in Table 10.4, content-attached motive positively influenced a spontaneous use of various strategies, and teachers' direct instruction of look-up strategy influenced students with low content-attached motive (Figure 10.2). Looking up unknown words is easy for students to perform; so it can be said that the effect of direct instruction was found only in the look-up strategy.

The results further revealed that as teachers use the own question answering approach, the strength of the relationship between content-attached motive and look-up strategy increased. This finding suggests that teachers' own question answering approach increased content-attached students' strategy use. This finding is opposite to the prediction of this study and may be explainable in terms of students' self-regulated learning skills. According to previous research studies, students perceiving high value in learning tend to also possess higher self-regulation skills (e.g., Pintrich, 1999; Pokay & Blumenfeld, 1990). Thus, students with high content-attached motive perceive what is needed during preparation and "regulate" their preparation strategy accordingly. Thus, it can be said that direct instruction of how to prepare for the next class is effective especially for students whose motivation for learning is low.

General discussion

Summary of findings from the two studies in this chapter

Study 1 built a relation model based on the assumption that students' perception about preparatory behaviors mediate relationships between teachers' teaching behaviors and students' preparation. In the final model, teachers' direct instruction of preparation positively and directly related to students' preparation. In addition, it also decreased students' perception of the cost of preparation and then positively influenced students' actual preparation. The model also suggested that teaching style requiring deep understanding increased both perceived utility and cost of preparation, and then perceived utility positively influenced and perceived cost negatively influenced students' preparation.

In Study 2, the relationship between students' strategies during preparation and teachers' teaching strategies was examined in more detail. The results showed that if teachers teach the macro-structure of texts, students' use of the look-up strategy decreased. The results also showed that if teachers teach the origins of each word or ask students how to translate sentences, students' use of the look-up strategy decreased. These results suggested that what and how teachers teach at school 'tell' students the needed preparatory behaviors and then influences their use of preparation strategies at home.

In addition, the results of Study 2 showed that if teachers encourage their students to examine unknown words and sentences with the use of a dictionary before the class, preparatory behaviors of students with low content-attached motive would increase. In addition, if teachers ask students how they translated some sentences in the textbook, students with high content-attached motive perceive the needed strategy and spontaneously use it.

Implications for practice

Direct instruction of preparation was found to have a positive direct relationship to students' learning preparation in Study 1, and it increased strategy use of students with low content-attached motive. Strictly speaking, however, this influence does not mean increasing the 'spontaneous' use of learning strategies. Although direct instruction of learning is important, the findings of the studies reported here suggest that teachers should pay careful attention to what they teach and how they teach in classroom lessons. In Study 2, it was revealed that as teachers explained the origins of meanings of each English word or asked students to answer their own translations, students' use of the look-up strategy increased. This finding may be generalizable to other school subjects. It suggests that if teachers explain not only each fact in the textbook but also the origins of the facts or ask students to explain what they thought about the contents, students might read the textbook and prepare for the next lesson more spontaneously. For instance, a mathematics textbook contains many facts such as formulas and how to solve mathematical problems. If teachers explain why the formulas are true or ask students to explain how they solved the problems, students may "understand" the needed preparatory behaviors better and spontaneously check a formula or the procedure for problem solving in the textbook during pre-class preparation.

Conclusion

Previous research about learning strategies showed that perceived goal structure affects students' learning strategy use (Lyke & Young, 2006; Nolen & Haladyna, 1990; Wolters, 2004). But classroom-level variables in these previous studies were not about teachers' "behaviors" but "goals" or "beliefs." Thus, it can be difficult for school teachers to apply such research findings to their daily educational practices in the classroom. The two studies reported in this chapter revealed the influence of teachers' teaching behaviors at school on students' learning behaviors at home. These findings have the potential to contribute to effective educational practices for enhancing students' spontaneous preparatory behaviors.

It is important to mention a limitation of the studies reported here. The results were based on self-reports, not actual behaviors. Self-reported measures can be influenced by respondents' knowledge about ideal instructional/learning behaviors. In future research, other measurements such as observation of daily instruction (for teachers' teaching behaviors) and what students write in their notebooks during preparation (for students' learning behaviors) should be gathered in investigating these relationships.

So far, research studies about how to teach effectively in daily classroom lessons (e.g., Kang, 2008) and about how to learn effectively at home (e.g., Alexander et al., 1998) have rarely been examined together. The results described in this chapter show that what and how school teachers teach in the classroom can affect their students' frequency and quality of preparation at home. Teachers' teaching behaviors in school and students' learning behaviors at home are not independent. The findings reported in this chapter highlight the need for further studies to examine how these two variables interact. Elucidating the connections between how teachers teach in daily classroom lessons and how students learn at home has the potential to contribute to new developments in strategies for learning and instruction.

Note

Tables and figures included in Study 2 have previously appeared in the paper detailed below. The *Japanese Journal of Educational Psychology* has given permission for the use of the tables and figures on the condition that the paper is referred to as the original source.

Shinogaya, K. (2014). Students' strategy used in preparation and lecture: The direct and moderate effects of teachers' teaching strategy. *Japanese Journal of Educational Psychology, 62*, 197–208.

References

Alexander, P. A., Graham, S., & Harris, K. R. (1998). A perspective on strategy research: Progress and prospects. *Educational Psychology Review, 10*(2), 129–154.

Ausubel, D. P. (1960). The use of advance organizers in the learning and retention of meaningful verbal material. *Journal of Educational Psychology, 51*(5), 267–272.

Barcikowski, R. S. (1981). Statistical power with group means as the unit of analysis. *Journal of Educational Statistics, 6*(3), 267–285.

Bonney, C. R., Cortina, K. S., Smith-Darden, J. P., & Fiori, K. L. (2008). Understanding strategies in foreign language learning: Are integrative and intrinsic motives distinct predictors? *Learning and Individual Differences, 18*(1), 1–10.

Elliot, A. J., McGregor, H. A., & Gable, S. (1999). Achievement goals, study strategies, and exam performance: A mediational analysis. *Journal of Educational Psychology, 91*(3), 549–563.

Horino, M., & Ichikawa, S. (1997). Learning motives and strategies in high-school students' English learning. *Japanese Journal of Educational Psychology, 45*(2), 140–147.

Kang, N.-H. (2008). Learning to teach science: Personal epistemologies, teaching goals, and practices of teaching. *Teaching and Teacher Education, 24*(2), 478–498.

Kreft, I., & De Leeuw, J. (1998). *Introducing multilevel modeling.* Thousand Oaks, CA: Sage.

Lyke, J. A., & Young, A. J. K. (2006). Cognition in context: Students' perceptions of classroom goal structures and reported cognitive strategy use in the college classroom. *Research in Higher Education, 47*(4), 477–490.

Murayama, K. (2003). Learning strategy use and short- and long-term perceived utility. *Japanese Journal of Educational Psychology, 51*(2), 130–140.

Murayama, K., & Elliot, A. J. (2009). The joint influence of personal achievement goals and classroom goal structures on achievement-relevant outcomes. *Journal of Educational Psychology, 101*(2), 432–447.

Nolen, S. B. (1988). Reasons for studying: Motivational orientations and study strategies. *Cognition and Instruction, 5*(4), 269–287.

Nolen, S. B., & Haladyna, T. M. (1990). Personal and environmental influences on students' beliefs about effective study strategies. *Contemporary Educational Psychology, 15*(2), 116–130.

Pintrich, P. R. (1999). The role of motivation in promoting and sustaining self-regulated learning. *International Journal of Educational Research, 31*(6), 459–470.

Pokay, P., & Blumenfeld, P. C. (1990). Predicting achievement early and late in the semester: The role of motivation and use of learning strategies. *Journal of Educational Psychology, 82*(1), 41–50.

Raudenbush, S. W., & Bryk, A. S. (2002). *Hierarchical linear models: Applications and data analysis methods.* Thousand Oaks, CA: Sage.

Sato, J. (1998). Effects of learner's perception of utility and costs, and learning strategy preferences. *Japanese Journal of Educational Psychology, 46*(4), 367–376.

Shimizu, K. (2005). *Gakuryoku wo sodateru [Enhancing students' achievement].* Tokyo, Japan: Iwanami syoten.

Shinogaya, K. (2008). Effects of preparation on learning: Interaction with beliefs about learning. *Japanese Journal of Educational Psychology, 56*(2), 256–267.

Shinogaya, K. (2010). Strategies in preparation for learning and during lectures: Using path analysis to develop a relational model. *Japanese Journal of Educational Psychology, 58*(4), 452–463.

Shinogaya, K. (2014). Students' strategy used in preparation and lecture: The direct and moderate effects of teachers' teaching strategy. *Japanese Journal of Educational Psychology, 62,* 197–208.

Tabachnick, S. E., Miller, R. B., & Relyea, G. E. (2008). The relationships among students' future-oriented goals and subgoals, perceived task instrumentality, and task-oriented self-regulation strategies in an academic environment. *Journal of Educational Psychology, 100*(3), 629–642.

Titsworth, B. S., & Kiewra, K. A. (2004). Spoken organizational lecture cues and student notetaking as facilitators of student learning. *Contemporary Educational Psychology, 29*(4), 447–461.

Tsai, C.-C. (2000). Enhancing science instruction: The use of 'conflict maps'. *International Journal of Science Education, 22*(3), 285–302.

Vansteenkiste, M., Simons, J., Lens, W., Sheldon, K. M., & Deci, E. L. (2004). Motivating learning, performance, and persistence: The synergistic effects of intrinsic goal contents and autonomy-supportive contexts. *Journal of Personality and Social Psychology, 87*(2), 246–260.

Wolters, C. A. (2004). Advancing achievement goal theory: Using goal structures and goal orientations to predict students' motivation, cognition, and achievement. *Journal of Educational Psychology, 96*(2), 236–250.

11

DEVELOPING REGULATION STRATEGIES THROUGH COMPUTER-SUPPORTED KNOWLEDGE BUILDING AMONG TERTIARY STUDENTS

Chunlin Lei and Carol K. K. Chan

Introduction

Substantial evidence has indicated that students' use of self-regulated strategies is related to their learning and academic performance (Boekaerts, Pintrich, & Zeidner, 2000; Zimmermann & Schunk, 2011). With increasing use of technology in classrooms, self-regulation in computer-supported learning environments has emerged as an important research strand in education (Azevedo, 2007; Azevedo & Aleven, 2013; Veenman, 2007; Winters, Greene, & Costich, 2008). Because computer-supported collaborative learning (CSCL) often involves students working in groups for shared tasks, there is a need for students not only to self-regulate their own learning but also to co-regulate the learning of other group members and of the group as a whole in socially shared regulation to accomplish learning (Järvelä & Hadwin, 2013; Winne, Hadwin, & Perry, 2013).

Although there has been growing interest in examining the nature of self-regulation and co-regulation and developing tools in computer-supported environments (Järvelä & Hadwin, 2013; Järvelä et al., 2015; Manlove, Lazonder, & de Jong, 2007; Winne & Hadwin, 2013), less effort has been invested in designing classroom learning environments that support students' spontaneous use of co-regulatory strategies. Of particular interest is how students can engage in self-regulation and co-regulation in communities of inquiry. Knowledge building communities (Scardamalia & Bereiter, 2006; 2014), which engage students in collective work with a high level of agency to develop improvable ideas, provide a productive learning environment to examine and to facilitate students' spontaneous use of regulation and strategies. The goals of this chapter are to examine instructional designs that support this regulation and to characterize regulated learning in the discourse.

Theoretical perspectives

Self-regulation and co-regulation in student learning

Self-regulated learning refers to processes whereby learners activate and sustain cognition and behavior directed toward personal goals (Zimmermann & Schunk, 2011). Self-regulated learners are better able to select and use strategies to achieve desired outcomes. Unfortunately, students often do not transfer or sustain the use of strategies that they learn (Pressley & McCormick, 1995). To address such problems, researchers have shifted from merely teaching students metacognitive strategies to embedding such strategies in group inquiry and communities of learners. One prominent example is the extension of research from reciprocal teaching (Brown & Palincsar, 1989) to communities of learners (Brown & Campione, 1994). As theories of learning have shifted from individual learning to community-based learning (Bereiter, 2002; Brown, Collins, & Duguid, 1989; Lave & Wenger, 1991), students are now enculturated into a community learning culture and helped to develop co-regulatory skills for collaborative inquiry.

Computer-supported learning environments have provided learners with opportunities for a high degree of self-control and self-direction in social contexts (Williams, 1996). When working collaboratively, students need to employ various types of self-regulatory processes such as planning, knowledge activation, monitoring, and reflection to make the collaboration effective (Azevedo, 2007). However, students often struggle with the open-ended learning environments (Winters et al., 2008) and do not necessarily use regulated strategies for deep understanding.

Whereas self-regulation strategies refer to the individual learner's deliberate planning and monitoring and the regulation of their progress toward completion of personal goals, co-regulation emphasizes the coordination of self-regulation among self and others, involving emergent interaction (Chan, 2012; Volet, Summers, & Thurman, 2009). Järvelä and Hadwin (2013) further distinguished between "self-regulation," "co-regulation," and "shared regulation" in CSCL environments; regulation can be viewed at different levels encompassing self, member(s), and the group; shared regulation usually involves students focusing on the group as a collective entity and coordinating with and complementing one another to achieve shared understanding.

While shared regulation investigates task performance and knowledge building examines sustained idea improvement, they are similar in that they both focus on the collective whole rather than individuals. In this chapter, we investigate how to design CSCL environments to facilitate learners' regulation, co-regulation, and collective regulation on learning and knowledge advances.

Knowledge building theory and approach

Scardamalia and Bereiter (2014) defined knowledge building as the production of new knowledge that adds value to the community. This model postulates that knowledge is improvable by means of continually refining the discourse through students' collective agency and responsibility. Emphasis is placed on socio-cognitive dynamics to enhance students' agency for spontaneous and sustained use of strategies at both individual and collective levels.

The goal of knowledge building is idea improvement and collective responsibility; agency, metacognition, and reflection are central to school life, extending from individual to social level. Bereiter and Scardamalia (1989, 1993) have proposed an account of intentional learning and expertise that illustrates high-level regulation of learning with learners setting knowledge building goals, as well as monitoring and evaluating their own and collective ideas. Regulated learning is also socially situated, and students working in a computer-supported intentional learning environment had been shown to be better able to monitor own, others', and group ideas compared to counterparts working in face-to-face conditions (Cohen & Scardamalia, 1998). Premised on the notion that learning is intentional, goal-directed, and collective, knowledge building focuses on epistemic agency and sustained idea improvement in a community context.

New media such as Knowledge Forum (KF) include affordances that can help students increase from self- to other regulation. KF is supported by networked technology, on which ideas (in the form of KF notes) can be publicized, shared, elaborated, explained, and refined (Figure 11.1). There are many affordances of KF, including a set of thinking prompts and modifiable scaffolds, such as "*My Theory*," "*I need to understand*", "*This theory cannot explain*," and "*Putting our knowledge together*," which help to shape students' discourse when they are engaged in collaborative knowledge building. Students can develop their ideas and questions prefaced by the scaffold: as such, these scaffolds help to identify as well as enhance students' metacognitive understanding and regulation (Figure 11.2).

Scardamalia (2002) proposed a system of 12 principles to facilitate the socio-cognitive and socio-technological dynamics of knowledge building; these are important for regulated learning and sustained use of strategies. Some key principles include:

- *Epistemic agency:* Students undertake agency and metacognitive work comparing different models to chart progress.
- *Improvable ideas:* Students view ideas as object of inquiry and seek to improve the quality of ideas collectively.
- *Community knowledge:* Students set inquiry goals that go beyond personal ones to embrace group and community goals.
- *Rising above:* Students monitor, evaluate, and synthesize taking ideas to a higher level to make further progress.
- *Transformative assessment:* Students work continually to reflect on their current state of knowledge and to exceed targeted goals.

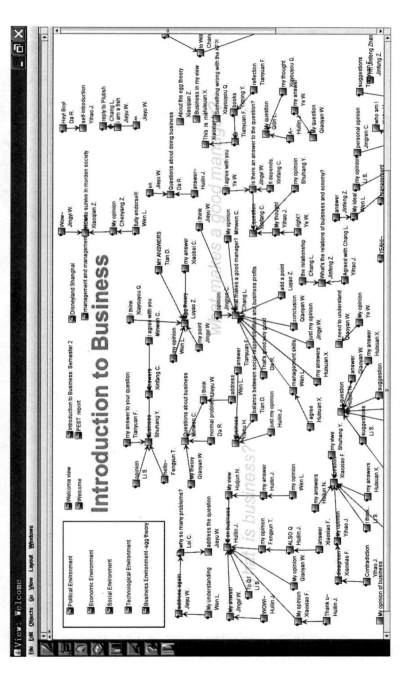

FIGURE 11.1 A Knowledge Forum (KF) view (the shaded square icons represent computer notes with links to other notes).

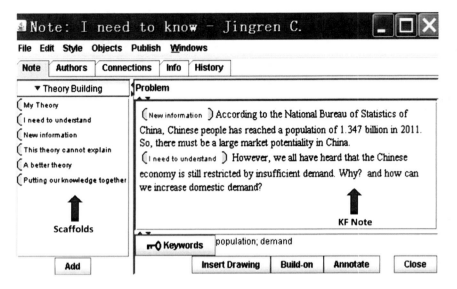

FIGURE 11.2 A Knowledge Forum (KF) note and scaffolds.

The principles themselves are abstract. However, when *idea improvement*, for example, becomes an explicit principle and norm in the community, it directs the community's focus to a deliberate and sustained regulatory effort to monitor, evaluate, and advance frontiers of knowledge. Scardamalia and Bereiter (2006) argued that classroom design should focus on principles rather than adherence to procedures or task completion to maximize student agency; with such agency, there would likely be more spontaneous use of strategies. In light of current debates about minimal versus guided instruction (Hmelo-Silver, Duncan, & Chinn, 2007; Kirschner, Sweller, & Clark, 2006;), these principles and epistemic standards highlight the importance of students taking responsibility to regulate their learning rather than carrying out tasks structured mainly by the teacher.

Knowledge building and reflective assessment

Assessment is at the heart of the student learning experience (Black & Wiliam, 1998). As such, assessment needs to adopt a socio-cognitive perspective in support of student learning and collaboration (Shepard, 2000). Reflective assessment, through a metacognitive process of reflecting on *what the students know, what they don't know, and how to bridge the gap*, empowers the students to take ownership of their own learning. Research has shown how the use of reflective assessment with students assessing their own inquiry can promote student metacognition and scientific inquiry (White & Frederiksen, 1998).

In knowledge building, reflective assessment provides students with "knowledge building principles" as epistemic scaffolds and as criteria for them to monitor and evaluate their learning. The principles can also be the learning goals; and students reflect on how they have achieved those goals as they monitor progress toward deeper understanding. Research in knowledge building has shown how students using e-portfolios in reflective assessment can engage in deeper inquiry (Lee, Chan, & van Aalst, 2006; van Aalst & Chan, 2007) and how reflective assessment can promote conceptual change (Chan & Lam, 2010) and metacognition among low achievers (Yang, van Aalst, Chan, & Tian, 2016).

Reflective assessment can be harnessed to engage students in co-regulation for meaningful learning and knowledge advancement, with the goal of students taking responsibility for *monitoring* their own and others' idea improvement. Although there has been considerable research evidence on knowledge building design and effects (Chan, 2013; Chen & Hong, 2016; Zhang, Scardamalia, Lamon, Messina, & Reeve, 2007), including those examining assessment (Lee et al., 2006; van Aalst & Chan, 2007), few have specifically examined the role of principles and regulatory strategies in conceptual learning. In this chapter, we propose that the emphases on principles, norms, and community dynamics in knowledge building are more likely to sustain students' use of active processing strategies. For instance, *epistemic agency* encourages students taking control of their own learning; *improvable ideas* places emphases on working together for coherent and improved understanding; and *community knowledge* focuses on advances of the whole learning community.

To summarize, this study aims to design and implement a computer-supported knowledge building environment, emphasizing the knowledge building principles and reflective assessment strategies, and evaluate the effects of this environment on students' learning outcomes and spontaneous use of self- and co-regulation strategies in the collaborative inquiry process. Specifically, we address the following research questions:

(1) What are the instructional effects of the principle-based knowledge building environment on students' domain understanding?
(2) What is the relationship between students' participation patterns and use of metacognitive scaffolds in KF and domain understanding?
(3) What characterize self-regulated, co-regulated, and collective regulatory strategies in their collaborative inquiry process, and how are they related to students' collective and individual knowledge advances?

Methods

Research context

Participants were students in two intact classes in the first year of a tertiary Sino-British program in a business-and-economics-oriented university in Shanghai, China. Both classes employed the knowledge building model using KF, but one incorporated a more intensive intervention including knowledge building principles. Thus, the study adopted a quasi-experimental design examining the effects of a principle-based knowledge building environment (KBP, $n = 30$) and a regular knowledge building environment (KBR, $n = 30$). Both classes were taught by the same teacher who had 12 years of teaching experience.

It was a two-semester course in 2010–2011, *Introduction to Business*, with two 90-minute lessons weekly for 12–14 weeks each semester. Class activities included student brainstorming, discussions and presentations, jigsaw reading, and knowledge-building talks, among others. After class, students employed KF to continue their learning, to pose questions arising from their inquiry, and to construct explanations on ideas discussed in class; problems and questions that emerged during the computer discourse were discussed in the class lessons.

Design of a knowledge building environment

Knowledge building environments focus on the production of new knowledge, artefacts, and ideas of value to the community (Scardamalia & Bereiter, 2014). With the support of KF, students write notes to articulate their ideas, express confusion, seek explanations, and co-construct new knowledge, using scaffolds described earlier. The principle-based environment placed emphasis on individuals' contribution to communal efforts and collective growth. Mediated by principles, students were facilitated toward self-regulation, co-regulation, collective regulation, and monitoring of ideas for improvement. Students deepened their discussions by creating or building onto notes in threaded thematic inquiries in the KF workspaces (see Figure 11.3).

There were mainly four intertwined aspects involved in both conditions:

1 *Forming a collaborative learning culture:* Students working in groups in the classroom community were encouraged and motivated to use KF to set their learning goals, pose relevant questions, and seek answers collaboratively. Opportunities were provided to become familiar with KF technology and to make their ideas public for collaborative inquiry.

2 *Developing progressive inquiry:* The course curriculum included several big core ideas. Through face-to-face and online discourse, students elaborated *what they know* and *what they want to know* about the topic. Students were engaged in a deepening cyclical inquiry process of questions, explanations, further questions, and further explanation (also see build-on structure in Figure 11.3). Students regulated and reflected on their knowledge gaps, to monitor their ideas as well as those of others for deeper understanding. Gradually, they learned to compare their ideas with those of others, identify similarities and inconsistencies therein, and chart their own course for knowledge advancement.

3 *Shared responsibility for community knowledge:* Group projects engaged students in regulated learning and inquiry; they had to help each other question, deepen their inquiry, evaluate, summarize, and synthesize ideas based on conjectures, viewpoints, and assumptions articulated by community members. They monitored both their own and the group's shared knowledge advances.

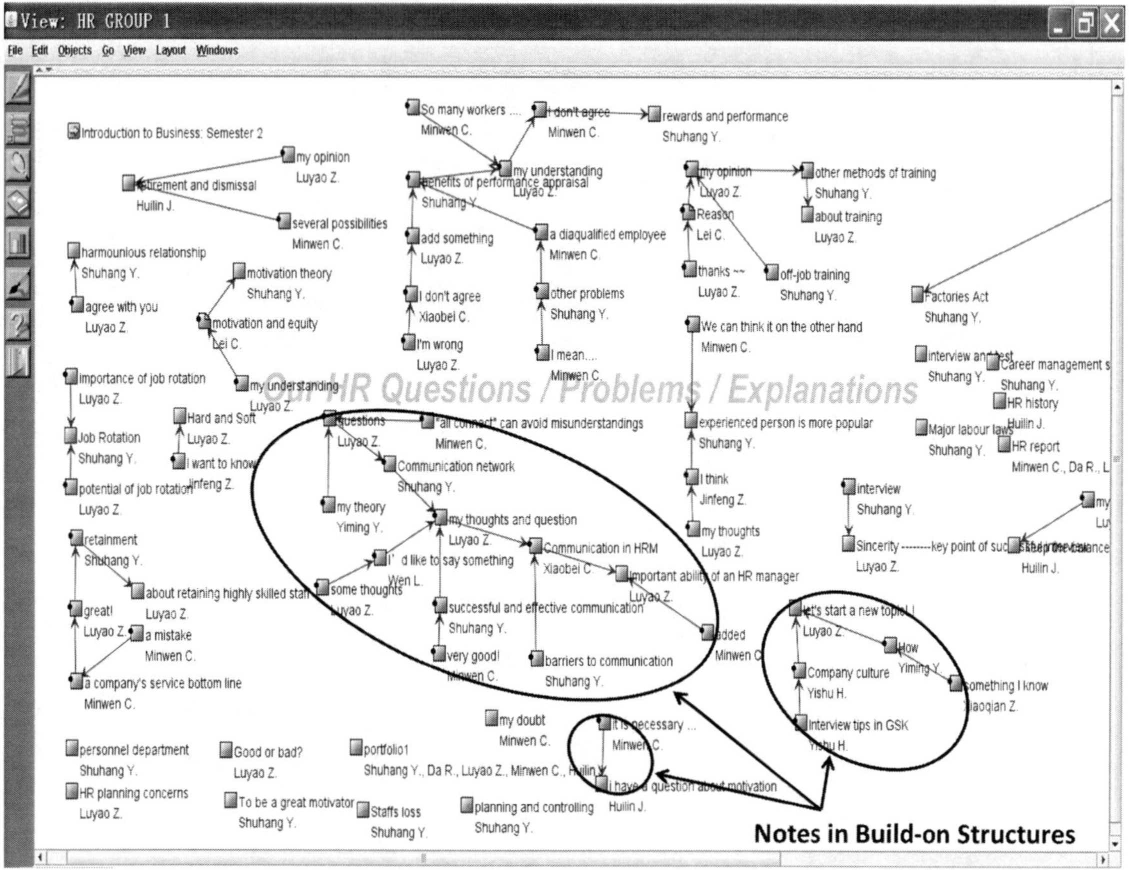

FIGURE 11.3 Students' build-on notes and thematic inquiries.

4   *Reflective assessment for deep understanding and knowledge building:* Reflective
     assessment involved students examining knowledge gaps in own and
     group understanding to advance collective knowledge. There were several
     components: (a) The regular posting of notes in KF emphasized students
     monitoring own and others' ideas and coordinating collective understanding.
     (b) Students took turns to summarize the KF discourse identifying high
     points and helped the class to reflect on their progress, using scaffolds to
     support monitoring of collective understanding, such as "*What we have
     achieved so far*" and "*What are some new questions?*" (c) E-portfolio assessments
     required students to select several clusters of their best notes for inclusion
     in a portfolio, in which they tracked and reflected on their inquiry trajec-
     tory to identify what were the promising questions and what require further
     inquiry.

Students in both classes experienced the four general components of knowledge building inquiry supported by KF, but there were also differences. For the
principle-based class, knowledge building principles were explicitly introduced,
discussed, and reflected upon so that students could set goals, monitor and evaluate
their learning processes, address knowledge gaps in the community, and coordinate
knowledge building efforts collectively. In the regular class, no explicit knowledge
building principles were introduced, but students were encouraged to use KF as a
new technological tool for communication and knowledge building.

Data sources

Domain understanding: A domain test with ten open-ended questions was given
at pretest and posttest to examine students' understanding of key business concepts relevant to the curriculum with specific questions such as "*When we talk
about the business environment, what do you know and what factors might be involved?*"
Students also wrote about "*What more [they] would like to know about the business
environment?*," including terminology they wanted to know. Both the pretest and
posttest were coded by two raters, using a seven-point scale developed jointly by
the researcher and a content teacher. The inter-rater reliability coefficients were .81
(pretest "*what I know*"), .89 (pretest "*what I want to know*"), .87 (posttest "*what I
know*"), and .91 (posttest "*what I want to know*").

Report writing was a regular course assessment, designed to assess understanding of a key business model and the ability to apply the model to authentic business
situations. The reports were marked by two raters, and the inter-rater reliability
coefficient was .92.

KF participation: KF includes the *Analytical Toolkit* (ATK), which provides data
on student participation and interaction (Burtis, 1998). ATK includes indices
which show how many notes a student created; whether the student used scaffolds
or key words in writing; the extent to which he/she read or built on others' notes;
and how often he/she revisited or revised his/her own notes. ATK indices also

mirror the online regulatory processes. Specifically, scaffolds (*I need to understand, my theory, putting our knowledge together, etc.*) are used as metacognitive prompts for students to reflect, monitor, and evaluate their thoughts, and their use indicates a certain level of regulation.

KF discourse and regulation strategies: Students' writing on KF was qualitatively analyzed to identify patterns of knowledge advances and use of self-regulatory, co-regulatory, and collective regulatory strategies.

Results

Instructional effects on students' domain understanding

The mean scores and standard deviations of the domain pretest for the KBP and KBR classes were 11.56 (2.66) and 11.20 (3.44), respectively; for the domain post-test, the values were 24.13 (3.31) and 20.97 (3.16), respectively. Paired sample t-tests indicated that both classes made gains from pretest to posttest (for the KBP class, $t(29) = 23.47$, $p < .001$, Cohen's $d = 4.37$; for the KBR class, $t(29) = 14.14$. $p < .001$, Cohen's $d = 2.59$). The findings thus show that both classes using knowledge building improved in domain understanding.

Further comparisons indicated that KBP had stronger effects. A repeated measure MANOVA (Time × Environment) revealed a main interaction effect between time and environment, Wilks' Lambda =.85, $F(1, 58) = 10.26$, $p < .01$, $\eta^2 = .15$. A significant main effect was also obtained for time, $F(1, 58) = 652.80$, $p < .001$, $\eta^2 = .92$; and for environment, $F(1, 58) = 6.61$, $p < .05$, $\eta^2 = .10$. These results show that both classes learned over time, but the KBP environment with principles and assessment was more conducive to fostering domain understanding compared to the KBR class that only used KF.

Relationship between KF participation, use of scaffolds, and domain understanding

KF participation indices show students' engagement as well as their regulation and metacognition. As discussed above, the scaffolds on KF signals students' reflection and monitoring of use of strategy (i.e., I need to understand, my theory); the use of revision shows students' iterative efforts to revise understanding; and use of references points to students' use of other ideas in the community. Over the whole instruction period, the KBP class produced a mean of 57.8 notes and the KBR class produced 24.4 notes for each student; these are high rates relative to other research on online forum participation in higher education (Hewitt, 2005).

Zero-order Pearson correlations were conducted to examine whether students' KF engagement was correlated to their post-domain test scores. Results (Table 11.1) indicate that domain understanding was related to the extent students posted new notes ($r = .49$), read notes ($r = .43$), building on others' notes ($r = .27$), use of thinking and metacognitive prompts to support their thinking ($r = .31$), and

TABLE 11.1 Zero-order correlations between ATK (Analytical Toolkit) indices and domain understanding for whole sample ($N = 60$)

		1	2	3	4	5	6	7	8
1	Notes created								
2	Scaffolds used	.74**							
3	Notes revision	.59**	.52**						
4	Reference notes	.66**	.60**	.43**					
5	Notes read	.65**	.60**	.35**	.45**				
6	Notes linked	.46**	.51**	.04	.54**	.37**			
7	Notes with key words	.26*	.38**	.11	.40**	.13	.47**		
8	Domain understanding	.49**	.31*	.22	.38**	.43**	.27*	.22	

$*p < .05$, $**p < .01$

references to others' KF notes ($r = .38$). Scaffolds were spontaneously used and selected by students, not imposed by teachers. The use of reference notes suggests co-regulatory and collective regulatory learning. Taken together, these findings suggest that students who engaged more actively in KF and employed more regulatory scaffolds in note-writing achieved a better understanding of business concepts and models, and their application.

Use of self-, co-, and collective regulatory strategies in the collaborative inquiry process

To examine what regulatory strategies students utilized in their collaborative inquiry, qualitative analyses were conducted to examine students' interaction patterns and KF discourse. We used content analysis (De Wever, Valcke, Schellens, & Van Keer, 2006), a common method involving assessing patterns of discourse based on different units of analysis. This study also adopted inquiry thread analysis (Zhang et al., 2007), categorizing and grouping the forum notes based on a shared key problem or thematic topic. Therefore, each inquiry thread represents a conceptual line of discussion/inquiry along a timescale, and may objectify the trajectory of the advancement of community knowledge.

Spontaneous use: Teacher- or student-initiated threads

The first analysis examined the relative roles of teacher and students in initiating and starting the inquiry threads to provide some preliminary evidence of student ownership and regulation of their knowledge gaps. Table 11.2 shows the number of inquiry threads initiated by either the teacher or the students in both the KBP and KBR classes. It appears that students in the KBP environment developed more ownership and were more able to initiate, regulate, and chart their learning goals and inquiries.

TABLE 11.2 Teacher- or student-initiated inquiry in KBP and KBR classes

	KBP, No. (%)	KBR, No. (%)
Student self-initiated inquiry	12 (52.2%)	4 (30.8%)
Teacher-led inquiry	11 (47.8%)	9 (69.2%)
Total	23 (100%)	13 (100%)

KBP = principled-based knowledge building environment; KBR = regular knowledge building environment.

Regulation strategies and relation with knowledge advances

To examine how students regulated their discourse for productive inquiry, we first examined KF discourse in terms of inquiry threads: specifically, we coded the threads (a cluster of notes) in line with knowledge building theory focusing on knowledge advancement shown in the threads. Generally, three discourse patterns emerged: low-level knowledge advances (LKA), moderate-level knowledge advances (MKA), and high-level knowledge advances (HKA) (Table 11.3).

Higher levels indicate greater student progress in conceptual understanding. We coded the threads of the KBP class into 7 LKA, 9 MKA, and 7 HKA and those of the KBR class into 7 LKA, 5 MKA, and 1 HKA, respectively. The inter-coder reliability was .83 (Pearson correlation using a random sample of 30% of the inquiry threads).

Characterization of regulatory strategies supported by the community: Within each inquiry thread, each computer note was examined for evidence of regulatory strategies. Three patterns including self-, co-, and collective regulation emerged (as discussed previously, see Järvelä & Hadwin, 2013). Self-regulation refers to students reflecting on their own ideas; co-regulation involves students working with others to monitor others' understanding, and collective regulation refers to students examining, monitoring, and regulating the community's collective understanding. We classified each kind of regulation into different levels depending on the extent of regulation, as exemplified below.

TABLE 11.3 Classification of inquiry threads in terms of knowledge advancement

Level	Description of the thread
Low (level 1)	The thread was not long, consisting of students' quick or naïve ideas and lacking a well-developed treatment of a business topic.
Moderate (level 2)	The thread shows students were able to respond to questions from various perspectives; a pool of business ideas was considered but repetition was found; there is some indication of constructive activity but lacks sustained inquiry of problems.
High (level 3)	In these threads, students were engaged in a question explanation intertwined process, identifying and addressing gaps in collective knowledge, negotiating meaning and formulating more sophisticated views toward business theories or concepts.

Self-regulation: With self-regulation, students monitor their own ideas; at level 1, it may include phrases such as "as far I know" or "I don't understand," such as:

> [My theory] Large population can be definitely a problem … we are in short of so many things because of the large population]. *I don't quite understand why we need to increase domestic demand.* The government can hardly supply so many citizens with enough resources.
>
> *(Excerpt #1, DT)*

At level 2, one student not only showed his/her awareness of own thinking but also provided a context for ideas or question:

> [I need to understand] *I've known that* business means the activity of buying or selling goods or services … *But how* can we make profit as much as possible, and how to run a company efficiently?
>
> *(Excerpt #2, RD)*

At level 3, there was clearer reflection on ideas or revision of ideas.

> [A better theory] Oh, *I'm really sorry that I did not express myself clearly.* I tended to believe that … When you ask why … I'm quite confused because I believe China doesn't need to stimulate the market … *But after talking with some of my classmates,* I *now* realized there are … I think *I can try to answer your question* in a more constructive way … we should strike a balance between
>
> *(Excerpt #3, DT)*

In this example, student DT gradually realized his own problems in understanding a business phenomenon and later tried to provide improved explanations. There was evidence of metacognition and realization of new ideas.

Co-regulation: Co-regulation refers to students monitoring others' ideas; three levels were identified. At level 1, students responded to others' ideas but mainly agreed or disagreed without providing further explanations.

> [My theory] I *agree with* the idea that management is maybe the most important factor in running an enterprise.
>
> *(Excerpt #4, WJY)*

At level 2, students interacted by asking for clarification of ideas or tried to help others to solve problems. They might ask what others mean by their ideas, or offer alternative ideas, as in this example:

> [My theory] *Maybe you can* interview some companies' managers, but it might be a little difficult. *Or maybe you can turn to* the internet *for some help* …
>
> *(Excerpt #5, JYH)*

At level 3, students enriched and refined ideas by working together.

> [My theory] … I *quite agree with* what you have already said. Here *I would like to add something*. A manager should … a clear goal in mind and achive the goal with minimum resources and maximaum effectiveness
>
> *(Excerpt #6, CXF)*

In this example, the student went beyond merely agreeing or disagreeing to add or supplement some new ideas, which enhanced participants' understanding.

Collective regulation: The third pattern, collective regulation, refers to students' collective monitoring or coordinating with rise above for the whole group's discourse. We again identified three levels of increasing complexity. At level 1, students mainly described ideas, which included a surface type of summary of *this person says what* and *another person says what* but nothing further to integrate the ideas. An example can be given as follows:

> [Putting our knowledge together] According to YSH– "the growth rate of GDP has reached …, so the economic environment is suitable for …"; *CXB* said – "Our economy is booming … economic environment include …"; … *As the classmates said*, China really has a favorable environment for business.
>
> *(Excerpt #7, YYM)*

At level 2, students are able to summarize ideas with some interpretation and integration, as in this example:

> [Putting our knowledge together] We have *a warm discussion on what is business*.[1]■business[2]■solve it[3]■personal opinion[4]■questions[5]■My idea[6]■My view. After the discussion, *we now have a basic conception of business. According to LC,* it is an approach to … *XQ said* business is a way of making profit … *HJ's idea* is that business is to focus on eight principles … *JF thought* business is associated with economy … I find a definition *from a business dictionary of the Internet*. It has three demisions … it is a complicated term, depending on your interpretation
>
> *(Excerpt #8, JHL)*

In this computer note, student JHL referred to other students' ideas, reinterpreted their meaning in her own words, and added some new findings into the discussion discourse, which enriched the collective knowledge of the community.

At level 3, students demonstrated higher agency in evaluating and synthesizing ideas; emergent questions might be generated to push the frontier of community knowledge. The following note shows an example:

> [Putting our knowledge together] … About why priracy is so frequent, *we have discussed a lot.*[1]■My view on piracy[2]■Partly because … [3]■Just my opinion[4]■to organize and integrate[5]■My view[6]■my view[7] *Now I want to bring*

a conclusion to this question:(1) High profit makes … *(2)* Piratical products meet the demands of … *(3)*Lack an awareness of IPR; *(4)* No strict rules to. … [I need to understand] Is there a possible way to lead to a 'healthy' development of "piracy"?

(Excerpt #9, LW)

In excerpt 9, student LW analyzed the group's notes and synthesized the ideas into coherent conclusions as a meta-discourse of what had been considered; he did not have closure but continued the inquiry and asked another question emerging from their new understanding that made further knowledge advancement possible in the group.

Regulation strategies and collective knowledge advances: Using the scheme described above, we rated the notes in all the threads in the KBP and KBR classes. Each was coded using a three-point scale on extent of regulatory strategies in the three areas of monitoring own ideas, monitoring others' ideas, and monitoring collective ideas (inter-rater reliability of .80, based on Pearson's correlation coefficient). The means and standard deviations of self-regulation, co-regulation, and collective regulation in the LKA, MKA, and HKA threads are summarized in Table 11.4.

Table 11.4 shows that there were higher ratings of regulation strategies for inquiry threads coded as indicating more knowledge advances. Multivariate analyses examined the presence of regulation comparing the inquiry threads in KBP and KBR classes. Follow-up univariate analyses revealed significant differences on two measures: co-regulation, $F (1, 34) = 10.19$, $p < .005$, $\eta^2 = .23$; and collective regulation, $F (1, 34) = 5.13$, $p < .05$, $\eta^2 = .13$. However, there was no significant differences in terms of self-regulation, $F (1, 34) = 0.82$, $p = .37$, $\eta^2 = .02$. These results suggest that students in the principle-based knowledge building environment were more likely to use co- and collective regulatory skills to attend and monitor others' and the whole group's discourse. Students in both classes utilized self-regulatory strategies, indicating that the KF environment facilitated students' self-monitoring of their own progress; the principle-based environment encouraged more use of community-based types of regulation.

TABLE 11.4 Means and standard deviations of SR, Co-R, and Col-R in LKA, MKA, and HKA threads in both KBP and KBR classes

KBP (Thread No. = 23)				KBR (Thread No. = 13)			
Threads (No.)	SR M (SD)	Co-R M (SD)	Col-R M (SD)	Threads (No.)	SR M (SD)	Co-R M (SD)	Col-R M (SD)
LKA (7)	1.29 (.49)	1.43 (.53)	1.14 (.38)	LKA (7)	1.43 (.53)	1.14 (.38)	1.00 (.00)
MKA (9)	2.11 (.78)	2.22 (.44)	1.89 (.78)	MKA (5)	2.20 (.45)	1.60 (.55)	1.60 (.54)
HKA (7)	2.57 (.53)	2.43 (.53)	2.57 (.53)	HKA (1)	2.00 (.00)	2.00 (.00)	2.00 (.00)

SR = self-regulation; Co-R = co-regulation; Col-R = collective regulation; LKA = low knowledge advances; MKA = moderate knowledge advances; HKA = high knowledge advances; M = mean; SD = standard deviation.

TABLE 11.5 Relations among high-level regulatory strategies (self, co, and collective regulations) and domain understanding

	1	2	3	4	5
1 SR(H)	–				
2 Co-R (H)	.17	–			
3 Col-R(H)	.62**	.48**	–		
4 Domain understanding	.40*	.18	.39*	–	

SR(H) = high-level self-regulation; C0-R(H) = high-level co-regulation; Col-R(H) = high-level collective regulation; * $p < .05$; ** $p < .01$.

Regulation strategies and individual domain understanding: Zero-order Pearson correlations examined whether regulation strategies (self-, co-, and collective regulation) were related to students' individual domain understanding assessed using combined students' domain tests and report writing. Table 11.5 shows significant correlations between high-level (levels 2 and 3) self-regulation and high-level collective regulation with domain understanding scores.

Discussion and implications

This study compared two knowledge building environments with tertiary business students in China, both using KF, with one emphasizing principle-based knowledge building. Students in the principle-based knowledge building environment outperformed their counterparts in the KF environment in domain understanding, participation, and spontaneous use of regulatory strategies. More than half of the inquiry threads were initiated by students themselves in the KBP environment, providing evidence of spontaneous strategy engagement. We also identified different patterns of regulation involving monitoring own ideas, others' ideas, and collective ideas. Analyses showed that with more regulatory activities, there was more progress on domain understanding. In the following, we discuss implications for knowledge building environments, reflective assessment, and the spontaneous use of self-regulated and co-regulated learning.

Knowledge building community and regulation

Although students' use of self-regulated strategies is strongly associated with better-quality cognitive processes and academic functioning, self-regulation skills do not automatically develop among learners (Schunk, 1989). There are also problems with spontaneous and sustained use of strategies. These problems extend to social aspects of regulation. We argue that spontaneous use of strategies needs to be developed in *a community of learners and inquirers*. Specifically, this study examined a knowledge building environment where students can pose questions, express confusion, ask for clarification, offer explanations, refine ideas, observe and monitor group progress. Individual learning usually lacks such a public modeling process, and students may find it difficult to set learning goals, monitor, and evaluate their learning and knowledge growth.

With distributed expertise, a group of students can discuss and compare different views and theories and employ different strategies examining own and others' learning while working on problems; such activities are believed to render positive effects on their self-regulation, co-regulation, and collective regulation. Our findings align with current research on regulated learning and CSCL (Järvelä & Hadwin, 2013). We have provided some initial evidence into students spontaneously taking more initiative and regulating their learning: they posed questions, monitored gaps in understanding, and pursued inquiry to extend their collective understanding.

Our qualitative discourse analyses illuminated and enriched students' self-regulation, co-regulation, and shared regulation (Järvelä & Hadwin, 2013) with a knowledge-building perspective. Our quantitative analyses indicated that students' engagement in self-regulation and collective regulation was significantly correlated with individual and collective knowledge advances. According to the knowledge building model, which emphasizes collective advances, we have identified patterns where students not only work on self, co-, and shared regulation on task performance, they are concerned with collective regulation in sustained idea improvement and the progress of the community. In the knowledge building environment, some students posed questions illustrating self-reflection and metacognition related to gaps in their own understanding; other students posed questions directly to their peers and elaborated responses as they co-regulated each other's understanding. Students also engaged in collective regulation and meta-discourse reflecting on what the group had examined, what knowledge advance has been made, and what new questions emerged in sustained inquiry. Collective cognitive responsibility is key to knowledge building and students need to work in an environment that sustains these three intertwined regulation practices in a cyclical manner.

Knowledge building principles and reflective assessment

A key design feature of this environment involves reflective assessment: asking students to focus on knowledge building principles and reflecting on their own and collective understanding. Students write reflective portfolio as well as conduct reflective classroom discourse reviewing what knowledge progress they have made. We propose that "rise above" or "meta-discourse" embedded in the reflective assessment practices contributes to students' co-regulation at a high level for collective advancement of knowledge in the community. By engaging in reflective practices, students are encouraged to develop social metacognition—they trace their community's learning progress, learning achievements, and learning gaps. Reflection prompted by scaffolds including "*what we have achieved so far*" and "what other questions we have" reinforce a collective awareness of the community's concerted efforts.

In addition, students employed knowledge building principles as criteria by which to monitor and evaluate their learning process, as well as to set goals for next-step inquiries. For example, when students used *community knowledge* as an epistemic standard, they attached importance to collective efforts for advancing community knowledge. They realized that they were not just learning to enrich their personal minds, but were embarking on a journey toward a collective endeavor. This community awareness differentiated the KBP and KBR classes. In the principle-based environment, a large number of notes were built on or connected to one another by means of "*adding a point,*" "*In addition to what you have mentioned, there are other …,*" or "*putting our knowledge together,*" indicating that helping group members or classmates to understand better for co-regulation and collective regulation became an ethos of the community. Without a deliberate effort to advance community knowledge, students in the non-principle–based environment might feel content with what was already in their minds, thus making the chance of contributing to community knowledge less viable.

In terms of design, we suggest that the dual approach of principles and assessment works together to enhance regulation and knowledge advances. Knowledge building principles provide parameters for students to engage themselves in co-constructing knowledge, and reflective assessment provides opportunities to reflect upon and consolidate their understanding of the principles, which reciprocally prompted them to adopt more refined regulated strategies to improve the quality of KF discourse.

Merely placing students together guarantees neither effective collaboration (Kreijins, Kirschner, & Jochems, 2003) nor high-quality collaborative discourse (Hewitt, 2005). This study suggests how principles can be effectively aligned with a CSCL context and with assessment practices. The focus on principles fosters collective agency and use of high-level regulation strategies to ensure deep learning and understanding, rather than surface information sharing, to take place in CSCL environments.

This study has several limitations. First, variables cannot be fully controlled in the real classroom settings of a quasi-experimental design. We may not have identified some other relevant factors affecting our results. Second, we classified regulatory discourse into different categories and levels; such characterizations are still tentative, and future studies can examine more dynamics and facets of regulation in the technology-enhanced environment.

The educational implications of the study are salient. This study demonstrated that spontaneous use of regulatory skills (including co- and collective regulation) could be fostered effectively in a community of learners mediated by knowledge building principles, which are epistemic standards and norms for the students. Instead of teaching students concrete procedures, we need to equip them with epistemic standards and reflective assessment so that they are able to chart and regulate their learning for deep understanding and knowledge building.

References

Azevedo, R. (2007). Understanding the complex nature of self-regulatory processes in learning with computer-based learning environments: An introduction. *Metacognition and Learning, 2*(2/3), 57–65.

Azevedo, R., & Aleven, V. (Eds.). (2013). *International handbook of metacognition and learning technologies*. Amsterdam: Springer.

Bereiter, C. (2002). *Education and mind in the knowledge age*. Mahwah, NJ: Lawrence Erlbaum Associates.

Bereiter, C., & Scardamalia, M. (1989). Intentional learning as a goal of instruction. In L. B. Resnick (Ed.), *Knowing, learning and instruction: Essays in honor of Robert Glaser* (pp. 361–392). Hillsdale, NJ: Lawrence Erlbaum Associates.

Bereiter, C., & Scardamalia, M. (1993). *Surpassing ourselves: An inquiry into the nature and implications of expertise*. Chicago: Open Court.

Black, P., & Wiliam, D. (1998). Assessment and classroom learning. *Assessment in Education: Principles, Policy and Practice, 5*(1), 7–74.

Boekaerts, M., Pintrich, P. R., & Zeidner, M. (Eds.). (2000). *Handbook of self-regulation*. San Diego, CA: Academic Press.

Brown, A. L., & Campione, J. C. (1994). Guided discovery in a community of learners. In K. McCilly (Ed.), *Classroom lessons: Integrating cognitive theory and classroom practice* (pp. 229–270). Cambridge, MA: MIT Press.

Brown, A. L., & Palincsar A. S. (1989). Guided, cooperative learning and individual knowledge acquisition. In L. B. Resnick (Ed.), *Knowing, learning, and instruction: Essays in honor of Robert Glaser* (pp. 393–451). Hillsdale, NJ: Lawrence Erlbaum Associates.

Brown, J. S., Collins, A., & Duguid, P. (1989). Situated cognition and the culture of learning. *Educational Researcher, 18*(1), 32–42.

Burtis, J. (1998). *Analytic toolkit for knowledge forum*. Toronto, Canada: The Ontario Institute for Studies in Education/University of Toronto.

Chan, C. K. K. (2012). Co-regulation of learning in computer-supported collaborative learning environments: A discussion. *Metacognition and Learning, 7*(1), 63–73.

Chan, C. K. K. (2013). Collaborative knowledge building: Towards a knowledge-creation perspective. In C. Hmelo-Silver, C. Chinn, C. K. K. Chan, & A. O'Donnell (Eds.), *The international handbook of collaborative learning* (pp. 437–461). New York, NY: Routledge/Taylor & Francis.

Chan, C. K. K., & Lam, C. K. (2010). Conceptual change and epistemic growth through reflective assessment in computer-supported knowledge building. In *Proceedings of the 9th International Conference of the Learning Sciences* (Vol. 1, pp. 1063–1070). Chicago: International Society of the Learning Sciences.

Chen, B., & Hong, H.-Y. (2016). Schools as knowledge-building organizations: Thirty years of design research. *Educational Psychologist, 51*(2), 266–288.

Cohen, A., & Scardamalia, M. (1998). Discourse about ideas: Monitoring and regulation in face-to-face and computer-mediated environments. *Interactive Learning Environments, 6*(1–2), 93–113.

De Wever, B., Valcke, M., Schellens, T., & Van Keer, H. (2006). Content analysis schemes to analyze transcripts of online asynchronous discussion groups: A review. *Computers & Education, 46*(1), 6–28.

Hewitt, J. (2005). Toward an understanding of how threads die in asynchronous computer conferences. *Journal of the Learning Sciences, 14*(4), 567–589.

Hmelo-Silver, C., Duncan, R. G., & Chinn, C. A. (2007). Scaffolding and achievement in problem-based and inquiry learning: A response to Kirschner, Sweller, and Clark (2006). *Educational Psychologist, 42*(2), 99–107.

Järvelä, S., & Hadwin, A. F. (2013). New frontiers: Regulating learning in CSCL. *Educational Psychologist, 48*(1), 25–39.

Järvelä, S., Kirschner, P. A., Panadero, E., Maimberg, J., Phielix, C., Jaspers, J., Koivuniemi, M., & Järvenoja, H. (2015). Enhancing socially shared regulation in collaborative learning groups: Designing for CSCL design tools. *Educational Technology Research and Development, 63*(1), 125–142.

Kirschner, P. A., Sweller, J., & Clark, R. E. (2006). Why minimal guidance during instruction does not work: An analysis of the failure of constructivist, discovery, problem-based, experiential, and inquiry-based teaching. *Educational Psychologist, 41*(2), 75–86.

Kreijins, K., Kirschner, P. A., & Jochems, W. (2003). Identifying the pitfalls for social interaction in computer-supported collaborative learning environments: A review of the research. *Computers in Human Behavior, 19*(3), 335–353.

Lave, J., & Wenger, E. (1991). *Situated learning: Legitimate peripheral participation.* New York: Cambridge University Press.

Lee, E. Y. C., Chan, C. K. K., & van Aalst, J. (2006). Students assessing their own collaborative knowledge building. *International Journal of Computer-Supported Collaborative Learning, 1*(2), 277–307.

Manlove, S., Lazonder, A. W., & de Jong, T. (2007). Software scaffolds to promote regulation during scientific inquiry learning. *Metacognition and Learning, 2*(2), 141–155.

Pressley, M., & McCormick, C. B. (1995). *Cognition, teaching, and assessment.* New York, NY: HarperCollins.

Scardamalia, M. (2002). Collective cognitive responsibility for the advancement of knowledge. In B. Smith (Ed.), *Liberal education in a knowledge society* (pp. 48–76). Chicago: Open Court.

Scardamalia, M., & Bereiter, C. (2006). Knowledge building: Theory, pedagogy and technology. In R. K. Sawyer (Ed.), *The Cambridge handbook of the learning sciences* (pp. 97–118). New York, NY: Cambridge University Press.

Scardamalia, M., & Bereiter, C. (2014). Knowledge building and knowledge creation: Theory, pedagogy and technology. In R. K. Sawyer (Ed.), *The Cambridge handbook of the learning sciences* (pp. 397–417). New York: Cambridge University Press.

Schunk, D. H. (1989). Social cognitive theory and self-regulated learning. In B. J. Zimmerman & D. H. Schunk (Eds.), *Self-regulated learning and academic achievement: Theory, research, and practice* (pp. 83–110). New York: Springer-Verlag.

Shepard, L. A. (2000). The role of assessment in a learning culture. *Educational Researcher, 29*(7), 4–14.

van Aalst, J., & Chan, C. (2007). Student-directed assessment of knowledge building using electronic portfolios. *Journal of the Learning Sciences, 16*(2), 175–220.

Veenman, M. J. (2007). The assessment and instruction of self-regulation in computer-based environments: A discussion. *Metacognition and Learning, 2*(2–3), 177–183.

Volet, S., Summers, M., & Thurman, J. (2009). High-level co-regulation in collaborative learning: How does it emerge and how is it sustained? *Learning and Instruction, 19*(2), 128–143.

White, B. Y., & Frederiksen, J. R. (1998). Inquiry, modeling, and metacognition: Making science accessible to all students. *Cognition & Instruction, 16*(1), 3–118.

Williams, M. D. (1996). Learner-control and instructional technologies. In D. H. Jonassen (Ed.), *Handbook of research of educational communications and technology* (pp. 957–983). New York, NY: Macmillan.

Winne, P. H., & Hadwin, A. F. (2013). nStudy: Tracing and supporting self-regulated learning in the Internet. In R. Azevedo & V. Aleven (Eds.), *International handbook of metacognition and learning technologies* (pp. 293–308). Amsterdam: Springer.

Winne, P., Hadwin, A. F., & Perry, N. E. (2013). Metacognition and computer-supported collaborative learning. In C. Hmelo-Silver, C. Chinn, C. K. K. Chan, & A. O'Donnell (Eds.), *The international handbook of collaborative learning* (pp. 462–479). New York, NY: Routledge/Taylor & Francis.

Winters, F. I., Greene, J. A., & Costich, C. M. (2008). Self-regulation of learning within computer-based learning environments: A critical analysis. *Educational Psychology Review, 20*(4), 429–444.

Yang, Y., van Aalst, J., Chan, C. K. K., & Tian, W. (2016). Reflective assessment in knowledge building by students with low achievement. *International Journal of Computer-Supported Collaborative Learning, 11*(3), 281–311.

Zhang, J. W., Scardamalia, M., Lamon, M., Messina, R., & Reeve, R. (2007). Socio-cognitive dynamics of knowledge building in the work of 9- and 10-year-olds. *Educational Technology Research and Development, 55*(2), 117–145.

Zimmerman, B., & Schunk, D. (Eds.). (2011). *Handbook of self-regulation of learning and performance.* New York, NY: Routledge.

PART III
Practice

12

THREE APPROACHES TO PROMOTING SPONTANEOUS USE OF LEARNING STRATEGIES

Bridging the gap between research and school practices

Shin'ichi Ichikawa, Yuri Uesaka, and Emmanuel Manalo

Introduction

Importance of improving students' learning skills, and associated problems that need to be overcome

Developing students' learning skills is now generally considered one of the crucial objectives of school education—at least as important as teaching the content of the various academic subjects usually offered in schools. This view is held not only at the school level but also more widely: for example, the OECD's (Organization for Economic Cooperation and Development) Centre for Educational Research and Innovation stressed the importance of developing learning strategies and "learning to learn skills" in students (OECD, 2008). Likewise, the National Research Council in the United States has emphasized the centrality of learning skills in the development of transferable knowledge and skills in the twenty-first century (Pellegrino & Hilton, 2012). In Japan, the Ministry of Education has also emphasized the importance of developing effective learning strategies and motivation to support life-long learning in school education.

Although, at the policy level, schools are expected to have responsibility for facilitating the development of students' learning skills, in reality students are not acquiring such skills sufficiently. This problem has been reported in a number of studies, including findings that students struggle in school learning because of inadequate proficiency in essential learning skills (Ichikawa, 1998), as well as due to the presence of gaps between teachers' expectations and students' actual frequency of use of appropriate learning strategies in their school work (Uesaka, Suzuki, Kiyokawa, Seo, & Ichikawa, 2014).

Three main reasons for the general deficiency in students' learning skills development in Japan are proposed here. Firstly, the instruction provided in schools to promote the development of learning skills is insufficient. Survey findings, for example, revealed that only a very limited number of elementary and junior high schools provide concrete support for promoting students' learning skills development, and many of those schools only provide students a booklet about the skills, which is not adequate to leverage the necessary changes in students' learning behaviors (Uesaka, Seo, & Ichikawa, 2012). Second, there is a general lack of other effective resources that students can use to improve their learning skills in Japan. There is no shortage of study aid and self-help books, and "jukus" (i.e., privately run institutes that provide extra tuition outside of regular school) are utilized by a large proportion of students. However, the books vary considerably in quality and make little or no use of pertinent findings from educational research, and the jukus primarily focus on helping students with preparation for entrance examinations. This general lack of focus on facilitating the development of students' learning skills was apparent in the findings of a survey in which "learning to learn" was reported by *none* of the student respondents when asked about their perceptions of the value of "jukus" (Japan Ministry of Education, Culture, Sports, Science and Technology, 2008).

The third reason, which is the one this chapter deals with, is the lack of concrete guidance from educational psychology about how such learning skills can actually be developed in students. In Japan, after World War II, educational psychology became a compulsory subject for those studying to become teachers in schools. However, even though the topics dealt with in educational psychology have, since around the 1980s, increasingly become more relevant to teaching and learning issues, the same problems that have been identified in other countries about the inadequacy of their impact on educational policy and school practices (e.g., De Corte, 2000; McInerney, 2005) have persisted as a problem in Japan. In essence, most research studies just report findings and do not propose concrete approaches, or they are quite detached from real educational contexts, making the possible applications of their findings hard to clearly see—let alone implement—in real classroom situations. Thus, how to bridge the gap between theory and research on the one hand, and educational practices on the other, remains a crucial challenge to address.

The aim of this chapter is to contribute to bridging that gap. It proposes three educational approaches (cognitive counseling, incorporation of learning strategies instruction in the curriculum, and thinking-after-instruction approach in class) developed based on research findings by the authors' research group. This chapter first discusses the design principles underpinning the educational approaches. Through the use of case studies, it then describes how these educational approaches work to promote the spontaneous use of learning strategies among students.

Design principles underpinning the three educational practice approaches

The three design principles underpinning the educational approaches are: direct engagement by researcher, promotion of student understanding of the relevant mechanisms of learning, and assessment of learning strategy use.

The first principle is that researchers should engage directly with schools in trialing and implementing methods for enhancing the learning strategies used by students. Ichikawa (1993) argued that researchers should engage in educational practices and practitioners should engage in research. This is contrary to the traditional view in Japan that educational psychology researchers should simply generate and provide new perspectives, while teachers should consider how to implement the ideas contained in those perspectives in their classrooms. It is, however, congruent with the "situated cognition" perspective in the learning sciences, which considers it essential that learning and cognitive processes be understood in natural contexts (e.g., Seifert, 1999). This approach to research is also fundamentally the same as that proposed in action research. For example, Carr and Kemmis (2004) argued that if research is to be truly useful in real educational contexts, the delineation between the work of researchers and practitioners needs to be eliminated. In practical terms, this means that educational researchers who are 'outside' the educational contexts "must become participants in the schools themselves" (p. 159).

The second principle is that students themselves should understand the important mechanism involved in how they learn, especially those associated with the learning strategies that are being promoted. Even in psychological research, the focus has largely been on instructing students rather than on promoting their understanding about learning processes. However, if students are simply provided "tips" for effective learning, they might not fully recognize the effectiveness of the strategies, and they may instead resort to using less effective strategies that require less effort to use. Including instruction about how the strategy being cultivated works, why it is effective, and what beneficial outcomes could be expected from its use has likewise been considered important in other instructional approaches like the "more comprehensive" strategy instruction described by O'Sullivan and Pressley (1984).

The third principle is that students' spontaneous use of learning strategies should be assessed. The tendency in many research studies and educational initiatives for cultivating students' use of learning strategies is to focus on performance outcomes (e.g., improvements in test results or other assessments) following experimenter-provided instruction on the strategies. However, conducting only such kinds of assessment does not reveal whether students would likely use the strategies spontaneously in other appropriate learning situations or contexts—which is very important if they are to become independent learners. Despite the importance of promoting "transfer of learning strategy" (cf. Borkowski, Carr, & Pressley, 1987; Uesaka, 2010), such promotion has not been sufficiently attended to in empirical studies in the learning strategy research area.

Use of cognitive counseling to promote learning strategy use transfer

What is cognitive counseling and how does it promote spontaneous use of learning strategies?

Cognitive counseling was proposed by Ichikawa (1989) as a practical research activity in which people (clients, who are usually students) who experience difficulties in cognitive aspects of their lives make individual consultations with people who possess expertise in cognitive psychology (counselors, who are psychological researchers or school teachers). In contrast to clinical counseling, in which support is provided for emotional or personal problems that people are experiencing, cognitive counseling—as its name suggests—targets cognitive problems (see Ichikawa, 2005, for more information about this activity in English).

In cognitive counseling, careful assessment is conducted through an initial interview. During assessment, not only problems relating to insufficient subject knowledge and skills, but also problems relating to learning strategy use, are evaluated. Furthermore, the cognitive counseling sessions provide opportunities for utilizing the real materials that the client is experiencing difficulties with as they aim to resolve the client's problems, which is unlike other individual tutoring approaches where the purpose is examining the effects of personal tutoring when providing instruction in some new knowledge or skill (and thus requiring the use of materials prepared by the experimenters/tutors instead—e.g., Chi, Siler, Jeong, Yamauchi, & Hausmann, 2001). By using authentic materials that deal with the client's real pressing issues, there is an expectation of higher likelihood of transfer because of similarities in surface characteristics to the client's real everyday learning situations (e.g., Day & Goldstone, 2012).

Another important feature of cognitive counseling is that it not only encourages change in learning strategy use (where this may be appropriate), but also change in beliefs about learning. Ichikawa (1998) defined student beliefs about learning as the student's ideas about how he or she learns (e.g., "The key to learning is to memorize knowledge without considering why we do so", "It is a good opportunity to identify my learning weaknesses when I fail in learning something"). Addressing such beliefs is important as previous research has shown that they influence learning-related behaviors (e.g., Ames & Archer, 1988).

Case study of cognitive counseling promoting spontaneous strategy use

The client in this case was an 8th-grade girl (14 years of age) living in Japan (see Uesaka, 2010, for further details). She sought cognitive counseling because her achievement gradually deteriorated when she entered junior high school. She reported spending a lot of time solving problems contained in a workbook provided in school, but her achievement did not improve—instead it declined further. She hoped to receive counseling advice in math as she was struggling the most in this subject.

The assessment of the client involved interviewing her about her daily learning behaviors and her perceptions about her learning difficulties, and giving her some problems to solve, observing how she approached solving those, and getting her comments about what she found difficult. The assessment revealed a number of problems which are represented in Figure 12.1. Those problems included practicing a lot without reflecting on what she was supposed to be learning or the learning processes she was engaging in. Perhaps most importantly, she did not consider the reasons for her failure in problem solving, so she made the same mistakes repeatedly. She lacked metacognitive learning strategies and was not able to learn or benefit from her learning experiences (including her experiences of failure). Her learning problems were considered to stem largely from her beliefs about the aversive nature of failing (making her dislike dealing with such situations) and the importance of amount of time on learning rather than the quality of it.

To address this client's learning problems, the goal set was for her to use "lesson induction" (Ichikawa, 1991) which is a metacognitive strategy in which the learner considers the reasons for each success or failure in problem solving or other learning task—and induces a "lesson" that can then guide future learning behavior. By asking her to reflect on the reasons why she failed in problem solving through the use of lesson induction, the counselor tried to help her develop a better understanding of how she could identify the procedures and other aspects of problem solving she had not yet learned. The counselor also encouraged her to write down the "lessons learned" in her notebook to make her think more about those lessons. However, for some time after the counselor taught her how to use lesson induction, this client did not use this learning strategy spontaneously—only using it when the counselor asked her to.

To address the problem that the client was not spontaneously using lesson induction in her learning at home, the counselor decided to focus on analyzing the reasons for failure in her problem solving, and aimed at making the client better aware of the benefits of using this metacognitive strategy. The counselor encouraged the client to "induce lessons" not only about mathematical knowledge but also about learning strategy use. One example of such a lesson was: "It is good to regularly consider and write down the reasons for failing to solve problems. It will contribute to finding out the weak points in one's approach to learning". One result of focusing on analyzing the reasons for failure during the counseling sessions was that she started to realize her tendency to repeat the same mistakes. In addition, she gradually managed to work out by herself what she did not understand in her problem solving, and was therefore able to take appropriate action to seek clarification of those. As a consequence, her academic performance started to improve, which led to an improvement in her learning motivation as well.

After the student realized the effectiveness of this strategy, her beliefs about learning were also transformed. One comment she made during counseling was,

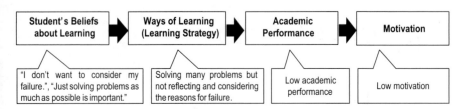

FIGURE 12.1 Situation of the client, as suggested by the assessment undertaken.

"This [lesson induction] is really good! I thought solving as many problems as possible was most important. But if I address the weaknesses in my learning, it is far more effective!" This comment clearly shows a shift in her beliefs about how to approach her learning. Moreover, following this apparent change in her beliefs about learning, she started to use lesson induction spontaneously in mathematics (i.e., without waiting for the counselor to advise or prompt her to do so). Toward the end of her cognitive counseling sessions, she also started to use lesson induction spontaneously even in science, in which she did not receive explicit encouragement for its use.

Discussion

This case study demonstrates application of the three design principles noted earlier. Firstly, the counselor was a researcher and cognitive psychologist who directly engaged in educational practice. Secondly, the client/student not only learned the learning strategy (lesson induction), but also learned how the learning strategy worked effectively in her actual learning situation. Evidence for this learning was shown by the student's declaration about the change in her conceptualization of learning. Thirdly, the counselor assessed the spontaneous use of a learning strategy in the student's own learning context, and made the effort to promote spontaneous use during the counseling sessions. The student cooperated with the activities that the counselor suggested, but did not evidence spontaneity in using the strategy until she better understood the personal worth of the strategy.

In the case described here, spontaneous strategy use was promoted not only in the subject dealt with during the cognitive counseling sessions (math), but also in another subject (science) not directly dealt with during the sessions. Thus, "transfer of learning strategy" (Borkowski et al., 1987; Uesaka, 2010) occurred. Figure 12.2 depicts the likely process by which the promotion of spontaneous use and transfer occurred. To address the problems that the client presented, the counselor focused on teaching and encouraging the use of a learning strategy in the subject of concern. Gradually, the client understood the connection between the use of the learning strategy and its contribution to her better problem solving performance, and the improvement in her academic performance enhanced

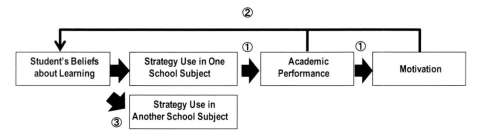

FIGURE 12.2 Process of learning strategy use promotion and transfer.

her motivation for study (① in Figure 12.2). These led to changes in her beliefs about learning (② in Figure 12.2)—particularly about the importance of the approach she used in learning. This change in her beliefs about learning led to her spontaneously applying the strategy in another subject (③ in Figure 12.2).

Development of special programs within the curriculum to promote spontaneous learning strategy use in schools

Learning strategy development within the curriculum

A recent development in the Japanese school curriculum is the inclusion of inter-disciplinary or cross-subject periods which teachers have the discretion to use for various learning integration or skills development work with students, including the provision of instruction in learning strategy use. However, learning strategy instruction was not included in the traditional Japanese curriculum, so many teachers feel that they lack the necessary knowledge and skills for its provision. Educational researchers therefore need to provide some guidance in this area, and one option is to collaborate with teachers so that teachers would later have a model for implementing the necessary development in other topic or subject areas. Ichikawa and Uesaka (2015) discussed how such development can be integrated within the current school curriculum. The case described here, which is based on a report by Fukaya et al. (2016), is one example of an approach to developing a specific aspect of learning strategy use. (Another example is provided in Chapter 14 in this book.)

Case study of special class sessions included in the curriculum

Learning strategies focused on in this case study

The learning strategies focused on were those that are necessary for effective communication with peers. Such strategies are important in students' everyday learning situations: they include strategies for effectively asking questions, expressing opinions, and monitoring others' understanding of information being conveyed. When appropriate communication strategies are used, collaboration with peers can be more beneficial and can help deepen students' understanding of what they are learning.

However, the quality of students' communicative strategies is not as good as educators and researchers might hope (e.g., Uesaka, Fukaya, Shinogaya, & Ichikawa, 2013). There are two basic problems. Firstly, when interacting in learning situations, students tend to ask superficial "what" questions rather than the more useful "why" or "how" questions that would lead to deepening their understanding (cf. Miyake, 1986). Secondly, students do not pay much attention to other students' understanding: for example, when explaining information to each other, students rarely ask their collocutors questions to check their understanding. Uesaka et al. (2013) believed that these problems originate from more fundamental problems in beliefs about learning: students tend to focus only on obtaining the "correct" answer. They neglect the importance of being able to explain reasons or mechanisms, and therefore do not use strategies like explaining in their own words to check their understanding. Thus, in this particular curriculum development, efforts were made to embed ways for improving students' learning beliefs and associated behaviors, alongside the provision of instruction on communication strategies for learning.

Brief description of the class sessions provided

The special class sessions were provided for first year students (320 students in eight classrooms) in one high school in Japan. The sessions comprised of four parts: Instruction (three sessions), Peer Tutoring-1 (one session), Feedback (one session), and Peer Tutoring-2 (one session).

In the Instruction sessions, lectures on the following topics were provided by a teacher or a researcher: relationship between learning strategy use and academic performance, three broad categories of learning strategies (metacognitive, cognitive, and resource use), and learning strategies relevant to peer communication. In the third of these sessions, how deep understanding can be achieved through effective communication was explained, and the students were given related exercises to do.

In the Peer Tutoring-1 session, the students were given four peer tutoring exercises to complete; these involved working in small groups, and taking on tutor and tutee roles. Ten minutes were allowed for each task, and worksheets provided to students included prompts to encourage communication with the use of "why" and "how" (rather than "what") questions.

In the Feedback session, a researcher provided feedback to students based on observation of the students' performance during the Peer Tutoring-1 session. The importance of communicating about "why" and "how" was emphasized. In addition, in order to check understanding, students in tutor roles were encouraged to ask students in tutee roles to explain what they had understood. The students were also encouraged to consider how they could use the strategies they had learned even when studying on their own (e.g., the use of self-explanation to check understanding).

In the Peer Tutoring-2 session, students were again given an opportunity to experience peer tutoring: this time they could decide the content of the tutoring based on what they were expecting would be included in the next regular class test. Students were asked to make groups of about four and to take turns at the tutor role.

Findings

To evaluate the effectiveness of this initiative, the quality of the students' communication in the two peer tutoring sessions and their spontaneous use of learning strategies were examined. The students' interactions in one of the eight classrooms (randomly selected) were audio recorded during the two peer tutoring sessions. The recordings were transcribed and each peer tutoring group's verbal output was coded 1 (affirmative) or 0 (negative) on seven aspects of interest. For example, if the students asked mainly "why" and "how" rather than "what" questions, then the "focus of questioning" aspect was coded as 1. Results from analysis of these data indicated that the overall quality of the students' communication improved from the first to the second session. For example, while some of the groups evidenced very low quality communication during the first session, none of the groups were in that category by the second session. This finding suggests that the instruction, practice, and feedback provided to students produced the desired improvements in the quality of their interactive communication.

The students' responses to a questionnaire that asked about their use of learning strategies were also examined. The questionnaire was administered three times: one month before (pre-test), one month after (post-test), and three months after (follow-up) the class sessions that were provided. The questionnaire included items like "I consider whether I can explain what I learned", which required responses on Likert-type scales. The students' scores on items that assessed use of self-explanation were significantly higher at post-test than at pre-test, and the higher level was maintained at follow-up. This finding suggests that the sessions provided to enhance the quality of students' communicative interactions in peer tutoring were also effective in promoting the students' spontaneous use of strategies relevant to their own individual learning.

Discussion

The approach described in this case study also incorporated the three design principles. Firstly, researchers were involved in designing and implementing the special classes in collaboration with school teachers so that a concrete model can be provided for the required development within the curriculum. Secondly, the students were not only instructed about effective strategies in communication, but also encouraged to understand why such strategies are facilitative of effective learning. Thirdly, the students' spontaneous use of the target learning strategies in communication, and in their own learning situations at home (transfer), was examined with the use of behavioral and survey data.

The findings from the project described here also indicate that effective learning strategies used in interactive peer learning/communication situations can be internalized by students for use in their own individual learning situations. This is congruent with earlier findings reported by Palincsar and Brown (1984) and Uesaka and Manalo (2007) where reading strategies and diagram use, respectively, were concerned. The findings from these earlier studies suggest that interactive peer learning/communication situations can facilitate students' awareness of the effectiveness of learning strategies they use during those situations, and as a consequence the students become more likely to subsequently use the strategies again in other learning situations (transfer).

Development of skills in learning strategy use through "thinking-after-instruction" approach in class

What is the "thinking-after-instruction" approach?

The use of the "thinking-after-instruction" approach in class was originally proposed by Ichikawa (2004, 2008) in an attempt to integrate two instructional approaches that are considered diametrically opposed to each other: discovery learning and receptive learning (Lee & Anderson, 2013). In this approach, students' thinking activity (discovery learning) follows teacher's direct instruction along with two additional phases to promote students' comprehension monitoring. More concretely, classroom instruction is conducted in four phases: (1) teachers' instruction (receptive learning), (2) comprehension checking, (3) deepening understanding (students' discovery learning), and (4) self-evaluation. It is therefore sequentially different to other instructional approaches that place discovering learning first and receptive learning second (e.g., Kapur & Bielaczyc, 2012). In addition, after receptive learning, the comprehension checking phase is included to encourage students to take appropriate steps to confirm their understanding. This checking comprehension phase is similar in idea to the "peer instruction" approach proposed by Mazur (1997) for teaching a physics course. After the deepening understanding phase, the self-evaluation phase is also included to encourage students to consciously consider what they have learned and what they have not.

The main purpose of the thinking-after-instruction approach is to deepen students' understanding of what they learn in class. It has, however, a secondary purpose—which is to promote effective learning strategy use. Many opportunities are provided for students to experience effective learning strategy use in classes where this approach is employed. An implicit expectation in the thinking-after-instruction approach is that students who experience the use of those learning strategies in class would acquire proficiency in their use and appreciate the benefits they bring to learning, and consequently they would internalize the use of those strategies and use them spontaneously in situations such as when they are learning at home. The third case study below (reported in more detail in Uesaka, 2014) describes a whole-school adoption of the approach.

Elementary school application of the thinking-after-instruction approach to promote spontaneous use of learning strategies

Kashiwajima Elementary School is a public elementary school in Japan that participated in a bigger research project aimed at enhancing students' academic achievement and competencies as effective citizens. As part of the project, the school also utilized the thinking-after-instruction approach in classroom teaching: it was used in teaching at least all math classes. Although teachers provided the classroom instruction, at the early stages of the project a researcher provided the thinking-after-instruction sessions to provide a model for conducting such sessions to the teachers. Also the first two authors of this chapter participated in teaching and providing advice to the school during the four years of the project. At the time of writing this chapter—which was after the project had been completed—teachers in this school were still using the approach in their classroom teaching.

This school especially focused on improving students' metacognitive learning strategies through use of the thinking-after-instruction approach. The framework for this approach is shown in Table 12.1. The first step occurred before class with preparatory reading: students were encouraged to check their understanding of the assigned reading materials, and to set concrete goals for what they should listen carefully to in class—especially to clarify what they might not have understood sufficiently. In the checking comprehension stage, students were provided problems to work on, or asked to explain key points "as a teacher might explain" (e.g., explaining how a formula is derived). At the end of each class, the students were asked to reflect again on what they had understood and what they had not sufficiently understood, so that they could better determine appropriate future learning behaviors (e.g., what to follow up on in study at home). To facilitate students' understanding of this cycle of learning, teachers also explicitly taught the students about the ideal learning process and displayed copies of good examples of notebooks in each classroom. As a result of these efforts, the academic achievement of students in this school started to improve as measured by standardized tests.

To answer the question of whether students in this school spontaneously used effective learning strategies, the notebooks of students in one classroom were examined, particularly concerning what students had written in one unit covered in grade 5 math (the unit was selected randomly, and the teacher was not informed of the selection until afterward). The results demonstrated that almost all of the students (29 students out of 30 students) prepared for each upcoming class by reading the textbook and clarifying what they understood, identifying what they did not understand, and specifying the goals they wanted to achieve in class. Analysis of the contents of what they wrote showed that, even when they were focusing on acquisition of procedural knowledge, half of students referred to the meaning of the procedure by connecting it with previously acquired knowledge. This kind of knowledge association can be considered as spontaneous use of a cognitive learning strategy. Several students who could not understand some information contained in their textbook, spontaneously wrote questions (e.g., "I am not sure why the decimal point should be moved"). Also in the self-evaluation stage of the thinking-after-instruction learning activities in class, half of the students referred not only to the procedures they learned, but also to their understanding of the meaning of

TABLE 12.1 Framework for using the thinking-after-instruction approach prior to and during class (parts relating to metacognitive learning strategies are underlined)

	Teacher's actions	Students' responsibilities
Before class: Preparatory reading	Encouraging students to read their textbooks to prepare for their upcoming classes.	Checking what they have understood and what they did not understand. Setting their own goals to achieve in class (especially in fifth and sixth grades) and writing these goals down in their notebooks.
In class: Teacher's instruction	Providing regular instruction, but taking care to also explain meanings rather than just telling students what to do.	Focusing on points that they do not understand when listening to teacher's instruction.
Checking comprehension	Asking students to solve problems, or to explain "as a teacher does" (conducted in pairs or small groups).	Checking own understanding; when they cannot solve or explain, becoming aware that they do not understand. The other member(s) of a pair (or group) should support to facilitate understanding.
Deepening understanding	Providing task(s) that require application of what students have learned; designed to further deepen students' understanding of learning materials.	Collaboratively solving assigned tasks with peers.
Self-evaluation	Asking students to reflect on what they have understood and what they have not understood.	Checking/identifying what they understood of the learning materials, and also what they have not sufficiently understood.

those procedures. Such comments indicated not only the acquisition of deeper understanding, but also of spontaneous use of a metacognitive learning strategy.

Discussion

This case example likewise shared the three design principles. Firstly, educational researchers also collaborated with the teachers in designing class instruction to promote skills development. Secondly, the teachers explicitly taught the students about effective learning processes—to ensure development of their understanding of the actual mechanisms involved in effective learning. Thirdly, the students' spontaneous use of learning strategies was assessed—in this case, in the students' learning at home, via the notes they were asked to make in preparatory reading and other homework activities.

The thinking-after-instruction approach shares parallel features with the cyclic framework of self-regulated learning, in which learning is conceptualized as having forethought, performance, and self-reflection phases (e.g., Zimmerman, 1989). In utilizing the thinking-after-instruction approach in this school, preparatory reading can be likened to the forethought phase; the teacher's instruction, comprehension checking, and deepening understanding components of the in-class session correspond to the performance phase; and the self-evaluation component is equivalent to the self-reflection phase. Analysis of the students' notes in their home learning revealed that the majority of them were spontaneously making use of appropriate learning strategies. As spontaneous strategy use is one indicator of self-regulated learning, this finding could be explained in terms of the thinking-after-instruction approach facilitating the students' application of the key phases of the self-regulated learning cyclic framework.

General discussion

This chapter described three case studies that illustrate how it may be possible to promote spontaneous learning strategy use among students in real educational contexts. In each case, evidence was gathered indicating that the students started using appropriate learning strategies spontaneously in their own learning situations—as a consequence of the interventions or instructions provided. In each case, the relevance and contributions of the three design principles in promoting spontaneous strategy use were explained. However, it is useful to briefly consider here some of the other instructional features the three cases shared that may have also contributed to such promotion.

The interventions employed in all three cases had a firm commitment to self-directed learning. Even though guidance and/or instruction were provided, the responsibility for the 'required' learning behaviors was always with the students. Such expectation on the student is very much in line with Knowles (1975, p. 18) concept of self-directed learning in which the learner takes the initiative in "diagnosing their learning needs, formulating learning goals, identifying human and material resources for learning, *choosing and implementing appropriate learning strategies* and evaluating learning outcomes" [italics added].

Closely connected to the expectation to take responsibility for learning behaviors is the valuing of strategies, which is both explicit and implicit in the three cases described. The students were not only provided explicit instruction about the value of the target learning strategies, but were also put in situations where they would experience the value of those strategies in achieving learning objectives. Those steps were also taken to ensure that students would be able to confidently use the strategies. Such experiences are important in facilitating internalization of the strategies—in other words, for the learner to consider those strategies as his or her own strategies to use (cf. Uesaka & Manalo, 2007). The importance that is placed here on communication to facilitate internalization of strategies resonates with Vygotsky's (1978) theory, in which interaction with significant others in the external environment is crucial for an individual to refine internal thinking processes and understanding. This internalization of strategies can also be understood in terms of Ryan and Deci's (2000) concept of "integrated regulation", where the regulatory behavior—in this case, use of the strategy—is assimilated to the self as it is viewed as being congruent with one's other values and needs.

Finally, in all three cases, metacognition was emphasized and cultivated: students were encouraged to consider connections between strategy use and learning performance outcomes, to check their own and their peers' understanding, to explain what they have learned as a teacher might do, and so on. Many of these metacognitive activities require articulation, either verbal (e.g., explaining to peers) or written (e.g., making notes). Such articulation is important in making students better aware of their thought processes and the connection of those to learning behaviors—including how, when, and where to use specific learning strategies. Borkowski et al. (1987) considered maturity in metacognitive ability as an essential determinant of whether an individual would engage in spontaneous use of appropriate learning strategies.

The three case studies described in this chapter illustrate how, in real educational settings, it is possible to promote students' spontaneous use of effective learning strategies. The approaches used can be modified and adapted to suit variations in learning environments and requirements of students. They are by no means the only approaches that can promote spontaneous strategy use, but the authors of this chapter hope that they can serve as useful models for teachers and other educators who are faced with challenges in the promotion of such strategy use.

References

Ames, C., & Archer, J. (1988). Achievement goals in the classroom: Student's learning strategies and motivation processes. *Journal of Educational Psychology, 80*(3), 260–267.

Borkowski, J., Carr, M., & Pressely, M. (1987). "Spontaneous" strategy use: Perspectives from metacognitive theory. *Intelligence, 11*(1), 61–75.

Carr, W., & Kemmis, S. (2004). *Becoming critical: Education, knowledge and action research.* London: RoutledgeFalmer.

Chi, M. T. H., Siler, S., Jeong, H., Yamauchi, T., & Hausmann, R. G. (2001). Learning from human tutoring. *Cognitive Science, 25*(4), 471–534.

Day, S. B., & Goldstone, R. L. (2012). Import of knowledge export: Connecting findings and theories of transfer of learning. *Educational Psychologist, 47*(3), 153–176.

De Corte, E. (2000). Marrying theory building and the improvement of school practice: A permanent challenge for instructional psychology. *Learning and Instruction, 10*(3), 249–266.

Fukaya, T., Uesaka, Y., Tanaka, E., Shinogaya, K., Nishio, S., & Ichikawa, S. (2016). Effects of a high school peer-tutoring program on the quality of students' interactions and learning strategy use. *Japanese Journal of Educational Psychology, 64*(1), 88–104.

Ichikawa, S. (1991). "Cognitive counseling" as practical cognitive study. In Y. Hakoda (Ed.), *The frontiers of cognitive science 1.* Tokyo, Japan: Saiensu-sha (in Japanese).

Ichikawa, S. (Ed.). (1993). *Cognitive counseling that supports learning: A new approach bridging psychology and education.* Tokyo, Japan: Brain Shuppan (in Japanese).

Ichikawa, S. (Ed.). (1998). *Assessment and instruction of learning skills: From a cognitive counseling approach.* Tokyo, Japan: Brain Shuppan (in Japanese).

Ichikawa, S. (1989). The idea of cognitive counseling and its development. *Japanese Psychological Review, 32*, 421–437.

Ichikawa, S. (2004). *Improving learning motivation and skills: Requested strategies for improving academic achievement.* Tokyo: Shogakukan (in Japanese).

Ichikawa, S. (2005). Cognitive counseling to improve students' metacognition and cognitive skills. In D. W. Shwalb, J. Nakazawa, & B. J. Shwalb (Eds.), *Applied developmental psychology: Theory, practice, and research from Japan* (pp. 67–87). Greenwich, CT: Information Age Publishing.

Ichikawa, S. (2008). *Designing a class with the "thinking-after instruction" approach.* Tokyo, Japan: Toshobunka (in Japanese).

Ichikawa, S., & Uesaka, Y. (2015). Learning skills to live in society and support for that. Curriculum Innovation Study Group at the University of Tokyo (Ed.), *Curriculum innovation: Toward the creation of new learning* (pp. 95–104). Tokyo, Japan: University of Tokyo Press (in Japanese).

Kapur, M., & Bielaczyc, K. (2012). Designing for productive failure. *The Journal of the Learning Sciences, 21*, 45–83.

Knowles, M. S. (1975). *Self-directed learning: A guide for learners and teachers.* New York: Association Press.

Lee, H. S., & Anderson, J. R. (2013). Student learning: What has instruction got to do with it? *Annual Review of Psychology, 64*, 445–469.

Mazur, E. (1997). *Peer instruction: A user's manual.* Upper Saddle River, NJ: Pearson-Prentice Hall.

McInerney, D. M. (2005). Educational psychology—Theory, research, and teaching: A 25-year retrospective. *Educational Psychology, 25*(6), 585–599.

Ministry of Education, Culture, Sports, Science and Technology in Japan. (2008). *A survey on actual situation of children's learning activities out of schools* (in Japanese). Retrieved May 10, 2014 from www.mext.go.jp/b_menu/houdou/20/08/__icsFiles/afieldfile/2009/03/23/1196664.pdf

Miyake, N. (1986). Constructive interaction and the iterative process of understanding. *Cognitive Science, 10*(2), 151–177.

OECD (Organization for Economic Cooperation and Development). (2008). *21st century learning: Research, innovation and policy: Directions from recent OECD analyses.* Paris: Author.

O'Sullivan, J. T., & Pressley, M. (1984). Completeness of instruction and strategy transfer. *Journal of Experimental Child Psychology, 38*(2), 275–288.

Palincsar, A. S., & Brown, A. L. (1984). Reciprocal teaching of comprehension-fostering and comprehension monitoring activities. *Cognition and Instruction, 1*(2), 117–175.

Pellegrino, J. W., & Hilton, M. L. (2012). *Education for life and work: Developing transferable knowledge and skills in the 21st century.* Washington, DC: National Academies Press.

Ryan, R. M., & Deci, E. L. (2000). Intrinsic and extrinsic motivations: Classic definitions and new directions. *Contemporary Educational Psychology, 25*(1), 54–67.

Seifert, C. (1999). Situated cognition and learning. In R. A. Wilson & F. C. Keil (Eds.), *The MIT encyclopedia of the learning sciences* (pp. 767–769). Cambridge, MA: MIT Press.

Uesaka, Y. (2010). How learning strategy use transfers across different school subjects: A case study on promotion of spontaneous use of "lesson induction". *Japanese Journal of Educational Psychology, 58*(1), 80–94 (in Japanese).

Uesaka, Y. (2014). Promoting meta-cognition coordinating classroom instruction and learning at home: Analysis of note-books in Kashiwajima elementary school in Kurashiki city. In Y. Uesaka & E. Manalo (Eds.), *New developments in theory and practices in learning strategy research: Findings from the third year of a JSPS-supported research project*, Working papers Vol. 3, October 2014 (pp. 63–74). Tokyo, Japan: The University of Tokyo(in Japanese).

Uesaka, Y., Fukaya, T., Shinogaya, K., & Ichikawa, S. (2013). Practices of peer-tutoring in high school (1): The reason why the quality of peer-tutoring did not improve. *Proceedings of the Annual Conference of the Japanese Association of Educational Psychology* (p. 601). Tokyo, Japan: Japanese Association of Educational Psychology (in Japanese).

Uesaka, Y., & Manalo, E. (2007). Peer instruction as a way of promoting spontaneous use of diagrams when solving math word problems. In D. S. McNamara & J. G. Trafton (Eds.), *Proceedings of the 29th Annual Cognitive Science Society* (pp. 677–682). Austin, TX: Cognitive Science Society.

Uesaka, Y., Seo, M., & Ichikawa, S. (2012). Examining the actual situation and problems of instruction about learning strategies in Japanese elementary school and junior high school. In Y. Uesaka & E. Manalo (Eds.), *Promoting students' use of effective learning strategies: Findings from the first year of a JSPS-supported research project*, Working papers, August 2012 (Vol. 1, pp. 22–26). Tokyo, Japan: The University of Tokyo (in Japanese).

Uesaka, Y., Suzuki, M., Kiyokawa, S., Seo, M., & Ichikawa, S. (2014). Using COMPASS (Componential Assessment) to reveal Japanese students' actual competence in the fundamentals of mathematics: Is it true that "students are generally fine with the fundamentals, and that the problems exist only in applications"? *Japanese Journal of Educational Technology, 37*, 397–417 (in Japanese).

Vygotsky, L. S. (1978). *Mind in society: The development of higher psychological processes.* Cambridge, MA: Harvard University Press.

Zimmerman, B. J. (1989). A social cognitive view of self-regulated learning. *Journal of Educational Psychology, 81*(3), 329–339.

13

CODING DOSAGE OF TEACHERS' IMPLEMENTATION OF ACTIVITIES USING ICAP

A video analysis

Glenda S. Stump, Na Li, Seokmin Kang, David Yaghmourian, Dongchen Xu, Joshua Adams, Katherine L. McEldoon, Matthew Lancaster, and Michelene T. H. Chi

Introduction

The ultimate goal of professional development is to facilitate teachers' spontaneous transfer of knowledge gained from education research to their teaching practice in order to improve student outcomes. Researchers in the field of teacher professional development agree that professional education should situate learning opportunities for teachers in the context of their work (e.g., Ball & Cohen, 1999; Kazemi & Hubbard, 2008) and that a professional development "curriculum" should be grounded in the tasks, questions, and problems of practice (Ball & Cohen, 1999, p. 20). Our intervention, instructing in-service teachers about the ICAP (*Interactive-Constructive-Active-Passive*) framework and its implementation, afforded them the opportunity to apply a theoretical framework in the context of their everyday activities. The instruction was grounded in the tasks that teachers perform on a frequent basis—designing ways to engage their students in learning. Our intervention was an effort to address the ubiquitous question of how student learning can be improved via teachers' instantiation of activities that elicit increased student engagement. In this chapter, we will report our methodology and results from a video analysis conducted to assess teachers' transfer of their learning about the ICAP framework from this professional development activity to their implementation of ICAP activities in the classroom.

The ICAP framework

The ICAP framework (Chi, 2009) links students' overt engagement behaviors to cognitive processes of knowledge change that facilitate learning. It not only explains discrepant findings in education research, but also prescribes characteristics that must be present for optimal learning to occur. The framework specifies four modes of behavioral engagement: *passive, active, constructive,* and *interactive.* When students are engaged in *passive* behaviors, such as listening to a lecture, or silently reading a passage of text, they are paying attention, or receiving information. This allows for "storing" of information without embedding it in a relevant schema, which eventually may detract from its retrieval in dissimilar contexts. *Active* engagement includes some type of motoric involvement in which students are manipulating the material to be learned in some way, such as highlighting or underlining a passage, matching a word to its definition, or solving a problem using a given formula. This manipulating behavior leads to the activation of prior knowledge and "integration" of the given information for later retrieval. When students engage in *constructive* behaviors, they generate some type of output containing new information that goes beyond what was given, or engage in the knowledge change process of "inferring." The inferences generated during this level of engagement serve to enrich relevant schema and better prepare students to transfer their understanding to novel situations. The fourth mode of engagement in the framework is the *interactive* level, in which students engage in the *constructive* process of inferring with another individual, or the knowledge change process of "co-inferring." During the exchange, they generate new insights together in a give-and-take manner.

The ICAP hypothesis posits that the four modes of engagement—*passive, active, constructive, and interactive*—are organized in a hierarchical manner and lead to differential effects on student learning. Behaviors enacted during the highest level of engagement (*interactive*) subsume those enacted in levels below it. For example, a student engaged at an *interactive* level is also generating information, which is *constructive*; when generating information, that student is also engaged in a motoric behavior, which is *active*; and when engaged in a motoric behavior, he or she is also paying attention, which is *passive*. As each level of engagement from *passive* to *interactive* leads to deeper processing of information, the ICAP hypothesis states that student learning during *interactive* activities will be greater than learning during *constructive* activities; learning during *constructive* activities will be greater than learning during *active* activities; and learning during *active* activities will be greater than learning during *passive* activities.

The ICAP hypothesis has been supported when multiple studies were reinterpreted using the ICAP framework (see Chi, 2009; Chi & Wylie, 2014; Fonseca & Chi, 2011 for a complete review). Several studies have shown results as predicted by the hypothesis in lab and naturalistic settings in which activities were implemented and controlled by the researchers (Menekse, Stump, Krause, & Chi, 2013). The current project was an effort to scale implementation of the ICAP framework to a larger sample of teachers than in previous implementations.

Project design

Successful implementation of ICAP in this study meant that teachers were able to transfer their learning about ICAP to their subsequent design and implementation of lessons. This study was part of a larger project designed to implement the ICAP framework in secondary and post-secondary settings. In the final year of the project, information about the framework was delivered as a professional development activity via an online module (the ICAP module) to in-service junior high and high school teachers. Teachers completed the module prior to the start of the school year.

The ICAP module consisted of a pretest, four units of instruction, and a posttest. It began with a general introduction about student engagement followed by an overview of module content. The teachers then completed a 68-question pretest before moving on to the first unit of instruction. The pretest took approximately 40 minutes to complete.

The first unit contained a description of the ICAP hypothesis along with principles of the ICAP framework. Twenty-one comprehension questions were embedded within the online material. Teachers were required to respond to the embedded questions before they could continue with the next activity. For questions that could be easily scored (e.g., multiple choice), teachers received immediate feedback regarding accuracy of their responses and were required to answer the item correctly before moving on to the next activity. However, the teachers' first response was recorded and used for scoring purposes. For questions that required human grading (e.g., short answer), teachers did not receive feedback, and they could move on to the next activity without ensuring their response was correct.

The second unit contained examples of activities at various ICAP levels and focused on the design of ICAP activities by providing practice with modifying or improving given instructional activities to fit criteria of a particular ICAP level. This unit contained 25 embedded comprehension questions. The third unit contained information about and practice with writing assessment items that would measure different levels of student learning from ICAP activities. There were 28 embedded comprehension questions in this unit. The fourth unit contained implementation tips as well as examples of lesson plans that were designed to align with a specific ICAP level. This unit did not contain comprehension questions. After completing the fourth unit, teachers completed a 68-question posttest that took approximately 40 minutes. Completion of the pretest, four units of the module, and posttest required approximately 2 hours.

In the months following completion of the ICAP module, teachers created lesson plans focused on teaching the same course content at different ICAP levels to two classes. Following submission of their lesson plans, teachers received feedback from members of the research team about their planned activities and student assessments. The feedback was provided to correct any misconceptions teachers had about the ICAP framework and to remind them about some specific aspects of ICAP levels related to student behaviors. The teachers revised their lesson plans as recommended by members of the research team and resubmitted them for further review.

Implementation of ICAP lessons

We considered teachers' correct implementation of their ICAP lessons in the classroom as evidence for successful transfer of their learning about the ICAP framework. In this context, transfer cannot be conceived of in the typical two-problem transfer paradigm as described by Lave (1988), in which learners first abstract the deep structure of a problem, recognize that a second problem has the same structure, and then realize that the same procedure applies to both. In our case, teachers were expected to make direct application of an explanatory concept (ICAP principles) to new instances well removed from their initial learning (Perkins & Salomon, 2012). This can be conceptualized as an instance of analogical reasoning in which the teachers mapped exemplars given in the ICAP module to their planned class activities (Gentner, 1983). Nokes (2009) explains that analogical reasoning is most commonly used in this type of situation because it is fast and efficient to the degree that the exemplar surface features and deep structure are a reasonable match to the new situation.

To evidence the degree of transfer by our 13 participating teachers, we videotaped each class in which they implemented their planned lessons. We then analyzed 65 videos for implementation of the lesson at a particular level of engagement from the teachers' perspective. Results from the video analysis helped us to determine if a class planned at a particular ICAP level by teachers (as evidenced in their lesson plans) was delivered at the intended level. We based the judgement of "delivered as intended" on the proportion of time allotted to activities at various levels of engagement (details of the coding will be presented below).

Data

Our data sources for this analysis were 65 class videos from 32 lessons along with written materials that teachers distributed to students during the lesson. Each lesson was delivered at a different ICAP level to two different classes, except for one lesson that was delivered at three different ICAP levels to three different classes. For example, one teacher developed a math lesson on ratios and delivered the lesson at an *active* level to one class and at an *interactive* level to another class. The class videos showed the entire class, which was approximately 50 minutes long for junior high students, and 90 minutes for high school students. A typical class involved a pretest; delivery of class content via lecture or readings; question and answer periods in which the teacher would ask questions of the entire class; individual activities such as writing question responses in journals, designing posters, or completing worksheets; activities in which students worked with a partner or group; and a posttest.

Activities were defined as student endeavors that occurred any time during the 50 minute class, such as note-taking during content delivery if the teacher lectured, or completing a worksheet or creating a poster after content delivery. Activities varied considerably in nature, length, and number between lessons. Some teachers designed lessons in which one activity extended over the majority of each class; other teachers initiated two or more shorter activities during a lesson. On average, the lessons contained between one and five activities, or an average of three for each class.

Procedure

Determination of boundaries in videos

Beginning and end boundaries on the video data were set at the beginning of each class (as the teacher began to give instruction or guidance related to the content of the lesson) and at the end of each class. The boundaries excluded time utilized for the pretest and posttest. If more than five minutes were devoted to transition from one portion of the class to another, e.g., teachers pairing up students, collecting worksheets, or students cleaning up, this time was also excluded. The remaining time represented between 80–100% of the total time per class. Boundaries between activities were determined to be the point at which one activity transitioned to another. These boundaries were established during phase 1 coding.

After boundaries were set, the time to be coded was parsed into one-minute segments. This allowed us to calculate the ICAP "dosage" in terms of the total number of minutes allocated for activities at a particular ICAP level. It also allowed us to check inter-rater agreement by making a minute-by-minute comparison of two rater's codes over the class period. The video coding was then conducted in two phases.

Phase 1 coding

During the first phase, we used the teachers' oral instructions for student activities, the content-related questions they asked during class, and any prompts they gave to students as cues to infer teachers' intention to implement activities at a particular ICAP level. We assigned a code to all minutes within the class boundaries using the following nomenclature: *passive, active, constructive, interactive, UTC* (unable to code – for the time in which an ICAP level could not be determined from teachers' oral instructions or activity descriptions), and *NC* (no code – for the short periods of time related to non-content instruction or time when students were forming groups, getting equipment, etc.).

Four activities were noted to be the most common—taking notes, completing worksheets, working with a peer, and responding to questions that teachers asked verbally during content delivery. Our coding rules for each of these activities are described below.

Taking notes: The ICAP level for time related to this activity was determined by *how* teachers orally told students to take the notes. A single activity could elicit different levels of student engagement, depending on the teacher's instructions or scaffolding during the activity. For example, if a teacher used a Power Point presentation to deliver a lecture for twenty minutes and orally told the students to take notes, those twenty minutes were coded as *active* because students were focusing on particular pieces of content and we assumed students were copying notes from the Power Point. Alternatively, if the teacher orally told students to take notes in their own words, or asked them to answer questions in their notes that required inferences about the content, those twenty minutes were coded as *constructive* because we assumed students were generating information beyond what was given.

Completing worksheets: The ICAP level for time used for this activity was determined by key words in the teachers' oral instructions. If key words suggesting manipulation of given information (such as "list the important concepts," "select the answer," or "match the items") were used, the related minutes were coded as *active*. If key words suggesting generation of inferences (such as "predict," "justify," "compare and contrast," "hypothesize," "generate a rule," "self-explain," "propose," "critique," or "create a table/concept map") were used, the related minutes were coded as *constructive*. If the teachers' verbal instructions did not explicitly reveal an ICAP level—for example, if the teacher stated, "Complete this worksheet," the related minutes were coded as *UTC* and recoded during phase two.

Working with a peer: The ICAP level for time related to this activity was coded as *interactive* if the teacher elicited at least a behaviorally interactive activity by instructing students with statements such as "talk to your partner," or "work together."

Responding to teachers' oral questions: The ICAP level for time used for this questioning activity was based on the type of question teachers asked and how many students were permitted to respond if an oral response was requested. If teachers asked questions that required students to recall a fact, such as "What makes up the coat of a virus?" and this fact had been presented during class, the related segments were coded as *active* because students were just recalling information that had been previously given. Key words from the 'remember' level of Bloom's taxonomy (Krathwohl, 2002) such as "define," "name," "list," "describe," or "restate" were often indicative of recall questions. On the other hand, if teachers asked questions that required students to make an inference or new connection between facts or concepts, the related minutes were coded as *constructive* because students were often generating information that had not been presented to them. Similar to evaluating the ICAP level of teachers' verbal instructions for worksheets, key words used when asking questions orally, such as "compare," "contrast," "justify," "defend," or "evaluate," were considered to be indicative of questions that required students to make inferences. These keywords are from the 'understand,' 'apply,' 'analyze,' 'evaluate,' and 'create' levels of Bloom's taxonomy, as tasks at those levels can require students to make inferences about given information. The exception to use of the above-mentioned words as key words was when the correct response had already been given and students merely had to recall it. For example, if teachers asked an inference question for which the answer had been previously discussed, we coded the allocated time as *active* because students were only required to recall the correct answer rather than making any new connections between concepts or generating any new understanding.

As mentioned earlier, the second consideration when coding time allocated to question and answer sessions was the number of students permitted to respond. If teachers asked an inference question and students answered by writing a response in their notes, the allocated time was coded *constructive* because all students were presumably writing responses. Similarly, if teachers told students to answer in unison to the same question, the allocated time was coded as *constructive* because again, all students (or at least a majority) were responding. However, if teachers told students to raise their hand to respond, and then called on only one student who raised his/her hand, the allocated time was coded as *passive*, because the majority of the students were not responding and may not have even contemplated a response to the question.

To summarize, during the first phase of coding, we examined the videos for teachers' oral instructions, questions, and prompts to determine the ICAP level that should have been elicited from their presentation to the students. We defined keywords, many borrowed from Bloom's taxonomy (Krathwohl, 2002) to code the ICAP levels of teachers' oral questions or instructions. In addition to the codes representing ICAP levels, we applied *UTC* for minutes in which the ICAP level was ambiguous from teachers' descriptions and *NC* for time that was not related to instruction or activities.

Phase 2 coding

The coding done in phase 1 was based strictly on the teachers' instructions, in terms of what the teachers orally asked students to do or to answer. However, it is not accurate to code only based on what teachers asked, without also coding for what teachers presented during the course of instruction, because what is presented in instruction can change the ICAP level of a question or an activity. Thus in this second phase of coding, we examined any written materials that accompanied the lessons and reviewed the information that teachers presented during class. Evaluation of Power Point presentations and readings as well as review of class lectures helped us to identify instances in which the answers to inference questions asked during activities had already been provided to students, thus converting *constructive* activities to *active* ones because students could simply recall an answer instead of generating it. Evaluation of the worksheets also helped to resolve any ambiguous segments that we were unable to code during the first phase (the cases in which teachers did not orally indicate the type of activity contained in the worksheet), and also helped us to determine if the activities were at one ICAP level or a mixture of levels. Our process of corroborating the accuracy of ICAP levels assigned during phase 1 is described in more detail below.

When reviewing materials for minutes that were coded as *passive* during the first phase, we examined for any directives that would increase students' level of engagement, such as a worksheet that provided spaces for note-taking during instruction. If such directives were found, the *passive* code was then changed to the appropriate ICAP level. When reviewing materials for segments that were previously coded as *active*, we examined the instructions, accompanying questions, or problems to confirm that they only asked students to manipulate the materials in some way, such as copying, selecting the correct answer from information given in class, using a given formula to solve a problem, or underlining important concepts. When reviewing materials related to the segments that were previously coded as *constructive*, we examined for directives to generate information in some manner, such as connecting previous knowledge to newly learned knowledge, using prior knowledge in a novel way, inducing or inferring new information from given information, making predictions related to newly learned principles, or deducing rules from observed patterns. Key words from Bloom's taxonomy, as described in the phase 1 coding description, were also used in this phase of coding as a guide to identify questions or activities that required recall versus inference-making. As described earlier, activities designated at this level could easily be converted from *constructive* to *active* if teachers presented the information elsewhere in the lesson that students were supposed to generate. Thus the classes were closely scrutinized to ascertain that the activities truly required students to exert generative cognitive effort instead of simply recalling information that they had been given. When reviewing materials for minutes that were previously coded as *interactive*, we examined the instructions, accompanying questions, or problems to confirm that they were *constructive* (required for true co-construction), rather than *active* activities in which students were asked to work in pairs. This coding was more stringent than during phase 1 when, rather than examine the nature of the activity, we considered the activity *interactive* if students were only asked to be behaviorally interactive (work together). However, in phase 2 we still could not determine whether students were actually co-constructing, which is the most stringent measure of *interactive* engagement as defined by ICAP.

Phase 2 coding also allowed us to assign minutes of an ICAP level within an activity if it was comprised of more than one level. For example, if after coding, half of the questions in a worksheet turned out to be recall questions (an *active* activity) and the other half were inference questions (a *constructive* activity), we coded 50% of the total minutes allocated for the activity as *active* and 50% as *constructive*.

To summarize, during the second phase of coding, we examined any written materials that accompanied the lessons to verify that they (materials) would contribute to or elicit engagement at the same ICAP level teachers articulated to their students. If the materials did not support student engagement at the ICAP level that teachers articulated, we recoded the associated minutes to the appropriate ICAP level.

Inter-rater agreement

During phase 1 coding, we randomly selected 23% of the data—four math classes, four science classes, four language arts classes, and three foreign language classes—to determine inter-rater agreement for our coding. The classes were assigned to six trained raters, ensuring that two raters independently completed coding for each class. Initial agreement between any two raters ranged from 39% to 100%, with only two classes having agreement lower than 85%. For those classes, the raters reviewed the coding protocol and recoded the classes until agreement reached 85%. The six raters then individually coded the remainder of the classes for phase 1.

During phase 2 coding, the same individuals served as second raters for the same fifteen classes. Initial agreement between any two raters ranged from 33% to 98%; this time, eight out of the 15 classes had inter-rater agreement lower than 85%.

The major source of discrepancy was determination of the proportion of questions or problems that belonged to the *active* or *constructive* category. The raters who coded the same class resolved this disagreement via discussion, and then recoded the segments, reaching an agreement of 85% for each of the eight classes. Six raters individually coded the remainder of the classes for phase 2.

Calculation of ICAP dosage and correct implementation

The final step of the video coding process was to calculate the proportion of class time teachers actually allocated to each ICAP level, based on our coding. These proportions were interpreted as the "ICAP dosage." We then determined whether teachers implemented classes as they intended by using two criteria related to ICAP dosage: 1) the plurality of time was allocated to the ICAP level stated on their lesson plan, and 2) the proportion of that time was greater than 30% of the total class time. For example, if a teacher designed a class to be *constructive* and allocated 45% of class time to *constructive* activities, 30% to *active* activities, and 25% to *passive* activities, the class was considered to be implemented correctly because the plurality of time was devoted to *constructive* activities and the time allocated was more than 30% of the total class time.

Results

When comparing the teachers' intended ICAP level for their classes (as stated in their lesson plans) with the ICAP dosage as determined by video coding, we found that overall, 37 of the 65 classes (57%) were not delivered at the ICAP level that the teacher intended, or what we will refer to as incorrectly implemented. That is, 57% of the classes did not allocate a plurality of the total class time (and greater than 30%) to the intended activity. Table 13.1 shows the number of classes that were actually implemented at each ICAP level (according to our two dosage criteria),

TABLE 13.1 Teachers' intended versus implemented class ICAP levels

Intended ICAP level (total classes intended at this level)	Implemented ICAP level using dosage criteria			
	Passive	Active	Constructive	Interactive
Passive (3)	**1.5 (50%)**	1.5		
Active (19)	2	**17 (89%)**		
Constructive (20)	3.5	11	**5.5 (28%)**	
Interactive (23)	4	13	1	**5 (22%)**

Numbers in **bold** denote classes that were implemented as intended; percentages were calculated from classes delivered as intended/total number of classes intended at this level. The classes in which time was allocated equally between activities were not considered to be implemented correctly.

out of the total number of classes intended at a given ICAP level. If the *passive* classes are ignored due to their low number, Table 13.1 shows that the highest proportion of classes implemented correctly was the *active* classes at 89%. Both the *constructive* and *interactive* classes had much lower rates of correct implementation, at around 25% on average.

We examined other data for factors that may have predicted the teachers' ability to effectively implement ICAP in their classes—teachers' responses to 16 posttest items related to application of ICAP principles from the online ICAP module. These questions asked teachers to explain their understanding of the ICAP framework and apply that understanding to given scenarios. There were four 'Improve' questions that asked teachers to apply their knowledge of ICAP to improve an activity to a higher level, and 12 'Explain' questions that asked them to define ICAP levels and describe activities that could be implemented at each level, or describe why an activity was classified at a particular ICAP level.

To see whether teachers could implement activities with greater fidelity to the ICAP framework if they understood it well, we examined scores from the three highest and three lowest scoring teachers on the 16 posttest items related to the four levels of ICAP. Although there was not a large enough sample to detect significant differences, the descriptive statistics shown in Table 13.2 reveal the differences in total score on the posttest ICAP items between low-scoring teachers (1–3) and high-scoring teachers (4–6). Table 13.2 also shows differences between the higher and lower-scoring teachers' performance when the 16 items were further broken down into the 'Improve' and 'Explain' categories. In addition, the teachers who scored highest on these posttest items also scored significantly higher on more difficult and discriminating posttest items from the entire test than teachers with lower scores, $t(4) = -3.674$, $p = .021$, demonstrating that, in general, they had a better understanding of ICAP.

TABLE 13.2 Teachers' scores for items on ICAP module post-test and subsequent implementation of lessons at correct ICAP level

Teacher	ICAP application question total score (N = 16 items)	ICAP application- 'improve' question score (N = 4 items)	ICAP application- 'explain' question score (N = 12 items)	Performance on difficult and high discrimination questions (N = 7 items)	Proportion of classes taught at intended ICAP level
1	62.5%	75%	45%	43%	.20
2	62.5%	75%	45%	57%	.67
3	62.5%	75%	45%	29%	.50
4	87.5%	100%	72%	71%	1.00
5	87.5%	100%	72%	86%	.50
6	93.7%	100%	81%	100%	.75

$N = 12$ teachers who took the posttest; data shown above represents teachers with lowest and highest scores; 'Application' questions were comprised of 'Improve' and 'Explain' questions.

The last column of Table 13.2 shows that higher-scoring teachers tended to deliver a higher proportion of classes at the intended ICAP level than teachers with lower scores. We calculated the proportion of classes that teachers implemented correctly by dividing the number of correct implementations by the total number of classes they planned. This suggests that teachers could transfer their understanding to correct implementation if they understood the ICAP module well.

Discussion

Overall, teachers did not appear to satisfactorily transfer their learning about the ICAP framework when implementing the lesson plans in their classrooms. When evaluating implementation of lessons in the classroom, evidence for transfer was considered to be a match between teachers' intended ICAP level for the class and the level they actually implemented based on our detailed analysis of time allocated for ICAP activities, materials prepared, and content presented. Our results showed that only 43% of the classes were implemented at the teachers' intended ICAP level, with a much higher percentage of classes intended as *active* implemented correctly (89%) than those intended as either *constructive* (25%) or *interactive* (22%).

From a cognitive perspective, one hypothesized reason for the teachers' failure to transfer is that teachers did not learn about ICAP deeply enough (Bransford & Schwartz, 1999; Bransford, Brown, and Cocking, 1999; Chi & VanLehn, 2012). This assumption is supported by our data here—that is, the three teachers who learned material about the ICAP framework more deeply were also more likely to transfer their understanding to practice, as evidenced by our comparison of correct implementation proportions from teachers who scored highest and lowest on 16 posttest application items.

It is interesting to consider how teachers' transfer of ICAP knowledge to practice is the same or different from traditional approaches to assessing transfer. As mentioned earlier, in the traditional transfer literature, transfer is typically conceived of in the context of the two-problem transfer paradigm (Chi & VanLehn, 2012; Lave, 1988), in which learners are expected to first abstract or induce the deep structure or principles underlying the first problem and then apply it to the second problem. In our case, teachers were given the deep structure of the ICAP framework—the cognitive processes associated with knowledge change at four levels of engagement—and exemplar activities for each level. They were then expected to make direct application of this information to their planned class activities, which seems to be an easier transfer than requiring them to first abstract the deep structure. Yet even when the deep structure was presented to them in the ICAP module, in terms of the principles and operational definitions of the ICAP framework, they did not apply ICAP correctly in multiple lesson contexts.

From an alternate viewpoint, researchers who have studied transfer suggest that multiple measures of transfer should be utilized to assess multiple dimensions of transfer (Nokes, 2009). Thus, taking an Actor Oriented Transfer perspective (Lobato, 2012), which removes the researchers' imposed criteria for successful transfer (in our case, "correctly implemented" meant that time allocated for the desired ICAP level was a plurality of the total class time, and greater than 30%), we examined teachers' implementation to determine if there was any transfer at all. From this different perspective, we noted that there was indeed some transfer by a majority of the teachers. As shown earlier in Table 13.1, the greatest number of classes teachers implemented incorrectly was those intended to be either *constructive* or *interactive*. However, in 13 of the 15 *constructive* classes that were incorrectly implemented (that is, they were implemented as either *passive* or *active*), teachers allocated an average of 8.8 minutes or 22% of their total class time to *constructive* activities. Similarly, in 14 of the 18 *interactive* classes that were incorrectly implemented, teachers allocated an average of 12.3 minutes or 19% of their total class time to *interactive* activities. For these classes, the percentage of class time allocated to *constructive* or *interactive* activities simply did not meet the plurality or 30% criteria we imposed and thus, by our rules, they were considered unsuccessful cases of transfer. Nevertheless, these teachers did allocate more time to *constructive* and *interactive* activities than teachers of the two *active* and two *passive* classes that were incorrectly implemented. In those four classes, teachers did not allocate any time to *constructive* or *interactive* activities at all.

For the intended *constructive* or *interactive* ICAP level classes, the lower amount of time allocated to activities at the intended ICAP level suggested the possibility that teachers considered the ICAP manipulation as an addendum to their former routines, implementing ICAP activities in addition to their usual class activity rather than considering the level of student engagement during the entire class period. To investigate this idea further, we reviewed teachers' initial plans for 22 lessons in which one class was planned at the *active* level and a comparison class was planned at either a *constructive* or *interactive* level. In 17 of the 22 lessons, teachers planned the same activities for both the *active* class and the *constructive* or *interactive* comparison class, adding only an additional activity or two at the intended ICAP level to the comparison class. This finding supports the idea that teachers may have delivered their class in the usual way and then added ICAP activities as an enhancement. This practice is certainly not detrimental to student learning if the usual class routine is highly engaging. However, if teachers continue a past practice of implementing a *passive* activity, such as lecture, for a majority of class time and then attempt to improve their class by adding a *constructive* or *interactive* activity for the last 10 minutes, they may not see any changes in students' learning outcomes due to their use of the ICAP framework.

It is important to note here that we did not tell teachers that all activities within a given class must meet the same intended ICAP level, or that a plurality of class time should be spent at the intended level, so it is not reasonable to hold teachers accountable for this information. We did find however, that the three teachers

TABLE 13.3 Class time allocated by teachers scoring high and low on post-test application items

Intended level	Constructive *classes*		Interactive *classes*	
	Average # of minutes allocated to *constructive* activities	Average % of class time allocated to *constructive* activities	Average # of minutes allocated to *interactive* activities	Average % of class time allocated to *interactive* activities
3 low-scoring teachers	19.00	25%	23.57	28%
3 high-scoring teachers	26.75	50%	32.75	69%

12 teachers took the posttest; data shown above represents teachers with lowest and highest scores.

who scored highest on the posttest application items not only implemented a greater proportion of classes correctly (as shown in Table 13.1), but in general they allocated a greater proportion of class time to intended ICAP level activities than the three low-scoring teachers, as shown in Table 13.3; thus again supporting our premise that teachers who understood ICAP more deeply were more likely to successfully transfer theory into practice by implementing activities that elicited a deeper level of student engagement.

Conclusion and recommendations

Taken together, our findings suggest several areas in which instruction about the ICAP framework can be improved to promote teachers' transfer of knowledge to their implementation in the classroom. Our findings when comparing the teachers who scored highest and lowest on the module posttest (as shown in Table 13.3) point clearly to the fact that teachers did not understand the ICAP framework deeply enough to implement activities that elicited higher levels of student engagement for any length of time during their classes. Therefore, we recommend that additional instructional strategies be utilized in subsequent versions of the module to increase deep learning of the ICAP framework.

In particular, teachers themselves need to engage more deeply in identifying the principles underlying the framework. Prior to being given information about ICAP, teachers could be asked to analyze contrasting cases (Schwartz & Bransford, 1998) of ICAP implementation, using video to show correct and incorrect applications of the framework. Comparing examples and non-examples of a concept to be learned assists the learner with three important transfer mechanisms: constructing generalizations, making connections between generalizations and examples, and making appropriate connections between different examples as part of analogical reasoning (Engle, Lam, Meyer, & Nix, 2012, p. 216). In this case, teachers' analysis of correct versus incorrect implementations of ICAP activities should prepare them to better understand the deep structure of the ICAP framework when it is presented. Additionally, the use of video as the media of instruction for the cases can provide a more engaging experience than text-based scenarios, and is recommended as a methodology that captures the complexity of classroom practice (Borko, Jacobs, Eiteljorg, & Pittman, 2008; Santagata, 2009).

Finally, our results suggest that an additional important point of emphasis for teachers new to ICAP is that utilizing ICAP is not an "add on," but rather a more holistic change in pedagogical approach. Instead of manipulating only one or two activities within a class to a higher level of engagement, teachers must consider students' level of engagement throughout the entire lesson, and adjust all of the instruction to engage students at the highest level that is reasonable. In our study, we explicitly asked teachers to transfer their knowledge of ICAP to their classroom practice. However, had we reframed the use of ICAP as a more holistic approach, it may have facilitated more successful spontaneous transfer of the ICAP framework from theory into practice.

Acknowledgments

The authors are grateful for support from the Institute of Education Sciences (Awards #R305A110090 and #R305A150432) to the last author for the projects "Developing Guidelines for Optimizing Levels of Students' Overt Engagement Activities," and "Developing and Revising Instructional Activities to Optimize Cognitive Engagement." They would also like to thank Emily Bogusch and Christiana Bruchok for their helpful comments on an earlier draft of this manuscript.

References

Ball, D. L., & Cohen, D. K. (1999). Developing practice, developing practitioners: Toward a practice-based theory of professional education. In L. Darling-Hammond & G. Sykes (Eds.), *Teaching as the learning profession* (pp. 3–31). San Francisco, CA: Jossey-Bass.

Borko, H., Jacobs, J., Eiteljorg, E., & Pittman, M. E. (2008). Video as a tool for fostering productive discussions in mathematics professional development. *Teaching and Teacher Education, 24*(2), 417–436.

Bransford, J., Brown, A. L., & Cocking, R. (Eds.). (1999). Learning and transfer. In *How people learn: Brain, mind, experience, and school* (pp. 39–66). Washington, DC: National Academy Press.

Bransford, J. D., & Schwartz, D. L. (1999). Rethinking transfer: A simple proposal with multiple implications. *Review of Research in Education, 24*(1), 61–100.

Chi, M. T. H. (2009). Active-constructive-interactive: A conceptual framework for differentiating learning activities. *Topics in Cognitive Science, 1*(1), 73–105.

Chi, M. T. H., & VanLehn, K. A. (2012). Seeing deep structure from the interactions of surface features. *Educational Psychologist, 47*(3), 177–188.

Chi, M. T. H., & Wylie, R. (2014). ICAP: A hypothesis of differentiated learning effectiveness for four modes of engagement activities. *Educational Psychologist, 49*(4), 1–25.

Engle, R. A., Lam, D. P., Meyer, X. S., & Nix, S. E. (2012). How does expansive framing promote transfer? Several proposed explanations and a research agenda for investigating them. *Educational Psychologist, 47*(3), 215–231.

Fonseca, B., & Chi, M. T. H. (2011). The self-explanation effect: A constructive learning activity. In R. Mayer & P. Alexander (Eds.), *The handbook of research on learning and instruction* (pp. 270–321). New York, NY: Routledge Press.

Gentner, D. (1983). Structure-mapping: A theoretical framework for analogy. *Cognitive Science, 7*(2), 155–170.

Kazemi, E., & Hubbard, A. (2008). New directions for the design and study of professional development: Attending to the coevolution of teachers' participation across contexts. *Journal of Teacher Education, 59*(5), 428–441.

Krathwohl, D. R. (2002). A revision of Bloom's taxonomy: An overview. *Theory into Practice, 41*(4), 212–218.

Lave, J. (1988). *Cognition in practice: Mind, mathematics, and culture in everyday life.* New York, NY: Cambridge University Press.

Lobato, J. (2012). The actor-oriented transfer perspective and its contributions to educational research and practice. *Educational Psychologist, 47*(3), 232–247.

Menekse, M., Stump, G. S., Krause, S., & Chi, M. T. H. (2013). Implementation of differentiated active-constructive-interactive activities in an engineering classroom. *Journal of Engineering Education, 102*, 346–347.

Nokes, T. J. (2009). Mechanisms of knowledge transfer. *Thinking & Reasoning, 15*(1), 1–36.

Perkins, D. N., & Salomon, G. (2012). Knowledge to go: A motivational and dispositional view of transfer. *Educational Psychologist, 47*(3), 248–258.

Santagata, R. (2009). Designing video-based professional development for mathematics teachers in low-performing schools. *Journal of Teacher Education, 60*(1), 38–51.

Schwartz, D. L., & Bransford, J. D. (1998). A time for telling. *Cognition and Instruction, 16*(4), 475–522.

14

DEVELOPMENT AND IMPROVEMENT OF A LEARNING STRATEGY USE ENHANCEMENT PROGRAM

Use of lesson induction and elaboration strategies

Mikiko Seo, Mengting Wang, Takeshi Ishizaki, Yuri Uesaka, and Shin'ichi Ichikawa

Introduction

Self-regulated learning is a key competence for our knowledge-based society. We need to continue learning new knowledge and skills after and outside of school education. Self-regulated learning requires many kinds of effective learning strategies (Pintrich & De Groot, 1990; Zimmerman, 1989; Zimmerman & Martinez-Pons, 1990). Pintrich, Smith, Garcia, and McKeachie (1993) proposed three main categories of learning strategies: cognitive, metacognitive, and resource management. Cognitive strategies refer to cognitive processing strategies by which learners memorize and understand information. For example, cognitive strategies include those involving rehearsal, elaboration, and organization of materials to be learned. Metacognitive strategies refer to mental functions learners engage in monitoring their own mental processing and in regulating their processing based on the results of monitoring. Resource management strategies refer to utilization of resources existing outside of the learner. Examples of external resources are other people and cognitive tools such as diagrams. Self-regulated learners can be described as persons who can progress their own learning using these kinds of strategies spontaneously.

Fostering self-regulated learning in school is a major topic in educational settings (e.g., Boekaerts, 1997; Japanese Ministry of Education, Culture, Sports, Science and Technology, MEXT, 2008). However, in Japan, a previous investigation has shown that less than half of middle school students learn in a self-regulated way (National Institute for Educational Policy Research, NIER, 2012). The findings of another study indicate that almost 70% of students are not familiar with effective learning strategies (Benesse Educational Research and Development Institute, 2006). These findings suggest that self-regulated learning training provided in classrooms is probably insufficient or ineffective.

More recently, we have developed a self-regulated learning strategy use enhancement program, focusing especially on metacognitive strategy promotion (Seo, Akasaka, Uesaka, & Ichikawa, 2013; Seo, Uesaka, & Ichikawa, 2012). The program has achieved some positive results. However, it was not always sufficient to promote students' spontaneity in strategy use for their self-regulated learning. The present study explores an improvement of our program.

What is needed for students to use learning strategies?

Previous research has pointed out that students do not always use learning strategies effectively and spontaneously (e.g., Garner, 1990). To consider the reasons for this problem, it is helpful to know findings about the development of children's strategic behaviors. Three levels can be identified in the development of children's memory strategies (Kinjou & Shimizu, 2009). The first level is knowledge deficiency, which is also referred to as "mediation deficiency." At this level, children lack knowledge about learning strategies and require explicit instruction about them.

The second level is production deficiency (Flavell, 1970). Some children do not use a learning strategy even if they already know them. Two reasons have been proposed. One is that children do not perceive well the benefit of using the strategy (Ichikawa, 1998). If children cannot perceive the benefit of a strategy, they would not use the strategy. Another reason is the absence of procedural knowledge for using the learning strategy. Procedural knowledge includes various skills for executing a learning strategy. For instance, using diagrams in mathematical problem solving requires various procedural skills that would enable the child to diagrammatically represent the situation described in the problem. Therefore, children at this level would have to recognize the effectiveness of the strategy and acquire the procedural skills related to using the strategy.

The third level is utilization deficiency (Miller, 1994). Children at this level use the learning strategy spontaneously but cannot use it effectively. They need certain skills to correctly apply the acquired strategy to new and related situations.

A recent study in Japan (Yoshida & Murayama, 2013) found that there is a gap between students and experts in their perceptions about effective learning strategies. In essence, students do not understand the reasons why the strategies are effective in learning. This finding suggests that it is important for students not only to perceive that a strategy is effective, but also to understand why it is effective. Therefore, our program addressed both components of perceiving and understanding the effectiveness of a learning strategy.

Framework of the formerly developed learning strategy use enhancement program

The learning strategy use enhancement program we developed earlier was called 'gakusyuhou-kouza' in Japanese (which basically translates to "lecture on learning strategies"). The program was provided by researchers and included lecture and practice about a learning strategy. The lecture was provided to give participants opportunities to experience cognitive psychology experiments and theoretical explanations with regard to the strategy (Seo et al., 2012, 2013). Experiencing the experiments was intended to facilitate perception of the effectiveness of the strategy. Understanding the effectiveness would be promoted by theoretical explanations based on psychology. To our knowledge, many traditional methods of strategy instruction consist of providing instruction on the strategies, followed by participants practicing the strategies. However, they often do not include opportunities for participants to explicitly perceive the benefits of using the strategies. Of course in our program, after the experiments and explanations, participants also practiced the strategies in the target learning settings, as we consider it important for students to apply the acquired strategies to new situations for strategy transfer.

In our previous research, we applied this framework to promote the use of a metacognitive strategy, lesson induction (LI: Ichikawa, 1991, 2005). Ichikawa (1991) had argued that it is important for learners to explicitly induce the lesson after they have finished daily learning. This strategy involves reviewing one's own cognitive processes, identifying the reasons for mistakes or successes, and inducing "the lesson" for future problem solving or learning. Gick and Holyoak's (1983) "schema induction" is abstracting the problem schema. Ichikawa's (1991, 2005) "lesson induction" is not inducing only the problem schema but also the relevant features of one's own cognitive processes. Ellis and Davidi (2005) have proposed a similar strategy as "after-event reviews." They showed that performance of learners improved when they drew lessons from successful and failed experiences.

We will provide an example. Given a calculation task: $-12 \times 45 \times 1/6$, many students firstly calculate -12×45. Some of them get the correct answer, but others get the wrong answer. In this case, applying the commutative law of multiplication, they could calculate $-12 \times 1/6 \times 45$ more easily, precisely, and quickly. In this case, a lesson—"It is important to check whether there is a way that I can calculate more easily"—can be derived. Our previous investigation revealed that only one-third of middle school students use this strategy in their learning (Seo et al., 2013). However, Uesaka (2010) reported that an eighth-grade student spontaneously started using LI in mathematics learning after receiving cognitive counseling, which is a form of personal tutoring based on cognitive psychology principles. This study was a single case study. For classroom implementation of similar principles, we have developed the learning strategy use enhancement program (Seo et al., 2012, 2013).

Let us now briefly describe the implementation and results of our former intervention (Seo et al., 2012, 2013). Thirty-seven eighth-grade students received two 90-minute instruction sessions in LI strategy use provided by a researcher. Most of the students perceived the effectiveness of the strategy and evidenced high motivation to use the strategy. The number of students who evidenced use of the strategy in a subsequent review practice task increased immediately following the lecture. However, about one month later, no student used the strategy any more.

The purpose of this study

In this study, we improved our formerly developed program and examined its effectiveness. We will point out issues about our program which needed to be improved and describe approaches we used to address those.

First, our former program, which consisted only of researcher-provided instruction, was not always sufficient to promote spontaneous strategy use. A likely reason was that the students had not sufficiently understood the subject they were learning. Adequate knowledge of the subject being learned is needed to use metacognitive strategies successfully. School teachers' support would be crucial to students' metacognitive strategy transfer as teachers provide subject learning instruction to students. Therefore, we added "school teacher-provided training" to our program.

Second, we needed to obtain evidence for the ecological validity of the program. In our previous research, we assessed students' learning strategy use by using an experimental task. Such behavioral measures have higher validity than self-report measures. However, the goal of our program was that students would acquire the ability to use the strategy in learning situations when the strategy could be effective. Thus, in the present study, we collected students' notebook data and analyzed the notes written by students so that we could examine whether strategy use transferred to real everyday learning.

Third, we needed to examine whether we can apply our framework to other self-regulated learning strategies. In this study, we developed the researcher-provided instruction for use of elaboration (EL) strategy. EL strategy is a cognitive deep-processing strategy that involves connecting new knowledge to existing ones and understanding the corresponding relationships (for a review, see Levin, 1988). Many previous studies have shown that elaboration promotes better memory performance (e.g., Stein & Bransford, 1979; Toyota & Tsujimura, 2000). Middle school students need to use this strategy. Students who instead use rote memorization cannot adapt well to middle school learning because the quantity and quality of the learning required increase greatly compared to the elementary school level.

Method

Overview

We conducted the study on 8th-grade students of a middle school in Japan. The students were put in one of two conditions, and the procedure used in each condition is shown in Figure 14.1. The first group was LI-EL condition and students in this group were provided researcher instruction about LI in Treatment 1 (May 2013), and about EL strategy in Treatment 2 (February 2014). The second group was EL-LI condition and students in this group were provided researcher instruction about EL in Treatment 1, and about LI in Treatment 2.

All the students had previously received school teacher-provided training about LI while they were in the 7th-grade. The teacher-provided training continued in both condition while they were in the 8th-grade.

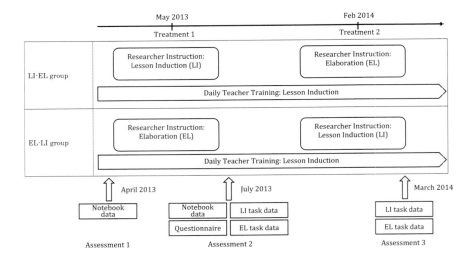

FIGURE 14.1 Intervention flow chart.

To examine the effects of those instructions, assessments were conducted several times during this one-year period. The first assessment (Assessment 1) was conducted in April 2013 before Treatment 1, during which notebook data of students were examined to evaluate the spontaneous use of LI. The second assessment (Assessment 2) was conducted in July 2013 after Treatment 1, during which notebook data were examined, tasks to assess the effects of instruction of LI and EL were administered, and questionnaires that gauged perception about the efficacy of the two targeted learning strategies and motivation to use those strategies were also administered. The reason why these cognitive variables, perception and motivation, were assessed is that spontaneous strategy use depends on perception of the efficacy of the strategies and motivation to use those strategies – as previously noted. The third assessment (Assessment 3) was administrated in March 2014 after Treatment 2 had been provided, and tasks to examine the effects of instruction of LI and EL strategy were used.

The hypotheses we examined were as follows. If the combination of researcher-provided instruction about LI and daily teacher-provided training is effective, we predicted that improvements in spontaneous use of LI from Assessment 1 to Assessment 2 (assessed using the notebook data) would be greater in the LI-EL condition than in the EL-LI condition (Hypothesis 1.1). Moreover, if the effects of the instruction in LI maintained as a consequence of teacher-provided training over the 9-month period, we predicted that students' use of LI in the LI-EL condition would be equivalent from Assessment 2 to Assessment 3 rather than decreasing (Hypothesis 1.2) (i.e., as might have been expected because they did not receive researcher instruction in LI for Treatment 2).

Furthermore, if the EL strategy instruction is effective, we predicted that the participants' spontaneous use of EL strategy in the experimental task administered at

Assessment 2 would be greater in the EL-LI condition than in the LI-EL condition (Hypothesis 2.1). Also, participants' spontaneous use of EL strategy in the LI-EL condition measured by the experimental task would increase from Assessment 2 to Assessment 3 (Hypothesis 2.2).

Participants and design

The participants were 162 8th-grade students (85 males, 77 females) belonging to five regular classes at a middle school in Japan. Students in the 8th-grade in Japan are between the ages of 13 and 14. Three classes (97 students) were assigned to the LI-EL group, and the other two classes (65 students) were assigned to the EL-LI group.

Treatment

School teacher–provided LI strategy training

Students received two types of teacher-provided LI strategy training. One was LI after a preliminary test before the students' examination. Students were given an LI session during the next lesson after the preliminary test. In the LI session, the teacher said to the students, "Find out the reasons for the mistakes you made in problem solving, and prepare to be able to correctly solve similar problems on the next occasion … If you can't find out the reason, can't understand or can't solve, you have to ask someone right away." So the teacher made opportunities for peer learning. Another type was the provision of LI session at the end of a lesson. Sometimes, following a regular class lesson, students were given LI sessions. At that time, the teacher said to the students, "In your notebooks, write down what you understand and what you don't understand."

Researcher-provided learning strategy instruction

The researcher-provided learning strategy instruction was a 50-minute lesson. Figure 14.2 shows the process involved. In the first phase, students experienced a cognitive psychology experiment and theoretical explanations with regard to the applicable strategy. To facilitate the students' perception of the effectiveness of the strategy, firstly students solved a problem prior to receiving information about the strategy, then the researcher instructed them on the strategy. The problems given to the students to try to solve were similar. In the second phase, students practiced applying the strategy to subject learning. Next, we describe the provision of this instruction where the LI and EL strategies were concerned.

LI strategy instruction: In the first phase, students were provided the challenge of solving a T-puzzle (Figure 14.3). Students were individually provided a T-puzzle which required them to make the "T" using the four pieces of the puzzle. After their first attempt, the students were informed of the right answer and the reason

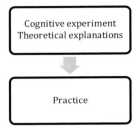

FIGURE 14.2 Process of the researcher-provided strategy instruction.

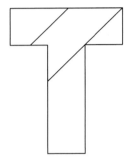

FIGURE 14.3 T-puzzle.

why they might not have been able to make the right "T" was discussed. That was the LI for the T-puzzle. Then, the students were provided the challenge of solving another two puzzles, with shapes like a tree and a house, which they should have been able to solve more easily by applying the lesson they had induced from the T-puzzle. Following this class 'experiment', students were provided theoretical explanations about the relationship between LI and transfer of learning.

In the second phase, the students were asked to apply LI to calculation tasks involving four arithmetic operations for practice. We designed the tasks so that they contained two important characteristics. One was that it would be easy to make errors in attempting to solve them without using basic principles like the distributive law (e.g., $12 \times (-5) + 14 \times 28 + 14 \times 72$). The other was that it would be easy to induce the appropriate lesson. The students worked on the tasks and then checked their answers individually. Then, they identified the reasons for any mistakes they made as well as the key point to solving the problems, and they wrote notes on those. The students were supported in inducing the lessons by being shown good and bad examples of the lessons they could induce. For instance, an example of a good one was "It is important to examine whether I can use some law about calculation or not before I start the calculation." An example of a bad one was "I will calculate more carefully next time!" At the end of the lesson, students worked on transfer tasks and their answers were checked in order to assess the effectiveness of LI.

EL strategy instruction: In the first phase, students experienced an EL experiment, which was a modified version of what Stein et al. (1982) used. At first, students were presented six short sentences and read them aloud. Every sentence described a man with a certain characteristic doing something (e.g., "The elderly man brought a picture story book"). After that, the students were asked to link the man's characteristic and his action on the list. Then, they checked their answers. Next, the students were introduced to the EL strategy that involved identifying the reason for connecting the man's characteristic to his action (e.g., "In order to read the picture story book to his grandchildren"). Again, students were asked to link the man's characteristic to his action and to compare that to their first performance. Following this class 'experiment', the students were provided theoretical explanations about the relationship between elaboration and memorization.

In the second phase, students practiced applying the EL strategy to geography learning. The topic was different areas of the world and their traditional housing (e.g., "the traditional Siberian house is built of log"). Students had already learned these when they were 7th graders. To start with, students were asked to link the area to its housing on the list. Then they checked their answers. Next, students were informed that it was important to use the EL strategy in the learning they were undertaking. The students, in the class as a whole, identified the reasons for connecting the area and its housing (e.g., "Log wood is plentiful in Siberia because the cool climate of the area promotes growth of coniferous forests"). At the end of the lesson, the students worked again on the same tasks and their answers were checked in order to assess the effectiveness of the EL strategy.

Measures and data collection

Perception of the effectiveness of the learning strategy and motivational belief about strategy use

Student perception of the effectiveness of the learning strategy and their motivational belief about strategy use were assessed using a questionnaire that consisted of two items. The item about perception of the effectiveness of the learning strategy was "How effective is this strategy in your learning?" Participants responded on a 4-point Likert-type scale that comprised the following: 1 (not effective), 2 (slightly effective), 3 (effective), and 4 (very effective). The item to assess motivational belief about the use of the strategy was "How often are you going to use the strategy in your learning?" Participants responded on a 4-point Likert-type scale that comprised the following: 1 (not going to use), 2 (rarely going to use), 3 (going to use sometimes), to 4 (going to use always).

Spontaneity of strategy use

Lesson induction: The spontaneity with which the students used LI as a strategy was assessed by examining the notes the students had made on the margins of their math notebooks and on the practice exercise paper they worked on.

Math notebook data were notes written following the checking of the answer of a calculation problem. These were often written in red pencil. Existence of the noted descriptions about the reasons for the mistakes and/or corrective measures in one problem to prevent such mistakes was coded as lesson induced. We collected the data during the month immediately prior to the provision of strategy instruction and during the month following strategy instruction.

The practice exercise paper data were collected in a similar manner to the math notebook data. The difference between the notebook data and exercise paper data was whether a time limit was imposed on the students in reviewing their problem-solving: it was only in the practice exercise that a time limit was imposed. We collected the data twice: following the provision of the first researcher-provided instruction (June 2013), and following the provision of the second instruction (March 2014).

EL strategy: We assessed the students' spontaneous use of the EL strategy by examining their written notes when they were learning their geography study materials. The written notes were gathered during two assessment occasions: following the first researcher-provided instruction (July 2013) and following the second instruction (March 2014).

The materials used during instruction and assessments were isomorphic in structure. During instruction, the material was about the relationships between areas of the world and the houses people live in. In the assessment in July, the material was about the relationships between different areas in China and the houses people live in. The material used in the assessment in March was about the relationships between areas of the world and the kinds of meals people eat.

Students were asked to learn the materials within 6 minutes for a test that followed. They were instructed to write notes as much as possible on the margins of worksheets. The written notes were coded using four categories: rehearsing, abstracting the information, associating the information (see Figure 14.4 for an example), and adding extra information (see Figure 14.5 for an example). The latter two (associating and adding) corresponded to use of the EL strategy. The inter-rater reliability scores, calculated as kappa coefficients, were acceptable ($\kappa = .70$ (July 2013), and .64 (March 2014)). Disagreements were resolved by discussion between the two raters.

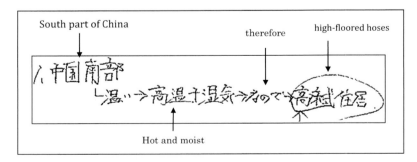

FIGURE 14.4   An example of the elaboration (EL) strategy: "Associating the information." The student connected key elements which were included in the learning material provided.

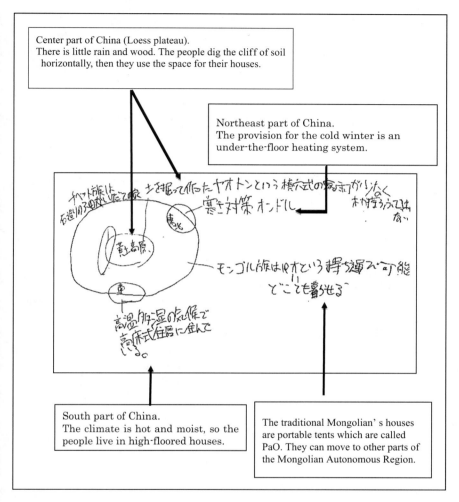

Center part of China (Loess plateau).
There is little rain and wood. The people dig the cliff of soil
  horizontally, then they use the space for their houses.

Northeast part of China.
The provision for the cold winter is an
under-the-floor heating system.

South part of China.
The climate is hot and moist, so the
people live in high-floored houses.

The traditional Mongolian' s houses
are portable tents which are called
PaO. They can move to other parts of
the Mongolian Autonomous Region.

FIGURE 14.5   An example of the elaboration (EL) strategy: "Adding extra information."
The student drew a diagram of information about China and incorpo-
rated features about the houses in the diagram. In this case, drawing the
diagram is adding extra information.

Results

We collected data for this study numerous times over a relatively long period of
time. We were not always able to obtain the desired data from all the students for
various reasons such as absence and non-submission of materials. The numbers of
students included in the analyses are shown in each result and table.

Preliminary analysis

To examine whether the students perceived the efficacy of the two targeted learning strategies, and had the motivation to use those strategies, participants' responses

to the questionnaires were analyzed. Regarding the LI strategy (n = 92), 94.6% of the students responded with "very effective" or "effective". Regarding the EL strategy (n = 64), the corresponding percentage was 96.9%. In response to the question about how often they were going to use the strategy in their learning, most of the students reported "going to use always" or "going to use sometimes" (LI = 98.9%; EL = 95.3%). These responses suggest that researcher-provided strategy instruction enhanced students' perception about the effectiveness of the strategies and their motivational beliefs about the strategy use.

Furthermore, the students' perception about the effectiveness of the strategy and their motivation for using the strategy were significantly correlated (LI: r = .54, p < .001; EL: r = .34, p < .01). This result suggests that when the students perceived greater effectiveness of the strategy they may be more strongly motivated to use that strategy.

Effects of LI interventions

In order to examine the combined effect of researcher-provided instruction and school teacher-provided training, students' spontaneous use of LI in their math class was analyzed. Figure 14.6 shows the changes in the proportions of the students using LI strategy in their math notebook before and after Treatment 1. Before the statistical analysis, the various pieces of work contained in students' notebooks were coded as "lesson induction strategy used" or "not used". Two raters independently carried out the coding and inter-raters agreement was 92%.

The proportions of students' spontaneous use of LI in their notebook were analyzed as an independent variable with a two-way design non-parametric test: 2 (group: LI-EL, EL-LI) × 2 (time: Assessment 1, Assessment 2). Results showed

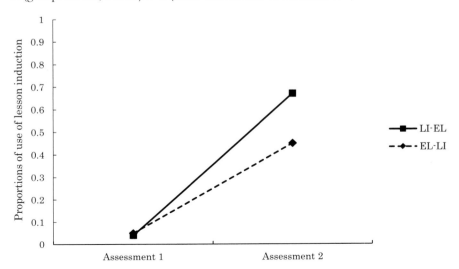

FIGURE 14.6 Change in the proportions of students who evidenced use of lesson induction (LI) in their math notebook.

TABLE 14.1   Numbers of the students who evidenced use of lesson induction (LI) in the practice exercise tasks

	Assessment 2	Assessment 3
LI-EL group ($n = 86$)	30 (35%)	56 (65%)
EL-LI group ($n = 65$)	16 (25%)	36 (55%)

a significant interaction between group and time ($z = 2.34$, $p < .05$). We used the fact that z-statistic about the difference within two paired proportions is approximately normally distributed under the null hypothesis. Before this analysis, we tested whether the proportions of students' spontaneous use of LI at Assessment 1 were equivalent in both LI-EL group and EL-LI group. No significant difference between the two groups was found. These results support Hypothesis 1.1. The LI-EL group students, who received researcher-provided instruction and teacher-provided training, used the LI strategy more compared to the EL-LI group students, who received only teacher-provided training.

To examine the maintenance of researcher-provided LI instruction combined with school teacher-provided training, the students' responses in the practice exercise tasks were analyzed. Table 14.1 shows the number of the students who used the LI strategy in the practice exercise tasks administered at Assessments 2 and 3. Hypothesis 1.2 predicted that participants' use of LI in the LI-EL group in the practice exercise tasks administered at Assessment 2 would be at a similar level as that at Assessment 3. The percentages of the participants who used the LI strategy spontaneously in the practice exercise tasks in Assessment 2 and Assessment 3 were analyzed using McNemar's test. The result revealed that the effect of time was significant ($\chi^2(1) = 17.78$, $p < .001$) – that is, the proportion of students who used the LI strategy actually increased between 1 month after receiving the researcher-provided instruction and about 9 months afterward. This result suggests that the combined effect of the researcher-provided instruction about LI and teacher-provided training not only maintained use but also promoted a subsequent increase in spontaneous use after a 9-month period. Thus, Hypothesis 1.2 was supported.

Effects of the EL strategy instruction

To examine the effect of instruction about EL strategy, participants' response to the experimental learning task administrated to evaluate the spontaneous use of elaboration was analyzed. Table 14.2 shows the number of students who used the EL strategy in Assessments 2 and 3. Hypothesis 2.1 predicted that the proportion of the EL-LI group's use of EL strategy in the experimental task at Assessment 2 would be larger than the proportion of the LI-EL group's use. To test this hypothesis, Pearson's Chi-squared test was used. The analysis revealed a significant group difference ($\chi^2(1) = 7.63$, $p = .006$). This result suggests that the EL-LI group which received researcher-provided instruction about EL strategy, used EL strategy significantly more than the LI-EL group students who had not received it at the period of Assessment 2.

TABLE 14.2 Numbers of students who evidenced use of the elaboration (EL) strategy in the experimental learning tasks

	Assessment 2	Assessment 3
LI–EL group (n = 75)	17 (23%)	33 (44%)
EL–LI group (n = 52)	23 (44%)	24 (46%)

Also, Hypothesis 2.2 predicted that the proportion of the LI–EL group's use of EL strategy in the experimental learning task would increase during the period between Assessments 2 and 3. To test this hypothesis, McNemar's test was used. The proportions increased significantly ($\chi^2(1) = 8.00$, $p = .005$), indicating that the students used EL strategy significantly more after they had received researcher-provided instruction compared to before.

We further examined whether the EL–LI group students, who used the EL strategy in the experimental learning task (Assessment 2), still used the strategy about seven months afterward (Assessment 3). The proportions of spontaneous use of EL in Assessment 2 and Assessment 3 were analyzed as the dependent variable, and McNemar's test was conducted with times of assessment (Assessments 2 and 3). The result found no significant difference between the proportions at Assessments 2 and 3, suggesting that the spontaneous use of EL was maintained.

Discussion

The main purposes of this study were (a) to investigate the combined effect of researcher-provided instruction and teacher-provided training on middle school students' LI strategy use, and (b) to examine the applicability of the EL strategy as a cognitive strategy in our framework of strategy instruction.

First, our results indicate that students who received both teacher-provided training and researcher-provided instruction used more LI strategy in their own math learning 1 month later compared to the students who received only teacher-provided training. Also, about 9 months following the researcher-provided instruction, they maintained LI strategy use. In contrast, Seo et al. (2013) reported that the students who received only researcher-provided instruction no longer used the LI strategy about 3 months later. These findings suggest that the combined program would be more effective compared to a single program of only teacher-provided training or only researcher-provided instruction. A possible reason for the emergence of the combined program effects might be meeting the following two conditions for LI strategy use. One is that almost all of the students who received the researcher-provided instruction evidenced clear perceptions of the effectiveness of the LI strategy and high motivation about using the strategy. The other is that the students who received the teacher-provided training were continuously supported to use LI strategy in math lessons and in their own learning.

Second, our findings about the EL strategy showed that students who had received the researcher-provided instruction about EL strategy used the strategy more spontaneously in the delay test after the instruction compared to students who had not received the researcher-provided instruction. Also, a comparison between pre-instruction and post-instruction indicates that the proportion of students who used EL strategy increased significantly. These findings suggest that our framework of strategy instruction can be applied to a different type of learning strategy. Furthermore, the students who received the researcher-provided instruction maintained the EL strategy use spontaneously over a long period of time (approximately 8 months) despite no intervention about EL strategy being provided by the teacher.

These findings imply that enhancement of using some types of strategies (e.g., LI strategy) may require a combination of researcher-provided instruction and teacher-provided instruction, while enhancement of using other types of strategies (e.g., EL strategy) may sufficiently be achieved by using only researcher-provided instruction. A possible explanation for the difference might be the relative ease-difficulty of applying the strategies to learning. LI would be a more difficult strategy that needs competence in metacognition, verbalization skills, and sufficient knowledge of learning contents. The acquisition and maintenance of such a difficult strategy would need the teacher's support in the regular classroom lessons that students receive. For example, the teacher could provide additional help to less competent students, show model examples that their peers had produced, and provide opportunities for talking about the strategies with their peers.

Implications for future research

Future studies need to examine in more detail the cognitive mechanisms involved in spontaneous learning strategy use. Our results indicate that some students did not/could not use the strategy although they perceived the effectiveness the strategy after the instruction. These findings could not be explained by the previous research concerning the reason for "production deficiency" mentioned in the Introduction section. Previous research suggested two reasons: absence of conditional knowledge, and absence of perception about the effectiveness of the strategy. However, in our intervention, almost of all students evidenced acquisition of these. Therefore, we need to explore different cognitive factors that may be the source of inability to use strategies.

The main aim of the acquisition learning strategies is to improve students' academic performance by self-regulated learning. It remains for future research to investigate whether the strategy enhancement program described here can promote not only strategy use but also improvements in academic performance.

Limitations of this study

Our study has several limitations. First, our findings about the effectiveness of the strategy use enhancement program were not obtained through a strict experimental design because of implementation in real regular classroom settings. Further study is therefore required to evaluate more precisely the effectiveness of this program.

Second, our descriptive data could not identify all the cognitive processes entailed in the students' strategy use. We used descriptive data as the measurement of strategy use. However, some students who had left no trace in their notebook and task paper might have used strategies in their mind. In the case of the LI strategy, some students could have identified the reasons for mistakes and induced lessons in their mind, but left no physical evidence for such undertaking. In the case of the EL strategy, some students could have understood the relationships between the study materials, but wrote nothing to indicate their understanding of those relationships. More sensitive means for assessment of the students' use of learning strategies need to be developed in future research.

Third, it is necessary to put more effort toward enhancing the reliability and validity of the measurements of students' perception of effectiveness and motivational beliefs. In this educational practice, conducted in a real school situation where constraints existed, we assessed each of those variables with only one item. To more sufficiently examine the mechanism of students' learning strategy use, we need to consider more robust ways to assess those variables.

In this study, the researcher delivered the aptly-named researcher-provided instruction. However, a researcher is not always necessary for such delivery. It should be possible for the schoolteacher to provide that instruction, if the teacher has sufficient understanding of the relevant psychological mechanisms and some training in the conduct of cognitive experiments.

References

Benesse Educational Research and Development Institute. (2006). *Gakushu kihon chousa [Survey report of learning attitude and learning behavior]*. Retrieved from http://berd.benesse.jp/shotouchutou/research/detail1.php?id=3227

Boekaerts, M. (1997). Self-regulated learning: A new concept embraced by researchers, policy makers, educators, teachers, and students. *Learning and Instruction, 7*(2), 161–186.

Ellis, S., & Davidi, I. (2005). After-event reviews: Drawing lessons from successful and failed experience. *Journal of Applied Psychology, 90*(5), 857–871.

Flavell, J. H. (1970). Developmental studies of mediated memory. In H.W. Reese & L. P. Lipsitt (Eds.), *Advances in child development and behavior* (pp. 181–211). New York: Academic Press.

Garner, R. (1990). When children and adults do not use learning strategies: Toward a theory of settings. *Review of Educational Research, 60*(4), 517–529.

Gick, M. L., & Holyoak, K. J. (1983). Schema induction and analogical transfer. *Cognitive Psychology, 15*(1), 1–38.

Ichikawa, S. (1991). Jissenteki ninchi-kenkyu to shiteno "ninchi counseling" ["Cognitive counseling" as a practical cognitive study]. In Y. Hakoda (Ed.), *The frontiers of cognitive science 1* (pp. 134–163). Tokyo, Japan: Saiensu-sha (in Japanese).

Ichikawa, S. (Ed.) (1998). *Ninchi kaunseringu kara mita gakusyuu houhou no soudan to shidou [Counseling and teaching study skills: A cognitive counseling approach]*. Tokyo: Brain Shuppan (in Japanese).

Ichikawa, S. (2005). Cognitive counselling to improve students' metacognition and cognitive skills. In D. W. Shwalb, J. Nakazawa, & B. J. Shwalb (Eds.), *Applied developmental psychology: Theory, practice and research from Japan* (pp. 67–87). Greenwich, CT: Information Age.

Kinjou, H., & Shimizu, H. (2009). Meta-kioku no shougai hattatsu [Lifelong development of metamemory]. In H. Shimizu (Ed.), *Metamemory: Monitoring and control processes in memory* (pp. 119–135). Kyoto, Japan: Kitaouji Shuppan (in Japanese).

Levin, J. R. (1988). Elaboration-based learning strategies: Powerful theory = powerful application. *Contemporary Educational Psychology, 13*(3), 191–205.

Miller, P. H. (1994). Individual differences in children's strategic behaviors: Utilization deficiencies. *Learning and Individual Differences, 6*(3), 285–307.

Ministry of Education, Culture, Sports, Science and Technology (MEXT). (2008). *Shin gakushu shidou youryou [The new courses of study]*. Retrieved from www.mext.go.jp/english/elsec/1303755.htm

National Institute for Educational Policy Research (NIER). (2012). *Zenkoku gakuryoku gakushu jyoukyou chousa [The report of national assessment of academic ability]*. Retrieved from www.nier.go.jp/12chousakekkahoukoku/index.htm (in Japanese).

Pintrich, P. R., & De Groot, E. V. (1990). Motivational and self-regulated learning components of classroom academic performance. *Journal of Educational Psychology, 82*(1), 33–40.

Pintrich, P. R., Smith, D., Garcia, T., & McKeachie, W. J. (1993). Reliability and predictive validity of the motivated strategies for learning questionnaire (MSLQ). *Educational and Psychological Measurement, 53*(3), 801–813.

Seo,M.,Akasaka,K.,Uesaka,Y.,& Ichikawa,S.(2013).Gakushu wo furikaeru chikara:"Kyoukun kinou" wo unagasu chugakkou kyoiku puroguramu no kaihatsu [Development and implementation of lesson induction strategy use enhancement program]. In Y. Uesaka & E. Manalo (Eds.), *Shinrigaku kara mita koukateki na manabikata no rikai to shien: Gakushu houryaku purojekuto H24-nendo-no kenkyuseika [Understanding and supporting students' learning strategy development: Findings from the second year of a JSPS-supported research project]*, Working papers, September 2013 (Vol. 2, pp. 29–39). Tokyo, Japan: The University of Tokyo (in Japanese).

Seo, M., Uesaka, Y., & Ichikawa, S. (2012). Kyokun kinou kouza no kaihatsu [Development of lesson induction strategy use enhancement program]. In Y. Uesaka & E. Manalo (Eds.), *Manabikata-no jouzu-na gakushusha-wo sodateru-tameni: Gakushu houryaku purojekuto H23-nendo-no kenkyuseika [Promoting students' use of effective learning strategies: Findings from the first year of a JSPS-supported research project]*, Working papers, August 2012 (Vol. 1, pp. 29–33). Tokyo, Japan: The University of Tokyo (in Japanese).

Stein, B. S., & Bransford, J. D. (1979). Constraints on effective elaboration: Effects of precision and subject generation. *Journal of Verbal Learning and Verbal Behavior, 18*(6), 769–777.

Stein, B. S., Bransford, J. D., Franks, J. J., Owings, R. A., Vye, N. J., & McGraw, W. (1982). Differences in the precision of self-generated elaborations. *Journal of Experimental Psychology: General, 111*(4), 399–405.

Toyota, H., & Tsujimura, M. (2000). The effects of self-regulated and self-choice elaboration on the memory of historical facts. *Bulletin of Nara University of Education, 49*(1) (Cultural and social science), 143–148 (in Japanese).

Uesaka, Y. (2010). How learning strategy use transfers across different school subjects: A case study on promotion of spontaneous use of "lesson induction". *Japanese Journal of Educational Psychology, 58*(1), 80–94 (in Japanese).

Yoshida, T., & Murayama, K. (2013). Why do students often fail to use learning strategies that experts have found effective? An intra-individual analysis. *Japanese Journal of Educational Psychology, 61*(1), 32–43 (in Japanese).

Zimmerman, B. J. (1989). A social cognitive view of self-regulated academic learning. *Journal of Educational Psychology, 81*(3), 329–339.

Zimmerman, B. J., & Martinez-Pons, M. (1990). Student differences in self-regulated learning: Relating grade, sex, and giftedness to self-efficacy and strategy use. *Journal of Educational Psychology, 82*(1), 51–59.

15

EPISTEMIC DESIGN

Design to promote transferable epistemic growth in the PRACCIS project

Clark A. Chinn, Ravit Golan Duncan, and Ronald W. Rinehart

Contemporary research in science education has promoted learning of content and reasoning practices through inquiry (Chinn, Duncan, Dianovsky, & Rinehart, 2013). Researchers have found that students learn science content better and gain greater competence in scientific reasoning under inquiry environments than under more traditional methods such as direct instruction (e.g., Minner, Levy, & Century, 2010; see Chinn et al., 2013). One goal of inquiry environments is to promote the ability to reason well not only in school but in spontaneous transfer to new topics and settings. We acknowledge, however, that many researchers working in classroom environments, including us, do not yet have evidence for transfer outside of classrooms.

Researchers have sought to design effective inquiry environments that promote robust growth in reasoning practices (e.g., Linn, Davis, & Bell, 2004; Sandoval & Reiser, 2004). We treat all these efforts as *epistemic design*—the design of learning environments to foster epistemic growth. Epistemic growth refers to improvement in a range of inclinations, understandings, and capabilities that enable people to achieve *epistemic* aims such as creating knowledge, good scientific explanations, well-justified models, compelling arguments, and so on. What makes these achievements *epistemic* is that they involve developing a representation of how the world is and/or how it works (Chinn, Rinehart, & Buckland, 2014). Robust epistemic growth will lead to spontaneous use of epistemic practices in and out of school.

Our purpose in this chapter is to sketch a theory of epistemic design, focusing on design for science classes. This chapter has the practice-based goal of explicating instructional principles of design that can promote such epistemic growth. Yet we also provide the theoretical rationale that undergirds the recommended design features. We ground our theory of epistemic design in our recent theoretical model of epistemic cognition, the AIR model (Chinn et al., 2014; Chinn & Rinehart, 2016b; Duncan & Chinn, 2016). The AIR model postulates that epistemic cognition comprises three components: epistemic **A**ims and values, epistemic **I**deals, and **R**eliable epistemic processes (REPs) for achieving epistemic aims. These three components provide the resources that people use to create and evaluate epistemic products such as knowledge claims, models, evidence, and arguments. In this chapter, we explain how each component is realized in our epistemic designs.

The outline of this chapter is as follows: We first provide a brief overview of our model-based inquiry project, called PRACCIS (Promoting Reasoning and Conceptual Change In Science); this provides needed background for our later discussions. Second, we explicate the components of the AIR model that are most relevant to our epistemic design work. Third, we discuss the implications of each component of the AIR model for epistemic design. Finally, we summarize and highlight several design features that are hallmarks of PRACCIS and why they are expected to promote epistemic growth that can transfer spontaneously to new settings.

Overview of PRACCIS: promoting reasoning and conceptual change in science

During the last 12 years, we have developed PRACCIS as an inquiry learning environment primarily for seventh-graders (12–13 years old). With its focus on model-based inquiry, PRACCIS follows recent trends emphasizing modeling as a core practice of science (e.g., Duschl & Grandy, 2008; Linn et al., 2004; Sandoval & Reiser, 2004). Through multiple design iterations working in collaboration with teachers, we have developed learning environments to promote both understanding of science content and growth in the epistemic practices of science, including argumentation, explanation, modeling, data interpretation, coordinating models with evidence, and communicating ideas. To date, PRACCIS includes learning environments for middle school life science topics such as cells, genetics (molecular and Mendelian), natural selection, and ecology. As we will discuss throughout this chapter, we have developed a variety of scaffolds and instructional approaches to promote epistemic growth in students' reasoning.

Students engage in a variety of modeling activities. In some lessons, students *develop and revise* their own original models based on evidence. In other lessons, students receive alternative models and use evidence to *choose among these models*. They frequently revise models that they have developed or encountered to better fit the evidence. Thus, students engage in a variety of activities, most of which involve comparing at some point two or more models against a body of evidence.

Two general forms of evidence are prominent in PRACCIS: (a) first-hand evidence that students gather themselves and (b) second-hand evidence (Hapgood, Magnusson, & Palincsar, 2004), in which students read reports of scientists' research that are rewritten to be accessible to them. A main thrust of our PRACCIS design has been to develop a range of evidence that students find engaging; these efforts have led to an increase in the use of video as components of evidence as well as evidence presented in various ways via computers, including interactive presentations of research reports, simulations of experiments, and blog posts.

Our approach to epistemic design takes a broadly sociocultural and dialogic view of processes of learning to reason (Reznitskaya & Gregory, 2013). Specifically, we assume that particular components of our epistemic design (e.g., particular scaffolds or particular moves recommended for teachers to use) foster particular forms of discourse. These forms of discourse are first experienced on the interpersonal plane and eventually appropriated into the students' own epistemic thinking, to be applied in future settings in and out of school.

We further assume that meta-level reflections on epistemic practices can promote epistemic competence and its transfer (Barzilai & Zohar, 2012; see Salomon & Perkins, 1989). In PRACCIS, these metacognitive reflections are pitched at a practical level rather than a highly abstract level (e.g., thinking about why a particular method of measurement is reliable rather than thinking about knowledge in general).

The AIR model of epistemic cognition

During the past half century, there has been a surge in research on people's epistemic or epistemological beliefs, personal epistemologies, epistemological development, epistemic cognition, and allied constructs (Greene, Sandoval, & Bråten, 2016). Chinn, Buckland, and Samarapungavan (2011) argued on philosophical and psychological grounds that prevalent frameworks for conceptualizing epistemic cognition excluded important epistemic dimensions and proposed a new, expanded conceptualization. The AIR model of epistemic cognition incorporates these new dimensions through the three components discussed below.

Epistemic aims are the goals that people set in particular situations, such as the goals of constructing a good scientific model, developing true beliefs, avoiding false beliefs, understanding a theory, creating strong arguments, and so on. People also place greater *value* on some specific epistemic products than others. For example, one may value knowledge of a cure for cancer more than knowledge about the history of type fonts, due to the practical usefulness of this knowledge for achieving the valued non-epistemic goal of health.

Epistemic ideals are the standards or criteria used to evaluate epistemic products such as explanations, knowledge claims, justifications, arguments, evidence, and so on. (We will use the terms *ideals* and *criteria* interchangeably.) Epistemic ideals can be applied to evaluate any kind of epistemic product. For example, epistemic ideals for evaluating models could include that good models (a) fit all the evidence, (b) provide an explanation of phenomena, (c) are clearly presented, (d) include mechanisms, and (e) are held with some tentativeness or uncertainty. Epistemic ideals for evaluating the strength of evidence could include that strong evidence (a) uses methods accepted by the community, (b) is diagnostic with respect to competing theories or models, and (c) addresses core parts of the model, not peripheral parts.

When people are strongly committed to epistemic ideals, they can be said to *value* them, and they are more likely to adopt aims that incorporate these ideals. For instance, a person who values the ideal that good models fit the evidence will be more likely to set aims to create and adopt such models.

Reliable epistemic processes (REPs) (see Goldman, 1986) are the manifold causal processes used to create and evaluate epistemic products. Epistemic processes are reliable to the extent that they are more likely to produce good epistemic outcomes (e.g., true beliefs, good models) than not (e.g., false beliefs, poor models). The AIR model posits that a very large "proportion" of epistemic cognition consists of a grasp of the causal processes used by people to produce epistemic products, such as the use of experiments and many other processes to develop scientific knowledge, the construction and administration of surveys to develop social science knowledge, the use of everyday observation processes to develop knowledge of one's surroundings, or the use of methods such as meta-analysis to combine evidence to reach judgments. The processes that people use to produce epistemic products (such as knowledge claims) vary in reliability, and sophisticated epistemic thinkers must be able to accurately evaluate the reliability of these processes.

REPs can be used both (a) creatively—to produce epistemic products—and (b) evaluatively—to appraise others' epistemic products. For example, consider a person who believes that a reliable journalistic process is for journalists to corroborate all claims through at least two independent sources, at least one of whom can be named in print, and both of whom are known both to the reporter and to her editor. If this person is herself a journalist, she can use this process creatively to guide her own knowledge-producing reporting; if she is instead reading a newspaper article and trying to evaluate the accuracy of its claims, she would reject a set of claims in the article that rested only on a single anonymous source.

Using the AIR model to frame epistemic design

In this section, we discuss our use of the AIR model to guide epistemic design, focusing in turn on Aims and values, Ideals, and REPs. We discuss Ideals and REPs at greater length because these components have been particularly influential in shaping PRACCIS designs.

Aims, values, and epistemic design

Like many other approaches to inquiry (e.g., Krajcik & Blumenfeld, 2006), PRACCIS units stem from driving questions that students explore in a series of epistemic activities, questions such as "How do genetics traits get passed on from parents to their children?" for genetics. Lessons within units often are guided by more specific driving questions, such as "Why have mountain sheep's horns become smaller over the last 50 years?" in a lesson in our natural selection unit.

Through these driving questions, some units seek to elevate the value of epistemic goals by connecting them to intrinsically valued questions, such as why do students share some traits with their mother and other traits with their father. Other units link epistemic goals to non-epistemic goals. For example, our unit on cell membranes is organized around the driving question, "How does lead get into cells?" We motivate interest in this question through activities introducing students to the severe health consequences of environmental lead poisoning. The epistemic goal of understanding cell membrane transport is thus linked to the non-epistemic goal of improving societal health.

PRACCIS also endeavors to encourage students to value models, evidence, and arguments that meet certain ideals and that are produced through particular REPs. For instance, as students come to believe that experimentation is a reliable process for producing knowledge, they should value the use of this process by themselves and others.

Ideals and epistemic design

Epistemic ideals have three characteristics that directly impact our epistemic design: (1) They are socially shared creations that guide production and evaluation of epistemic products such as models. (2) They are situated. (3) They are undergirded by meta-epistemic justifications and are thus improvable. In this section, we explicate each characteristic and show how each guides our epistemic design.

Epistemic ideals are socially shared resources that guide creation and evaluation of epistemic products. Scientific communities develop and enact epistemic ideals for evaluating epistemic products such as theories, models, and evidence (Toulmin, 1972). These ideals are shared by many members of communities of practice as they work to create knowledge and evaluate each other's knowledge claims. For example, a theory that fails to account for the availability of evidence will be rejected for failing to meet a central ideal (Longino, 2002).

The development of shared epistemic ideals is a central feature of epistemic design in PRACCIS. Every PRACCIS class develops its own set of public, community-developed epistemic ideals for models, evidence, and/or arguments. For example, each PRACCIS class develops its own ideals for good models at the outset of their modeling work (Pluta, Chinn, & Duncan, 2011). The instruction begins with students working with six pairs of models that vary in purpose and quality. Without any instruction beyond the information that "models provide explanations," students discuss in pairs which (if either) model is better, and why. At that point, all students individually write a list of six characteristics of good models, based on their discussions with their partner to that point. Teachers then lead a class discussion that generates a set of criteria for the full class based on what the individuals have developed. Each class's criteria is posted publicly. All classes we have worked with develop appropriate criteria; an example of one class's criteria is presented in Figure 15.1. The criteria thus generated become norms for all students in the class to follow. All students have agreed to them and thus they have a guiding influence as genuine shared ideals that govern the class's epistemic work.

Using analogous instructional activities, we have worked with students to facilitate the development of criteria for good evidence and good arguments, as well. Figure 15.2 shows one class's list of criteria for good evidence, which the class used to evaluate evidence throughout the school year.

By engaging students very directly with developing and using epistemic ideals for good models, good evidence, and good arguments, our intent is to build

> Clearly answers the question.
> Provides visual aides and words.
> Easy to read and understand.
>   + organized.
> Gives most information (all you have).
>   --correct info
> No unnecessary words--Keep it simple
> Supported by/based on evidence
>   --shows data
>   --background research
> Steps/states in order (if appropriate)
> Explains why or how--answers question.
> There's an example of how it works
>   (if appropriate)
> <u>Audience</u> = classmates
> None of the evidence contradicts the model.
> Realistic, makes sense
> Make sure evidence is correct

FIGURE 15.1 One class's criteria for good models, posted on the wall.

> • Validity
> • Trustworthiness
> • Sample size
> • Proper comparisons
> • Accurate, unbiased measures

FIGURE 15.2 One class's criteria for good evidence, posted on the wall.

competence with one of the three core features of epistemic cognition. Class discourse supports the use of these criteria. Students use them when evaluating their own and others' work. They hold themselves and each other accountable to these criteria through peer review processes that are analogous to those used by scientists. Rubrics based on students' own shared criteria may be developed to support these evaluations.

Because students develop these criteria themselves as a social community and regularly use them to create and evaluate models, evidence, and arguments, we hypothesize that they develop a level of commitment that can support future, spontaneous use of these criteria. Spontaneous use of epistemic criteria is unlikely if students have no commitment to them. Further, commitment should lead students to *value* models, evidence, and argument that meet the shared criteria that students have developed themselves. For example, if students are committed to the idea that good models should fit the evidence, this commitment can transfer to other topics outside of the life sciences, and even to topics in other areas of science.

Situativity of ideals: Ideals are not monolithically applied in uniform ways across topics and settings. For example, one reasonable ideal for good models is that good models fit all the high-quality evidence. Yet the details of determining what counts as evidence or as high-quality evidence will vary substantially from one topic to another. In evolutionary biology, this involves integrating a broad range of diverse evidence ranging from fossil evidence to experiments investigating effects of selective pressures. In cell biology, it requires examination of very different kinds of evidence involving various procedures to examine structures and biochemical processes of cells. The ability to apply the ideal "fit with high-quality evidence" will require that students learn to tailor this ideal to particular situations.

The implication of the situativity of ideals for epistemic design is that students must learn to apply and tailor ideals flexibly to particular situations. Some might argue that epistemic criteria such as those used in PRACCIS are too rigid and generalized to capture the situated nature of scientific thinking. However, PRACCIS avoids such generalized rigidity through the encouragement of discourse that tailors the criteria to particular situations, using the following three design features.

First, there is *varied exposure*. PRACCIS engages students in using these criteria across many different lessons and units, on diverse topics ranging from human health and inheritance of traits to the mechanisms of genetic HIV resistance and natural selection. The great variety of topics in which the class-developed ideals are used affords students many opportunities to grasp how the ideals can be adaptively tailored to different situations.

Second, PRACCIS explicitly encourages a form of discourse that articulates how ideals are to be tailored to situations. An example of such *discourse tailoring ideals to situations* would be a statement that a particular model of photosynthesis fails to "show all the steps" (one of the class's community criteria for good models) because it does not show any steps involving chloroplasts. Because the class has seen evidence showing that chloroplasts are involved in converting light to glucose, they begin to appreciate that showing all the steps in cell biology means including steps that involve cell organelles like chloroplasts. Such statements enrich students' understanding of how "showing all the steps" is to be instantiated with topics involving cell organelles. We postulate that such discourse promotes adaptive use of epistemic ideals to different settings that can facilitate adaptive use in future transfer settings.

Third, PRACCIS encourages occasional talk at a *meta-epistemic level* about conditions that differentiate the application of the same ideals to different situations. For example, our principles of epistemic design encourage teachers and students to pose questions such as, "We said that this model of photosynthesis shows all the steps, and that the model two weeks ago showing why mountain sheep are getting smaller horns also shows all the steps. But the models are very different! How is it that *both* of them meet the criterion of showing all the steps?" Through questions like this, teachers can facilitate a meta-epistemic understanding of how to adaptively apply epistemic ideals to different situations.

Ideals are justified through meta-epistemic justifications. A central claim of the AIR model is that epistemic ideals are not and should not be arbitrary conventions (Chinn & Rinehart, 2016a, 2016b). Rather, ideals themselves can and should be justified through *meta-epistemic justifications*. A meta-epistemic justification is a justification for a general epistemic statement such as "good models fit the evidence." For example, a meta-epistemic justification of this statement might be the argument that models should fit the evidence because, without such fit, the model will not reflect the way the world behaves. Or one might argue that models should be expected to fit *most* of the evidence but not *all* of the evidence because some evidence will turn out to be flawed and erroneous, so that trying to fit a model to *all* evidence could actually decrease the quality of a model.

The implication of meta-epistemic justifications for epistemic design is that PRACCIS encourages teachers and students to explicitly discuss these meta-epistemic justifications at appropriate junctures in lessons. One such juncture is when students initially develop their class criteria for good models, good evidence, and so on. When discussing these criteria, teachers are encouraged to explicitly ask students to explain their reasons for their criteria, and also to discuss which criteria are most important (which encourages students to consider the meta-epistemic justifications underlying the criteria). Here is one class's discussion about which of two criteria is more important: incorporating visual aids or ensuring that the model stays on topic.

Student 1:   Because, um, things are more important than visual aids like you need everything to stick on topic, that's more important than visual aids, so stick on topic should be number one.

Teacher: Student 2, what do you think of that?

Student 2:   I agree, but it shouldn't be number one because I think that, um, diagrams and pictures and explanations are more important than just sticking on topic. Well it's very important ...

...

Student 3:   Well, if you have, if you have good um like text and evidence and good pictures, that won't even matter if the model that they're involved in doesn't relate to the topic because if the topic is like how like the water cycle and like you have a picture of like a volcano erupting but it's a really detailed picture and it's got evidence supporting how it erupts, that's not gonna matter because it doesn't relate to the topic ...

The epistemic design goal of eliciting discussions centered on meta-epistemic justifications of criteria is to encourage students to articulate the reasons why their criteria are valid. When students grasp the reasons behind the criteria, we postulate that they will be more likely to use these criteria both inside and outside of class, because they now have reason to think that these criteria are valuable, and thus worth adopting and pursuing.

Because ideals are themselves justifiable, ideals can improve as our arguments for and against different ideals change. Our PRACCIS designs include opportunities for the revision of epistemic ideals. For example, although all classes in our studies that have developed model quality criteria have included a criterion involving fit with evidence in some fashion, they may see this as a relatively less important criterion. Later, they may elevate fit with evidence to a more prominent place as they come to appreciate that support that fit with evidence is really essential to models. Further, students may refine this criterion over time, such as shifting to a more sophisticated criterion that models should fit as much of the high-quality evidence as possible. Revisions of criteria create additional opportunities for meta-epistemic discussions about justifications for ideals and why they should be changed.

Summary: Figure 15.3 summarizes the main theoretical arguments of this section about how selected components of PRACCIS designs can foster transferrable epistemic growth. Our designs include meta-epistemic discussions that establish community epistemic ideals and that later refine these ideals. Then students use these ideals daily in their modeling work of creating, revising, and evaluating models, evidence, and arguments in their inquiry classes. These criteria appear explicitly and implicitly in their discourse as they weigh models against evidence. Students gain experience working with ideals across diverse topics and configurations of models of evidence. Through regular successful use of the ideals, together with reflecting on why these ideals are justified (meta-epistemic justifications) as well as how they are tailored to particular situations, students gain a commitment to these ideals and an adaptive grasp of how to use them across situations. These competencies, in turn, are expected to promote spontaneous use of these ideals in new settings.

Reliable processes and epistemic design

Next we discuss reliable epistemic processes (see Goldman, 1986) and how these have shaped our principles of epistemic design. REPs have three characteristics exactly parallel to those of ideals: (1) They are socially shared practices that guide production and evaluation of epistemic products. (2) They are situated. (3) They are undergirded by meta-epistemic justifications and are thus improvable. In this section, we discuss how these three characteristics guide our epistemic design.

REPs are social practices that guide production and evaluation of epistemic products. REPs can be classified into several broad categories including (cf. Goldman, 1999):

- Individual processes, such as observation and perception, memory, reading and evaluating multiple websites alone, identifying patterns in one's own experiences, the exercise of virtues such as being open-minded, and so on.
- Individual and social methods, which are more formal procedures such as processes of statistical analysis, titration of chemicals, conducting controlled experiments, conducting meta-analyses of prior studies, and so on. These may be executed by groups or by individuals.
- Group processes such as argumentation, internal criticism, group brainstorming, responding to anomalies in a research group, distributing roles and tasks within a group, sharing information, and so on.
- Institutional processes such as journal review processes, processes of public peer critiques, grant funding processes, processes used by media entities to corroborate sources, and so on.

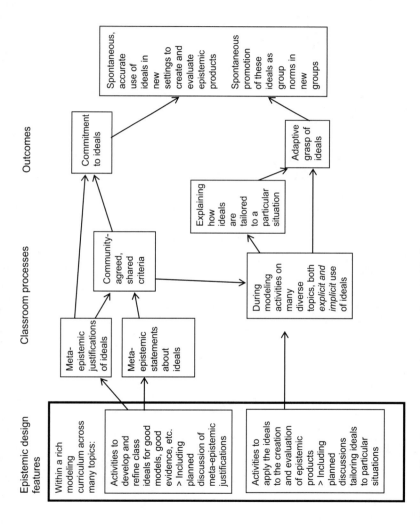

FIGURE 15.3 Design and learning processes related to epistemic ideals.

Many of these processes are inherently social, such as argumentation and peer review. But even those processes that are potentially individual are infused with social influences. For example, an individual designing and implementing an experiment must be aware of the research community's judgments about which procedures are viewed as reliable and which are not. Moreover, in science experiments are usually designed and implemented collaboratively by teams.

These processes are used regularly to produce knowledge claims, and one can evaluate others' knowledge claims by evaluating whether these processes have been used. For example, evaluating the findings of a research report requires evaluating the reliability of the various processes used to conduct the study and analyze the data.

The implication for PRACCIS is that students should engage extensively in social processes of knowledge production using REPs to create and evaluate epistemic products. Like most designers of inquiry environments, we strive to design challenging tasks that individuals cannot resolve effectively alone, so that input from some or many classmates is needed to reach the best judgment. Further, we strive to promote the argumentation practices that are emphasized in research as an REP that is central to science. Our design principles further specify that students should be explicitly encouraged to reflect on their group processes—what makes them more versus less effective—thus gaining metacognitive knowledge of reliable and unreliable group processes that they themselves engage in. White and Frederiksen (1998) have documented the effectiveness of such group reflections.

In PRACCIS designs, one of our central scaffolds, the Model-Evidence Link (MEL) matrix, is intended to encourage creative and evaluative use of REPs. Figure 15.4 shows an example of a MEL matrix; using this scaffold, students engage in several REPs, most commonly through discussion with classmates. Students use the MEL matrix in Figure 15.4 after they have thoroughly examined the four pieces of evidence that are included in the matrix, in the context of evaluating two competing models explaining why some humans are genetically resistant to HIV. First, the students use different types of arrows to denote whether each of the available pieces of evidence *supports, strongly supports, contradicts, strongly contradicts,* or *is irrelevant to* each model. This supports the practice of coordinating models with evidence and encourages reflection on why some evidence is stronger than other evidence. It also encourages the process of systematically tabulating all of the available evidence, thereby avoiding selective use of evidence or ignoring of one or more models under consideration. Thus, the scaffold embodies a reliable epistemic process for resolving disagreements between conflicting models by coordinating multiple models with multiple pieces of evidence so as to determine which model (if any) is best supported by the evidence. This enables students to coordinate evidence with models to make reasoned decisions about how to resolve the disagreement between the models.

A second feature of MEL matrices is the series of small boxes next to each piece of evidence. In these boxes, students rate the *quality of evidence* on a scale of 0 to 3, with 0 indicating evidence so poor that it should be neglected, 3 indicating very

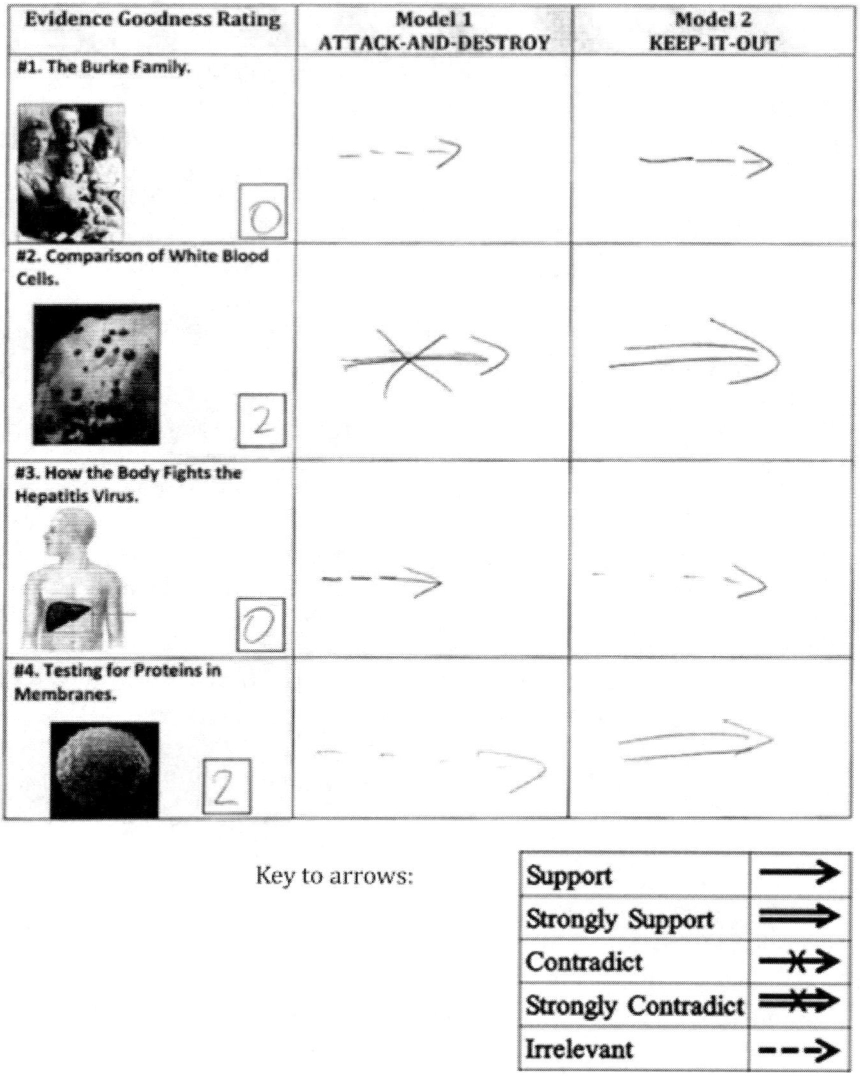

Evidence Goodness Rating	Model 1 ATTACK-AND-DESTROY	Model 2 KEEP-IT-OUT
#1. The Burke Family.		
#2. Comparison of White Blood Cells.		
#3. How the Body Fights the Hepatitis Virus.		
#4. Testing for Proteins in Membranes.		

Key to arrows:

Support	⟶
Strongly Support	⟹
Contradict	⟶×⟶
Strongly Contradict	⟹×⟹
Irrelevant	⟶ ⟶

FIGURE 15.4 A Model-Evidence Link (MEL) matrix.

high-quality evidence that should be weighted very heavily, and 1 and 2 indicating intermediate levels of evidence quality. A hallmark of PRACCIS designs is that we regularly incorporate low-quality evidence within the evidence sets that students evaluate; for example, evidence may be merely anecdotal, or it may involve studies with flaws such as poor measures or confounded experiments. In creative processes of assembling evidence and coordinating evidence with models, students using the MEL matrices thus weigh both quantity and quality of evidential support.

Students' ratings of evidence quality also spur discussions about the reliability of processes used by others to gather and report evidence. Thus, students learn to evaluate a variety of processes (both reliable and unreliable) that are used to produce scientific evidence and associated knowledge claims. In our implementations of PRACCIS, students do regularly engage in argumentation about the quality of evidence, thus engaging in reflection on the reliability of evidence-producing processes (Rinehart, Duncan, & Chinn, 2014). In fact, low-quality evidence is particularly potent at spurring such discussions (Zimmerman, Chinn, & Duncan, 2016) and is responsible for deeper considerations of evidence as shown in students' written argumentation (Rinehart, Chinn, & Duncan, 2015).

In summary, MEL matrices are thus designed both to promote a reliable, systematic, process for creatively coordinating theories and evidence, and to foster discussions that engage students in evaluations of the reliability of the various good and poor processes that scientists and others (including themselves) use to produce evidence.

Situativity of REPs: Like ideals, REPs are highly situated in that every REP is subject to conditions that affect its reliability in particular situations. For example, observation is, in general, a reliable process for finding things out, but it is only reliable under certain conditions: stimuli are not vague or degraded, distances are not too great, lighting is good, strong theoretical biases are not engaged, and so on. Eyewitness testimony frequently fails to meet these conditions, and because many jurors are unaware of these conditions and overestimate the reliability of eyewitness observation, they render erroneous judgments in trials. All REPs have such conditions, including all types of scientific methods. Experimentation, for instance, yields meaningful findings only if all variables (including hidden ones) are controlled, measures are not biased with respect to conditions, experimental conditions sufficiently simulate situations to which one wants to generalize, and so on. Appropriate conditions interface with detailed domain knowledge; for instance, knowing exactly what variables need to be controlled in an ecology experiment depends on knowing the many details of the environment and its organisms to identify which casually relevant confounds might emerge.

The implications of the situativity of REPs for epistemic design in PRACCIS are exactly analogous to the implications of the situativity of ideals that we discussed earlier. (1) *Varied exposure.* Students discuss the quality of evidence—and, therefore, the reliability of the processes used to produce the evidence—across many topics, thereby affording opportunities to see how conditions vary across contexts, and hence the reliability of processes vary accordingly. (2) *Discourse tailoring REPs to particular situations.* As with ideals, PRACCIS encourages students to apply general REPs to particular science content (e.g., considering the applicability of the generally reliable method of experimentation to a particular case). Such discourse could articulate why the conditions on particular REP are or are not applicable to a particular situation (e.g., a student could argue that a particular experiment is not useful because it employs hamsters rather than humans to investigate something about human health; other students might offer counterarguments leading to refinement of ideas about when animals can and cannot be used to provide insights about human health). (3) *Meta-epistemic discourse about conditions.* Finally, students might occasionally articulate general meta-epistemic statements about the conditions affecting the reliability of processes (e.g., observation is not reliable when the scientist has strong beliefs, unless some form of blind measurement is used).

Meta-epistemic justification of REPs: As with ideals, the reliability of epistemic processes is not established by fiat. There are philosophical and empirical justifications for believing that putatively reliable processes are in fact reliable. These are meta-epistemic justifications supporting the reliability of the processes. For example, the reliability of experimentation can be argued for on philosophical grounds as well as pointing empirically to clear advances that have emerged in certain fields as a result of using experiments. The reliability of double blind studies emerges from empirical research showing the effects of biases when doctors or patients know which condition patients are in.

As with ideals, epistemic design in PRACCIS encourages not only discussions that explore the reliability of epistemic processes and the conditions under which processes are reliable, but also explicit discussions of justifications for the claims made about the reliability of these processes. Here is one example: In a discussion of the reliability of having hotel guests count local animals such as arctic foxes and salmon as a means to determine the population sizes of these animals, students in one PRACCIS class offered many reasons why such counting procedures are unreliable, including that one needs training and expertise to be able to identify foxes and salmon, that this way of counting animals can be unreliable because the animals may be shy and not show themselves to people, and that the process is too haphazard and unsystematic to yield accurate results. The students thus strengthened their collective articulated understanding of counting processes through these meta-epistemic justifications for why this particular counting process was unreliable. We expect that a deep understanding of the reasons why processes are reliable or unreliable under specified conditions is more likely to transfer to future settings than a sketchy or rote understanding of a process.

In our studies, we have found that students often have nonnormative ideas about the reliability of processes. For example, many students initially find anecdotal reports of the cause of a disease more persuasive than scientific studies. Similarly, we have found that some students argue vigorously that it is more reliable to determine the amount of algae in a pond by evaluating the color of the pond than by weighing samples of algae, and their reasoning makes sense given their limited knowledge of scientific methods: they believe that eyeballing the color takes *all* the algae into account, whereas sampling does not account for *all* the algae. Addressing such alternative conceptions mandates a curriculum that gives students information about the reliability of methods and opportunities to debate them; PRACCIS does both. Students develop a grasp of which processes are reliable and *why* they are reliable, thus developing a commitment to using these processes and to expecting others to use them.

Design   Discourse   Outcomes

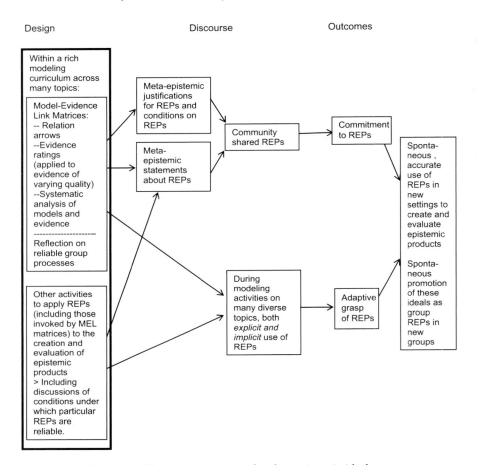

FIGURE 15.5 Design and learning processes related to epistemic ideals.

Summary: Figure 15.5 summarizes selected PRACCIS design features intended to support transferrable development in students' use of REPs to create and evaluate epistemic products. MEL matrices are a tool designed to promote discussions of critical reliable processes: First, the evidence ratings encourage discussions about the reliability of processes used to produce evidence. Second, the matrices encourage the use of reliable processes for coordinating evidence with models and weighing the evidence to resolve disagreements between conflicting models. In addition, students' reflection on their own group processes supports growth in knowledge of social REPs that groups can use to promote knowledge advancement. Meta–epistemic discussions across diverse topics promotes adaptive grasp of the conditions under which REPs apply to different situations, together with a commitment to use the REPs to create and evaluate epistemic products. All of this is intended to support committed, adaptive use of these REPs in settings requiring spontaneous transfer.

Summary: Epistemic design to promote transferrable epistemic growth

Throughout this chapter, we have discussed principles of epistemic design grounded in the AIR model of epistemic cognition and implemented in our PRACCIS project. PRACCIS incorporates design features used by many other inquiry projects, such as organizing lessons around driving questions, engaging students in argumentation, and affording students rich, varied opportunities to use evidence to construct and revise models. But there are also some distinctive hallmarks of PRACCIS designs, and the AIR model provides a theoretical rationale for these hallmarks. We close by summarizing these hallmarks of PRACCIS. All of these represent instructional techniques that teachers could incorporate into their own inquiry lessons.

1   *A strong focus on choosing among competing models:* Nearly all PRACCIS lessons ask students to evaluate competing models. This design feature promotes mastery of the important class of reliable processes for resolving disagreements or controversies. As students gain adaptive facility in resolving various conflicts, they should be better prepared to reason about controversies encountered in the real world.

2   *Public, community criteria:* In PRACCIS designs, students take the lead in developing public, community criteria for good models, good evidence, and/or good models. This establishes community norms to which individuals as well as the class community are committed, and which then guide the development and evaluate of epistemic products within the classrooms. Students thus share a commitment to significant epistemic ideals that can improve their epistemic thinking across settings.

3   *MEL matrices:* The MEL matrices have two distinct components. First, the evidence quality ratings afford opportunities for students to discuss (and argue about) evidence quality, and thereby to reflect on the reliability of processes used to produce evidence. Increased understanding of REPs for producing evidence is expected to be generally useful in and out of school settings. Second, they are designed to provide a reliable epistemic process for coordinating models and evidence—taking the quality and quantity of evidence supporting and contradicting each model into account, as well as the strength of evidential support. This is a generalizable approach that can be used to systematize thinking about evidence and models in many contexts.

4   *Evidence of varying quality:* PRACCIS exposes students to evidence of varying quality (from very good to very poor), which we regard as essential to promoting competence in evaluating evidence. The discussions around evidence quality across diverse evidence supports a more robust understanding of how REPs are (and are not) applicable across different situations.

5   *Distinctive approaches to discourse:* Finally, guided by principles foundational to the AIR model, our approach to epistemic design privileges several forms

of discourse surrounding epistemic ideals and reliable epistemic processes. *Discourse tailoring ideals and REPS to situations* helps students grasp the connections between more general epistemic constructs (ideals and REPs) and the specific situations. *Meta-epistemic discourse about conditions* can also help students articulate conditions under which epistemic ideals and reliable processes do and do not apply, making their knowledge more sensitive to different conditions and thus more transferable. Finally, *discourse focused on meta-epistemic justifications* can play a central role in helping students change prior conceptions about ideals and processes, and helping them develop a robust appreciation of the value of the ideals and processes that they are discussing in class.

Our goal in this chapter has been to show how one can develop a set of epistemic design principles that are thoroughly grounded in a model of epistemic cognition. In this way, we have striven not only to show how instructional designs can promote spontaneous transfer of ideas, but also to show how every element of those designs is grounded in theory.

Note

This material is based upon work supported by the National Science Foundation under Grant No. 1008634. Any opinions, findings, and conclusions or recommendations expressed in this material are those of the author(s) and do not necessarily reflect the views of the National Science Foundation. We are very grateful to Sarit Barzilai, Andy Elby, Toshio Mochizuki, Na'ama Av-Shalom, Leah Hung, Brandon Mauclair-Augustin, Hebbah El-Moslimany, Jing Yang, and Randi Zimmerman for very helpful comments on earlier drafts of this manuscript.

References

Barzilai, S., & Zohar, A. (2012). Epistemic thinking in action: Evaluating and integrating online sources. *Cognition and Instruction, 30*(1), 39–85.

Chinn, C. A., Buckland, L. A., & Samarapungavan, A. (2011). Expanding the dimensions of epistemic cognition: Arguments from philosophy and psychology. *Educational Psychologist, 46*(3), 141–167. doi:10.1080/00461520.2011.587722

Chinn, C. A., Duncan, R. G., Dianovsky, M., & Rinehart, R. (2013). Promoting conceptual change through inquiry. In S. Vosniadou (Ed.), *International handbook of conceptual change* (2nd ed., pp. 539–559). New York, NY: Taylor & Francis.

Chinn, C. A., & Rinehart, R. W. (2016a). Advances in research on sourcing: Source credibility and reliable processes for producing knowledge claims. *Reading and Writing, 29*, 1701–1717.

Chinn, C. A., & Rinehart, R. W. (2016b). Epistemic cognition and philosophy: Developing a new framework for epistemic cognition. In J. A. Greene, W. A. Sandoval, & I. Bråten (Eds.), *Handbook of epistemic cognition.* New York: Routledge.

Chinn, C. A., Rinehart, R. W., & Buckland, L. A. (2014). Epistemic cognition and evaluating information: Applying the AIR model of epistemic cognition. In D. Rapp & J. Braasch (Eds.), *Processing inaccurate information: Theoretical and applied perspectives from cognitive science and the educational sciences* (pp. 425–453). Cambridge, MA: MIT Press.

Duncan, R. G., & Chinn, C. A. (2016). New directions for research on argumentation: Insights from the AIR framework for epistemic cognition. *German Journal of Educational Psychology, 30*(2–3), 155–161.

Duschl, R. A., & Grandy, R. E. (Eds.). (2008). *Teaching scientific inquiry: Recommendations for research and implementation.* Rotterdam, The Netherlands: Sense Publishers.

Goldman, A. I. (1986). *Epistemology and cognition.* Cambridge, MA: Harvard University Press.

Goldman, A. I. (1999). *Knowledge in a social world.* Oxford, UK: Oxford University Press.

Greene, J. A., Sandoval, W. A., & Bråten, I. (Eds.). (2016). *Handbook of epistemic cognition.* New York: Routledge.

Hapgood, S., Magnusson, S. J., & Palincsar, A. S. (2004). Teacher, text, and experience: A case of young children's scientific inquiry. *Journal of the Learning Sciences, 13*(4), 455–505.

Krajcik, J. S., & Blumenfeld, P. C. (2006). Project-based learning. In R. K. Sawyer (Ed.), *The Cambridge handbook of the learning sciences* (pp. 317–333). Cambridge, UK: Cambridge University Press.

Linn, M. C., Davis, E. A., & Bell, P. (Eds.). (2004). *Internet environments for science education.* Mahwah, NJ: Erlbaum.

Longino, H. E. (2002). *The fate of knowledge.* Princeton, NJ: Princeton University Press.

Minner, D., Levy, A. J., & Century, J. (2010). Inquiry-based science instruction—what is it and does it matter? Results from a research synthesis years 1984 to 2002. *Journal of Research in Science Teaching, 47*(4), 474–496.

Pluta, W. J., Chinn, C. A., & Duncan, R. G. (2011). Learners' epistemic criteria for good scientific models. *Journal of Research in Science Teaching, 48*(5), 486–511.

Reznitskaya, A., & Gregory, M. (2013). Student thought and classroom language: Examining the mechanisms of change in dialogic teaching. *Educational Psychologist, 48*(2), 114–133.

Rinehart, R. W., Duncan, R. G., & Chinn, C. A. (2014). A scaffolding suite to support evidence-based modeling and argumentation. *Science Scope, 38*(4) 70–77.

Rinehart, R. W., Chinn, C. A., & Duncan, R. G. (2015, August). Bad evidence makes for good learning: An analysis of science students' argumentation. Paper presented at the 16th meeting of the European Association for Research on Learning and Instruction, Limassol, Cyprus.

Salomon, G., & Perkins, D. N. (1989). Rocky roads to transfer: Rethinking mechanisms of a neglected phenomenon. *Educational Psychologist, 24*(2), 113–142.

Sandoval, W. A., & Reiser, B. J. (2004). Explanation-driven inquiry: Integrating conceptual and epistemic scaffolds for scientific inquiry. *Science Education, 88*(3), 345–372.

Staley, K. W. (2004). *The evidence for the top quark: Objectivity and bias in collaborative experimentation.* Cambridge, UK: Cambridge University Press.

Toulmin, S. E. (1972). *Human understanding: The collective use and evolution of concepts.* Princeton, NJ: Princeton University Press.

White, B. Y., & Frederiksen, J. R. (1998). Inquiry, modeling, and metacognition: Making science accessible to all students. *Cognition and Instruction, 16*(1), 3–118.

Zimmerman, R. M., Chinn, C. A., & Duncan, R. G. (2016, April). *Disagreement resolution strategies during student inquiry: Applying the AIR model of epistemic cognition.* Poster presented at the annual meeting of the American Educational Research Association, Washington, DC.

16

EXPLORING THE SCOPE AND BOUNDARIES OF INQUIRY STRATEGIES

What do young learners generalize from inquiry-based science learning?

Ala Samarapungavan, Jamison Wills, and Lynn A. Bryan

Introduction

Transfer is understood as the adaptation and use of knowledge acquired or learned in one context to novel contexts or situations (Bransford & Schwartz, 1999; Perkins & Salomon, 1992). Questions of how, why, and when we take something learned previously and use it in a seemingly new context or situation have long preoccupied psychologists, educators, and philosophers. The origin of the term *transfer* is attributed to the psychologist Thorndike who, along with his colleagues (Thorndike & Woodworth, 1901), conducted some of the earliest laboratory investigations of transfer. Based on their investigations, Thorndike and colleagues concluded that spontaneous transfer was rare and depended on the existence of identical elements between the contexts of training and of transfer. However, some contemporaries (e.g., Judd, 1908) disagreed, arguing that thinking skills are generalizable beyond the specific elements of the training context. Following Thorndike's footsteps, there has been a long and fruitful history of experimental studies of transfer in the laboratory. This research has yielded insights into the conditions that foster transfer as well as the mechanisms of transfer (e.g., Gentner & Colhoun, 2010; Holyoak, Junn, & Billman, 1984; Kershaw, Flynn, & Leamarie, 2013; Price & Driscoll, 1997). Salomon and Perkins (1989) proposed two varieties of transfer: *high road transfer*, which is deliberate transfer through mindful abstraction, and *low road transfer*, which is automatic transfer through extensions of varied practice. Salomon and Perkins have noted that successful educational systems foster both high road and low road transfer and that each type of transfer is useful in different contexts.

More recently, work in the area of transfer has expanded from purely cognitive accounts to consider environmental, social, and motivational factors (see Schwartz & Martin, 2004, Schwartz, Varma, & Martin, 2008). Researchers have shown that collaborative learning contexts can foster the transfer of learning (Fleming & Alexander, 2001; Kirschner, Paas, & Kirschner, 2009; Kirschner, Paas, Kirschner, & Jansen, 2011; Schwartz, 1995). Kapur's (2010, 2014) work on the role of productive failure in mathematics learning highlights the importance of student agency in originating or generating new knowledge during initial learning for future transfer.

Our perspective on the question of transfer is influenced by the writings of John Dewey who grappled with the educational challenges of fostering practical knowledge that can guide and be embodied in action as one goes about the business of living (Dewey, 1960, 1963). Dewey's ideas about praxis—for example, the fluidity, generativity, and adaptability of knowledge required as scientists engage in the practices of inquiry (1960)—are particularly relevant to our work. Over the past decade, Samarapungavan and her collaborators have engaged in a program of research that examines how students in the primary grades learn science in the context of model-based, content-rich inquiry environments. Specific examples of this work include the *Scientific Literacy Project* (SLP; Mantzicopoulos, Patrick, & Samarapungavan, 2005), which focused on life science learning in kindergarten students, and the *Modeling in Primary Grades* (MPG) project (Samarapungavan, Bryan, & Giordano, 2012), which explored second-grade students' learning about the particulate nature of matter.

Although we do not explicitly adopt the language of transfer to frame our program of research, it is our hope that the learning environments we help design will allow students to develop new knowledge that is fluid, adaptable, and useful over a wide range of contexts. In short, our goal is to support students' ability to transfer knowledge in the ways that Dewey envisioned.

In the next section, we provide a brief overview of the program of research on young children's school-based science conducted by the lead author's research group and discuss how elements of our pedagogical approach connect to considerations of transfer. Drawing from our prior work, we provide examples of spontaneous transfer by young children as they engage in science learning. When we refer to spontaneous transfer, we mean simply that no explicit cues about prior relevant examples are provided in the transfer situation. Our examples of transfer are drawn both from our analyses of children's thinking in situ as they engage in classroom discourse about their investigations during science learning, as well as from formal individual assessments of learning. We conclude with a discussion of some of the cognitive and social factors that influence the scope and limits of transfer of science learning in young children and their implications for the design of science instruction.

Designing inquiry environments to support science learning in the early years: Considerations of transfer

The theoretical framework we adopt assumes that learning in major conceptual domains such as science is predicated, at least in part, on the development of distinct domain-specific knowledge structures and processes—for instance, explanatory principles, models, reasoning patterns, and patterns of activity. Research in human cognition and cognitive development over the last three decades supports the development of domain-specific knowledge as a critical aspect of science learning (Brown, 1990; Gelman & Brenneman, 2004; Spelke & Kinzler, 2007). For example, Brown and Kane (1988) have shown than even preschoolers can transfer knowledge to new contexts when the base and target context share an underlying causal structure that is well understood.

A second key assumption is that learning is socially situated and knowledge is negotiated and realized in specific cultural contexts and practices (Boyd & Richerson, 2005; Driver, Asoko, Leach, Mortimer, & Scott, 1994; Greeno, 1998). This assumption is consistent with a rich body of literature in the area of science studies which describes scientific knowledge and practice as grounded in and shaped by specific sociocultural and historic contexts (Giere, 1988; Knorr-Cetina, 1999; Laudan, 1990; Laudan et al., 1986). Our goal in working with teachers is to help them design learning environments that recreate important aspects of science in the classroom (cf. Chinn & Malhotra, 2002; National Research Council, 2012; Singer, Marx, Krajcik, & Chambers, 2000). We try to create investigative frameworks that allow young learners to engage in productive and meaningful investigations.

The examples we use to illustrate our approach come primarily from two projects. *SLP* (Mantzicopoulos et al., 2005) examined life science learning in U.S. kindergarten classrooms. MPG (Samarapungavan et al., 2012) examined U.S. second-graders' physical science learning about the particulate nature of matter. Additional examples will be drawn from the first author's current research on students developing models of experimentation and evidence in biology (Samarapungavan, in press).

The most obvious set of candidates for knowledge transfer in our projects are the core disciplinary principles that are needed to explain (as well as predict and/ or manipulate) a wide range of phenomena. For example, a deep understanding of life-supporting relationships among structures, behaviors, and biological functions in organisms, populations, and ecosystems, and of the principles and mechanisms of natural selection that shape them constitute core biology knowledge. This core knowledge is applicable (i.e., should transfer) across the full range of biological phenomena. The transfer of core disciplinary principles allows children to entertain and evaluate plausible mechanisms for the occurrence of novel phenomena as well as to rethink explanations for phenomena that they have encountered routinely in their daily lives.

A second set of candidates for knowledge transfer belong to realm of meta-knowledge about science and the practices of scientific inquiry. In our projects, these are realized in praxis when students engage in constructing, evaluating, and revising scientific models as they conduct and reflect upon investigations centered on biological or physical science phenomena. These intricate connections between core disciplinary content and the practices of scientific inquiry are further elaborated in the specific examples of transfer we discuss below.

Leveraging the past: Transfer of core domain knowledge in support of learning

A first design principle in our projects is that each investigation must align with children's existing cognitive resources as they begin cycles of scientific inquiry, as indicated by developmental research. For the SLP project, curriculum units focused on a series of investigations about living things because developmental research indicates that even very young children employ biological concepts to categorize natural kinds (e.g., to distinguish between living and non-living things or between plants and animals), to make causal inferences, and to predict biological phenomena (Greif, Nelson, Keil, & Guitierrez, 2006; Inagaki & Hatano, 2004, 2006; Medin & Atran, 2004; Spelke & Kinzler, 2007). Additionally, young learners possess certain core capacities for scientific reasoning such as the ability to make inferences from evidence and to attend to empirical anomalies (e.g., Zimmerman, 2000).

The MPG project leverages children's early capacities and experiences to support the learning of scientific concepts that have traditionally been considered too difficult to introduce in the early elementary school years (Fensham, 1994). Developmental research has found that children between the ages of three and seven think that tiny particles too small to be visible to the naked eye (e.g., particles of sugar or salt) can exist in aqueous solutions and that the properties of solutions, such as taste or drinkability, may be affected by these particles (Au, Sidle, & Rollins, 1993; Rosen & Rozin, 1993). Wiser and Smith (2008) proposed introducing instruction on the nature of matter in upper elementary school, yet MacDonald and Bean (2011) found that second graders who engaged in informal museum learning activities can construct an understanding that microscopic material entities can be studied indirectly.

In MPG, we build upon children's emerging ideas of scale, from objects that are too large to be seen directly, such as the earth or the solar system, to those that are too small to be seen directly, such as germs. MPG leverages this developing sense of scale to help young students to: (a) imagine the materiality of visible substances in terms of the microscopic particles that comprise them, and (b) to model how the arrangement and motion of these particles relate to macroscopic phenomena such as differences in the appearance and behavior of a substance in a solid, liquid, or gas physical state or during phase transitions such as melting, freezing, evaporation, or condensation (Samarapungavan, Bryan, Wills, & Yuksel, 2015).

Our first design principle speaks to a key point about transfer. Although much psychological research has focused on transfer as an outcome or product of learning, it is important to consider the role of transfer as a key resource or input during the course of school learning. Effective pedagogy depends on successfully leveraging students' prior knowledge and reasoning capacities to engage them in a bootstrapping process of developing new ideas, practices, and habits of mind from what came before. In other words, school science learning depends on the ability of young learners to "transfer in" relevant knowledge.

Some of the transfer of core domain knowledge that occurs in our projects is cued rather than spontaneous. For example, when teaching an investigative unit on life cycles, a teacher might use question prompts to engage kindergarten students in a comparison of how they are similar to or different from other family members. However, we have observed that as young learners' fluidity with inquiry grows through their ongoing engagement in communities of practice, they come to see themselves as collaborative agents working towards shared goals of understanding and creating knowledge. For example, once a teacher has established norms and routines for discourse around scientific inquiry, children routinely engage in instances of continued spontaneous transfer during small group and whole class inquiry activities and discourse. Two examples of such spontaneous transfer are discussed below.

The first example is drawn from a lesson about the growth and development of living things in the SLP project with kindergarten students. The unit focused on an investigation of the life cycle of the monarch butterfly in which children studied the growth and development of eggs placed on the leaves of live milkweed plants as the larvae hatched, advanced through the caterpillar phase, pupated, and eventually emerged as adult butterflies and were released outdoors (Samarapungavan, Mantzicopoulos, & Patrick, 2008).

The teacher introduced the unit by asking her kindergarten students what it meant for a living thing to grow. She reminded them of their own growth and asked if they could think of ways in which living things change as they grow and develop over time. At first the children focused exclusively on changes in size, saying that living things get "bigger" or "taller" as they develop. When the teacher showed the kindergarten students pictures of a monarch butterfly and asked them what it might have looked like when it was born, a typical initial response was a "baby butterfly" that came out of its mother's "tummy," and that looked just like its mother only smaller.

However, as the children broke into small groups to discuss what they thought would happen and to draw models predicting the ways in which two species (people and monarch butterflies) developed, some children spontaneously began to recall more qualitative changes in humans over time. For example, one child shared that he knew that he was born with "no hair" on his head from his baby pictures. Yet another spontaneously shared that their new puppy was learning to "go potty outside."

Kindergarteners initially did not know the stages of metamorphosis for the monarch butterfly. However, by reflecting on what they knew about their own about growth and development or that of their pets, kindergarteners were able to transfer the expectation that they should look for qualitative changes that monarch butterflies might undergo over their life cycles and planned to look for such changes in their investigations. Some children wondered if butterflies learned special sounds to "talk" as they grew older or if they were born with "whiskers" (most likely a reference to insect antennae) or would grow them later.

A second example is drawn from an MPG lesson on phases of matter with second grade students (Samarapungavan et al., 2015; Samarapungavan & Bryan, 2015).

On the first day, students explored the macroscopic or visible properties of matter in solid, liquid, and gas phases, considering a number of exemplars for each state (e.g., a block of wood, sawdust, sand, cloth, air in bubble wrap, water, liquid dish soap, etc.). They concluded that a solid typically holds its shape while liquids spread out evenly to take the shape of their containers. At first the students were unsure about gases, but after observing the air rush out of a large balloon and thinking about what happens to air that they exhale, the students concluded gases like air spread out "all over the room."

On the following day, the teacher engaged the students in a modeling exercise in which they divided a block of wood into smaller and smaller pieces (e.g., half a block, a quarter block, an eighth) until they were asked to imagine dividing the smallest visible pieces (flecks of sawdust) to the point at which each piece was so small that it was invisible. The children were asked to draw models of what these smallest invisible particles of wood might look like.

Following this activity, the teacher told students the class would use "human models" to show what the smallest possible particles of matter in a solid (a wooden Popsicle stick) looked like. The teacher taped off a "jar" shape on the floor and asked a small group of students to imagine each of them was one of those smallest possible particles of wood. She asked them to work together to model or show how these particles behaved to form the visible stick. At first the group of modelers stood haphazardly on the floor. As the onlookers began to provide feedback, one of the children in the modeling group spontaneously curled up on her hands and knees into a little sphere in the jar. The other group members promptly followed suit and under the continued direction of their classmates, they moved themselves closer together into a symmetrical arrangement with two of the "spheres" touching the bottom of the jar.

Next, the teacher asked another group of students to model particles of water. The second group started by arranging itself in a similar manner to the first group, but their classmates decided that because water moved to take the shape of its container, the particles should be further apart and should move around more (e.g., "no – water squishes about," "spread out a little more"). By the time the teacher called upon a third group to model particles of air, the new modelers took their positions in the jar, jiggling around loosely. Then two of them started rolling out of the jar as the onlookers called out "all over, they are going all over the room." The class had spontaneously transferred ideas about differences in the arrangement and movement of particles in solid and liquid phases to model the gas phase.

Bootstrapping cognitive resources: Developing fluidity in the practices of science

Our projects build upon the pedagogical principles of guided inquiry (Brown & Campione, 1994). We start with the assumption that science can be viewed as a community of practice, with shared cognitive resources (Samarapungavan et al., 2008; Samarapungavan, Patrick, & Mantzicopoulos, 2011). Drawing from Giere

(2002, 2004), we think of science as the collective cultural practices of articulating, testing, evaluating, and refining or revising models of the world. Our projects represent initiations of young learners into these cultural practices of science. A key challenge of instructional design is to incorporate appropriate instructional supports that allow young learners to develop fluidity in the practices of science. Examples of supports "hard-wired" into our instructional designs include the topic of study, investigational context, and tools and artifacts for data collection. Other supports are more contextual as teachers model inquiry and scaffold students' model construction and discourse through prompts, questions, and requests for clarification, elaboration, and justification.

Further, our projects employ varied inscriptional tools that are used to support the development of fluency with modeling practices during inquiry. Idea boards are used to record students' ideas during whole class discussions and to encourage them to revisit and revise these ideas over the course of their investigations. Each student maintains a science notebook during investigations to record important aspects of inquiry (e.g., questions or predictions, plans for observation and collection of evidence, what data were collected, what conclusions were drawn from the data etc.). After making sense of their data and discussing what they found out in the investigation, students work collaboratively in small groups to develop posters to share what they learned with others. The use of such inscriptional tools further serves to scaffold students' fluidity in the practices of science. We present some examples of such developing fluidity that illustrate generative transfer as it is enacted in classroom discourse around scientific inquiry.

Hypothesis testing: One interesting example comes from kindergarten classroom discourse during an SLP pre-inquiry activity that was designed to help young learners understand science as an approach to investigating and making sense of the world around them (see Samarapungavan et al., 2008, p. 878). The teacher passed a tulip bulb around for students to examine and asked them to try and figure out what it was. The children advanced varied guesses, suggesting that the object was a "nut," a "potato," or an "onion." The teacher maintained epistemic press by asking the students to justify their guesses and to see if they could figure out a way to come to a consensus. As the kindergartners became comfortable with the argumentation practices the teacher was facilitating, they drew upon their prior knowledge to offer justifications for their claims. For example, one child claimed it was a nut because "it's brown and hard." Others disagreed, saying it was "too big for a nut." Some children argued that it was an onion because it had "a peel," or "a skin," and was "white and squishy inside."

Although the students agreed that the bulb was plant material, they could not reach consensus on its identity. As their arguments offered no way out of the impasse, the teacher simply continued to provide epistemic press for over half an hour, urging the children to think about how they could figure out "a way to find out what it is," given their different claims. Eventually, one student hesitantly suggested that they bury the bulb in the ground and "wait for it grow." She had spontaneously transferred her knowledge about the life cycle of plants to suggest

an alternate path to identification. The class quickly converged around her suggestion, treaching consensus around an empirical test that would help them resolve
their arguments.

Our pedagogical approach harnesses both students' domain-specific knowledge
(e.g., about biological growth and development) and their more general cognitive
faculties (e.g., causal, and mechanistic reasoning) to scaffold the early emergence of
important scientific practices such as the construction of empirical tests to resolve
theoretical impasses. On the one hand, the child who proposed planting the tulip
bulb drew from her biological knowledge of plant growth to come up with an
empirical test. The proposed test was seen as a plausible way forward by her classmates, presumably because they shared this background knowledge. On the other
hand, the idea of an empirical test itself was slow to emerge. The first half hour of discussion focused on categorical reasoning and the use of the bulb's visible properties
to determine its identity. The idea for the test eventually emerged under conditions
of persistent epistemic press in the social context of the theoretical impasse.

We have evidence that individual members of our primary grade communities
of practice can transfer such knowledge out to novel problems. In the SLP project, Samarapungavan et al. (2011) found that fewer than 2% of SLP kindergarten
students could propose a test of two competing hypotheses on a pretest interview
question on the individually administered Science Learning Assessment (described
in Samarapungavan et al., 2008, 2011). In contrast, 44% of these students were able
to propose a plausible hypothesis test on a posttest item with novel content after
engaging in the SLP inquiry units. A comparison group of kindergarten peers who
received routine science instruction instead of the SLP curriculum showed no such
gains (2% on pretest, 3% on posttest) (Samarapungavan et al., 2011).

Models of investigation: As young learners engage in inquiry, varied design issues
relating to ongoing investigations become problematized in their discourse. For
example, discussions about the adequacy of the experimental set up, the duration
or frequency of observations, or accuracy of measurement often emerge as students
encounter problems during their investigations. We regard such learning phenomena as exemplars of emerging enacted epistemic knowledge about the practices of
scientific inquiry.

In the SLP project, kindergarten students learned the basics of simple measurement as part of an early unit in which they practiced measuring the fit of their
feet to shoe sizes, using a standard foot ruler. In a later unit, they measured and
recorded the growth of monarch caterpillars daily until they pupated. The students worked in pairs to hold up and cut lengths of string equal to the length of
the caterpillars they were studying. They then measured their lengths of string
in inches using a standard foot ruler and recorded the measurements in their
science notebooks. In this context, kindergarteners showed spontaneous attention to the precision and accuracy of their measurements of caterpillar growth.
Consider the following exchange between kindergartners: One child pointed to a
caterpillar on a milkweed plant and told the classroom assistant, "He is five inches."
The classroom assistant responded, "Five inches? How do you know?" At this

point, a second small group member from the same work station, referring to the same caterpillar, pointed to her science notebook record and interjected, "This is two, two inches." The first child looked over at the second child's notebook, then realigned his string on the ruler and re-measured the length of the string (see Samarapungavan et al., 2008, p. 882). In this example, students transferred considerations of the accuracy of measurement from a unit taught several weeks prior to their current investigations.

A second example comes from a pilot project on fourth graders' models of investigation conducted by the lead author. In the context of a unit on plant growth, the teacher initially asked student dyads to design experiments to examine the effect of variables such as the temperature and amount of water on seed germination. Bean seeds were planted in identical plastic cups, each with same amount of soil. To examine the effects of water, dyads chose a range of values, operationalized as a number of pipette drops (the teacher had provided dyads with pipettes to encourage precise measurement).

Problems arose because several dyads chose large contrasts in the amount of water (e.g., 2 vs. 2000 drops) but were unable to physically manipulate and keep track of their pipetting accurately after the first few drops. The students began to joke around or fudge their data. One dyad squeezed all the water from their pipette into a seed cup without counting but recorded the amount as 5000 drops. For some dyads, the task morphed from that of giving seeds a pre-specified amount of water to that of being able to perfect the skill of pipetting.

After discussing these observations with us, the teacher refocused the lesson as an opportunity for students to think about reliability and accuracy in experimental procedures. The following day, she engaged the students in a discussion of the difficulties they had encountered. Several students acknowledged that they could not accurately measure high amounts of water with pipettes and had no idea how much water each seed was getting. The teacher then asked dyads to work on addressing these problems. No specific instructions or suggestions were provided. The students spontaneously generated a variety of plausible strategies to improve the reliability and accuracy of their experiments such as:

(a) Specialization: Some students were recognized as being more skilled at pipetting, and it was suggested that these students should do the pipetting for the class (e.g., "Maya is really good at it. She should always do drops.").
(b) Training: Some students proposed pre-experimental training in pipetting techniques (e.g., "We should do lots of practice before we start") to increase their skill and accuracy.
(c) Changes in instrumentation: Some students proposed using other instruments to yield more reliable measures (e.g., "we can use – a spoon for less water, and we can use a cup for more water, it's easier to do the same each time").

Each of these solutions represented examples of spontaneous transfer from prior knowledge, allowing students to propose more effective models of investigation.

However, the teacher also provided explicit epistemic press or demand that motivated students to evaluate and revise to their investigative designs.

Models of data: As students engage in the practices of data collection and interpretation, they also develop fluidity with models of data. Models of data are qualitative and quantitative ways of representing investigative results in order to interpret and communicate findings. An example is drawn from the MPG project as second graders engaged in an investigation of evaporation (Samarapungavan, et al., 2012, 2015;). The activity employed a balance scale with two identical cups, each filled with the same volume of water at room temperature and mounted on each end of the scale. A heat lamp positioned over one of the two cups was left on overnight. On the next day the students examined the amount of water left in each cup. An example of a data model from this experiment can be found in Figure 16.1. The transfer of the data model occured on a post-intervention interview question as the student explained steam rising from a kettle with water that was being heated. She correctly described particles of water in the kettle moving more vigorously and some escaping into the air as heat was added. As part of her account, she spontaneously recalled her data model of evaporation from the classroom experiment several weeks prior ("I drew a model in class, with the lamp. Some water went in the air when it got hot."). We interpret this as an example of a developing fluency with data models in which the child transfers and connects macroscopic data models from specific experimental investigations to more abstract theoretical particle models of phase transitions.

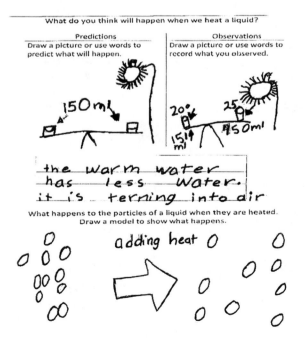

FIGURE 16.1 Models of data in MPG (Modeling in Primary Grades) project.

Epistemic knowledge about the practices of scientific inquiry: Through their participation in inquiry practices, even young learners begin to abstract epistemic knowledge about scientific inquiry. For example, following their experiences with constructing and using particulate models of matter in the MPG project, second graders began to articulate epistemic knowledge about the nature and purposes of modeling. In the first year, the MPG curriculum did not include explicit discussion of the nature and purposes of models and modeling (Samarapungavan et al., 2015). Particulate models were introduced contextually by asking children to draw or model how the smallest possible pieces of matter exemplars might be arranged or move. Nonetheless, during the post-interview, several students said that the smallest particles were not visible to the naked eye and spontaneously added that models were needed to think about things that were too small to work with directly.

Kindergarten students in the SLP project showed evidence of a generalized understanding of the importance and function of record keeping during inquiry (Samarapungavan et al., 2008; Samarapungavan et al., 2011). As they progressed through the 20 week curriculum, they began to spontaneously request which ideas the teacher should write down or record on class idea boards. They also asked if they could use their science notebooks during investigations instead of being prompted to use them by the teachers. When students worked to create posters for reporting their findings, they spontaneously referred to their notebooks records to aid in poster production.

In the preceding sections, we have provided examples of positive transfer from varied model-based inquiry learning projects. The classroom-based examples of transfer discussed, though not specifically cued, occur in co-regulative task contexts. Such co-regulation is predicated on the coordination of individual knowledge and skill among group members engaged in shared tasks. However, knowledge that emerges through co-regulated activity cannot be reduced to the sum of its parts (i.e., the knowledge of individual members). Beyond the shared and co-produced knowledge that is reflected in group outputs (e.g., investigation reports), individual members also carry new knowledge into new tasks and social contexts (e.g., on individual posttests). Collectively, these examples illustrate how the pedagogy of model-based inquiry learning can support powerful, generative science learning. However, our research also suggests boundaries on the scope of transfer, as we discuss in the final section.

Constraints on transfer for young learners

Our program of research indicates certain conditions under which transfer may be especially difficult for young learners. Many of these constraints have been discussed in the literature, typically in research on learning in adolescents and adults. Our research extends these considerations to the context of early science learning.

Ontology: Chi and her associates (Chi, 2005; Slotta & Chi, 2006) have suggested that the ontological category assigned by learners to an entity imposes constraints on the imputed behaviors and properties for that entity. Chi et al. suggest that novices assign entities such as heat, light, and sound to the ontological category of material substances and therefore find it difficult to understand such phenomena as arising from microscopic processes at operating at the particulate level.

In the MPG project, we observed that second graders found it very difficult to model sound as produced through the transfer of vibrational energy across particles in a medium, even with extensive support. We are not sure at present whether these difficulties stem from children's conceptions of sound itself as a material substance, or rather if they think of sound as disembodied or immaterial entity that is sensed by a special organ (the ear) (see Lautrey & Mazens, 2004; Mazens & Lautrey, 2003). Although we are still analyzing these data, it appears that ontological barriers make it difficult for young learners to understand sound.

The interactive and discourse structure of classrooms: The structure of classroom interaction and discourse during inquiry are critical to facilitate students' fluidity with the practices of scientific inquiry (Roth & Welzel, 2001; Samarapungavan, 2008, 2011; Seymour and Lehrer, 2006; Windschitl et al, 2008a, b). This requires the refinement of teachers' existing pedagogical content knowledge to develop a repertoire of productive strategies for facilitating student science discourse. For example, teachers need to be able to "see" the emerging science in children's classroom discourse (Hammer & van Zee, 2006). Over the course of our research we have found that epistemic press or demand as students puzzle to explain complex phenomena is a key factor in generating fluidity with practices of scientific inquiry (such as model evaluation and revision, explanation, and argumentation).

Conclusions and directions for future research

Our program of research indicates that young children transfer core knowledge and reasoning strategies, developed through their informal experiences with the natural world, to build new knowledge and skill in the classroom. Additionally, our research indicates that children are able to transfer the knowledge and skills that they construct during formal science learning to novel contexts in and out of school. Some of the most powerful examples of transfer in our projects are based on students' developing mastery of inquiry practices. Our research indicates that the epistemic demands of the classroom social context play a key role in supporting students' developing fluidity of scientific practice. These epistemic demands are realized through the structure and norms of group interaction and discourse under the guidance of teachers. They require considerable pedagogical content knowledge on the part of teachers for successful implementation. Further research is needed on effective models of teacher professional development which allow teachers to sustain and transfer effective inquiry pedagogies in the absence of research support.

Acknowledgments

The research described in this paper was supported by grants from the U.S. Department of education (#R305K050038) and from the National Science

Foundation (#1222853). The opinions expressed are those of the authors and do not represent views of the U.S. Department of Education or the National Science Foundation. We greatly appreciate the involvement of the teachers, parents, and children who participated in the research.

References

Au, T. K., Sidle, A. L., & Rollins, K. B. (1993). Developing an intuitive understanding of conservation and contamination: Invisible particles as a plausible mechanism. *Developmental Psychology, 29*(2), 286–299.

Bransford, J. D., & Schwartz, D. L. (1999). Rethinking transfer: A simple proposal with multiple implications. *Review of Research in Education, 24*, 61–100.

Boyd, R., & Richerson, J. (2005). Solving the puzzle of human cooperation. In S. Levinson & N. Enfield (Eds.), *Evolution and culture* (pp. 105–132). Cambridge, MA: MIT Press.

Brown, A. L. (1990). Domain-specific principles affect learning and transfer in children. *Cognitive Science, 14*(1), 107–133.

Brown, A. L., & Campione, J. C. (1994). Guided discovery in a community of learners. In K. McGilly (Ed.), *Classroom lessons: Integrating cognitive theory and classroom practice* (pp. 229–270). Cambridge, MA: MIT Press/Bradford Books.

Brown, A. L., & Kane, M. J. (1988). Preschool children can learn to transfer: Learning to learn and learning from example. *Cognitive Psychology, 20*(4), 493–523.

Chi, M. T. (2005). Commonsense conceptions of emergent processes: Why some misconceptions are robust. *The Journal of the Learning Sciences, 14*(2), 161–199.

Chinn, C. A., & Malhotra, B. A. (2002). Epistemologically authentic inquiry in schools: A theoretical framework for evaluating inquiry tasks. *Science Education, 86*(2), 175–218.

Dewey, J. (1960[1933]). *How we think: A restatement of the relation of reflective thinking to the educative process* (New edition). Lexington, MA: D. C. Heath and Company.

Dewey, J. (1963[1938]). *Experience and education.* New York: Collier Books.

Driver, R., Asoko, H., Leach, J., Scott, P., & Mortimer, E. (1994). Constructing scientific knowledge in the classroom. *Educational Researcher, 23*(7), 5–12.

Fensham, P. (1994). Progression in school science curriculum: A rational prospect or a chimera? *Research in Science Education, 24*(1), 76–82.

Fleming, V. M., & Alexander, J. M. (2001). The benefits of peer collaboration: A replication with a delayed posttest. *Contemporary Educational Psychology, 26*(4), 588–601.

Gelman, R., & Brenneman, K. (2004). Science learning pathways for young children. *Early Childhood Research Quarterly, 19*(1), 150–158.

Gentner, D., & Colhoun, J. (2010). Analogical processes in human thinking and learning. In *Towards a theory of thinking* (pp. 35–48). Berlin/Heidelberg: Springer.

Giere, R. N. (1988). *Explaining science: A cognitive approach.* Chicago, IL: University of Chicago Press.

Giere, R. N. (2002). Discussion note: Distributed cognition in epistemic cultures. *Philosophy of Science, 69*(4), 637–644.

Giere, R. N. (2004). How models are used to represent reality. *Philosophy of Science, 71*(5), 742–752.

Greeno, J. G. (1998). The situativity of knowing, learning, and research. *American Psychologist, 53*(1), 5–26.

Greif, M. L., Nelson, D. G. K., Keil, F. C., & Gutierrez, F. (2006). What do children want to know about animals and artifacts? Domain-specific requests for information. *Psychological Science, 17*(6), 455–459.

Hammer, D., & van Zee, E. H. (2006). *Seeing the science in children's thinking: Case studies of student inquiry in physical science.* Portsmouth, NH: Heinemann.

Holyoak, K. J., Junn, E. N., & Billman, D. O. (1984). Development of analogical problem solving skill. *Child Development, 55*(6), 2042–2055.

Inagaki, K., & Hatano, G. (2004). Vitalistic causality in young children's naive biology. *Trends in Cognitive Sciences, 8*(8), 356–362.

Inagaki, K., & Hatano, G. (2006). Young children's conception of the biological world. *Current Directions in Psychological Science, 15*(4), 177–181.

Judd, C. H. (1908). The relation of special training to general intelligence. *Educational Review, 36*, 28–42.

Kapur, M. (2010). Productive failure in mathematical problem solving. *Instructional Science, 38*(6), 523–550.

Kapur, M. (2014). Productive failure in learning math. *Cognitive Science, 38*(5), 1008–1022.

Kershaw, T. C., Flynn, C. K., & Gordon, L. T. (2013). Multiple paths to transfer and constraint relaxation in insight problem solving. *Thinking & Reasoning, 19*(1), 96–136.

Kirschner, F., Paas, F., & Kirschner, P. (2009). Individual and group-based learning from complex cognitive tasks: Effects on retention and transfer efficiency. *Computers in Human Behavior, 25*(2), 306–314.

Kirschner, F., Paas, F., Kirschner, P., & Janssen, J. (2011). Differential effects of problem-solving demands on individual and collaborative learning outcomes. *Learning and Instruction, 21*(4), 587–599.

Knorr Cetina, K. (1999). *Epistemic cultures: How the sciences make knowledge.* Cambridge, MA: Harvard University Press.

Laudan, L. (1990). *Science and relativism: Some key controversies in the philosophy of science.* Chicago, IL: Chicago University Press.

Laudan, L., Donovan, A., Laudan, R., Barker, P., Brown, H., Leptin, J., . . . Wykstra, S. (1986). Scientific change: Philosophical models and historical research. *Synthese, 69*(2), 141–223.

Lautrey, J., & Mazens, K. (2004). Is children's naive knowledge consistent? A comparison of the concepts of sound and heat. *Learning and Instruction, 14*(4), 399–423.

MacDonald, T., & Bean, A. (2011). Adventures in the subatomic universe: An exploratory study of a scientist–museum physics education project. *Public Understanding of Science, 20*(6), 846–862.

Mantzicopoulos, P., Patrick, H., & Samarapungavan, A. (2005). The Scientific Literacy Project: Enhancing young children's scientific literacy through reading and inquiry-centered adult–child dialog. *Institute of Education Sciences*, Grant Award (#R305K050038).

Mazens, K., & Lautrey, J. (2003). Conceptual change in physics: Children's naive representations of sound. *Cognitive Development, 18*(2), 159–176.

Medin, D. L., & Atran, S. (2004). The native mind: Biological categorization and reasoning in development and across cultures. *Psychological Review, 111*(4), 960–1044.

National Research Council. (2012). *A framework for K-12 science education: Practices, crosscutting concepts, and core ideas.* Committee on a Conceptual Framework for New K-12 Science Education Standards. Board on Science Education, Division of Behavioral and Social Sciences and Education. Washington, DC: The National Academies Press. Retrieved from www.nap.edu/read/13165/chapter/1

Perkins, D. N., & Salomon, G. (1992). Transfer of learning. In *International encyclopedia of education* (2nd ed., pp. 2–13). Oxford: Pergamon Press.

Price, E. A., & Driscoll, M. P. (1997). An inquiry into the spontaneous transfer of problem-solving skill. *Contemporary Educational Psychology, 22*(4), 472–494.

Rosen, A. B., & Rozin, P. (1993). Now you see it, now you don't: The preschool child's conception of invisible particles in the context of dissolving. *Developmental Psychology, 29*(2), 300–311.

Roth, W.-M., & Weizel, M. (2001). From activity to gestures and scientific language. *Journal of Research in Science Teaching, 38,* 103–136.

Salomon, G., & Perkins, D. N. (1989). Rocky roads to transfer: Rethinking mechanism of a neglected phenomenon. *Educational Psychologist, 24*(2), 113–142.

Samarapungavan, A. (in press). Construing scientific evidence: The role of disciplinary knowledge in reasoning with and about evidence in scientific practice. In F. Fischer, K. Engelmann, J. Osborne, & C. Chinn (Eds.), *Interplay of domain-specific and domain-general aspects of scientific reasoning and argumentation skills.* New York, NY: Taylor & Francis.

Samarapungavan, A., & Bryan, A. L. (2015, April). Modeling in primary grades (MPG): Science learning through content rich inquiry. As part of symposium. *Toward Building a Foundation for Teaching and Learning Elementary Science: Highlighting Six NSF Projects.* National Association for Research in Science Teaching (NARST).

Samarapungavan, A., Bryan, A. L., & Giordano, N. (2012). Modeling in the Primary Grades (MPG): Science learning through content-rich inquiry. *National Science Foundation,* Grant Award (Award # 1222853).

Samarapungavan, A., Bryan, A. L., Wills, J., & Yuksel, T. (2015, April). *Examining second graders' emerging particulate models of matter in the context of learning through model-based inquiry.* Paper presented at the Annual Meeting of the American Educational Research Association, Washington, DC.

Samarapungavan, A., Mantzicopoulos, P., & Patrick, H. (2008). Learning science through inquiry in kindergarten. *Science Education, 92*(5), 868–908.

Samarapungavan, A., Patrick, H., & Mantzicopoulos, P. (2011). What kindergarten students learn in inquiry-based science classrooms? *Cognition and Instruction, 29*(4), 416–470.

Samarapungavan, A., Tippins, D., & Bryan, L. A. (2015). A Modelling-based inquiry framework for early childhood science learning. In K. Trundle (Ed.), *Research in early childhood science education* (pp. 259–277). Heidelberg, Germany: Springer.

Schwartz, D. L. (1995). The emergence of abstract representations in dyad problem solving. *The Journal of the Learning Sciences, 4*(3), 321–354.

Schwartz, D. L., & Martin, T. (2004). Inventing to prepare for future learning: The hidden efficiency of encouraging original student production in statistics instruction. *Cognition & Instruction, 22*(2), 129–184.

Schwartz, D. L., Varma, S., & Martin, L. (2008). Dynamic transfer and innovation. In S. Vosniadou (Ed.), *Handbook of conceptual change* (pp. 479–506). Mahwah, NJ: Erlbaum.

Seymour J. R., & Lehrer, R. (2006). Tracing the evolution of pedagogical content knowledge as the development of inter animated discourses. *The Journal of the Learning Sciences, 15,* 549–582.

Singer, J., Marx, R. W., Krajcik, J., & Clay Chambers, J. (2000). Constructing extended inquiry projects: Curriculum materials for science education reform. *Educational Psychologist, 35*(3), 165–178.

Slotta, J. D., & Chi, M. T. (2006). Helping students understand challenging topics in science through ontology training. *Cognition and Instruction, 24*(2), 261–289.

Spelke, E. S., & Kinzler, K. D. (2007). Core knowledge. *Developmental Science, 10*(1), 89–96.

Thorndike, E. L., & Woodworth, R. S. (1901). The influence of improvement in one mental function upon the efficacy of other functions. *Psychological Review, 8*(3), 247–261.

Windschitl, M., Thompson, J., & Braaten, M. (2008a). Beyond the scientific method: Model-based inquiry as a new paradigm of preference for school science investigations. *Science Education, 92*, 941–967.

Windschitl, M., Thompson, J., & Braaten, M. (2008b). How novice science teachers appropriate epistemically discourses around model-based inquiry for use in classrooms. *Cognition & Instruction, 26*, 310–378.

Wiser, M. & Smith, C. L. (2008). Learning and teaching about matter in grades K-8: When should the atomic-molecular theory be introduced? In S. Vosniadou (Ed.), *International handbook of research on conceptual change* (pp. 205–239). New York, NY: Routledge.

Zimmerman, C. (2000). The development of scientific reasoning skills. *Developmental Review, 20*(1), 99–149.

17

PMC-2E

Conceptual representations to promote transfer

Cindy E. Hmelo-Silver, Rebecca Jordan,
Suparna Sinha, Yawen Yu, and Catherine Eberbach

Complex systems are an important part of the world we live in. Complex causal systems are characterized by the following five characteristics (Assaraf & Orion, 2010; Vattam et al., 2011): (1) hierarchical structures, (2) subsystems that exhibit natural outcomes or engineered functions, (3) causal elements, (4) causal event chains giving rise to system mechanisms and outcomes, and (5) causal event chains varying in temporal and spatial dimensions. Novices, however, tend to focus exclusively on visible and stable structures (Hmelo, Holton, & Kolodner, 2000; Mintzes, Trowbridge, Arnaudin, & Wandersee, 1991). Indeed, it is the multiple levels of organization, variable connections and components, invisible elements, and dynamic processes (Hmelo-Silver & Azevedo, 2006) that combine to make complex systems challenging to understand.

The United States' Next Generation Science Standards (NGSS Lead States, 2013) highlight the value of engaging in systems thinking, relating structure and function, and engaging in scientific practices such as modeling to address themes that cross-cut the sciences. Here we address the role of a conceptual representation, focusing on structure and mechanism, and models in scientific systems thinking. Conceptual representations are the big ideas in a domain that help organize knowledge and guide knowledge construction. These can be particularly important for dealing with complex systems phenomena. The synergy of conceptual representations and the scientific practice of modeling can help make complex phenomena accessible to learners.

External representations such as pictures, models, and conceptual representations have been successfully used to help students meet the cognitive demand of reasoning with systems. Suthers, Girardeau, and Hundhausen (2003) showed that visual representations influenced discussion and made both phenomena and interrelations salient. In addition, the practice of modeling has resulted in students generating more dynamic and complex explanations of system-level phenomena (Nersessian, 1992; Schwarz & White, 2005).

Models and simulations, in particular, afford opportunities for learners to externalize their thinking and test ideas—essentially providing a vehicle by which mental models can be externalized. Discussion of these models is associated with increased learning outcomes. Lehrer and Schauble (2012) demonstrated the importance of collective participation and discussion in learning through modeling practices. With particular regard to complex systems, models have been a platform to represent multiple levels of organization (Buckley, 2000). Further, the ability to test and revise system elements has been argued as being critical to science learning (NGSS, 2013). Liu (2008) demonstrated that group engagement in epistemic practices and discussions while using simulations is associated with improved individual learning outcomes.

Simply asking students to model complex systems, however, may prove unsatisfying because it is such an open-ended task. Without a means to articulate ideas in models, students can conflate system processes and continue to represent ideas as narratives that are simply accompanied by arrows (e.g., Jordan, Gray, Brooks, Honwad, & Hmelo-Silver, 2013). We, however, have found that providing students with a conceptual representation as a learning frame can help them to make their ideas visible in a model. We have accordingly developed and used the PMC conceptual representation, with which learners frame their thinking around a particular phenomenon or ecological pattern (P); generate or recall plausible mechanisms (M) that may result in (P); and explore the parts or components, both visible and invisible (C), that interact to result in (M and P). This PMC conceptual representation is used in conjunction with instruction that provides a platform for finding or generating evidence in support of mechanistic explanations (Figure 17.1). This representation provides an external language for students to self-direct learning and express their ideas in models. Paired with this conceptual representation, models can further aid students in developing and refining their ideas. With computers being so ubiquitous, we can have students create models quickly through programs like Ecomodeler (ecomodeler.jonnybomb.com) and simulations with NetLogo (netlogo.com). Ecomodeler, in particular, allows students to also capture and support their Explanations with Evidence (= 2E). The PMC-2E syntax is embedded in the modeling tool such that students and their teachers are aware that their model must consider these aspects of PMC-2E. Early evidence supports the notion that our conceptual representation enhances system-level learning (Jordan, Sorenson, & Hmelo-Silver, 2014).

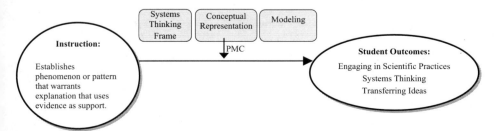

FIGURE 17.1 Complex systems learning.

Complex system learning and its associated instruction is not solely teaching about systems but with systems. As mentioned earlier, it is important for learners to be steeped in the practice of making ideas visible through conceptual modeling and in the practice of scientific modeling where they develop, test, and refine ideas. Pairing the PMC representation with external frames and appropriate analogies that are meaningful and embedded in the curricula may be valuable in promoting learning transfer. This is relevant because students find it challenging to transfer understanding of mechanistic behavior (Sinha, 2013). A possible explanation for this is that while some conceptual entities map on directly to parts of the system, others are more abstract and may not be clearly associable to any component of the system (Chin & Brown, 2000). So children's difficulties in constructing mechanistic explanations may lie in their struggles to first identify and causally relate the relevant entities of the particular mechanism, and then to place these causal relations mentally into a dynamic sequence (Metz, 1991). In the remainder of this chapter, we provide an example of how we have used different lenses to explore transfer in our PMC-guided learning environments.

Perspectives on transfer

Given the ubiquity of complex systems in the natural world, transferring ideas about complex system learning from one context to another is critical for scientific reasoning. Research suggests that instruction designed to support inquiry focuses primarily on assessing content accuracy and less on reasoning, argumentation and other science practices (Hmelo-Silver, Liu, Gray, & Jordan, 2015; Marx et al., 2004). Transferring disciplinary content from one system to another is certainly important. However, Russ, Coffey, Hammer, and Hutchinson (2009) argued that "certain aspects of inquiry are ultimately more valuable than correctness" (p. 641) and proposed that mechanistic reasoning is central to scientific inquiry. The goal of our research is to observe students' abilities to generalize their understanding of complex systems. To do so, the research reported in this study draws upon two contrasting theoretical lenses of transfer—traditional analogical transfer (Reed, 2012) and actor-oriented transfer (AOT; Lobato, 2006)—to shed light on students' abilities to (1) transfer mechanistic reasoning skills and ideas about ecosystem processes within a technology-rich learning environment and (2) use it solve new problems.

Cognitivist theorists propose that transfer is a process of abstraction, generalization, and transformation of representations between contexts (Greeno, Collins & Resnick, 1996). This traditional perspective of transfer is viewed as transformation of schemata between situations. However, sociocultural learning theorists believe that transfer is a process of adaptation to affordances and constraints in new environment (Greeno, 1998). The traditional analogical view of transfer looks for evidence of transfer from an expert view of a correct solution (Gick & Holyoak, 1983). In contrast, AOT shifts focus from an expert perspective to how the actor (student) perceives similarities between new problems with their own prior experiences (Lobato, 2006).

Analogical transfer

Transfer is defined as the application of knowledge learned in one context to other contexts (Barnett & Ceci, 2002). It occurs if two situations (i.e., the base situation and the target situation) are analogous, meaning that they share common patterns of relationships between elements in the situation, problem, or context (Reed, 2012). The base situation is the context in which some knowledge or skill is initially learned, whereas the target is the novel context to which knowledge or skills will be applied. For transfer to occur, individuals need to align relationships that connect elements in both the base and target situation (Reed, 2012). However, this is hard to achieve even when the situations are closely related—what is termed as *near transfer* (Barnett & Ceci, 2002). This is because transfer requires students to have a deep and comprehensive understanding of the base situation (Brown, Kane & Long, 1989). Students need to draw abstractions from the learning situation, to generalize them in new situation, and to perceive precisely which elements are invariant across situations. Alternate theories of transfer such as the actor-oriented perspective shed light on learners' process of generalization.

Actor-oriented transfer

The underlying assumption of AOT is the need for a shift from the observer's (expert's) perspective to a consideration of how the actor (learner) constructs similarities between the new problem and prior experiences (Lobato, 2006). Evidence for transfer from this perspective is found by scrutinizing a given activity for any indication of influence from previous activities. Analysis of transfer from an actor-oriented perspective draws upon qualitative research methods to identify possible influences of past experiences.

Prior research in AOT has focused on mathematics education and the professional development of teachers (Lobato, Rhodamel & Hohensee, 2012; Sinha et al., 2013). Our present research adds to the transfer literature by exploring the implications of dual perspectives—traditional and actor-oriented—in the area of ecosystems understanding among middle school students.

Methods

This study is part of a project that investigates a technology-rich curricular unit that facilitates student understanding of aquatic ecosystems (Hmelo-Silver, Eberbach, & Jordan, 2014). One hundred and sixty-four students collaborated in groups of three to four to participate in the study that comprised of a curricular unit spread out over 6–7 weeks in the academic school year in two middle school classrooms. Students were grouped heterogeneously to reflect mixed gender, ethnicity, and ability.

Classroom context

During the course of the curricular unit, students engaged in scientific inquiry by reasoning about problems related to aquatic ecosystems. Multiple problems related to aquatic ecosystems, albeit situated in varying contexts (such as aquariums, ponds and ocean) set the stage for inquiry. Students were encouraged to reason about such problems using the phenomena-mechanisms-components (PMC) framework. Phenomena refer to the problem or outcome under investigation. Components are the entities that display specific behaviors or mechanisms based on their properties. Mechanisms are characterized as causal explanations of how phenomena occur. They are typically used to explain how a phenomenon comes about or how some significant process works. In addition, the tool provided support for students to link *evidence* to the model that was serving as their evolving *explanation*.

Technologies such as NetLogo simulations (Wilensky & Reisman, 2006; see Figure 17.2) and the predecessor to Ecomodeler, the Ecological Modeling Toolkit (EMT) (Vattam et al., 2011; see Figure 17.3), afforded opportunities for students to use the PMC-2E framework to understand dynamic processes and to create models of their evolving understanding.

Problem description and data sources

Traditional transfer: All 164 participants individually completed a pre- and posttest in which they were asked to draw images of an aquatic ecosystem and a rainforest ecosystem. In addition, students determined if there were connections in the form of relationships between various components in each ecosystem. Drawings of the aquatic ecosystem and rainforest ecosystem served dual purposes. First, at the pre-test stage the drawings allowed us to examine students' baseline performance and to identify pre-existing differences in understanding between the two ecosystems. Second, comparing the drawings at the pre and post stage allowed us to look at learning (in the base aquatic system) and transfer (to the rainforest system).

Actor-oriented transfer: Drawing from our participant pool we interviewed 38 students from ten small groups. After the last day of curriculum implementation, three researchers interviewed each student individually. We designed the interview to assess students' generalization of mechanistic reasoning and to make sense of new problems related to aquatic ecosystems. In the first problem, students were shown

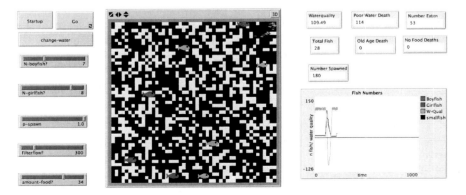

FIGURE 17.2   Net logo simulation.

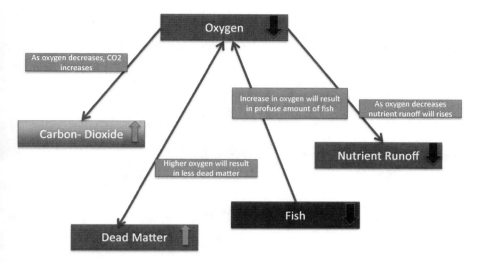

FIGURE 17.3   Ecological Modeling Toolkit (EMT).

a paper copy of their group-generated EMT model depicting factors that may have led to fish dying suddenly in a local pond. The students were then asked to label the model in terms of PMC and explain their reasoning. In the model (see Figure 17.4), the entire problem reflected the phenomena; the rectangular boxes represented components that were linked together by explanations of their mechanistic behavior.

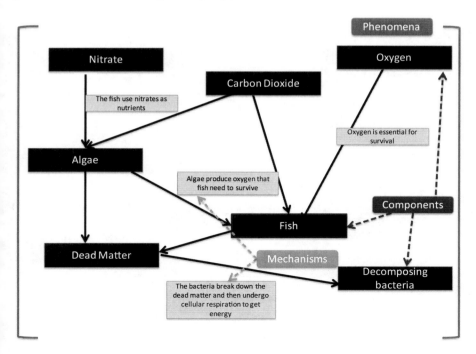

FIGURE 17.4   Labeling EMT model with PMC framework.

In the second problem, students were told that there has been a sudden increase in geese population around a lake that has resulted in changes to the aquatic eco-system. They were shown three versions of EMT models—the first consisting only of components (Figure 17.5), the second had only mechanisms but no components (Figure 17.6), and the third consisted of numerous components, mechanisms connecting them and phenomena (Figure 17.7).

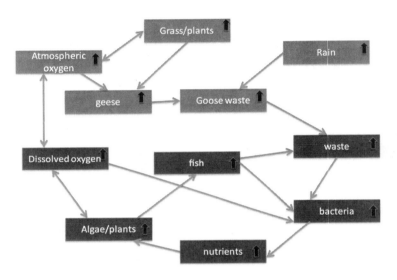

FIGURE 17.5 Components–based model of geese problem.

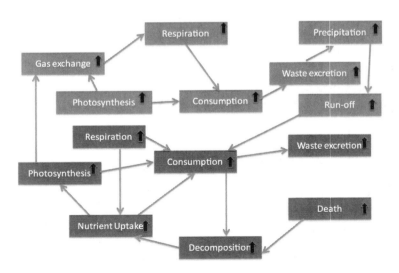

FIGURE 17.6 Mechanisms–based model of geese problem.

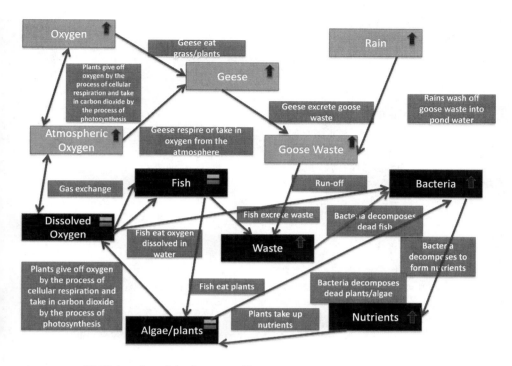

FIGURE 17.7 PMC-based model of geese problem.

Students were first asked to rank each model on a scale of one to three, with three being the most complete explanation about what happened to the lake ecosystem as a result of the overpopulation of geese. Next, students labeled the model they had ranked the highest (in terms of PMC) and were asked to explain the criteria for making their selection. Interviews were recorded and transcribed. The interview sought to identify ways in which students spontaneously constructed similarities using PMC in a new context. It allowed us to look at how they interpreted the way that PMC could be used, rather than focusing on what the researchers considered a "correct" application.

Data analysis

Traditional transfer of specific ecosystem processes. To examine the extent to which students were able to transfer what they learned in an aquatic system to a rainforest system, we coded their drawings in each of two ecosystems. We examined the extent to which students could provide evidence of understanding the processes of photosynthesis, respiration and decomposition in the base system (aquatic ecosystem) and the transfer system (rainforest ecosystem). To accomplish this, we developed coding schemes based on expert understanding of photosynthesis, cellular respiration, and decomposition. The three system concepts all include four

TABLE 17.1 Learning and transfer scoring

Level	Numbers of components in photosynthesis, respiration, decomposition
0	No components
1	Single component included
2	2/4 components plus some relationships or 3 of 4 components without showing any relationships among them
3	3/4 components and some evidence of relationships among them

The 0–3 scale represents a continuum from 0 indicating no evidence of understanding and a 3 indicating good evidence of understanding. Specifically for photosynthesis and respiration, students had to mention both aspects of gas exchange to reach 3 points. Coding was conducted for the aquarium and rainforest systems.

learning and transfer levels ranging from zero to three (Table 17.1). To examine overall effects, we ran a 2×2×3 ANOVA with contexts (aquatic ecosystem and rainforest ecosystem), time (pre-test and posttest), and processes (photosynthesis, respiration, and decomposition) as within-subject factors. A research assistant coded 20% of the sample in order to ensure reliability. Inter-rater agreement was 99% for photosynthesis, 97.5% for respiration, and 98% for decomposition.

Photosynthesis is a chemical process that converts carbon dioxide into organic compounds by using energy from the sun and releasing oxygen (Brown & Schwartz, 2009; Hogan & Fisherkeller, 1996). Based on this definition, we divided photosynthesis into four elements:

(1) Photosynthesis is a process
(2) Gas is exchanged—plants absorb CO_2 and plants release O_2
(3) Plants use energy from sunlight
(4) Organic compounds are produced.

Initially, we coded each student's pre- and posttests for presence or absence of each element. For example, if students mentioned the growth of trees, plants make their own food, and sunlight or energy from the sun connected to plant growth, we would code presence of three elements.

For instance, Figure 17.8 is an example of one student's inclusion of sun and plants in which the student annotated, "sun gives light and food source for plants." On this basis, we coded for the presence of two components: plants use energy from sunlight and organic compounds are produced. We also coded the presence of gas exchange because the student annotated "trees give out O_2 and take in CO_2." Thus, this student's final score is 3 as he or she mentioned three components and made connections between them. Similarly, for the rainforest ecosystem, the student also received a final score of 3 because the student included these same components.

Respiration is a set of the metabolic processes using oxygen that takes place in the cell of organisms to convert biochemical energy from nutrients into Adenosine

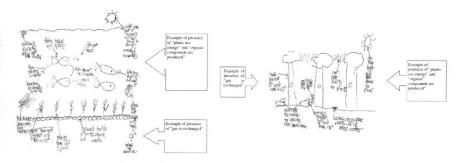

FIGURE 17.8 Student's coded drawings of aquatic and rainforest system.

Triphosphate (ATP) then releasing waste product—CO_2 (Hogan & Fisherkeller, 1996). According to this definition, we divided cellular respiration into four elements:

(1) Respiration is a process.
(2) Respiration is essential for all living things.
(3) As part of respiration, energy is released.
(4) Plants/animals breathe in O_2 and release CO_2.

We coded and scored each student's pre- and posttests for presence or absence of each element. We were liberal in our application of the codes. For example, referring to the fact that respiration is a dynamic process, the code *dynamic* could be coded if students mentioned that an animal eats for nutrients or for energy. We coded this liberally because as long as students mentioned food and energy, it indicated students were beginning to think the role of food in respiration—the first step towards thinking of cellular respiration. The way we coded respiration as essential for all living things is consistent with how we coded the first component. Students received credit if they indicated fish or animals need oxygen for survival or if they articulated the relationship between levels of O_2 and fish survival (e.g., low oxygen level kills fish).

Decomposition is the metabolic process that breaks down materials into simpler components by living organisms. This process requires oxygen and releases nutrients (Hogan & Fisherkeller, 1996). Based on this definition, we divided decomposition into four elements:

(1) Bacteria are essential to the ecosystem.
(2) Bacteria decomposes using oxygen.
(3) The process of decomposition releases nutrients such as nitrate.
(4) Bacteria breaks down material.

Students' pre and posttests were coded for presence and absence of each element. For example, we coded "bacteria are essential to the ecosystem" as long as students mentioned the beneficial role of bacterial played in an ecosystem.

AOT of mechanistic reasoning: To trace generalization of mechanistic reasoning from an AOT lens, we compared each student's labeled model in task 1 (group model explaining cause of sudden death of fish) with that in task 2 (effect of over population of geese on lake ecosystem). We identified items they labeled as identical in terms of PMC in both tasks and also kept track of areas where they exhibited differences (i.e., identified phenomena in one task as the entire model and in the other had it labeled as a mechanism). Because our goal was to observe generalization of mechanistic reasoning, we were not focusing on assessing conceptual accuracy. Along with the labeled model artifacts, we also reviewed transcribed interview responses for indicators that would allow us to observe how students viewed similarities between the two tasks and made use of mechanistic reasoning. For example, if a student identified photosynthesis as a mechanism in both diagrams, this would be consider transfer from the cognitive perspective, but from an AOT perspective, it would also be transfer if that student identified photosynthesis as a component in both diagrams. Although not canonically correct, this would provide a formative window into the students thinking and show how students were using ideas experienced previously, even if not accurately.

Results

Our findings indicate variations in the extent to which students' transferred their understanding between the aquatic and rainforest ecosystems and the processes they followed to reason about problems related to aquatic ecosystems. Findings from a traditional lens gave us participants' transfer from a canonical perspective. The AOT perspective complemented the findings of the traditional perspective by helping us trace possible sources of students' generalizations.

Traditional transfer

Overall, our results suggest that students demonstrated some learning of systems processes in the aquatic system and transferred these to the rainforest system. Descriptive statistics are shown in Table 17.2.

Because we had specific hypotheses about learning and transfer, we conducted a series of planned contrasts. For all three ecosystem processes, there were significant pre to post test gains in the aquatic system, as expected ($t(195) = 10.65$,

TABLE 17.2 Means and standard deviation of scores (levels) by context and time of tests

Systems	Photosynthesis		Respiration		Decomposition	
	Pre	Post	Pre	Post	Pre	Post
Aquatic system	0.02 (0.13)	0.59 (0.71)	0.01 (0.08)	0.38 (0.59)	0.00 (0.00)	0.10 (0.35)
Rainforest system	0.01 (0.11)	0.42 (0.60)	0.00 (0.00)	0.16 (0.40)	0.00 (0.00)	0.01 (0.08)

8.56, 3.51 for photosynthesis, respiration, and decomposition respectively, all $p <= .001$). Students demonstrated significant gains in the rainforest ecosystem for photosynthesis ($t(167) = 8.97$, $p < .001$) and respiration ($t(167) = 5.09$), $p < .001$) but not for decomposition ($t(167) = 1.00$, $p = .32$). Thus we have some evidence of transfer occurring based on what increased scores for two of the ecosystem processes in the rainforest. These results while statistically significant are still small in magnitude, with all the means being less than one. Through the actor-oriented lens, we provide evidence that suggests that these traditional transfer measures are an underestimate of what students transferred.

Actor-oriented lens

Our analysis indicated that students' generalizations could broadly be categorized into four categories (see Table 17.3). We observed 30% students generalizing all three aspects of PMC thinking across the contexts. Approximately 60% of the students demonstrated at least partial PMC transfer of one or two of the three aspects. Very few students displayed no evidence of transfer at all. From an AOT perspective we were intrigued by the high levels of transfer we observed within the data set.

As we compared students' labeling of models, it was evident that a majority of students generalized the concepts of components and phenomena. We observed that students either circled the entire model or focused on the primary problem under investigation when asked to label phenomena. Additionally, almost all the students were quick to tag components as factors that may have led to the problem. In the following excerpt, for example, a student explains his criteria for identifying components and phenomena, first in problem 1 and next in problem 2:

> I thought the death of the fish going up was the phenomenon because everything is pointing at it. All the components are pointing at it, and they're all saying why the fish are dying, and I thought that these were some components because they're all saying why the fish are dying or saying that they are factors of the death of fish.
>
> Geese would be the phenomenon because, as you said before, the problem is that there's a high increase in geese population, and it's affecting the ecosystem in the fish. I had grass and plants as a component because it is pointing to the geese, and it says that it attracts geese 'cause geese eat it.

TABLE 17.3 Frequencies of students' generalization of PMC

Students	Levels of PMC transfer				
	No transfer	Only C transfer	Only P & C transfer	Only M & C transfer	PMC transfer
n = 36	3	13	7	1	12

Analysis from an AOT perspective indicated that this student likely used his prior understanding of phenomena and components for mechanistic reasoning to make sense of the new problem in terms of changing populations of animals. In response to problem 1, he identified the increase in fish deaths as the phenomenon in the primary problem under investigation (i.e., the *P* of PMC). He appeared to have applied this criterion of focusing on the underlying problem during problem 2 when he responded that the phenomenon in this case is a high increase in geese population. Similarly, when identifying components, he drew attention to the relevance of factors that are responsible for the fish dying in task 1. He used the same approach to determine components in task 2. AOT helped us trace the source of his generalization of phenomena and components.

Conflation of understanding of mechanisms: Given the extent to which students' generalized components and phenomena, we were intrigued, but not surprised, to note that understanding the role of mechanisms is one of the most complex aspect of mechanistic reasoning. During the interviews, 20 students asked researchers to define mechanisms, despite the use of this term throughout the unit. Additionally, we observed students labeling components, such as nutrients and dissolved oxygen as mechanisms. From an AOT perspective we attributed this conflation to two factors. First, students found it challenging to identify causal mechanisms because some behaviors exhibited by components were visible and others invisible (Feltovich, Coulson, & Spiro, 2001). It is possible that this led them to focus on interactions between invisible and visible components as the criteria for identifying mechanisms. This suggests that some students may not have been aware of the causal mechanisms that explain how phenomena occur in both tasks. Such students may have generalized a partial understanding of mechanistic reasoning.

Second, given that both components and mechanisms in EMT models are rectangular boxes, it is also possible that students' conceptual conflation may be a result of the similar superficial representation. This suggests that surface features of representations may lead students to perceive conceptual similarity.

Conclusions

The goal of this chapter was to examine the prospects for transfer in learning environments guided by the PMC-2E framework, but in examining transfer, we need to look beyond the established norms of assessing accuracy as the sole indicator for transfer of scientific understanding. Our results stress the importance of integrating subjective experiences, affordances of the curriculum and interactions with the environment to shed light on participatory practices that influence transfer in inquiry based learning contexts. We anticipate our findings will serve as a foundation for future research in this area.

Overall we need to consider ways that conceptual representations such as PMC-2E can focus students towards productive generalizations. This is especially true in traditional transfer. Given that students indicated a lower transfer effect than we had hoped, we hypothesize that this may be a result of curriculum design. At the beginning of the curriculum, students were asked to investigate an overarching question: why did fish die suddenly in the local pond? We conjecture that this may have limited students' understanding of these processes to aquatic ecosystem and in turn made their transfer to rainforest ecosystem harder. Research by Lobato and her colleagues (2012) supports our hypothesis, as they emphasize that different features of tasks and representations can influence what students notice and subsequently transfer from their learning experiences. Alternatively, having students consider how the aquatic ecosystems were one example of many possible ecosystems might have promoted increased generalization of the ecosystem processes to other classes of ecosystems.

Our findings in these middle school science classrooms are consistent with findings from the study conducted by Lobato et al. (2012) in mathematics classrooms. From the AOT perspective we found that many students acquired a superficial understanding of the PMC framework, which in turn influenced their sense making in new problems but also that a substantial number of students also began to think about the larger phenomena and mechanisms that cut across different problems. Sinha (2013) presented an additional fine-grained analysis that indicates additional ways that students transfer mechanistic reasoning strategies (the M in PMC) to new problems. Our findings suggest that technologies that promote the modeling and simulation of complex systems afford opportunities for students to consider mechanistic behavior of components. Students' collaborative engagement with modeling tools influences their individual thinking regarding the extent to which they generalize mechanistic reasoning to make sense of new problems.

Taking the AOT perspective is a particularly appropriate route for examining spontaneous transfer of the PMC framework as a strategy for thinking about systems. This perspective was designed to illuminate and capture spontaneous transfer – in particular, in ways that may differ from the expert conceptions of spontaneous strategy use (Lobato, 2006). Here, although students were prompted to label their diagrams with PMC labels, they were not told how to use them or to draw similarities between the two tasks. The goal of using a conceptual representation as an instructional frame was a strategy designed to promote spontaneous transfer to new systems. We argue that by simply delineating the parts and processes within the system encourages students to attach a more generalized meaning to system elements without specific prompts.

Together our results provide evidence that the PMC framework supports spontaneous transfer to new contexts. A conceptual representation, such as PMC, allows learners to attach generalizations to what they are learning. With these generalizations, learners will have access to cognitive resources that will likely prove productive when confronted with a novel context.

Acknowledgments

This research was funded by Institute of Education Sciences (IES) grant # R305A090210. Conclusions or recommendations expressed in this paper are those of the authors and do not necessarily reflect the views of IES.

References

Assaraf, O. B. Z., & Orion, N. (2010). Systems thinking skills at the elementary school. *Journal of Research in Science Teaching, 47*(5), 540–563.

Barnett, S., & Ceci, S. J. (2002). When and where do we apply what we learn? A taxonomy for far transfer. *Psychological Bulletin, 128*(4), 612–637.

Brown, A. L., Kane, M. J., & Long, C. (1989). Analogical transfer in young children: Analogies as tools for communication and exposition. *Applied Cognitive Psychology, 3*(4), 275–293.

Brown, M. H., & Schwartz, R. S. (2009). Connecting photosynthesis and cellular respiration: Preservice teachers' conceptions. *Journal of Research in Science Teaching, 46*(7), 791–812.

Buckley, B. C. (2000). Interactive multimedia and model-based learning in biology. *International Journal of Science Education, 22*(9), 895–935.

Chin, C., & Brown, D. E. (2000). Learning in science: A comparison of deep and surface approaches. *Journal of Research in Science Teaching, 37*(2), 109–138.

Collins, A., Greeno, J., & Resnick, L. B. (1996). Cognition and learning. In B. Berliner & R. Calfee (Eds.), *Handbook of educational psychology.* New York: Simon & Schuster MacMillan.

Feltovich, P. J., Coulson, R. L., & Spiro, R. J. (2001). Learners' (mis)understanding of important and difficult concepts. In K. D. Forbus & P. J. Feltovich (Eds.), *Smart machines in education: The coming revolution in educational technology* (pp. 349–375). Menlo Park, CA: AAAI/MIT Press.

Gick, M. L., & Holyoak, K. J. (1983). Schema induction and analogical transfer. *Cognitive Psychology, 15*(1), 1–38.

Greeno, J. G. (1998). The situativity of knowing, learning, and research. *American psychologist, 53*(1), 5–26.

Greeno, J. G., Collins, A. M., & Resnick, L. B. (1996). Cognition and learning. In D. Berliner & R. Calfee (Eds.), *Handbook of educational psychology* (pp. 15–41). New York, NY: MacMillian.

Hmelo, C. E., Holton, D. L., & Kolodner, J. L. (2000). Designing to learn about complex systems. *The Journal of the Learning Sciences, 9*(3), 247–298.

Hmelo-Silver, C. E., & Azevedo, R. (2006). Understanding complex systems: Some core challenges. *The Journal of the Learning Sciences, 15*(1), 53–61.

Hmelo-Silver, C. E., Liu, L., Gray, S., & Jordan, R. (2015). Using representational tools to learn about complex systems: A tale of two classrooms. *Journal of Research in Science Teaching, 52*(1), 6–35.

Hogan, K., & Fisherkeller, J. (1996). Representing students' thinking about nutrient cycling in ecosystems: Bidimensional coding of a complex topic. *Journal of Research in Science Teaching, 33*(9), 941–970.

Jordan, R. C., Gray, S. A., Brooks, W. R., Honwad, S., & Hmelo-Silver, C. E. (2013). Process based thinking in ecosystem education. *Natural Sciences Education, 42*(1), 68–74.

Jordan, R., Sorenson, A., & Hmelo-Silver, C. E. (2014). A conceptual representation to support ecological systems learning. *Natural Sciences Education, 43*(1), 141–146.

Lehrer, R., & Schauble, L. (2012). Seeding evolutionary thinking by engaging children in modeling its foundations. *Science Education, 96*(4), 701–724.

Liu, L. (2008). *Trajectories of collaborative scientific conceptual change: Middle school students learning about ecosystems in a CSCL environment* (PhD dissertation). Rutgers The State University of New Jersey, New Brunswick, NJ.

Lobato, J. (2006). Alternative perspectives on the transfer of learning: History, issues and challenges for future research. *Journal of the Learning Sciences, 15*(4), 431–449.

Lobato, J., Rhodamel, B., & Hohensee, C. (2012). "Noticing" as an alternative transfer of learning process. *Journal of the Learning Sciences, 21*(3), 433–482.

Marx, R., Blumenfeld, P., Krajcik, J., Fishman, B., Soloway, E., Geier, R., Tal, T. (2004). Inquiry-based science in the middle grades: Assessment of learning in urban systemic reform. *Journal of Research in Science Teaching, 41*(10), 1063–1080.

Metz, K. E. (1991). Development of explanation: Incremental and fundamental change in children's physics knowledge. *Journal of Research in Science Teaching, 28*(9), 785–797.

Mintzes, J. J., Trowbridge, J. E., Arnaudin, M. W., & Wandersee, J. H. (1991). Children's biology: Studies on conceptual development in the life sciences. In S. M. Glynn, B. K. Britton, & R. H. Yeany (Eds.), *The psychology of learning science* (pp. 179–202). Hillsdale, NJ: Erlbaum.

Nersessian, N. (1992). How do scientists think? Capturing the dynamics of conceptual change in science. In R. N. Giere (Ed.), *Cognitive models of science* (pp. 3–44). Minneapolis, MN: University of Minnesota Press.

NGSS Lead States. (2013). *Next generation science standards: For states, by states.* Washington, DC: National Academies Press.

Reed, S. K. (2012). Learning by mapping across situations. *Journal of the Learning Sciences, 21*(3), 353–398.

Russ, R. S., Coffey, J. E., Hammer, D., & Hutchinson, P. (2009). Making classroom assessment more accountable to scientific reasoning: A case for attending to mechanistic thinking. *Science Education, 93*(5), 871–891.

Schwarz, C. V., & White B. Y. (2005). Metamodeling knowledge: Developing students' understanding of scientific modeling. *Cognition and Instruction, 23*(2), 165–205.

Sinha, S. (2013). *Exploring student engagement and transfer in technology mediated environments* (PhD dissertation). Rutgers University, New Brunswick, NJ.

Sinha, S., Gray, S., Hmelo-Silver, C., Jordan, R., Eberbach, C., Goel, A., & Rugaber, S. (2013). Conceptual representations for transfer: A case study tracing back and looking forward. *Frontline Learning Research, 1*(1), 3–23.

Suthers, D., Girardeau, L., & Hundhausen, C. (2003, June). Deictic roles of external representations in face-to-face and online collaboration. In B. Wasson, S. Ludvigsen, & U. Hoppe (Eds.), *Designing for change in networked learning environments. Proceedings of the International Conference on Computer Support for Collaborative Learning* (pp. 173–182). Dordrecht, The Netherlands: Kluwer Academic.

Vattam, S., Goel, A., Rugaber, S., Hmelo-Silver, C., Jordan, R., Gray, S., & Sinha, S. (2011). Understanding complex natural systems by articulating structure-behavior-function models. *Educational Technology & Society, 14*(1), 66–81.

Wilensky, U., & Reisman, K. (2006). Thinking like a wolf, a sheep, or firefly: Learning: Biology through constructing and testing computational theories – an embodied modeling approach. *Cognition and Instruction, 24*(2), 171–209.

18

DUDE, DON'T START WITHOUT ME!

Fostering engagement with others' mathematical ideas

Noreen M. Webb, Megan L. Franke, Nicholas C. Johnson, Angela C. Turrou, and Marsha Ing

Researchers, policy makers, and practitioners increasingly realize that engaging students as active participants in conversations in classrooms is central to the development of their skills and understanding. For example, the United States' Common Core State Standards for Mathematical Practice calls for students at all grades to be able to "construct viable arguments and critique the reasoning of others," which includes students communicating and justifying their conclusions, listening to and responding to others' arguments, deciding whether they make sense, and asking useful questions to clarify or improve the arguments (National Governors Association Center for Best Practices & Council of Chief State School Officers, 2010, pp. 6–7). This paper examines how students can interact with each other in beneficial ways and how the teacher supports productive engagement among students. A main focus is illustrating how students spontaneously transfer ways of engaging with each other that they experience in contexts with teacher support to contexts when the teacher is not present.

Elaborating one's thinking and engaging with others' ideas are at the heart of many researchers' perspectives on productive classroom dialogue. In Mercer's (1996) exploratory talk, students jointly consider, evaluate, challenge, and justify hypotheses. Mercer contrasts exploratory talk with disputational talk (characterized by disagreements but little constructive criticism of suggestions) and cumulative talk (characterized by positive but uncritical building upon each other's suggestions). Similarly, in Barron's (2000) highly coordinated groups, students propose ideas for joint consideration and closely attend to and acknowledge each other's ideas, repeat others' suggestions, and elaborate on others' proposals.

A related conception of productive dialogue is co-construction, a term often used to characterize interaction in which students contribute different pieces of information and build upon others' explanations to jointly create a complete idea or solution (Forman & Kraker, 1985; Hatano, 1993). In co-construction, students acknowledge, clarify, correct, add to, build upon, and connect each other's ideas and suggestions (Hogan, Nastasi, & Pressley, 2000). Such reasoning about fellow discussants' ideas is also at the heart of transactive discussions or transactive dialogues (Azmitia & Montgomery, 1993; Berkowitz & Gibbs, 1985; Kruger, 1993; see also Goos, Galbraith, & Renshaw, 2002), high-level co-regulation (Volet, Summers, & Thurman, 2009), and shared regulation (Iiskala, Vaurus, Lehtinen, & Salonen, 2011; Roschelle & Teasley, 1995).

The potential benefits of such interaction are many. Offering ideas to others, listening to others' ideas, and having their ideas challenged all encourage students to monitor their own thinking. Students may recognize their own misconceptions or contradictions or incompleteness in their ideas (Forman & Cazden, 1985; Whitebread, Bingham, Grau, Pino Pasternak, & Sangster, 2007) and, consequently, re-examine, question, and revise their ideas and beliefs, seek new information, fill in gaps in their understanding, develop new ideas, reconcile conflicting viewpoints, build new connections between pieces of information or concepts, and link new information to information previously learned (Bargh & Schul, 1980; Brown, Campione, Webber, & McGilly, 1992; Chi, 2000; Wittrock, 1989). By monitoring the degree to which they understand each other's thinking, extending others' ideas and applying them in new ways, acknowledging divergent interpretations, and resolving inconsistencies between ideas proposed, students can also construct shared meanings (Roschelle, 1992), which may facilitate communication and learning.

Much empirical research supports the hypothesized benefits of active student participation for student learning (e.g., Brown & Palincsar, 1989; Chinn, O'Donnell, & Jinks, 2000; Howe et al., 2007; Nattiv, 1994; Saxe, Gearhart, Note, & Paduano, 1993; Slavin, 1987; Veenman, Denessen, van den Akker, & van der Rijt, 2005; Webb & Palincsar, 1996; Yackel, Cobb, Wood, Wheatley, & Merkel, 1990). For example, sharing explanations that are complex (e.g., reasons elaborated with further evidence, explanations that integrate multiple concepts), elaborated, or fully detailed is positively correlated with learning outcomes (e.g., Roscoe & Chi, 2008; Webb et al., 2008, 2009), as is engaging with others' ideas at a high level (e.g., Webb et al., 2014). Moreover, training students to provide elaborated descriptions of their own ideas and to engage with others' ideas has positive effects on learning outcomes (e.g., Gillies, 2004; Howe & Tolmie, 2003; Mercer, Dawes, Wegerif, & Sams, 2004).

To understand how to promote beneficial dialogue in classrooms, researchers often study the role of the teacher. Teachers can set ground rules and guidelines for participation, such as supporting ideas with reasons (Baines, Blatchford, & Kutnick, 2009) or discussing alternatives before making decisions (Mercer, Wegerif, & Dawes, 1999). They can also establish norms for desired communication, such as expecting that students will probe and challenge each other's thinking to be able to understand it better (Yackel, Cobb, & Wood, 1991). They can assign students roles to play such as the active listener who detects errors and omissions in other students' summaries (O'Donnell & King, 1999) or the tutor who confirms correct responses and remediates incorrect responses (Fuchs et al., 1997). They can also require specific activities such as asking each other high-level questions about the material to encourage elaboration (King, 1992; Mevarech & Kramarski, 2003).

Teachers can also encourage productive dialogue by asking students probing and clarifying questions to press them to elaborate on their ideas, helping students confront discrepancies in their thinking, asking students to paraphrase other students' ideas, and asking students for their opinions about other students' ideas (Chinn, Anderson, & Waggoner, 2001; Franke et al., 2015; Gillies, 2004, 2006; Gillies & Boyle, 2008; Kazemi & Stipek, 2001; Michaels, O'Connor, & Resnick, 2008; O'Connor, Michaels, & Chapin, 2015; Smagorinsky & Fly, 1993; Waggoner, Chinn, Yi, & Anderson, 1995; Webb et al., 2008, 2009, 2014).

What is less well understood is the extent to which students can interact with each other productively when the teacher is not present to specifically guide them, and the moves the teacher can make to support students when they are apart from the teacher. We address these issues in the context of a fourth-grade mathematics classroom whose teacher was committed to engaging students with each other's mathematical ideas. We report on the specific ways in which students engaged with each other's ideas during dyadic conversations that occurred apart from the teacher, specific moves that the teacher made to encourage productive interaction, and ways in which students' discussions seemed to respond to, or even incorporate, the teacher's moves.

Methods

The sample includes a teacher and her students ($n = 32$) from a fourth grade classroom from a public elementary school in a large urban area. This teacher was selected based on her preparation in principles of Cognitively Guided Instruction (Carpenter et al., 1999), where she engaged in learning about the development of children's mathematical thinking, and her commitment to creating an environment that valued detailed student explaining, sharing of ideas, and disagreeing.

We worked with this teacher for six months. At three time points (three days per time point in January, March, and May; a total of nine days) during the 2013–2014 academic year, we videorecorded student and teacher interactions and collected all student work for each observation day using a data collection procedure that made it possible to identify which student was speaking even during simultaneous pair conversations. Three days per time point were necessary to collect data on all students (six pairs of students per day) with minimal disruptions in instruction. The results presented in this chapter are based on in-depth analyses of data from the three days at one time point (May) for all students (16 pairs).

For each observation day, the teacher followed her usual practices for structuring the lessons. The mathematical content across all observations was multiplication and division. Each lesson began with a 10–20 minute number sense activity (e.g., "Decompose 783 any way you'd like") designed to elicit a wide range of student ideas during a whole-class discussion (e.g., $(7 \times 100) + (40 \times 2) + (3 \times 1)$). During this warm-up time, the teacher provided brief opportunities for students to turn and engage with their partner or to engage with the whole class about an idea posed by another student.

The lesson then continued with 30–40 minutes of problem solving, during which students worked in pairs to solve multi-digit multiplication and division word problems. Each problem included a story context with multiple number sets. For example, one story problem was "A hammer factory produces hammers for $___ each. How many hammers can Home Depot buy for $ ___?" This problem had three number sets: ($6, $954); ($15, $600); ($26, $1,040). Student dyads worked through the number sets at their own pace and often attempted multiple strategies for each number set. During this extended pairshare portion of the class, students largely worked independently from the teacher; the teacher circulated among the pairs, spending various amounts of time with the pairs.

After the extended pairshare time, the teacher facilitated a 10–15-minute whole-class wrap-up discussion of purposefully selected strategies from students' work during pairshare time. During this time, students had opportunities to engage with their partner or with the whole class about the strategies being shared.

Our primary interest in this chapter is the specific ways in which students engaged with each other around the mathematics (especially when the teacher was not present) and the specific moves that teachers made to encourage this engagement. We present data on student interactions from the extended pairshare portion of the class when students worked independently from the teacher in pairs, and data about specific teacher moves with students that occurred throughout the entire lessons.

Results

Students' engagement with each other's mathematical ideas

Overview of student engagement in pairs: Of the 16 student pairs we observed, the large majority (12 pairs, 75%) showed sustained and synchronous engagement with each other's ideas during the entire extended pairshare portion of the lesson. (The remaining four pairs showed limited engagement, often working independently for long stretches of time.) These 12 pairs exhibited two basic patterns of interaction. In one pattern, students in the pair took turns taking the lead on suggesting a strategy for solving the problem and moving the solution forward. When one student assumed the lead, the other student engaged in the strategy by asking questions about it, challenging specific details, checking calculations, repeating steps, and adding or modifying steps.

In the other pattern, students worked jointly to develop their problem-solving strategy, with no student apparently taking the lead. Students kept close tabs on each other's work and on the emerging strategy. They checked each other's calculations, as well as what students had written on their papers, and suggested the next steps to take. Students in some of these pairs also asked each other questions about why they suggested certain steps, challenged each other's calculations and suggestions, revoiced each other's ideas, and evaluated and questioned the joint strategy being developed.

Students' moves to engage with each other's mathematical ideas: Students displayed a variety of moves with which they engaged with each other's mathematical ideas. They asked general and specific questions about each other's ideas, restated or revoiced others' ideas, noted similarities or differences between their own ideas and another student's ideas, challenged work proposed by another student or work that they produced jointly with another student (and often proposed an alternative strategy), kept tabs (verbally or nonverbally) with the work that another student was doing, and added on to ideas that another student proposed. Table 18.1 provides examples of each category of moves displayed by students.

TABLE 18.1 Student moves to engage in each other's mathematical ideas

Engagement move	*Example of student engagement move*
Asks a general question about other's idea	• How do you know? • Do you think it will work? • Wait, why do you think that? • You have to explain better. What did you get?
Asks a specific question about other's idea	• Where did you get the 5 from? • Four times 15? Or four times, what did you mean? • What do you mean, "all 4s"? • But what are you going to do with the 16?
Restates/revoices other's idea	• Oh, yeah, let's just take away one. • So 80 plus 40, we could do that? • So you're saying that we could do another four times 12? • So first you're saying you decided that six times 4 was 24. And then six times 3 was 18. But you knew that was only 42. So that is seven times. So that's why you added the 7 to the 90. That's 97.
Notes similarities/ differences between one's own ideas and other's ideas	• I just did this. But I did it a different way. • I think we should do something… different. • So you're saying that for the first strategy, you want to do what we did yesterday. • It's almost like similar to skip counting, but actually we're subtracting.
Challenges (or sees a problem with) other's idea or work created jointly; may offer an alternative	• 600 times anything will be too much. • Let me think. This one has to be wrong. • You can count by 5s, you know. • Let's do something more efficient. Like 50 times 2.
Keeps tabs on other's idea	• Oh! I see what you're doing. • Do you disagree with me or do you agree? • Hold up. Where did we stop? • How many do you have? (counts the number on partner's paper) 15. OK. • Dude, why did you start without me?

(Continued)

Engagement move	Example of student engagement move
Adds on to other's idea	• [S1: First we could do six times …]* S2: Maybe six times 100?
	• [S1: 153 left. We need to get to that.] S2: Maybe we could do four times 25, and that equals 100.
	• [S1: Not 100 because that would be 600. So maybe something lower.] S2: Maybe we could do six times 70?
	• [S1: Add by 25s] S2: Umm … we could do … you know how 25 plus 25 equals 50? So maybe we could add the 50s to go faster.

*The text in brackets represents the idea offered by one student (here, labeled S1) prior to the additional details offered by another student (here, labeled S2).

To illustrate the moves that students drew upon as they engaged with each other's mathematical ideas, we give two extended examples.

Illustration 1: Students challenging each other's ideas and their joint ideas: The first extended example shows two students, Melissa and Daria, solving the measurement division problem about purchasing hammers presented earlier; the excerpts below come from Melissa and Daria working with the numbers 6 and 954 (meaning, how many $6 hammers can Home Depot buy for $954).

The pair began by reading the problem together and discussing how they might start figuring out "six of how many will get us to 954." Based on an idea that Daria suggested, they first worked together (for about six minutes) to solve the problem using 6×100, then 6×50, and 6×9 to form 954. Then the pair moved on to a second problem-solving strategy for the same set of numbers. In the excerpt below, Melissa initiated the discussion (line 1) and Daria responded by inviting Melissa to provide the idea for the second strategy (line 2).

1 *Melissa:* What's another strategy?
2 *Daria:* Would you like to go next?
3 *Melissa:* I was thinking of skip counting, like, sort of like your strategy like skip counting 6 until we get 900, and then we count how many, so if we get, like, 50, we put 50 times on the side.
4 *Daria:* Ok (nods).
5 *Melissa:* So, 6.
6 *Daria:* Can I just do a little edit to yours – instead of doing 6 how many times, wouldn't it be faster to do it by twelves?
7 *Melissa:* So we count by twelves, so we group two sixes?
8 *Daria:* Yes.

In accepting Daria's invitation to suggest an approach, Melissa proposed the strategy to count by sixes (line 3). Daria initially agreed (line 4) but as Melissa started to carry out the strategy, Daria challenged Melissa's idea by suggesting what she termed an "edit" to Melissa's proposal (line 6). Daria's "edit" doubled Melissa's counting by sixes approach to instead count by twelves. Melissa agreed and showed that she understood this by rephrasing and adding onto Daria's suggestion, specifically, relating the counting by twelves to two of her sixes (supporting multiplicative reasoning; line 7).

The pair proceeded by using Daria's modification of Melissa's strategy. Over the course of the next four minutes, they added twelves together. After adding twelves up to 144, Daria stopped and challenged the pace of their strategy (line 9). Daria's challenge led Melissa to suggest an alternative (faster) approach: counting upwards from 144 by hundreds instead of by twelves (line 10).

9 *Daria:*   144, I feel like we should be doing something faster
10 *Melissa:*   We are barely on 144 and we have to go to 900, so do you want to count by hundreds?
11 *Daria:*   Sure.
12 *Melissa:*   So 144 plus 100 is 244
13 *Daria:*   So we are going by hundreds then
14 *Melissa:*   244, then 344 right
15 *Daria:*   Yes.

After this, the pair proceeded to add by hundreds to get to 954. They then had to relate their strategy to the original problem, that is, they had to determine how many sixes were in 100 in order to figure out how many hammers they could buy. They did eventually solve the problem correctly by keeping track of the 16 sixes in each 100 (accounting for 96 in each 100) and then combining the extra fours in each 100.

This extended example shows the pair engaged in two challenges. In the first, one student (Daria) challenged the other student's (Melissa) idea (line 6). In the second, Daria challenged the pair's joint work by noting their approach was going to take a long time (line 9). In both cases Melissa readily acknowledged Daria's challenges, showed that she understood Daria's suggestions and concern, and explicitly connected with Daria's ideas. Specifically, in the first challenge exchange, Melissa responded by restating Daria's idea, adding on to it, and connecting it to her own idea by noting that counting by twelves is equivalent to counting by groups of two sixes. In the second challenge exchange, Melissa responded to Daria's challenge by repeating Daria's concern and addressing it by suggesting a faster strategy (counting by hundreds instead of by twelves).

Illustration 2: Sustained and synchronous student engagement with a range of moves: The second example involves a lengthy interaction between two students, Luciana and Josie, who drew on a range of moves in synchronous and sustained ways. These moves included asking general and specific questions, revoicing others' ideas, keeping tabs on what their partner was doing, and making connections to previous work by noting similarities/differences in their ideas. A number of these moves appeared to be in service of Luciana making sense of Josie's proposed strategy.

The students were working on the problem "Wilbert Grant School wants to buy more basketballs for the school. If new basketballs cost $4 each, how many basketballs can the school buy with $553?" They spent four minutes reading the problem together, discussing what they understood about the context and what they were trying to figure out, and briefly revisiting their work from the previous day.

Following this discussion, Josie proposed a strategy for them to try (line 1 below). Luciana asked several questions about Josie's idea, starting with why they should use Josie's approach (lines 2, 4, 6). Luciana's questioning and expression of confusion led Josie to explain her idea in more detail, to clarify it, and to provide a rationale for it (lines 3, 5, 7).

1	*Josie:*	Wait, actually, we could maybe do 553 and subtract it with 4 dollars.
2	*Luciana:*	Why subtract?
3	*Josie:*	Because you can know how many balls you can have.
4	*Luciana:*	But I know how many balls we can have, but why do you want to do subtracting?
5	*Josie:*	Because you're almost like skip counting by fours, like you're sub-tracting by 4's, and then like the four, then we represent, that's one basketball, and then we keep going and going and going until we reach up to zero.
6	*Luciana:*	Ok, but I'm still confused why you want to subtract four. Like, don't you want to do, like, multiplying?
7	*Josie:*	I think we should do something different.

Luciana continued with specific questions about the details of Josie's strategy, focusing on how it would be represented on paper (line 8) and how Josie would know when to stop counting (line 14). Luciana interspersed her questions with her own revoicing of Josie's idea (lines 12, 16).

8	*Luciana:*	Ok, so how would you represent the subtracting on your paper?
9	*Josie:*	Subtract it, like, we put 553 dollars, right? Subtract four … [Josie starts writing on her paper, Luciana looks at Josie's paper and begins to write on her own] and we know we're going to subtract by fours.
10	*Luciana:*	Oh, so that's what you're doing?
11	*Josie:*	Like almost like skip counting.
12	*Luciana:*	Oh, so you're saying that we can do that like 553 minus four (gesturing with her hands)
13	*Josie:*	Four dollars.
14	*Luciana:*	But I have another question. How would you know when to stop?
15	*Josie:*	When it reaches zero.
16	*Luciana:*	So you're saying that we're skip counting 553 all the way to 0 (gestures) … by fours?

Luciana's continued questioning demonstrated her desire to understand her partner's strategy in its entirety, and her revoicing, gesturing, and comments about the overall strategy communicated her understanding of the idea. Engaging in specific questioning, responding and revoicing, and noting similarities and differences gave the pair opportunities to make sense of mathematical operations in an in-depth manner, specifically, considering the relationships among subtracting, multiplying, and skip counting.

Especially striking about this extended example is its interplay among mathematical understanding and detailed student engagement that occurs throughout the pair's interaction. In particular, one student (Luciana) tried to understand another student's idea (Josie's) comprehensively enough to take it on for herself. Her questions provided the opportunity for the pair to work through their understanding of how their various mathematical strategies were related—specifically, the mathematical similarities and differences between their ideas of multiplying (partial products), skip counting (likely by fours), and repeated subtraction—and why some strategies would be inefficient for the quantities involved. This substantive mathematical conversation had strong potential to develop these students' conceptual understanding of the operation of how quantities are related within a division problem context.

Teacher moves to support students' engagement with each other's mathematical ideas

The teacher supported the student engagement moves described in the previous section (see Table 18.1) by using the moves herself as she engaged with the class or with individual students and by supporting students to use them while they were engaged with other students (Table 18.2). Table 18.2 provides just a few examples of the many ways in which teachers supported these student moves.

TABLE 18.2 Teacher moves to support students to engage in each other's mathematical ideas

Engagement move	Example of teacher move to support student engagement
Asks a general question about other's idea	**Melissa, what were you and Daria thinking?** *With your partner, I want you to each share your two ideas. Tell them how you know. Your partner can say, How do you know that for sure? How did you get that?*
Asks a specific question about other's idea	**How many basketballs did you buy first?** *Guys? What do you think?* Are you sure about this part (points to 40 x 2)? *Can you talk to your neighbor about how it's going to work?*
Restates/revoices other's idea	**I heard Hannah say that we know that we need four mosquitoes in 1 hour.** *Can you just talk about what was the first step that these partners took together. [Say]: "First, these partners". Go. What did they do first? [Pairs start talking]*

Notes similarities/ differences between one's own ideas and other's ideas	**Should we keep going until we land on … Charles, do you remember what you were doing the other day? Why did you stop? He landed on something special, wasn't it? It was an easier number.**
	Can you guys see any connections between the red and the blue strategy? … Turn and tell your neighbor how they are connected.
Challenges (or sees a problem with) other's idea or work created jointly; may offer an alternative	**Did you guys hear what she said? Should she repeat it? Cause some of you might disagree.**
	T: Do you disagree or agree?
	S: Disagree
	T: Talk to him! [say] "Nathan, I'm disagreeing because…" Go ahead.
Keeps tabs on other's idea	**I see lots of eyebrows [raised] … That means we're noticing something that we want to talk about.**
	So Charles, do you see the strategy that Jose is using?
Adds on to other's idea	**T: How many 12s, if we added them together like Anabelle's saying, would be nice and easy to work with? Daisy: Five 12s… 60.**
	T: Anabelle and Daisy I am going to combine your idea.
	Jaclyn: Well, I know that 26 times 10 equals 260.
	T: Can you talk about how this would help Jaclyn? Go ahead and turn and talk.

The **bolded** examples show the teacher enacting a particular move; the *italicized* examples show the teacher supporting students to take up a particular move. While the above examples are presented individually, it is important to note that these moves occur within (and are excerpted from) complex interactions. Within a single interaction the teacher may draw upon a multitude of moves in-the-moment.

The following extended example shows how the teacher drew on a range of moves that supported the students to engage with each other's mathematical ideas. This episode occurred during whole-class discussion following the extended pairshare time, with students seated on the rug in the front of the class. The mathematical problem being discussed was the basketball problem from the previous example. The teacher began by choosing two students' strategies to highlight particular mathematical ideas. Josie and Luciana (see Figure 18.1: left side) and Dante and James (see Figure 18.1: right side) had written their strategies next to each other on the board in different colors.

Two student-generated strategies were shown on the board for the problem: "Wilbert Grant School wants to buy more basketballs for the school. If new basketballs cost $4 each, how many basketballs can the school buy with $553?" The teacher started the class conversation by noting that they were going to discuss two strategies and that one of the strategies, the one on the left (the strategy in red), had not been finished, that the students working on it had become frustrated, and the class was going to help complete it. She asked students to talk to their neighbor about the red strategy ("What did they do first? What did they do next? What should they

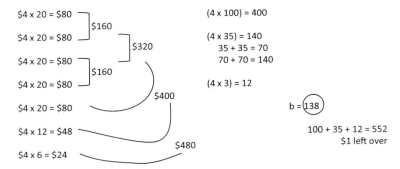

$4 x 20 = $80 ⎤
              ⎥ $160
$4 x 20 = $80 ⎦
                   ⎤ $320
$4 x 20 = $80 ⎤ ⎦
              ⎥ $160
$4 x 20 = $80 ⎦
                   $400
$4 x 20 = $80

$4 x 12 = $48
                   $480
$4 x 6 = $24

(4 x 100) = 400

(4 x 35) = 140
35 + 35 = 70
70 + 70 = 140

(4 x 3) = 12

b = 138

100 + 35 + 12 = 552
$1 left over

FIGURE 18.1 Student work on board. The strategy on the left was written in red and the strategy on the right was written in blue.

do down here? Go ahead and tell your partner."). Her questions, while general, invited the students to engage around the pair's strategy and attend to the steps that the pair carried out.

Following the brief pairshare, the teacher called on Jeremiah to share his ideas about the pair's strategy (line 1 below). Shortly after Jeremiah began explaining, when another student jumped in to tell Jeremiah that he could not follow what he was saying (line 5), the teacher encouraged Jeremiah to slow down while signaling that students needed to be able to follow his explanation (line 6). The teacher revoiced what Jeremiah said (line 10), asked Jeremiah a specific question about his explanation (a question that focused on making sure that the class understood that 20 represented the number of basketballs being bought, line 12), and asked questions of the class to make sure they were keeping tabs on Jeremiah's explanation (lines 14, 16).

1	*Teacher:*	Jeremiah, do you want to share? What can we do with it? Can you start the conversation and other people will join in?
2	*Jeremiah:*	First they did four times 20 and then that equals 800.
3	*Other students:*	80!
4	*Jeremiah:*	80. And then …
5	*Other student:*	That is so fast. Not even I could understand you.
6	*Teacher:*	Jeremiah, people would like to really hear what you are saying, could you slow down for them?
7	*Jeremiah:*	First they did four times 20 and then that equals 800.
8	*Other students:*	80!
9	*Jeremiah:*	80.
10	*Teacher:*	80. Ok.
11	*Jeremiah:*	Then they did another four times 20 and that equals 80 …
12	*Teacher:*	Wait, are you saying they got 20 balls first?
13	*Jeremiah:*	Yeah. And then they did another four times 20 and that equals another 80.

14	*Teacher:*	Ok. Class, what is 80 plus 80?
15	*Students:*	160.
16	*Teacher:*	Are we good so far?

Soon thereafter, the teacher opened the class for further discussion. She asked the class if students wanted to comment on what had been discussed (line 17 below). She summarized for the class what portion of the strategy had been discussed, and invited a student (Jaclyn) to add on to what had been shared. After Jaclyn started explaining, the teacher asked her a question to help her clarify her point (line 19). The teacher then turned the conversation to the second strategy written on the board (the blue strategy), and invited the class to note similarities between the second strategy and their own strategy (line 21). Rather than expressing a general invitation, she was specific about elements in the strategy that she wanted students to focus on, and used her questions to support students to compare the two strategies.

17	*Teacher:*	Ok. Do you have any comments or do you think it worked so far? Does anyone want to comment on what has happened here? I'm going to draw a line. At that point, they had $400 spent. Then they added 48 more and 24 more and they got $480. Jaclyn, you are noticing something? Go ahead.
18	*Jaclyn:*	I'm noticing that they got really close to where they are supposed to be ... where their answer is supposed to be. They are supposed to be at 553 but then ...
19	*Teacher:*	So they are not done yet?
20	*Jaclyn:*	Yes.
21	*Teacher:*	Ok, I'm going to stop. They need to do some more work don't they? Because they have more money to spend. Ok? Let's look at this strategy over here. Did anyone use something similar to this today? Did anyone buy 100 basketballs on your first order? [Three students raise their hands] Only three? Did anyone use four times 100 as a quick known fact? Raise your hands if you did. I want to see. [Several students raise their hands] Ok. And they ordered 35 balls, another 35, and a 12. Here's what I want to look at. Can you guys see any connections between the red and the blue strategy? ... Turn and tell your neighbor how it is connected. [Students talk to each other]

In summary, this example shows the teacher demonstrating and/or supporting students to carry out a variety of engagement moves: asking specific questions about others' ideas, restating or revoicing others' ideas, noting similarities and/or differences between one's own ideas and others' ideas, challenging others' ideas, keeping tabs on others' work, and adding on to others' ideas.

In addition to supporting students to use the engagement moves during the whole-class portions of the lesson, the teacher also carried out a significant amount of this work with students during the extended pairshare time. For example, when working with a pair who struggled to work together and who were unsure about how to generate a strategy for solving the basketball problem, the teacher supported the pair in both figuring out a strategy they might use to solve the problem and in using the engagement moves of asking general questions and keeping tabs on each other's ideas.

1	*Teacher:*	Andrea, can you ask her a question about beginning thinking so we can get ready? What do we do as mathematicians when we get first get a new problem?
2	*Andrea:*	Write it out, talk about it.
3	*Teacher:*	So we could talk about it first. Savannah, do you want to ask her a question first? What could you ask her to help get us started?
4	*Savannah:*	[silent]
5	*Teacher:*	So could you say, "Andrea what is one thing that we know?" Can you ask her that? Go ahead and ask her.
6	*Savannah:*	What is one thing that we know?
7	*Andrea:*	Well, 4, 4 plus
8	*Teacher:*	What does the 4 represent?
9	*Savannah:*	How much basketballs cost.
10	*Andrea:*	How much money?
11	*Teacher:*	How much money what?
12	*Pair:*	How much money one costs
13	*Teacher:*	Does one basketball cost? [Andrea nods] So $4 is how much they cost. [turns to Andrea] Now you get to ask Savannah another question. You get to say "Savannah, what is something else that we know?"
14	*Andrea:*	[to Savannah] So what else do we know? (Teacher walks away)

The teacher adapted her support in-the-moment in situationally specific ways. She did not simply provide a general reminder to Andrea and Savannah to ask each other questions, but rather, when her initial invitation (line 3) did not result in them asking questions, the teacher provided specific guidance and support to help them see when and how to ask questions that would help them make progress in developing a strategy for solving the problem by focusing them on the context and relationships within the problem (lines 5, 8, 13). She did not make the move for them without first providing them the opportunity to do so themselves. At the same time, the teacher helped the pair keep tabs on one another's ideas by pressing the students to elaborate their thinking (here, explaining what the number four represented, lines 7–13).

Conclusions

In this study, we set out to examine how students can interact in ways that are beneficial for learning–specifically, engaging with each other's mathematical ideas–even when the teacher is not present to specifically guide them, and how teachers can support students to engage in such constructive interaction. Using close analysis of interaction in a classroom whose teacher was committed to developing students' ability to engage with others' mathematical ideas, we found that a large proportion of students showed sustained and synchronous engagement with each other's ideas during collaborative mathematics conversations even without direct teacher intervention.

We uncovered several important features of the support that the teacher provided to students to help them engage with each other's ideas. First, the teacher worked continuously throughout the lesson and during moment-to-moment interactions with students to provide them support to learn how to engage with each other's ideas. Within each interchange with students (e.g., during a class discussion about a particular student's problem-solving strategy), she herself used, and encouraged students to use, multiple engagement moves such as revoicing, questioning, and challenging others' ideas. She followed up initial offers to engage with supporting moves to help students engage more deeply with the details in the ideas being shared.

Second, the teacher intimately connected her support of students' engagement with others' ideas to the mathematical concepts underlying the lessons and the mathematical details in students' ideas. She did not merely ask whether students used a similar or different problem-solving strategy, but she highlighted essential elements within the mathematics for students to attend to (e.g., specific numbers that represented key quantities in the mathematics problem).

Our results showed that the teacher support was successful in promoting spontaneous student engagement in new contexts without the teacher being present. That is, students were able to transfer what they learned and experienced while interacting with the teacher to contexts without direct teacher involvement. In particular, the majority of students in the classroom we studied continued to engage with each other at a high level (e.g., revoicing, questioning, challenging, and adding onto each other's ideas) and attend to the mathematical details of each other's ideas in dyadic discussions without the teacher being there to guide them.

An important next step will be to investigate how teacher moves for supporting student engagement with others' ideas develop in relation to the many other dimensions of teacher practice that may influence students' engagement, such as the norms established in the classroom around communication in general (e.g., expectations about sharing explanations and justifying solutions), the norms concerning engagement with others' ideas in particular (e.g., expectations about disagreeing with others), and how the teacher positions students as capable and valuable contributors to mathematical conversations in general and to the development of mathematical ideas in particular. Investigating teacher practice comprehensively will be essential for understanding more fully how students can be supported to engage with each other's ideas at a high level in contexts with, and without, explicit teacher guidance.

Acknowledgment

This research was supported by grants from the Institute of Education Sciences of the U.S. Department of Education (#R305A100181), the Spencer Foundation, and the Academic Senate on Research, Los Angeles Division, University of California. The views expressed in this paper are the authors' alone and do not reflect the views or policies of the funding agencies. We wish to thank the teachers who contributed their expertise to our research.

References

Azmitia, M., & Montgomery, R. (1993). Friendship, transactive dialogues, and the development of scientific reasoning. *Social Development, 2*(3), 202–221. doi:10.1111/j.1467-9507.1993.tb00014.x

Baines, E., Blatchford, P., & Kutnick, P. (2009). *Promoting effective group work in primary schools*. London: Routledge.

Bargh, J. A., & Schul, Y. (1980). On the cognitive benefits of teaching. *Journal of Educational Psychology, 72*(5), 593–604. doi:10.1037/0022-0663.72.5.593

Barron, B. (2000). Achieving coordination in collaborative problem-solving groups. *Journal of the Learning Sciences, 9*(4), 403–436. doi:10.1207/S15327809JLS0904_2

Berkowitz, M. W., & Gibbs, J. C. (1985). The process of moral conflict resolution and moral development. *New Directions for Child and Adolescent Development, 1985*(29), 71–84. doi:10.1002/cd.23219852907

Brown, A. L., Campione, J. C., Webber, L. S., & McGilly, K. (1992). Interactive learning environments: A new look at assessment and instruction. In B. Gifford & M. C. O'Connor (Eds.), *Changing assessments: Alternative views of aptitude, achievement, and instruction* (pp. 121–211). New York: Kluwer Academic.

Brown, A. L., & Palincsar, A. S. (1989). Guided, cooperative learning and individual knowledge acquisition. In L. B. Resnick (Ed.), *Knowing, learning, and instruction: Essays in honor of Robert Glaser* (pp. 393–451). Hillsdale, NJ: Lawrence Erlbaum.

Carpenter, T. P., Fennema, E., Franke, M. L., Levi, L. W., & Empson, S. B. (1999). *Children's mathematics: Cognitively guided instruction*. Portsmouth, NH: Heinemann.

Chi, M. T. H. (2000). Self-explaining expository texts: The dual processes of generating inferences and repairing mental models. In R. Glaser (Ed.), *Advances in instructional psychology: Educational design and cognitive science* (pp. 161–238). Hillsdale, NJ: Erlbaum.

Chinn, C. A., Anderson, R. C., & Waggoner, M. A. (2001). Patterns of discourse in two kinds of literature discussion. *Reading Research Quarterly, 36*(4), 378–411. doi:10.1598/RRQ.36.4.3

Chinn, C. A., O'Donnell, A. M., & Jinks, T. S. (2000). The structure of discourse in collaborative learning. *Journal of Experimental Education, 69*(1), 77–97. doi:10.1080/00220970009600650

Forman, E. A., & Cazden, C. B. (1985). Exploring Vygotskian perspectives in education: The cognitive value of peer interaction. In J. V. Wertsch (Ed.), *Culture, communication and cognition: Vygotskian perspectives* (pp. 323–347). New York, NY: Cambridge University Press.

Forman, E. A., & Kraker, M. J. (1985). The social origins of logic: The contributions of Piaget and Vygotsky. *New Directions for Child and Adolescent Development, 1985*(29), 23–39. doi:10.1002/cd.23219852904

Franke, M. L., Turrou, A. C., Webb, N. M., Ing, M., Wong, J., Shin, N., & Fernandez, C. H. (2015). Student engagement with others' mathematical ideas: The role of teacher invitation and support moves. *Elementary School Journal, 116*(1), 126–148.

Fuchs, L. S., Fuchs, D., Hamlett, C. L., Phillips, N. B., Karns, K., & Dutka, S. (1997). Enhancing students' helping behavior during peer-mediated instruction with conceptual mathematical explanations. *Elementary School Journal, 97*(3), 223–249. doi:10.1002/cd.23219852904

Gillies, R. M. (2004). The effects of communication training on teachers' and students' verbal behaviours during cooperative learning. *International Journal of Educational Research, 41*(3), 257–279. doi:10.1016/j.ijer.2005.07.004

Gillies, R. M. (2006). Teachers' and students' verbal behaviours during cooperative and small-group learning. *British Journal of Educational Psychology, 76*(2), 271–287. doi:10.1348/000709905X52337

Gillies, R. M., & Boyle, M. (2008). Teachers' discourse during cooperative learning and their perceptions of this pedagogical practice. *Teaching and Teacher Education, 24*(5), 1333–1348. doi:10.1037//0022-0663.90.4.746

Goos, M., Galbraith, P., & Renshaw, P. (2002). Socially mediated metacognition: Creating collaborative zones of proximal development in small group problem solving. *Educational Studies in Mathematics, 49*(2), 193–223.

Hatano, G. (1993). Time to merge Vygotskian and constructivist conceptons of knowlwedge acquisition. In E. A. Forman, N. Minick, & C. A. Stone (Eds.), *Contexts for learning: Sociocultural dynamics in children's development* (pp. 153–166). New York: Oxford University Press.

Hogan, K., Nastasi, B. K., & Pressley, M. (2000). Discourse patterns and collaborative scientific reasoning in peer and teacher-guided discussions. *Cognition and Instruction, 17*(4), 379–432. doi:10.1207/S1532690XCI1704_2

Howe, C. J., & Tolmie, A. (2003). Group work in primary school science: Discussion, consensus and guidance from experts. *International Journal of Educational Research, 39*(1–2), 51–72. doi:10.1016/S0883-0355(03)00073-9

Howe, C., Tolmie, A., Thurston, A., Topping, K., Christie, D., Livingston, K., . . . Donaldson, C. (2007). Group work in elementary science: Towards organisational principles for supporting pupil learning. *Learning and Instruction, 17*(5), 549–563. doi:10.1016/j.learninstruc.2007.09.004

Iiskala, T., Vauras, M., Lehtinen, E., & Salonen, P. (2011). Socially shared metacognition of dyads of pupils in collaborative mathematical problem-solving processes. *Learning and Instruction, 21*(3), 379–393. doi:10.1016/j.learninstruc.2010.05.002

Kazemi, E., & Stipek, D. (2001). Promoting conceptual thinking in four upper-elementary mathematics classrooms. *Elementary School Journal, 102*(1), 59–80. doi:10.1086/499693

King, A. (1992). Facilitating elaborative learning through guided student-generated questioning. *Educational Psychologist, 27*(1), 111–126. doi:10.1207/s15326985ep2701_8

Kruger, A. C. (1993). Peer collaboration: Conflict, cooperation, or both? *Social Development, 2*(3), 165–182. doi:10.1111/j.1467-9507.1993.tb00012.x

Mercer, N. (1996). The quality of talk in children's collaborative activity in the classroom. *Learning and Instruction, 6*(4), 359–377. doi:10.1016/S0959-4752(96)00021-7

Mercer, N., Dawes, R., Wegerif, R., & Sams, C. (2004). Reasoning as a scientist: Ways of helping children to use language to learn science. *British Educational Research Journal, 30*(3), 359–377. doi:10.1080/01411920410001689689

Mercer, N., Wegerif, R., & Dawes, L. (1999). Children's talk and the development of reasoning in the classroom. *British Educational Research Journal, 25*(1), 95–111. doi:10.1080/0141192990250107

Mevarech, A. R., & Kramarski, B. (2003). The effects of metacognitive training versus worked-out examples on students' mathematical reasoning. *British Journal of Educational Psychology, 73*(4), 449–471. doi:10.1348/000709903322591181

Michaels, S., O'Connor, C., & Resnick, L. B. (2008). Deliberative discourse idealized and realized: Accountable talk in the classroom and in civic life. *Studies in the Philosophy of Education, 27*(4), 283–297. doi:10.1007/s11217-007-9071-1

National Governors Association Center for Best Practices & Council of Chief State School Officers. (2010). *Common core standards mathematics.* Washington, DC: Authors.

Nattiv, A. (1994). Helping behaviors and math achievement gain of students using cooperative learning. *The Elementary School Journal, 94*(3), 285–297. doi:10.1086/461767

O'Connor, M. C., Michaels, S., & Chapin, S. H. (2015). "Scaling down" to explore the role of talk in learning: From district intervention to controlled classroom study. In L. B. Resnick, C. Asterhan, & S. N. Clarke (Eds.), *Socializing intelligence through talk and dialogue* (pp. 111–126). Washington, DC: American Educational Research Association.

O'Donnell, A. M., & King, A. (1999). *Cognitive perspectives on peer learning.* Mahwah, NJ: Erlbaum.

Roschelle, J. (1992). Learning by collaborating: Convergent coneptual change. *Journal of the Learning Sciences, 2*(3), 235–276. doi:10.1207/s15327809jls0203_1

Roschelle, J., & Teasley S. D. (1995). The construction of shared knowledge in collaborative problem solving. In C. E. O'Malley (Ed.), *Computer-supported collaborative learning* (pp. 69–97). Berlin, Germany: Springer-Verlag.

Roscoe, R. D., & Chi, M. T. (2008). Tutor learning: The role of explaining and responding to questions. *Instructional Science, 36*(4), 321–350. doi:10.1007/s11251-007-9034-5

Saxe, G. B., Gearhart, M., Note, M., & Paduano, P. (1993). Peer interaction and the development of mathematical understandings: A new framework for research and educational practice. In H. Daniels (Ed.), *Charting the agenda: Educational activity after Vygotksy* (pp. 107–144). London: Routledge.

Slavin, R. E. (1987). Ability grouping and student achievement in elementary schools: A best-evidence synthesis. *Review of Educational Research, 57*(3), 293–336. doi:10.3102/00346543057003293

Smagorinsky, P., & Fly, P. K. (1993). The social environment of the classroom: A Vygotskian perspective on small group process. *Communication Education, 42*(2), 159–171. doi:10.1080/03634529309378922

Veenman, S., Denessen, E., van den Akker, A., & van der Rijt, J. (2005). Effects of a cooperative learning program on the elaborations of students during help seeking and help giving. *American Educational Research Journal, 42*(1), 115–151. doi:10.3102/00028312042001115

Volet, S., Summers, M., & Thurman, J. (2009). High-level co-regulation in collaborative learning: How does it emerge and how is it sustained? *Learning and Instruction, 19*(2), 128–143. doi:10.1016/j.learninstruc.2008.03.001

Waggoner, M., Chinn, C., Yi, H., & Anderson, R. C. (1995). Collaborative reasoning about stories. *Language Arts, 72*(8), 582–589.

Webb, N. M., Franke, M. L., De, T., Chan, A. G., Freund, D., Shein, P., & Melkonian, D. K. (2009). Teachers' instructional practices and small-group dialogue. *Cambridge Journal of Education, 39*(1), 49–70. doi:10.1080/03057640802701986

Webb, N. M., Franke, M. L., Ing, M., Chan, A., De, T., Freund, D., & Battey, D. (2008). The role of teacher instructional practices in student collaboration. *Contemporary Educational Psychology, 33*(3), 360–381. doi:10.1016/j.cedpsych.2008.05.003

Webb, N. M., Franke, M. L., Ing, M., Wong, J., Fernandez, C. H., Shin, N., & Turrou, A. C. (2014). Engaging with others' mathematical ideas: Interrelationships among student participation, teachers' instructional practices and learning. *International Journal of Educational Research, 63*(1), 79–93. doi:10.1016/j.ijer.2013.02.001

Webb, N. M., & Palincsar, A. S. (1996). Group processes in the classroom. In D. Berliner & R. Calfee (Eds.), *Handbook of educational psychology* (pp. 841–873). New York, NY: Macmillan.

Whitebread, D., Bingham, S., Grau, V., Pino Pasternak, D., & Sangster, C. (2007). Development of metacognition and self-regulated learning in young children: The role of collaborative and peer-assisted learning. *Journal of Cognitive Education and Psychology, 6*(3), 433–455. doi:10.1891/194589507787382043

Wittrock, M. C. (1989). Generative processes of comprehension. *Educational Psychologist, 24*(4), 345–376. doi:10.1207/s15326985ep2404_2

Yackel, E., Cobb, P., & Wood, T. (1991). Small-group interactions as a source of learning opportunities in second-grade mathematics. *Journal for Research in Mathematics Education, 22*(5), 390–408. doi:10.2307/749187

Yackel, E., Cobb, P., Wood, T., Wheatley, G., & Merkel, G. (1990). The importance of social interaction in children's construction of mathematical knowledge. In T. J. Cooney & C. R. Hirsch (Eds.), *Teaching and learning mathematics in the 1990s* (pp. 12–21). Reston, VA: National Council of Teachers of Mathematics.

19

SUPPORTING TEACHERS' SPONTANEOUS USE OF TALK MOVES DURING INQUIRY DIALOGUE

Alina Reznitskaya, Ian A. G. Wilkinson, and Joseph Oyler

In this chapter, we discuss a professional development program designed to help classroom teachers use a special kind of discourse, called *inquiry dialogue*. Walton (1998) proposed a useful classification of six dialogue types and described their characteristic goals and norms. Following Gregory (2006), who related Walton's work to education, we suggest that inquiry dialogue is most aligned with the pedagogical goals of supporting the development of students' argumentation skills and promoting deep understanding of subject matter. This is because the goal of inquiry dialogue is to collectively find the most reasonable answer, rather than to win over an opponent (as in persuasion dialogue) or to reach an agreement by making concessions (as in negotiation dialogue). Thus, inquiry dialogue, as compared to other dialogue types, evokes normative argumentation processes and evaluation standards, such as those used by professionals in academic disciplines. For example, the goal of working toward the most reasonable answer compels participants not only to defend their own positions and critically examine those of others, but also to give up their viewpoints in the face of previously overlooked evidence or faulty reasoning (Gregory, 2006). The professional development program described in this chapter was specifically focused on promoting teachers' use of inquiry dialogue. We believe that clarity in goals and norms of dialogic engagement helps to support teacher learning and spontaneous use of new discourse practices.

Although the term 'inquiry dialogue' has not been typically used in studies of classroom discourse, our work is largely informed by previous studies on various dialogue-intensive approaches to classroom instruction (Alexander, 2008; Commeyras, 1994; Kuhn, 2010; Osborne, 2010; Resnick, Asterhan, & Clarke, 2015; Trickey & Topping, 2004; Wells, 2000). These studies have examined and documented the potential of productive classroom dialogue to support the development of students' argumentation skills (i.e., the ability to comprehend, formulate, and evaluate arguments) and deep understanding of subject matter knowledge.

This research has also shown that facilitating discussions that share features with inquiry dialogue is a serious challenge for novice and experienced teachers (Alvermann & Hayes, 1989; Juzwik, Sherry, Caughlan, Heintz, & Borsheim-Black, 2012; Nguyen, Anderson, Waggoner, & Rowel, 2007). This is not surprising because such discussions entail a major transformation in teacher use of talk, from explaining established facts and principals to scaffolding student co-construction of knowledge through argumentation. "To invite students to articulate and explore their ideas … is to require that teachers hear those ideas, diagnose their virtues and weaknesses, and incorporate them into the substance of instruction … This is a new role for teachers whose practice has been defined by traditional goals and methods, and it comes with different and strenuous intellectual demands" (Hammer & Schifter, 2001, p. 442). Moreover, as opposed to more predictable traditional lessons, each discussion is largely unique, since it heavily depends on student participation. It represents a novel space where teachers need to improvise to make moment-to-moment decisions regarding the amount and type of involvement. Thus, effective facilitators need to not only know various facilitation skills but also be able to spontaneously apply these skills in new contexts, as they react to specific student contributions during each discussion.

To illustrate the effective use of inquiry dialogue, let us consider an excerpt from a discussion in a fifth-grade language arts classroom. The teacher facilitating the discussion participated in our professional development program on the use of inquiry dialogue in text-based discussions (Reznitskaya & Wilkinson, 2015; Wilkinson et al., 2017). Prior to this discussion, students read an article about a boy named Zack, who was paralyzed after suffering a concussion during a football game. Next, they gathered in a circle to discuss a question, "Who is responsible for Zack's injury?"

Teacher: So who would like to start us off this morning? Okay, Jerry.

Jerry: Well, I think the one responsible for Zack's injury would be the coach, because he was the one who let Zack play when he shouldn't, because he knew that he already had an injury.

Andrew: I disagree with Jerry because it actually said in the passage that Zack thought that his team needed help, so he decided to go in, 'cause the coach wasn't trained to find a concussion. So, he decided to go in on his own, without the coach telling him to. 'cause the coach wasn't trained to see a concussion.

Lily: I agree with Andrew because … you wouldn't let … If you know we got hurt and we insisted to go back into something like that, you would at least make sure that we're okay. And I think Zack's coach probably did that … I think Zack's coach probably made sure that he was okay, so it's not all of his fault. He, as an adult, should say "No, maybe you could go back in next time." But it's not only his fault.

Teacher: So wait, how is that agreeing with Andrew? 'Cause Andrew says it's not the coach's fault, but you're …

Lily: Yeah, I don't think it's the coach's fault either.

Teacher: But you said, "As an adult he should know." I'm just… I want you to just clarify.

Lily: Well okay, I agree with Andrew, like everything that he said, but it's not complete… Okay, I just agree with Andrew, like what he said … The coach didn't say "Zack, get back in here." Zack wanted to and he went in on his own.

Kate: I disagree with Jerry. I don't find that it's the coach's fault because in the paragraph it says they, the coaches weren't trained at that time to know what brain concussion looks like. 'cause brain concussions are invisible injuries, it says it in this story, so, I don't find that it's the coach's fault and …

Jerry: But Zack was hurt …

Kate: Yeah, but he said he was all right, so how is the coach supposed to know?

Teacher: Ok, so let's let him respond to that. They challenged you, right? So now let's let Jerry respond … We had a few challenges, so let's let Jerry maybe respond to that challenge, and maybe, I don't know …

Jerry: But if you see someone fall down very hard on their head and come back to the bench, saying that they're alright, the coach should know that they've been in an injury, and the coach should not let them play.

Students in this discussion are addressing an open-ended, contestable question that does not have a single right answer. During the discussion, the teacher largely releases control over the flow of discourse to the students. We see students asking questions, self-nominating, and evaluating each other's answers. There are exchanges with consecutive student turns without teacher interruption. As students discuss their positions on the question of who is responsible for the injury, they provide elaborated explanations of the reasoning behind their views and refer to text information for evidence. The teacher does not dominate the discussion, speaking less than students. Her deliberately chosen questions serve to advance the inquiry further: she asks students to clarify how their ideas connect with those of other group members (i.e., "So, wait, how is that agreeing with Andrew?") and encourages the discussion of an opposing perspective (i.e., "They challenged you, right? So now let's let Jerry respond").

Studies of class discussions that share features with inquiry dialogue reveal a considerable consensus as to what constitutes effective dialogic engagement (e.g., Alexander, 2003; Applebee, Langer, Nystrand, & Gamoran, 2003; Billings & Fitzgerald, 2002; Mercer & Littleton, 2007; Soter et al., 2008). Here, we draw on these studies to highlight three important characteristics of inquiry dialogue. First, inquiry dialogue is initiated by a central question that is "fundamentally open or divergent … in terms of allowing a broader degree of uncertainty in what would constitute an adequate answer" (Burbules, 1993, p. 97). Such central questions elicit thinking at higher cognitive levels, including the formulation, analysis, and evaluation of arguments. During inquiry dialogue, these questions invite students to engage in a collective and disciplined search for the most reasonable answer.

Second, in inquiry dialogue, as in similar types of discussions, students assume more control and responsibility over the form and content of discourse (Nystrand, 1997; Nystrand, Wu, Gamoran, Zeiser, & Long, 2003; Resnick & Schantz, 2015). As a result, classrooms are transformed into learning communities, where participants meet on terms of equality and take on key roles in navigating class communication: they ask questions, participate in managing speaking turns, and challenge each other's claims. Importantly, we believe that the release of responsibility from a teacher to students needs to be "gradual" (cf. Pearson & Gallagher, 1983). In other words, initially (and when necessary) teachers need to model the desired behaviors by using effective facilitation strategies. For example, a teacher can ask a student to clarify a vague remark by saying, "Can you explain this again?" This request for clarification will eventually be 'picked up' by students and used in relevant situations, thus enhancing the learning experience of the individual and the group.

Third, participating in inquiry dialogue, or other types of discussions focused on co-constructing arguments, is inherently metacognitive (Kuhn & Dean, 2004; Splitter & Sharp, 1996). Metacognition includes the awareness of the content and process of one's thinking and the ability to monitor and regulate thought processes in ways that can improve performance (Flavell, 1985; Kuhn & Dean, 2004). During inquiry dialogue, teachers can help students pay attention to the quality of group argumentation by being "procedurally strong, but substantively self-effacing" (Splitter & Sharp, 1996, p. 306). This means that instead of giving students the right answers, teachers can focus on "strengthening the procedures of inquiry" (Splitter & Sharp, 1996, p. 301). They need to enforce the norms of inquiry dialogue, as well as to encourage effective use of talk to help students co-reason together.

Professional development programs designed to promote dialogue-intensive approaches to instruction previously relied on the use of talk moves to help teachers develop the necessary facilitation skills (e.g., Beck, McKeown, Sandora, Kucan, & Worthy, 1996; Michaels & O'Connor, 2015). O'Connor and colleagues defined *talk moves* as "families of utterances that help teachers in the moment-to-moment micro-interactional challenges of orchestrating student discussion" (O'Connor, Michaels, & Chapin, 2015, p. 112). During inquiry dialogue, skilled facilitators deliberately use a particular cluster of these discursive devices to help students engage in collaborative and rigorous argumentation. For example, suppose that during a discussion of a contestable question, such as who should be held responsible for a player's concussion, students all line up on the same side of the issue. A teacher can step in and ask students to propose alternative positions and reasons (i.e., *If another fifth-grader disagreed with you, what would she say?*). This talk move helps to improve the quality of argumentation by prompting students to think about opposing views previously overlooked by the group, thus making their arguments more comprehensive and nuanced.

Through the use of effective talk moves, teachers can help their students transform a directionless conversation into a collaborative and rigorous inquiry. Also, as they model and support effective use of language, teachers play an important role in socializing students into new ways of speaking and thinking. Yet, not much is known about how to help teachers acquire the necessary skills and knowledge to effectively facilitate inquiry dialogue. In the next section, we describe our efforts to identify and evaluate instructional activities and materials that promote teachers' learning and spontaneous use of talk moves during inquiry dialogue in elementary language arts classrooms.

Helping teachers learn to facilitate inquiry dialogue

Earlier in this chapter, we illustrated the use of inquiry dialogue in a fifth-grade classroom. The teacher was able to make moment-to-moment decisions about the use of talk moves that served to enhance the quality of student argumentation. In other words, this teacher was successful at transferring her knowledge of effective facilitation to a new context of a classroom discussion about a concussion during the football game. In this section, we describe our year-long professional develop-ment program designed to foster teachers' spontaneous use of talk moves during the discussions of assigned readings in elementary school classrooms.

Overview of the program

In this three-year research project, we worked collaboratively with teachers to identify and organize instructional content that supports teachers' use of inquiry dialogue and related pre- and post-discussion activities. Each year, we implemented a version of the program and collected data from teachers and students to assess program effectiveness and inform its revisions. Examples of the data used to revise the program include structured focus group interviews with participating teachers, videotaped classroom discussions, and pre- and post- measures of teacher beliefs and knowledge related to the use of inquiry dialogue for promoting argumentation skills (e.g., Wilkinson et al., 2017).

The design of our program was informed by general principles of effective professional development described in earlier studies (e.g., Elmore, 2002; Wei, Darling-Hammond, Andree, Richardson, & Orphanos, 2009; Yoon, Duncan, Lee, Scarloss, & Shapley, 2007). These principles include: the involvement of teachers in planning and undertaking professional development; the collective participa-tion of groups of teachers; intensive and sustained support; and the integration of professional development into the daily lives of teachers. We also learned from pre-vious professional development efforts that specifically focused on helping teachers acquire new discourse practices (e.g., Alvermann & Hayes, 1989; Juzwik et al., 2012; Kucan, 2009; Michaels & O'Connor, 2015). This research emphasized the importance of engaging teachers in the analysis of their own discussions through the use of videos and transcripts (e.g., Juzwik et al., 2012) and highlighted the value of helping teachers view talk moves as tools that have specific functions and contexts of use (Michaels & O'Connor, 2015).

Study participants came from school districts in two states in the United States: Ohio and New Jersey. In year 1, we worked with a total of 10 fifth-grade teachers and their students (six in Ohio and four in New Jersey). In year 2, 13 fifth-grade teachers participated at both sites (six in Ohio and seven in New Jersey). Teaching experience of participants ranged from 2 to 26 years.

Challenges and accomplishments

Our first challenge was to identify instructional objectives of the program to help teachers develop coherent pedagogical frameworks that integrate both theoretical and practical knowledge. As noted by Richardson, Anders, Tidwell, and Lloyd (1991), real transformation of classroom communication

> will happen only when teachers think differently about what is going on in their classrooms, and are provided with the practices that match the different ways of thinking. The provision of practices without theory may lead to misimplementation or no implementation at all. . . . Changing beliefs without proposing practices that embody those theories may lead to frustration.
>
> *(p. 579)*

Below are the instructional goals of our program that represent a mix of relevant theoretical knowledge and related practical skills:

1   To help teachers develop views about knowing, teaching, and learning that are aligned with the use of inquiry dialogue;
2   To raise teacher awareness about the use of classroom language to achieve specific pedagogical goals;
3   To help teachers understand argumentation and criteria for evaluating arguments;
4   To provide teachers with a repertoire of talk moves to facilitate inquiry dialogue.

To accomplish these goals, we designed a year-long professional development program. In the Year 2 iteration of the program, teachers participated in a two-day workshop, 7 two-hour study group meetings, 6 coaching sessions, and a half-day workshop. We used a variety of instructional activities and materials in our program, including peer debriefing, collaborative analysis of transcripts and videos of classroom discussions, co-planning a unit around a text, and practicing inquiry dialogue.

Le us now describe specific learning experiences and materials we believe to be particularly helpful for supporting teachers' spontaneous use of effective talk moves during class discussions. For example, one aspect of our program that was highly valued by teachers was coaching. During coaching sessions, teachers viewed and critiqued their own classroom discussions with the help of an experienced discourse coach who supported teachers' ongoing development and reflection. Revisiting their own classroom interactions and watching them in "slow motion" provided teachers with an opportunity to examine how a particular talk move used or skipped at a given moment could open (or restrict) opportunities for student learning. The coaches were careful to frame the reflection as a non-judgmental collegial exercise, avoiding telling teachers what they should have done, and instead encouraging them to engage in a careful reflection on the possibilities of using language to enhance the quality of students' argumentation.

During coaching and throughout the program, we also developed and used a systematic measure to evaluate the quality of teacher facilitation and student argumentation, called the Argumentation Rating Tool (ART) (Reznitskaya & Wilkinson, in press). The ART is an observational rating scale designed to examine teacher-student interactions during inquiry dialogue in elementary language arts classrooms. Users of the ART view short segments of classroom discussions of assigned readings, apply a set of evaluation criteria, and rate the quality of argumentation on a 6-point scale. Designed to support professional development and research efforts, the ART aims to engage practitioners in a systematic assessment of their practice, informing and structuring the process of change. Figure 19.1 presents the structure of the ART, and Tables 19.1 and 19.2 illustrate two of the practices.

Figure 19.1 shows that the ART is organized around four criteria of quality argumentation: (1) consideration of diverse perspectives, (2) clarity of language and argument structure, (3) acceptability of reasons and evidence, and (4) logical validity of inferences. We developed these criteria based on the normative models proposed by scholars in the field of argumentation (e.g., Govier, 2010; Nussbaum, 2011; Toulmin, 1958; Walton, 1996). We then linked the four criteria to a set of eleven practices, which we identified through a comprehensive review of theoretical, empirical, and pedagogical literature on the use of classroom discussions focused on argumentation (e.g., Billings & Fitzgerald, 2002; Chinn, Anderson, & Waggoner, 2001; Gregory, 2007). For example, the clarity criterion is supported by the use of four practices, including clarifying meaning, connecting ideas, labeling moves and parts of an argument, and tracking the line of inquiry.

Next, as shown in Table 19.1 and Table 19.2, we provided a detailed description of each practice, by including a short overview of an underlying principle behind

FOUR CRITERIA OF QUALITY ARGUMENTATION DURING DISCUSSION

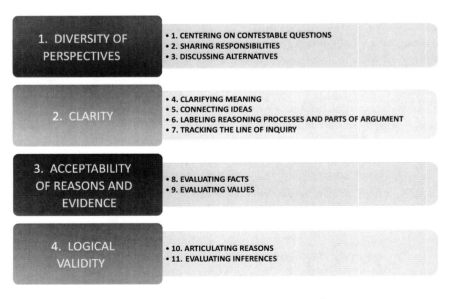

FIGURE 19.1   The structure of the Argumentation Rating Tool: connecting 4 criteria to 11 practices

Criterion #1. Diversity of perspectives: we explore different perspectives together

Practice		Advancing		Developing		Not yet	
		6	5	4	3	2	1
3. Discussing alternatives	**Teacher**	The teacher **prompts students to take into account missing perspectives** overlooked by the group, whenever students fail to consider alternative viewpoints. **Teacher questions are well-focused,** inviting students to carefully examine their disagreement. • *Which part are you disagreeing with?* • *Let Molly respond to this.* • *If someone disagreed with you, what would they say to argue against you?* • *So far, we haven't heard from anyone who never had a pet – I wonder if they think the same way.* • *Is this the only explanation?* • *We have a number of examples already. Can anyone offer a counter-example?*		The teacher makes an effort to invite multiple interpretations. However, he **may miss opportunities** to probe for alternative perspectives, especially when students' answers are consistent with the predetermined plan for the lesson. The prompts for alternative perspectives are overly general. There may be clear content boundaries for the discussion. The teacher **may constrain and refocus the discussion** in a predetermined direction. • *Anybody else?* • *Does anyone disagree?*		There are **few, if any, opportunities** for students to consider alternative points of view to the correct answer given in the text or by the teacher. *That's right, Rachel. And then what happened?*	
	Students	Students **consistently bring up alternative viewpoints.** These multiple viewpoints are seriously considered and challenged by group members. • *I disagree with Jeff because …* • *Well, some people might say that he cheated when he ran across the lake.* • *But, Don, what about that time in the story when …?* • *I disagree with all of you and think that he should tell because …* • *I guess if someone disagreed, they might say that …*		Students **occasionally** bring up or explore alternative viewpoints. Disagreement is rare.		Students **do not** bring up and discuss alternative viewpoints.	

TABLE 19.2 Selected practice from the Argumentation Rating Tool: clarifying meaning

Criterion #2. Clarity: we are clear in the language and structure of our arguments

Practice		Advancing		Developing		Not yet
	6	5	4	3	2	1
4. Clarifying meaning *(Teacher)*		The teacher **asks students to clarify their ideas** and to restate each other's responses, whenever necessary. She closely paraphrases, re-voices, and **distills student responses**, helping to highlight key ideas. The teacher often **follows up with a student** to make sure the paraphrasing is accurate. *(Is that what you were saying?)* • *I hear you saying … Is that what you mean?* • *Can someone else say what you understand his point to be? …Jose, is that what you meant?* • *So are you saying that …?* • *How are you using the word …?* • *Are you making a distinction between … and …?* • *What characteristics make someone "an adult" …?* • *How is cheating different from lying?* • *How is this similar to …? Would this be the same as …?* • *Ok, so it looks like we can't move forward without first clarifying what we mean by …*		The teacher **occasionally** checks for clarity and asks students to explain their answers. When paraphrasing, the teacher **may change the original meaning** of student answers to emphasize specific points that students should not miss. The teacher sometimes selectively adds or subtracts information from student answers in order to fit in with a predetermined purpose for the lesson. Questions are often **overly general**. • *Is everyone following so far?* • *Is this clear? Any questions?* • *Can you explain more?*		The teacher may ask students to simply **repeat right answers.** Incorrect, incomplete, or unclear answers from students often remain unexamined. *Say it again, Jorge, so that everyone can hear the right answer.*
(Students)		Students **paraphrase their own and each others' answers,** offer definitions, give examples, and otherwise work to clarify meaning, whenever necessary. They check with each other to make sure the group understands the ideas accurately and completely. • *What I think Jose was saying is that …* • *Mirabai and I were using the same word to mean different*		Students **occasionally** paraphrase their own answers, but not those of their peers. Students reformulate their ideas to clarify what they mean, instead of repeating what they originally said. • *What I meant was that nobody is*		Students **do not** paraphrase answers. They may repeat correct answers about specific facts from the text. They don't have opportunities to clarify or reformulate more complex thoughts.

this practice and by listing examples of specific verbal prompts, or talk moves used to set it in motion. For instance, as can be seen in Table 19.2, when working on clarifying meaning, the teacher can use the following talk moves: "I hear you saying ... Is that what you mean? Can someone else say what you understand his point to be? How are you using the word ...?"

Another feature of the ART enables teachers to evaluate whether or not their use of talk moves during discussions helps to elicit intended student responses. Following Mercer (2008), we believe that talk moves should be interpreted in relation to the context of a given discussion, since the same move can have distinct meanings and encourage different student responses. For example, a teacher question "What do we mean by privacy?" can be followed by a student recall of a dictionary definition or by a group inquiry into this complex construct. This is why the ART contains related items that purposefully match teacher and student actions. For example, in Tables 19.1 and 19.2, there are two related descriptions for each practice, one for the teacher and one for the students.

Students who participate in inquiry dialogue are expected to eventually internalize important argumentation practices and related talk moves and to use them without additional prompting from the teacher. For example, students will learn to introduce alternative perspectives and clarify ambiguous terms. As a result, at the more advanced stages (ratings 5 and 6), teacher involvement should decrease. In order to reflect expected changes in the levels of involvement, we qualified the descriptions of teacher practice in the ART. For example, as shown in Table 19.2, teachers should ask students to clarify "whenever student statements lack precision." This wording highlights the importance of teacher responsiveness to the development of group's reasoning. Thus, the ART does not simply reward teachers for using more talk moves during a discussion. Instead, it focuses on whether or not teachers *missed opportunities* to improve the quality of argumentation. In other words, the ART assesses whether or not teachers could spontaneously react to student contributions and change their use of talk depending on the needs of the group and the developing competencies of the students.

In our professional development program, we used the ART to structure coaching sessions around specific argumentation criteria, practices, and talk moves, thus helping teachers to 'develop an ear' for quality of argumentation during the discussion. Consider, for example, the following excerpt of a teacher examining her facilitation with a coach, as they view and evaluate a recently videotaped discussion with the use of the ART. Both the coach and the teacher watched the video before the coaching session.

Coach: Alright ... [Reading from the ART] *Clarify their ideas, restate each other's responses.* So what are you thinking on this one?

Teacher: Well, I marked at least three times in that part that we watched where I did do that. So, "Let me make sure I'm understanding ..." or "So you're saying ..." I did, I marked three times when I heard myself do that ... But I always kind of said the same thing each time. And when I look down at this list [referring to the ART], there are other ways that I could be saying it too. Like, I would like to do more of these others, instead of just saying, "I hear you saying ..." or "What do you mean by that?"

Coach: Yeah. I was going to say, I saw the move pretty frequently. So I think you're doing a good job. But I do like, like this, "Can someone else say ..."

Teacher: Right. And I like, "How are you using that word?" Or this is when I could have, well that would be more evaluating their evidence, but ... I know there's more that I can do with that ... I use the same one over and over.

Coach: So maybe in that, like, five-fourish area? [referring to the ART ratings]

Teacher: Yeah, that's what I would say.

Coach: I mean, I think you're doing it. But I think if you want to use a little more nuanced language ... [Reading from the ART] *Students paraphrase their own and each other's answers.*

Teacher: Hmmm. They did a little bit ... Like, "I think it's true when you say duh-duh-duh-duh, but ..."

Coach: Yeah.

Teacher: They do a little bit, but they're not taking over the teacher-type role in that yet... To help people understand what they're trying to say or what others are saying.

Coach: Yeah.

Teacher: So I would say "*Developing*"? [referring to the ART ratings]

Coach: Yeah, they're in the middle. Yeah, "*Developing.*" I have to say, I haven't seen, I mean I haven't seen that yet with kids. Where they paraphrase for each other. You know, that's a pretty, like ...

Teacher: Yeah, high level.

Coach: Yeah. Be interesting to see if we get there ... Okay. [Reading from the ART] *Clear in the language and structure of our arguments.* I feel like this is one you have to really be thinking about. [Reading from the ART] *The teacher clarifies the group's reasoning by making visible the connections among students' ideas.* So ...

Teacher: [Referring to the ART ratings] I would say "*Developing*" for me ... Especially this part, [Reading from the ART] *Students give redundant answers, they make points already made by others.* Sometimes they would say that. And I didn't really do a whole lot of talking ... And that's a fine line. Like, you want them to have the conversation, but knowing when to step in ...

Coach: Yeah, I mean, that's the name of the game: pulling back and stepping in and knowing what that balance is ... I mean the kids are doing a fairly good job of making their responses interrelated and connected.

In the above segment, the teacher and the coach systematically evaluate the video-taped discussion in relation to the ART's criterion of clarity. The coach starts by reading the ART description of a given practice related to encouraging clarity (i.e., Practice # 4: Clarifying Meaning, see Table 19.2 for details). Then, she asks the teacher an open-ended question, "So what are you thinking on this one?" This prompts the teacher to engage in evaluation of the ways in which addressing the clarity criterion manifested itself through her use of specific talk moves, as well as her students' contributions during the course of the discussion.

During this evaluation, the teacher identifies specific instances in the video where she used talk moves related to clarification of meaning, thus engaging in evidence-based assessment of her practice (e.g., *"Well, I marked at least three times in that part that we watched, where I did do that. So, "Let me make sure I'm under-standing ..." or "So you're saying ..." I did, I marked three times when I heard myself do that"*). The teacher then critically reflects on her use of the moves. Through this reflection, she recognizes her limited use of language, and sets a new goal for herself to increase the variety of moves in her future discussions (i.e., *"And when I look down at this list, there are other ways that I could be saying it too. Like, I would like to do more of these others, instead of just saying, "I hear you saying ..." or "What do you mean by that?")*. The ART helps the teacher to learn about multiple ways to address the clarity criterion during the discussion, offering specific examples of relevant talk moves.

During coaching, the teacher and the coach also use the rating scale from the ART to place each practice on the continuum from "Not Yet" to "Developing" to "Advancing." This is another activity that allows the teacher to critically analyze her facilitation, discovering what her challenges are and gaining new insights on how to address them. For example, in the above excerpt, the teacher appears to be struggling with finding the right balance between being procedur-ally strong and allowing the students to take more ownership of the discussion. (e.g., *I would say "Developing" for me ... Especially this part, [Reading from the ART] "Students give redundant answers, they make points already made by others." Sometimes they would say that. And I didn't really do a whole lot of talking ... And that's a fine line. Like, you want them to have the conversation, but knowing when to step in ...*). The coach echoes the teacher's interpretation, pointing out the fundamental tension present in facilitating inquiry dialogue: knowing when to intervene to enhance the intellectual rigor of the discussion vs. when to relinquish control over the discourse to her students.

The topics discussed during coaching can emerge from concerns that the teacher brings to the session or from the discussion segments identified by the coach. In both cases, however, the structure of a coaching session usually involves: 1) the use of the ART descriptions and the rating scale to focus on specific practices and talk moves from the video, 2) critical reflection on these practices and talk moves, and 3) collaborative identification of the goals for future discussion. From our thematic analysis of the data collected during focus group interviews with teachers, we learned that teachers valued engaging in a systematic reflection on their prac-tice and receiving specific feedback from the coach to be used during subsequent discussions. Below are representative quotes:

The coaching has been phenomenal. Watching the video with a coach and getting feedback on how I could have made a different move has helped me transfer that right into my teaching. It has also helped when I would watch by myself and feel like something had gone wrong, but didn't know what to do in the moment. Then, I would show that to the coach, and they would help me figure out what to do next time.

The feedback, I think, is great, too, because I know I've taken things that the coach specifically said and I've said, "Oh, I am going to work on using that thing you just said in my next discussion," which I did.

A couple of things [the coach] brought up that I just simply had never even considered, that he called out and said, "You maybe could have done this here." And I hadn't even considered what he had mentioned until he said it, and then it seemed very obvious to me.

As can be seen from the above quotes, teachers appreciated having an opportunity to evaluate their progress with an experienced colleague in a systematic and supportive manner. Coaching sessions provided a forum within which teachers were able to discuss their practice as facilitators, thus heightening their awareness about the use of talk during class discussions. Our analysis of teacher facilitation of the discussions conducted before and after professional development showed statistically significant and practically important improvements in teacher spontaneous use of talk (Wilkinson et al., 2017). We believe the coaching with the ART, along with other features of our program, contributed to this welcome change.

Conclusion

Informed by prior work in professional development and our own ongoing study, we are developing a set of design principles to guide future iterations of our program. Two of the emerging principles, illustrated in this chapter, are as follows:

- Teachers should have multiple opportunities to reflect on their discourse practices through systematic and collaborative analysis of video and transcripts of discussions;
- Teachers' use of talk moves to promote argumentation is contingent on the quality of group arguments and should be taught in the context of analysis of argumentation.

We believe that coaching using the ART has the potential to support teachers' spontaneous use of talk moves in several ways. First, it helps teachers to become more cognizant of relevant aspects of classroom talk, to monitor the extent to which students are engaging in collaborative and rigorous argumentation, and to intervene when discussion goes awry. Previous research has shown that, despite having some general notions about the use of discussions, many teachers lack understanding of specific ways in which classroom talk can support student learning

(Nystrand et al., 2003). Further, teachers often have difficulty recognizing discrepancies between their expressed commitment to "open-forum discussions" and their actual use of the traditional recitation script, during which they might dominate and control interactions (Alvermann, O'Brien, & Dillon, 1990). The use of the ART during coaching operationalizes the construct of inquiry through group argumentation by identifying effective practices and talk moves to be used during facilitation. Thus, it helps teachers to develop a better theoretical knowledge of the intended pedagogy and to link that knowledge to verbal and social acts that support classroom application.

Coaching with the ART also serves as a mechanism for identifying challenges teachers face in their facilitation and for determining new strategies to try out in response to those challenges. For example, assigning and comparing ART ratings during coaching supports teachers in critical evaluation of their practice, inviting them to discover and address problems with spontaneous transfer. Other researchers have used a similar protocol during coaching with an observational tool called the *Talk Assessment Tool for Teachers* (TATT) (Wilkinson, Reninger, & Soter, 2010). In a qualitative study involving eight teachers from elementary and middle school classrooms, Wilkinson et al. examined the educative value of the TATT. They concluded that use of the TATT during coaching helped to enhance teachers' awareness of features of classroom discourse and allowed teachers to "make reasoned judgments" to improve their discussion practices.

Finally, coaching with the ART helps to orient teachers to the essentials of argumentation and to situate their learning in the context of inquiry dialogue. For example, as teachers work with coaches to evaluate argumentation using the ART, they practice identifying specific talk moves that might be effective at addressing a given problem with student arguments. In other words, teachers begin to see that the choice of a talk move is contingent on student argumentation. Connecting talk moves to argumentation criteria through the use of the ART helps teachers to learn how to transfer their knowledge of talk moves to future class discussions, thus supporting spontaneous use of language to enhance the quality of group argumentation.

References

Alexander, R. J. (2003). *Talk for learning: The first year.* Northallerton, UK: North Yorkshire County Council.

Alexander, R. J. (2008). *Essays on pedagogy.* New York: Routledge.

Alvermann, D. E., & Hayes, D. A. (1989). Classroom discussion of content area reading assignments: An intervention study. *Reading Research Quarterly, 24*(3), 305–335.

Alvermann, D. E., O'Brien, D. G., & Dillon, D. R. (1990). What teachers do when they say they're having discussions of content area reading assignments: A qualitative analysis? *Reading Research Quarterly, 25*(4), 296–322.

Applebee, A. N., Langer, J. A., Nystrand, M., & Gamoran, A. (2003). Discussion-based approaches to developing understanding: Classroom instruction and student performance in middle and high school English. *American Educational Research Journal, 40*(3), 685–730. doi:10.3102/00028312040003685

Beck, I. L., McKeown, M. G., Sandora, C., Kucan, L., & Worthy, J. (1996). Questioning the author: A year-long classroom implementation to engage students with text. *The Elementary School Journal, 96*(4), 385–414.

Billings, L., & Fitzgerald, J. (2002). Dialogic discussion and the Paideia seminar. *American Educational Research Journal, 39*(4), 907–941. doi:10.3102/00028312039004905

Burbules, N. (1993). *Dialogue in teaching: Theory and practice.* New York: Teachers College Press.

Chinn, C. A., Anderson, R. C., & Waggoner, M. A. (2001). Patterns of discourse in two kinds of literature discussion. *Reading Research Quarterly, 36*(4), 378–411. doi:10.1598/RRQ.36.4.3

Commeyras, M. (1994). Promoting critical thinking through dialogical-thinking reading lessons. *The Reading Teacher, 46*(6), 486–494.

Elmore, R. F. (2002). *Bridging the gap between standards and achievement: The imperative for professional development in education.* Washington, DC: Albert Shanker Institute.

Flavell, J. H. (1985). *Cognitive development* (2nd ed.). Englewood Cliffs, NJ: Prentice Hall.

Govier, T. (2010). *A practical study of argument* (7th ed.). Belmont, CA: Wadsworth Publishing Company.

Gregory, M. (2006). Normative dialogue types in philosophy for children. *Gifted Education International, 22*(2–3), 160–171.

Gregory, M. (2007). A framework for facilitating classroom dialogue. *Teaching Philosophy, 30*(1), 59–84.

Hammer, D., & Schifter, D. (2001). Practices of inquiry in teaching and research. *Cognition & Instruction, 19*(4), 441–478.

Juzwik, M. M., Sherry, M. B., Caughlan, S., Heintz, A., & Borsheim-Black, C. (2012). Supporting dialogically organized instruction in an English teacher preparation program: A video-based, web 2.0-mediated response and revision pedagogy. *Teachers College Record, 114*(3), 1–42.

Kucan, L. (2009). Engaging teachers in investigating their teaching as a linguistic enterprise: The case of comprehension instruction in the context of discussion. *Reading Psychology, 30*(1), 51–87.

Kuhn, D. (2010). Teaching and learning science as argument. *Science Education, 94*(5), 810–824. doi:10.1002/sce.20395

Kuhn, D., & Dean, D. (2004). Metacognition: A bridge between cognitive psychology and educational practice. *Theory into Practice, 43*(4), 268–273. doi:10.1207/s15430421tip4304_4

Mercer, N. (2008). The seeds of time: Why classroom dialogue needs a temporal analysis. *The Journal of the Learning Sciences, 17*(1), 33–59.

Mercer, N., & Littleton, K. (2007). *Dialogue and the development of children's thinking: A socio-cultural approach.* London, UK: Routledge.

Michaels, S., & O'Connor, C. (2015). Conceptualizing talk moves as tools: Professional development approaches for academically productive discussion. In L. B. Resnick, C. A. Asterhan, & S. N. Clarke (Eds.), *Socializing intelligence through academic talk and dialogue* (pp. 347–362). Washington, DC: American Educational Research Association.

Nguyen, K., Anderson, R. C., Waggoner, M., & Rowel, B. (Eds.). (2007). *Using literature discussions to reason through real life dilemmas: A journey taken by one teacher and her fourth-grade students.* Hillsdale, NJ: Erlbaum Associates.

Nussbaum, E. M. (2011). Argumentation, dialogue theory, and probability modeling: Alternative frameworks for argumentation research in education. *Educational Psychologist, 46*(2), 84–106. doi:10.1080/00461520.2011.558816

Nystrand, M. (1997). *Opening dialogue: Understanding the dynamics of language and learning in the English classroom*. New York: Teacher College Press.

Nystrand, M., Wu, L., Gamoran, A., Zeiser, S., & Long, D. A. (2003). Questions in time: Investigating the structure and dynamics of unfolding classroom discourse. *Discourse Processes, 35*(2), 135–198.

O'Connor, C., Michaels, S., & Chapin, S. (2015). "Scaling down" to explore the role of talk in learning: From district intervention to controlled classroom study. In L. B. Resnick, C. Asterhan, & S. N. Clarke (Eds.), *Socializing intelligence through talk and dialogue*. Washington, DC: American Educational Research Association.

Osborne, J. (2010). Arguing to learn in science: The role of collaborative, critical discourse. *Science, 328*(463). doi:10.1126/science.1183944

Pearson, P. D., & Gallagher, M. C. (1983). The instruction of reading comprehension. *Contemporary Educational Psychology, 8*(3), 317–344.

Resnick, L. B., Asterhan, C. S. C., & Clarke, S. N. (2015). *Socializing intelligence through academic talk and dialogue*. Washington, DC: American Educational Research Association.

Resnick, L. B., & Schantz, F. (2015). Talking to learn: The promise and challenge of dialogic teaching. In L. B. Resnick, C. S. C. Asterhan, & S. N. Clarke (Eds.), *Socializing intelligence through academic talk and dialogue*. Washington, DC: American Educational Research Association.

Reznitskaya, A., & Wilkinson, I. A. G. (2015). Professional development in dialogic teaching: Helping teachers promote argument literacy in their classrooms. In D. Scott & E. Hargreaves (Eds.), *Learning, pedagogy and assessment* (pp. 219–232). UK: Sage.

Reznitskaya, A., & Wilkinson, I. A. G. (in press). *The most reasonable answer: Helping students build better arguments together*. Boston, MA: Harvard Education Press.

Richardson, V., Anders, P., Tidwell, D., & Lloyd, C. (1991). The relationship between teachers' beliefs and practices in reading comprehension instruction. *American Educational Research Journal, 28*(3), 559–586.

Soter, A., Wilkinson, I. A. G., Murphy, P. K., Rudge, L., Reninger, K., & Edwards, M. (2008). What the discourse tells us: Talk and indicators of high-level comprehension. *International Journal of Educational Research, 47*, 372–391. doi:10.1016/j.ijer.2009.01.001

Splitter, L. J., & Sharp, A. M. (1996). The practice of philosophy in the classroom. In R. F. Reed & A. M. Sharp (Eds.), *Studies in philosophy for children: Pixie* (pp. 285–314). Madrid, Spain: Ediciones De La Torre.

Toulmin, S. E. (1958). *The uses of argument*. Cambridge, UK: Cambridge University Press.

Trickey, S., & Topping, K. J. (2004). Philosophy for children: A systematic review. *Research Papers in Education, 19*(3), 365–380. doi:10.1080/0267152042000248016

Walton, D. (1996). *Argument structure: A pragmatic theory*. Toronto, Canada: University of Toronto Press.

Walton, D. (1998). *The new dialectic: Conversational contexts of argument*. Toronto, Canada: Univeristy of Toronto Press.

Wei, R. C., Darling-Hammond, L., Andree, A., Richardson, N., & Orphanos, S. (2009). *Professional learning in the learning profession: A status report on teacher development in the United States and abroad*. Dallas, TX: National Staff Development Council.

Wells, G. (2000). Dialogic inquiry in education: Building on the legacy of Vygotsky. In C. D. Lee & P. Smagorinsky (Eds.), *Vygotskian perspectives on literacy research* (pp. 51–85). New York, NY: Cambridge: University Press.

Wilkinson, I. A. G., Reninger, K. B., & Soter, A. (2010). Developing a professional development tool for assessing quality talk about text. In R. T. Jimenez, V. J. Risko, D. W. Rowe, & M. Hundley (Eds.), *59th yearbook of the national reading conference* (pp. 142–159). Oak Creek, WI: National Reading Conference.

Wilkinson, I. A. G., Reznitskaya, A., Bourdage, K., Oyler, J., Nelson, K., Glina, M., . . . Kim, M.-Y. (2017). Toward a more dialogic pedagogy: Changing teachers' beliefs and practices through professional development in language arts classrooms. *Language & Education, 31*(1), 65–82.

Yoon, K. S., Duncan, T., Lee, S. W.-Y., Scarloss, B., & Shapley, K. (2007). Reviewing the evidence on how teacher professional development affects student achievement. *Issues & Answers Report, 33.* Retrieved from https://ies.ed.gov/ncee/edlabs/regions/southwest/pdf/REL_2007033.pdf

CONCLUSION

Some take-home messages on how it may be possible to promote greater spontaneity in students' use of learning and reasoning strategies

Emmanuel Manalo, Yuri Uesaka, and Clark A. Chinn

Integrating the many possible solutions to the problem

The 19 chapters of this book indicate that it remains a problem that many students fail to spontaneously use appropriate learning and reasoning strategies in situations when it would be helpful to do so. The chapters, however, also demonstrate that researchers have developed a strong body of knowledge about how to prevent or overcome this problem. Researchers have designed interventions, programs, and learning environments that can promote the desired spontaneity. Furthermore, many of the mechanisms underlying successful promotion of spontaneous strategy use are understood, which makes it possible to draw out crucial principles for educational practice.

Each of the 19 chapters of this volume articulates its perspectives and conclusions clearly; so chapter summaries will be dispensed with. Instead, this conclusion lays out an integration of the findings and key message of the chapters in combination, thereby drawing out what may be useful for readers in terms of understanding, addressing, and further investigating spontaneity in strategy use.

So, what is necessary for students to develop spontaneity in employing effective learning and reasoning strategies? Taken together, the chapters of this book indicate that spontaneous strategy use is supported when a set of conditions is in place during educational experiences. These conditions are characteristics of students, learning environments, and the teachers who interact with students within these learning environments. The basic components of these conditions and the connections between them are summarized in the model depicted in Figure 20.1. In this model, the student conditions could be considered as close to essential: without meeting those conditions, students are unlikely to use appropriate learning and reasoning strategies spontaneously in situations that would benefit from their use. The teacher and environmental conditions, on the other hand, are necessary for

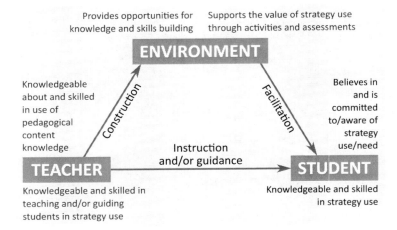

Provides opportunities for
knowledge and skills building

Supports the value of strategy use
through activities and assessments

ENVIRONMENT

Knowledgeable
about and skilled
in use of
pedagogical
content
knowledge

Construction

Facilitation

Believes in
and is
committed
to/aware of
strategy
use/need

TEACHER

Instruction
and/or guidance

STUDENT

Knowledgeable and skilled in
teaching and/or guiding
students in strategy use

Knowledgeable and skilled
in strategy use

FIGURE 20.1   Teacher, environment, and student conditions for spontaneous strategy use to occur.

promoting development of the student conditions. The learning environment can be viewed as the designed curriculum or instruction in which students interact (e.g., scaffolds embedded in technology or materials to support student learning). The teacher's role includes the teacher's various activities during instruction, which are in turn guided by his or her own knowledge and beliefs. When students learn in contexts where the teacher and environmental conditions specified in Figure 20.1 are absent, fewer students will manifest spontaneous strategy use. However, some students may still do, and the likely reason for this is that those students had already developed the needed knowledge and values in other learning situations. But it is likely that those other learning situations involved teachers and learning environments that did meet the conditions shown in Figure 20.1.

Student conditions

Many of the chapters in this volume confirm or lend support to what previous authors like Borkowski, Carr, and Pressley (1987) and Garner (1990) have claimed: students need (1) sufficient knowledge about the target learning strategies and (2) awareness of and commitment to the value of using them, if they are to use those strategies spontaneously. To begin with the first condition, Manalo and Henning (Chapter 6) identified poor knowledge about effective vocabulary learning strategies and how to use them as the culprit that explains why many students use poor strategies despite their being cognizant of those strategies being ineffective. Shinogaya (Chapter 10) demonstrated that teaching students a learning strategy, such as how to prepare for an upcoming class, reduces students' perception of cost associated with the use of that strategy—and more importantly, it increases their spontaneous use of that strategy.

Based on their research findings in diagram use in problem solving and communication, Uesaka and Manalo (Chapter 4) concluded that, if students are to use learning strategies spontaneously, one crucial requirement is that they be provided the necessary training so that they become knowledgeable and skilled in what strategies to use and how to appropriately use those strategies. Another important point related to this is that knowledge and skills development reduces the cognitive processing cost of using strategies: in other words, if students know how to use a strategy well, it demands less mental effort for them to use it than if they are not so familiar with its use. Stadtler, Bromme, and Rouet (Chapter 3) came to the same conclusion about the need for training in the use of search, evaluation, and integration skills in online multiple documents reading; they argued that students need strong skills in searching, evaluating, and integrating multiple documents, which requires in turn well-routinized basic reading skills. Wecker and Hetmanek (Chapter 5) proposed not only the provision of appropriate training but also ample opportunities and a broad array of diverse tasks for student practice—so that subsequent use of the new target learning strategies becomes more automated.

The three case studies described by Ichikawa, Uesaka, and Manalo (Chapter 12) indicate that, in authentic education settings, tangible results can be obtained in promoting student spontaneity in the use of various appropriate learning strategies—particularly when adequate attention is paid to instructional design. An essential component of the design they described is the provision of more comprehensive instruction so that students understand the mechanisms involved in how they learn, how the target learning strategy works and hence why it is effective, as well as how and when to use it. It is important to note, however, that the promotion of spontaneous use of some learning strategies could be more difficult than others—as Seo, Wang, Ishizaki, Uesaka, and Ichikawa (Chapter 14) also pointed out. In the school practices that Seo et al. described, the use of a metacognitive learning strategy (lesson induction) required additional teacher encouragement and support before students started manifesting self-initiated use of it.

Having sufficient knowledge about the strategy to use, however, does not guarantee that students will actually invoke its use. This is part of the reason why many teachers frustratingly find that, despite providing lots of instruction about effective learning and reasoning strategies, many students still fail to use them of their own volition. Thus, a second condition for spontaneous strategy use is a commitment to use the strategies. This commitment arises from a belief in and/or awareness of the value or need for the strategies in question. This condition is congruent with Borkowski et al.'s (1987) view that, to produce spontaneous strategy use, attributional beliefs need to be retrained so that students more clearly perceive the connections between their actions, the strategies they use, and the success and failure outcomes that follow. Garner's (1990, p. 521) comment that "children and adults are unlikely to invoke strategies demanding time and effort if they believe the strategies will not make any difference" likewise conveys the importance of student beliefs and awareness. Findings from the Manalo and Henning study (Chapter 6) provide support for this claim: They reported that most of the students did not use the "better" strategies they had described because of their awareness that those strategies—despite the greater amounts of time and effort they demanded—did not reliably lead to better test outcomes. As noted, however, the "better" strategies were *not* really better in the sense of being more effective, because many of the students in that study were deficient in their knowledge about vocabulary learning strategies.

The necessity of belief in and/or awareness of the value or need for strategies was clearly demonstrated through the manipulations utilized in the Fukaya (Chapter 9) and Shinogaya (Chapter 10) studies. The Fukaya study showed that increasing students' awareness of the inadequacy of their understanding of the material being learned (via explanation generation and self-evaluation tasks) led to an increase in their spontaneous strategy use (i.e., use of organization strategy), suggesting that awareness of learning needs instigates employment of strategies that address those needs. In the Shinogaya study, adjustments in the way the teacher taught in class (so that greater emphasis was placed on deep understanding) led to an increase in student perceptions about the utility of a particular word learning strategy (dictionary look-up of the meaning of unknown words)—and their spontaneous use of that strategy.

Wecker and Hetmanek (Chapter 5) argued that it is necessary to make students aware of deficiencies in their current learning performance, how those deficiencies can be attributed to suboptimal strategies they are using, and how new strategies can improve their performance. Ichikawa et al. (Chapter 12) described how similar procedures of awareness raising and attribution can successfully promote spontaneous use of more effective and appropriate strategies in case studies of real educational practices. In fact, they emphasized "change in student beliefs about learning" as a crucial component in the process of learning strategy use promotion and transfer. In the Seo et al. studies (Chapter 14), a similar change in perception about the effectiveness of the target learning strategy (brought about by the provision of hands-on demonstrations and instruction) was considered to be a key contributor to subsequent spontaneous strategy use.

Uesaka and Manalo (Chapter 4) explained that student beliefs about learning (which they defined as orientation toward either valuing the process of understanding to arrive at the correct answer, or simply seeking to obtain the required answer) is a moderator of the effects that interventions (aimed at improving student skills in strategy use and perceptions about the efficacy of the strategy) can have in enhancing spontaneity in strategy use. This means that, apart from beliefs about learning strategies, *beliefs about learning itself* can influence such spontaneity. If students are only interested in getting the right answer, they are unlikely to benefit from interventions provided for improving their self-initiated use of effective learning strategies. Stadtler et al. (Chapter 3) made a similar observation where students' epistemic beliefs (i.e., their beliefs about the nature of knowledge, and the criteria for and processes involved in knowing) are concerned: If students believe that knowledge is complex and more tentative, they exhibit greater spontaneous effort at integrating knowledge from different sources. In contrast, if they believe that knowledge is just a collection of simple facts and is unchanging, they tend not to make such effort. These observations indicate the important influence that beliefs have on the strategies that students invoke in their attempts at learning.

The student conditions can be viewed not only as knowledge, skills, and beliefs that students acquire and internally possess, but also as changes in the students' patterns of interaction within their communities of learning (e.g., their classroom, school, home).[1] From this latter perspective, the development of appropriate student conditions would arise from the process of strategies being discussed and used within the relevant communities, where norms are collectively developed to support the use of those strategies. Thus, as Chinn, Duncan, and Rinehart (Chapter 15) pointed out, students develop knowledge of and valuing of strategies that is interconnected with community patterns of interaction and the norms that support those interactions. There are different ways by which such development of knowledge and values can occur. For example, Hmelo-Silver, Jordan, Sinha, Yu, and Eberbach (Chapter 17) discussed how the necessary student understanding that leads to transfer could emerge from their collaborative interactions with technology. On the other hand, Lei and Chan (Chapter 11) stressed how, in a knowledge-building environment, students take collective responsibility for the development of community knowledge—and that collective responsibility essentially drives the spontaneous transfer that occurs.

Hence, the take-home message as far as student conditions are concerned is that, to promote greater spontaneity in strategy use, students must develop, firstly, adequate knowledge and skills in the strategy they should be using and, secondly, beliefs and awareness about the value or need for using that particular strategy. Further, the development of those conditions can be considered as being inseparable from the community of learning that the student engages with: the knowledge and values that the student develops are closely linked with and supported by community patterns and norms of interaction. Research findings reported or reviewed in the preceding chapters attest to increases in spontaneous strategy use when the manipulations or interventions used provided for these conditions. Conversely, in the absence of these conditions, corresponding failures in spontaneous invocation of the target strategies had been manifested.

Teacher conditions

Although it is the student who needs to spontaneously use learning and reasoning strategies, the teacher has an indispensable role in promoting that spontaneity—a role which the chapters of this book suggest he or she can more effectively fulfil if certain conditions are met. Those conditions are that the teacher is able to (1) apply pedagogical content knowledge (PCK, explained below) to the design and implementation of learning environments, and (2) provide instruction and/or guidance in the use of learning strategies (which could also be considered as requiring—at least in some cases—the application of PCK) (see Figure 20.1). PCK here pertains to the teacher's "subject matter knowledge *for teaching*," which includes "the ways of representing and formulating the subject that make it comprehensible to others," as well as "an understanding of what makes learning of specific topics easy or difficult: the conceptions and preconceptions that students of different ages and backgrounds bring with them to the learning of those most frequently taught topics and lessons" (Shulman, 1986, p. 9).

PCK includes the knowledge to construct or adapt a learning environment to support complex learning through inquiry and problem solving, and to effectively orchestrate learning activities within that environment. Several chapters in this book dealing with instructional design explicitly or implicitly indicate the need for teachers to have high levels of proficiency in this kind of knowledge for spontaneous strategy use to be facilitated. For example, Samarapungavan, Wills, and Bryan (Chapter 16) stressed that the teacher needs considerable PCK of this kind in order to successfully design and implement content-rich inquiry classrooms that support not only construction but also transfer of knowledge and skills. Chinn et al. (Chapter 15) described basic principles of epistemic design to promote epistemic competence and subsequent spontaneous transfer: It is clear that the teacher needs sufficient PCK to orchestrate learning in a classroom community that implements such principles. Likewise, Kapur, Lee, and Lee's (Chapter 1) argument that the design of classroom tasks and activities needs to elicit students' prior knowledge (before instruction is provided) is dependent on the teacher having the necessary PCK to successfully conceptualize, create, and implement such a design.

Apart from the teacher's competence in applying PCK to the learning environment, the other teacher condition that contributes to the promotion of spontaneous use of learning and reasoning strategies is possession of knowledge and skills in teaching and/or guiding students specifically in strategy use.[2] Oyama (Chapter 2) argued that, to promote students' spontaneous use of questioning as a strategy for learning, it is necessary for teachers to employ scaffolding, reciprocal teaching, and assessment and feedback provision to improve not only students' quality of questioning but also their perceptions about the usefulness and manageability of using that strategy. Webb, Franke, Johnson, Turrou, and Ing (Chapter 18) reported classroom findings that teacher support in developing students' engagement with each other's ideas—and connecting those others' ideas with essential elements in what the students were learning in a mathematics class—promoted the students' subsequent engagement with each other in *new contexts*—without the teacher being present. Similar effects of teacher support and modeling were reported by Shinogaya (Chapter 10) where use of preparation strategies were concerned: the more the teacher focused in class on the meaning aspects of English words the students were learning (as a foreign language), the more the students subsequently looked up meanings of words in a dictionary during their independent preparation (at home) for the following day's class. In fact, Tanaka's (Chapter 7) findings suggest that the teaching styles used by teachers have a significant influence on the strategies that students spontaneously use. Her findings indicate that the following teaching styles are facilitative of the use of deeper processing strategies when learning: encouraging and allowing time for students to think for themselves, building knowledge connections, and linking information being taught to the realities of daily life.

Because of the problem of many teachers not having the necessary depth of knowledge and skills to effectively promote learning strategies acquisition among their students, one of the principles underpinning the educational approaches that Ichikawa et al. (Chapter 12) described is direct engagement by researchers in educational practices in schools—so that mutual professional development and learning could occur for both teachers and educational researchers. Reznitskaya, Wilkinson, and Oyler (Chapter 19) also emphasized the importance of teacher professional development and support if they are to acquire the necessary capabilities in implementing approaches for promoting student use of thinking and reasoning strategies. They explained how engaging students in inquiry dialogue is not an easy task for both novice and experienced teachers, and how the provision of appropriate professional development as well as tools (e.g., for examining the quality of interactions during inquiry dialogue) can be considered vital in helping teachers reach the necessary levels of capability.

Thus, the take-home message as far as the teacher side of things is concerned is that teachers also need to have particular kinds of knowledge and skills if they are to contribute to the promotion of spontaneous strategy use in students. More specifically, they need PCK, and knowledge and skills about how competencies in strategy use can be developed in students. Inadequacies in these kinds of knowledge and skills would render teachers unable to successfully construct the necessary learning environments or to provide the necessary instruction or guidance to students. To this end, teacher professional development is indispensable.

Environmental conditions

The learning environment includes the curriculum, activity structures, problems and activities, materials, and technologies that students engage with while learning. The learning environment is more likely to promote spontaneous strategy use if certain conditions are met. The chapters of this book suggest that those requirements are, firstly, that the environment provides opportunities for student-driven knowledge and skills building and, secondly, that it supports the value of strategy use through activities and assessments that are provided.

A number of the chapters in this volume examined the role of learning environments, with a focus on how participation in activities leads to the appropriation of the norms and practices of those activities. Lei and Chan (Chapter 11) described how a computer-supported knowledge-building environment effectively elicited students' spontaneous use of self-regulation, co-regulation, and collective regulation strategies to monitor their own and their community's learning. Knowledge building here pertains to the production of new knowledge that adds value to the learner's community, and knowledge-building environments are those where knowledge is improvable by means of continuously refined discourse with the learner's collective agency and responsibility. Lei and Chan explained that such environments emphasize *intentionality of learning, goal-directedness, and metacognition.* There is collective cognitive responsibility for creating knowledge as a class (with the distinctive focus in knowledge building on class-level knowledge rather than individual knowledge). Chinn et al. (Chapter 15) likewise described some of the characteristics of learning environments that facilitate spontaneous use of thinking and reasoning strategies in science. These environments should create a classroom culture in which students develop and share criteria (or norms) for good models, good evidence, and so on. They develop other norms for what counts as reliable epistemic processes for producing knowledge. Through participating in the creation and implementation of these community norms, students are expected to develop a commitment to them that will transfer to new settings.

Hmelo-Silver et al. (Chapter 17) described their PMC-2E (phenomena-mechanisms-components & explanations with evidence) framework and how it supports students in being able to generalize their conceptual understandings (in science) to novel contexts. According to them, the success of PMC-2E in promoting such transfer is due to it allowing students to *attach generalizations to what they are learning*, which in turn leads them to access cognitive resources that are useful in novel contexts. This kind of priming and linking of cognitive resources is also one of the objectives behind Samarapungavan et al.'s (Chapter 16) emphasis on *soliciting students' prior knowledge and reasoning capacities* to engage them in the process of developing new ideas, practices, and ways of thinking in content-rich inquiry classrooms. Likewise, Kapur et al. (Chapter 1) argued that, through the use of design methods such as "Productive Failure," students are able to spontaneously *generate multiple representations and solutions* to the problem they are presented, which has the effect of facilitating the construction of new knowledge based on prior knowledge.

As noted at the beginning of this section, the other environmental condition that appears necessary is that it must support the value of strategy use to students. This condition was also emphasized in the projects discussed above, all of which sought to promote strong community norms within the classroom as well as strong practices for using the strategies during classroom sensemaking. This environmental condition is congruent with Ames and Archer's (1988) finding that students who perceive an emphasis on mastery goals in their classroom (i.e., development of new skills are considered important, the process of learning is valued, and achievement is seen as dependent on effort) employ more effective learning strategies compared to those who instead perceive an emphasis on performance goals (i.e., natural ability and normatively high scores are considered important).

Several chapters in this volume emphasized that spontaneous strategy use depends on the provision of instruction that enables students to appreciate the value of strategies. Wecker and Hetmanek (Chapter 5), for example, argued that spontaneous strategy use is dependent on the student becoming aware of shortcomings in their current levels of performance, and being able to see—and understand—the performance benefits that follow from the use of new and more effective strategies. One way of raising such awareness is through the use of reciprocal teaching or peer instruction, which is advocated in several of the chapters (e.g., Oyama in Chapter 2, Uesaka & Manalo in Chapter 4, Stump et al. in Chapter 13). For instance, Uesaka and Manalo explained that, when students have to teach or explain something to their peers, they receive feedback about how they are managing through the reactions and responses of their interlocutors that they observe. Such feedback includes indicators of both successes and failures in comprehension, which leads to spontaneous use of alternative strategies (e.g., asking a question to seek clarification, constructing a visual representation to support the verbal explanation) when necessary, and to insights about what strategies produce the most successful outcomes. Importantly, such insights can then lead to spontaneous reuse of the successful strategies in future similar—or even novel—learning and instruction situations.

The tests and assessments that students receive in their learning environment can also significantly impact their perceptions about the value of strategy use. Suzuki and Sun's (Chapter 8) findings suggest that tests should be perceived by students as having genuine value to their own selves (e.g., as a means of improving their learning, and not just as a tool for enforcing study). They explained that if students perceive such value, they are more likely to use effective learning strategies of their own volition. Fukaya's (Chapter 9) results support this notion: When students were required to explain what they had learned and carry out self-evaluation of how much they had learned, their awareness of inadequacies in their understanding improved, and this in turn led to an increase in their use of effective learning strategies.

The take-home message therefore when considering the environmental conditions of spontaneous strategy use facilitation is that the learning environment needs to support student-driven knowledge and skills building, as well as to enable students to come to appreciate personally the value of investing effort in the use of effective strategies. Some instructional approaches focus on communicating these ideas persuasively to students; others take the approach of engaging students in communities in which strategies are needed for meaning making, and learners within communities develop and enact collective norms that manifest the value of these strategies. The absence of either or both conditions will almost certainly lead to a reduction in spontaneous strategy use. An environment that is deficient in providing opportunities for student-driven knowledge and skills building will likely fail in inculcating robust understanding of and solid competencies in the use of learning and reasoning strategies. On the other hand, an environment that does not foster an appreciation of the value of employing effective strategies would likely leave most students relying on the use of strategies that require the least amounts of effort and time—even if they are fully cognizant of and capable of using the most effective and appropriate strategies.

Concluding comments on addressing the problem of spontaneous strategy use

The most important message from the 19 chapters of this book is that there are genuine, viable solutions to the problem of spontaneous strategy use: It is possible to promote greater spontaneity in students' use of learning and reasoning strategies. Students are more likely to reliably employ effective strategies on their own volition when certain conditions are in place. Starting with the students, they need to be knowledgeable and well skilled in the use of the strategies most appropriate to use in their particular learning situations. Furthermore, they need to be aware that those strategies are appropriate for the learning situations they encounter, and that the use of those strategies would be beneficial—and hence worth their effort and time. But for the students to attain this state, their teachers and learning environments need to have met their respective conditions, as well.

The learning environment needs to provide students with opportunities for self-directed knowledge and skills building: in other words, the environment needs to be one that encourages students to take adequate responsibility for their learning—and not to simply wait for their teachers to tell them what they should do, when, and how. Furthermore, through the activities engaged and assessments administered in that environment, the value of strategy use should be supported. This can be achieved through persuasive communications and experiences that change students' knowledge and values, as well as through participation in communities that engage in practices that emphasize strategy use and norms that support their value.

Teachers need to have sufficient knowledge and skills in two areas: the teaching of their subject content (referred to here as PCK), and the provision of instruction or guidance in cultivating knowledge and skills in strategy use. If teachers have sufficient proficiency in these, they would be able to construct learning environments that would meet the conditions mentioned in the previous paragraph. They would also be able to teach or guide students in strategy use. For teachers to meet such requirements, appropriate professional development and support are required. It is possible to design instructional methods and learning frameworks that deliver excellent results in research-based evaluations, but it is not reasonable to expect teachers to implement those methods and frameworks without providing them with sufficient training and support. The findings of the Stump et al. study (Chapter 13) clearly show this.

As a final note, a flexible and multi-perspective approach to promoting spontaneity in students' learning and reasoning strategies use is advocated here. There is no one single correct way of promoting the use of such strategies. Instead, there are numerous, alternative ways—as the findings reported in the chapters of this book demonstrate. Rather than rigidly advocating only one particular approach, it is important for teachers to draw from their PCK and consider the different models and approaches that have been presented to determine what might work best in the specific educational contexts where they are operating. To that end, the authors sincerely hope that this book will prove to be an informative and useful resource.

Acknowledgment

The authors would like to thank Christoph Daniel Schulze for the construction of the diagram shown in Figure 20.1.

Notes

1 Two perspectives or "metaphors" for understanding learning were discussed by Sfard (1998): the acquisition and the participation metaphors. In brief, the acquisition metaphor considers "the human mind as a container to be filled with materials" (p. 5) and the learner essentially becomes the owner of those materials. In contrast, the participation metaphor considers learning as the process of "becoming a member of a certain community" and, for the learner, it results in "the ability to communicate in the language of this community and act according to its particular norms" (p. 6). To varying degrees, the contributing authors of this volume can be considered as coming primarily from one or the other of these perspectives. The editors consider these perspectives equally important in formulating and implementing solutions to the central problem about spontaneity in strategy use that has been posed.

2 This form of knowledge and skills has both domain-general and domain-specific aspects to it. For example, teaching diagram use to aid communicative effectiveness could be considered as largely requiring domain-general knowledge in that the knowledge about construction of diagrammatic representations to supplement spoken or written information to aid clarity could apply to a wide range of subject disciplines. In contrast, teaching diagram use in problem solving could be considered as requiring content-specific knowledge or PCK; for example, diagrams that would be helpful in solving math word problems are different from diagrams to solve philosophical or logic problems, so that the knowledge for these strategies would be a form of PCK. The important point is that teachers need to have sufficient domain-general and domain-specific knowledge (PCK)—as appropriate to the situation—to teach and/or guide students in strategy use.

References

Ames, C., & Archer, J. (1988). Achievement goals in the classroom: Students' learning strategies and motivational processes. *Journal of Educational Psychology, 80*(3), 260–267.

Borkowski, J., Carr, M., & Pressley, M. (1987). "Spontaneous" strategy use: Perspectives from metacognitive theory. *Intelligence, 11*(1), 61–75.

Garner, R. (1990). When children and adults do not use learning strategies: Toward a theory of settings. *Review of Educational Research, 60*(4), 517–529.

Sfard, A. (1998). On two metaphors for learning and the dangers of choosing just one. *Educational Researcher, 27*(2), 4–13.

Shulman, L. S. (1986). Those who understand: Knowledge growth in teaching. *Educational Researcher, 15*(2), 4–14.

INDEX